The Character of John Adams

*The Institute of Early American History and Culture
is sponsored jointly by
The College of William and Mary in Virginia
and The Colonial Williamsburg Foundation.*

John Adams, 1783.

Oil by John Singleton Copley.
(Detail of Figure 2.)
Courtesy of the Harvard University Portrait Collection,
Cambridge, Mass.

The Character of John Adams

by Peter Shaw

Published for
the Institute of Early American
History and Culture
Williamsburg, Virginia
by The University of
North Carolina Press
Chapel Hill

Copyright © 1976 by The University of North Carolina Press
All rights reserved
Manufactured in the United States of America
ISBN 0-8078-1254-4
Library of Congress Catalog Card Number 75-14306

Library of Congress Cataloging in Publication Data

Shaw, Peter, 1936–
   The character of John Adams.

   Includes index.
   1. Adams, John, Pres. U.S., 1735–1826.
I. Institute of Early American History and Culture,
Williamsburg, Va. II. Title.
E322.S54   973.4'4'0924 [B]   75-14306
ISBN 0-8078-1254-4

To my wife, Penelope

Preface

    John Adams's lifelong struggle with the temptations of popularity and fame was not apparent to his contemporaries, but it contributed to his lack of popularity while he lived and until recent years to his relative obscurity among the founders of the nation. The nineteenth-century custodian of Adams's reputation was his grandson Charles Francis Adams, who during the 1850s published the *Works of John Adams* with a biography. The judicious "Mr. Adams" of this edition resembled the obscure Charles Francis rather than his embarrassingly hotheaded ancestor. In 1933 Gilbert Chinard initiated modern revaluations with his aptly titled *Honest John Adams*. But in their search for a usable past the American writers of the 1920s and 1930s championed not Adams but Jefferson and Hamilton, while the imaginations of schoolboys continued to find the stuff of legend in their textbook portrayals of Washington, Franklin, and Paine. The one exception was typical of Adams's bad luck with publicity. Ezra Pound, who found a version of his own cranky originality in Adams, devoted one of the longest and least known sequences in American poetry to him in his *Cantos*.

Beginning in the 1940s there were signs of change. Catherine Drinker Bowen's warm biographical study covered Adams's early years, and in the 1950s for the first time the great cache of Adams Family Papers at the Massachusetts Historical Society, containing unexpurgated texts of John Adams's diary, autobiography, and personal letters, was opened unconditionally to researchers. In essay reviews of the published volumes of the Adams Papers and later in specialized studies, Adams was rescued from the respectable obscurity contrived by his grandson. Page Smith reintroduced Adams to the public in a detailed two-volume biography, and the intellectual history of Zoltán

Haraszti, Edmund S. Morgan, and Bernard Bailyn made Adams a newly crucial figure. In recent years Adams has been studied as a diarist, political writer, diplomat, president, and as a letter writer and sage in his letters to Jefferson during retirement. Adams would have been pleased to find so many of his activities and services being discussed—while noting the neglect of his career in Massachusetts politics and in the Continental Congress. But I wonder if he would have noticed that, ironically, his personality is once again being lost through appreciative rehearsals of his fragmented careers.

Instead of touching on all the events of Adams's life I have attempted to view his character, thought, and acts as a whole. As far as possible I have placed him in the context of his time and place as well as in the light of his Puritan intellectual and emotional heritage. The Adams Papers have opened to view the colorful side of Adams with such impact that he is in danger of going from a nonentity to a character: explosive of temper, all too quotably biting in his criticism of others, consumedly envious, brutally awkward in company. On the other hand, Adams continues to be treated as a judicious political leader and political scientist, which he was not. If I have had a formula for reconciling the public and private Adams it has been to intellectualize his behavior and to personalize his ideas. His behavior appears less eccentric when viewed in the context of its origins in the village life of eighteenth-century Massachusetts. His politics and ideas appear less abstractly motivated when they are viewed in light of the evolution of his character.

While I have brought the habits of a literary training to this study of Adams, my conscious reliance has been on the brilliant work of the last decade by American historians of the colonial and Revolutionary periods. I have tried to introduce Adams to readers outside the profession of American history without sacrificing the standards of historical scholarship. If the word "interdisciplinary" had not come to connote the avoidance of all disciplines rather than the use of more than one, I would have subtitled this work "an interdisciplinary study."

The inspiration to write about John Adams came from Alfred Kazin. Stages of the manuscript have been read with different but crucial result by Professor Sacvan Bercovitch, L. H. Butterfield, Heywood Gould, Professor William C. Stinchcombe; my wife, to whom this book is dedicated; and my editor, Norman S. Fiering. L. H. Butterfield, Marc Friedlaender, and the staff of the Adams Papers helped me at every juncture, as the footnotes partially indicate. Research was done at the New-York Historical Society, the Columbia University library, and the New York Public Library, New York City; the library of the State University of New York at Stony Brook; the Yale University library, New Haven, Connecticut; and the Massachusetts Historical Society, Boston. I thank the following institutions for permission to quote from their manuscript collections: the Pennsylvania Historical Society, Philadelphia, for the Vanderkemp Papers; the New-York Historical Society, for the Osgood Papers; and the Massachusetts Historical Society, for the Dana Papers.

Support of my research came from a half sabbatical leave from the State University of New York at Stony Brook, summer grants from the State University of New York Research Foundation and the American Council of Learned Societies, and a fellowship from the National Endowment for the Humanities. The book was written in an office donated by Bernard Gould, to whom I am indebted with every line I write.

I have had to quote Adams in several forms, none of them exactly as he set down the words: Charles Francis Adams's regularized versions, the published text of the Adams Papers, and my own, slightly less edited transcriptions from the Adams Papers microfilms. I have supplied initial capitals and periods for sentences lacking them; have expanded the y, or the thorn, in abbreviations such as ye, to th; and have put into lowercase the medial capital s. But I have let stand irregularities that only an editor should touch, notably Adams's capital s at the beginning of a word and his grammatically unnecessary dashes. Words supplied conjecturally by the Adams Papers editors in most cases are indicated in the notes instead of inserted in brackets as in their edition.

New York City
July 1974

Contents

Illustrations

The Character of John Adams

I know not the Reason but there is some Strange Attraction between the North Parish in Braintree and my Heart. It is a remarkable Spot. It has vomited Forth more Fire than Mount Etna. It has produced three mortals, Hancock and two Adams's, who have, with the best Intentions in the World, set the World in a blaze. . . . Glorious however as the flame is, I wish I could put it out.–Some People say I was born for such Times. It is true I was born to be in such times but was not made for them. They affect too tenderly my Heart.

John Adams to Abigail Adams
The Hague, August 15, 1782

 I
Ambition
1735–1756

One hundred years after arriving in the New World the Adams family was well established in Braintree, Massachusetts, a small town about twelve miles from Boston, located in what is now called Quincy. Succeeding generations worked and enlarged the forty acres acquired in 1638 by the immigrant, Henry Adams. They maintained his malt brewery and farm, became ministers and town officers, and in the third generation Deacon John Adams became the town's cordwainer, or shoemaker. In 1735, when his son John was born, Deacon Adams was a militia officer, both tithe and tax collector for Braintree, and a recently elected selectman, or town manager. His older brother had been sent to Harvard College to become a minister, and the deacon planned to send his own first son there.

When the deacon married into the prominent Boylston family, he set a precedent for later Adamses of social advance through marriage instead of business. That he was determined to have his son become a minister (for that was what Harvard College signified to him) was a measure both of his economic progress—he could afford to spare a hand from the work of the farm—and of his idealism, for it would be only with some difficulty that he could support that son at school. John Adams was expected to continue the family struggle for improvement. He began by resisting but ended by carrying it further than anyone could have expected.

"From his Mother," John Adams wrote in his autobiography, "probably my Father received an Admiration of Learning as he called it, which remained with him, through Life, and which prompted him to his unchangeable determination to give his first son a liberal Education." In his sketchy autobiographical account of his youth Adams concentrated on his father's obsession with education and on his own resistance to it. After being "very early taught to read at home" and at a school run by a neighbor across the way, Adams was sent to the local public school. He found the teacher, Joseph Cleverly, so "indolent" and inattentive that he became a "truant": "I spent my time as idle Children do in making and sailing boats and Ships upon the Ponds and Brooks, in making and flying Kites, in driving hoops, playing marbles, playing Quoits, Wrestling, Swimming, Skaiting and above all in shooting, to which Diversion I was addicted to a degree of Ardor which I know not that I ever felt for any other Business, Study or Amusement."[1] When he was about ten and his father admonished him for squandering his chance for an education, he answered that he did not wish to go to college. When his father asked, "What would you do Child?" he replied, "Be a Farmer."

Luckily Deacon Adams's ambition took the form of calm determination rather than repressive absolutism. To his son's saucy reply the deacon responded: "A Farmer? Well I will shew you what it is to be a Farmer. You shall go with me to Penny ferry tomorrow Morning and help me get Thatch. I shall be very glad to go Sir.—Accordingly next morning he took me with him, and with great good humour kept me all day with him at Work. At night at home he said Well John are you satisfied with being a Farmer. Though the Labour had been very hard and very muddy I answered I like it very well Sir. Ay but I dont like it so well: so you shall go to School to day. I went but was not so happy as among the Creek Thatch."[2] The autobiographer's closing remark captured the stubbornness of

1. L. H. Butterfield *et al.*, eds., *The Diary and Autobiography of John Adams* (Cambridge, Mass., 1961), III, 256, 257, hereafter cited as *Diary and Autobiography*. It was in a later account of his youth that Adams called himself a "truant." John Adams to Benjamin Rush, Jan. 11, 1813, Adams Papers microfilm, Reel 121 (microfilm edition published by the Massachusetts Historical Society, Boston, which owns the originals), hereafter cited as Adams Papers, Reel 121, etc.

2. *Diary and Autobiography*, III, 257–258.

refused to admit his weariness—at ten he was
⌐ and had to puff to keep up with the other boys.
nt also obscured the grounds of his defiance—his
:e to provide him with an intellectual challenge.
on Adams recalled being persuaded rather than
⸜ return to school by his father's favorite appeal
When a fool has a prize in his hands, he has no
:e it."
:o be sett down for a fool," Adams returned to
⸜⸜ instead of working at his prescribed Latin—
. s only entrance requirement—he began to study
⸜⸜netic on his own in protest at what he regarded as Mr.
⸜⸜everly's laziness. "My School master neglected to put me
into Arithmetick longer than I thought was right, and I resented it," he later explained.[3] The pattern of initial, apparently
motiveless defiance growing into self-righteousness became a
familiar one in Adams's life. In order wholeheartedly to com-
mit himself to a task, it seemed, he needed someone to denounce and the chance to make his own actions appear as an
exemplary demonstration of the virtues he had found lacking in
another. This time he persuaded his father to change him to a
private tutor (a Mr. Marsh), dedicated himself to his Latin, and
was able to enter Harvard about a year later at the usual age of
sixteen.

The atmosphere in John Adams's childhood home seems to
have been moralistic but not unbending. Although he recalled
that his grandmother kept a book of strict precepts for children,
he did not indicate that her regime was enforced with especial
severity, or indeed that it was enforced at all. Adams recollected
that after he was caught by his first schoolteacher for having
gone off to shoot birds, he had the temerity to beg his father
and mother to let him go out to the marshes again "to kill wild
fowl and to swim"—and that they let him go.

His parents gave John Adams the gift of freedom. Running

3. Adams to his grandson John, Feb. 2, 1820, Adams Papers, Reel 124; *Diary and Autobiography*, III, 258. On Adams's youthful pudginess see L. H. Butterfield *et al.*, eds., *The Earliest Diary of John Adams* (Cambridge, Mass., 1966), 50n.

about in the semiwilderness around Braintree, learning to smoke at the age of eight when other boys were at work, he developed the taste for independence that marked his life. His father's strict principles—Adams called him "the honestest Man I ever knew"—were combined with "parental Kindness."[4] The deacon's resultant personality encouraged a distinct ethical bias without inhibiting independence.

When he was twenty-three and living at home while making his way as a lawyer, Adams recounted a revealing family squabble in his diary. Complaining about the expense of boarding two servant girls, his mother declared: "I wont have all the Towns Poor brought here, stark naked, for me to clothe for nothing. I wont be a slave to other folks folk for nothing. . . . [You] want to put your Girls over me, to make me a slave to your Wenches." As a selectman Deacon Adams was an overseer of the poor; evidently he brought into his own home those for whom he could make no other arrangements. Like his son in his later political disputes, he began by controlling his anger, then "had his Temper roused at last, tho he uttered not a rash Word, but resolutely asserted his Right to govern." Stubbornly he carried out his town office at financial cost that angered his wife ("she fretts, squibs, scolds, rages, raves"). With a young man's love of order Adams wrote: "Passion, Accident, Freak, Humour, govern in this House." But if the family atmosphere lacked "Cool Reasoning" from the point of view of John Adams at the age of twenty-three (during the spat he "quitted the Room, and took up Tully to compose myself"), it contrasted favorably with the oppressive surroundings still common in the homes of his contemporaries.[5]

While his father set its moral tone, Adams's mother seems to have dominated emotionally in the household. Little is known of Mrs. Susanna Adams beyond her having been a strong woman physically. She outlived her husband, remarried at fifty-

---

4. *Diary and Autobiography*, III, 258n, 256, 276. John Demos reports youths at work between the ages of six and eight into the 18th century. *A Little Commonwealth: Family Life in Plymouth Colony* (New York, 1970), 140–141.

5. *Diary and Autobiography*, I, 65–66.

seven, and died at eighty-eight. Adams associated her with wayward emotion and intellectual disorder—weaknesses of his own. When he married he reproduced in his home the essential conditions of his own childhood. He harangued but "never dictated to" his children, and he concerned himself with their psychological well-being. He chose a wife who held up to the children the highest moral principles in the name of their father yet relied on persuasion rather than force.[6] Adams, nearly ruining himself financially in the public interest, left it to his wife to manage the household during the youth of his children, thereby making her, like his mother, its emotional center in practice if not inclination.

By the time he finished his education Adams forgot his early resistance to it; thereafter he treated his youth as a period of ruinous freedom from parental authority. "Ran over the past Passages of my Life," he wrote in 1760: "Little Boats, water mills, wind mills, whirly Giggs, Birds Eggs, Bows and Arrows, Guns, singing, pricking Tunes, Girls &c. Ignorance [on the part] of Parents, Masters Cleverly, Marsh, Tutors Mayhew &c. [at Harvard]. By a constant Dissipation among Amuzements, in my Childhood, and by the Ignorance of my Instructors, in the more advanced years of my Youth, my Mind has laid uncultivated so that at 25, I am obliged to study Horace and Homer.—Proh Dolor!" After resisting his father's wishes Adams made them his own and then exceeded them. At Harvard, demanding more of himself than was asked for became a habit: "I soon perceived a growing Curiosity, a Love of Books and a fondness for Study, which dissipated all my Inclination for Sports, and even for the Society of the Ladies. . . . I got my Lessons regularly and performed my recitations without Censure."[7]

Adams had begun the narrowing and restricting process that

6. Page Smith, *John Adams* (Garden City, N.Y., 1962), II, 1017. For Adams and his wife on their children see John Adams to Abigail Adams, July 1, 1774, and Abigail Adams to John Quincy Adams, June [10?], 1778, and to John Thaxter, Aug. 19, 1778, all in L. H. Butterfield *et al.*, eds., *Adams Family Correspondence* (Cambridge, Mass., 1963–), I, 118, III, 37, 78, hereafter cited as *Adams Family Correspondence*.

7. *Diary and Autobiography*, I, 131, III, 261–262.

he identified with achievement. For the next ten years he tried to tame his spirit—by methods that ranged from periodically attempting to avoid the stimulus of company, especially the ladies', to adopting one handwriting where he had begun with several. In narrating his college years he emphasized his youthful effort to regularize his spirit. At the time he told himself, "I should moderate my Passions, regulate my Desires." But he could not help "devouring Books without Advice and without Judgment"—another lifelong habit. Adams strove for but never achieved the kind of genius represented by "Order, Method, System, Connection, Plan."[8]

Nor did he grow less defiant. When his mother and aunt visited him during his sophomore year they found his room lacking even the modest conveniences of the time, for he was "loth to burden my father with the expence." Yet, by persisting in mathematical and scientific studies inappropriate to a preparation for the ministry he continued to oppose his father's will. This grew clear when he considered taking up the law instead of the ministry. In his autobiography he offered a series of rationalizations, any one of which sufficiently justified him but that taken together suggested uneasiness with his plan. He recalled that at a student club formed for the purpose of holding literary and dramatic readings, "I was as often requested to read as any other, especially Tragedies, and it was whispered to me and circulated among others that I had some faculty for public Speaking and that I should make a better Lawyer than Divine."[9]

But his choice of a profession was not simply a matter of following a natural bent toward public speaking, a skill that served as well in a pulpit as a courtroom. Actually Adams was justifying a decision made before he went to college to avoid the stuffiness of the ministry. Continuing his autobiographical

8. Butterfield *et al.*, eds., *Earliest Diary*, 77; Adams to Rush, Jan. 11, 1813, Adams Papers, Reel 121; Butterfield *et al.*, eds., *Earliest Diary*, 73. The quotations on passions and order are from 1758.

9. Adams to John Quincy Adams, Jan. 12, 1824, Adams Papers, Reel 124; *Diary and Autobiography*, III, 263. Adams recalled his scientific enthusiasm in letters to Samuel Sewall, Nov. 23, 1821, Adams Papers, Reel 124, and to Francis Adrian Vanderkemp, Sept. 3, 1815, Vanderkemp Papers, Pennsylvania Historical Society, Philadelphia.

explanations, though he nowhere else spoke of any influence over his life by relatives, Adams introduced as one of his primary considerations a concern for his uncles' "most illiberal Prejudices against the Law." His father he made his last and least concern, for, "Although my Fathers general Expectation was that I should be a Divine, I knew him to be a Man of so thoughtful and considerate a turn of mind, to be possessed of so much Candor and moderation, that it would not be difficult to remove any objections he might make to my pursuit of Physick or Law or any other reasonable Course."[10] In fact, Adams's leaning toward the insecure and still only barely respectable legal profession amounted to a daring move for a young man without means.

But it was a move of a piece with his independent nature. During his college years he attended an "Ecclesiastical Council" at his father's house, at which the local minister was examined and criticized for his opinions and "his Conduct, which was too gay and light if not immoral." Such councils—"frightful engines" of intellectual oppression Adams called them about a year later—"never failed to terrify" him. His "Inclination . . . was to preach," but the religious establishment threatened his "liberty to think." At his graduation from college Adams understandably hesitated at committing himself to the law instead of the ministry. Only a couple of dozen men in the province were practitioners, the people still held the idea of a lawyer in distrust, and it was understood to be a suitable profession only for young men of means. Had he been born wealthy, his letters during his retirement suggest, he would have undertaken a career as an essayist. As it was he accepted the post of Latin master—schoolmaster, really—for the town of Worcester, Massachusetts, after its minister had been sufficiently impressed with his graduation–exercise Latin performance to offer him the job. Schoolteaching was not quite a profession, but his

10. *Diary and Autobiography*, III, 263. Adams told the story of deciding against the ministry before going to college when he was an old man. See Donald H. Stewart and George P. Clark, "Misanthrope or Humanitarian? John Adams in Retirement," *New England Quarterly*, XXVIII (1955), 228–229.

uncle, cousin, and many others had taken it up before going into the ministry. Outside of the approved trinity it was the one respectable source of income available to a graduate who needed time to accustom himself and his family to the idea of his becoming something other than a minister.[11]

From his upbringing in nearby Braintree, John Adams knew well the life of a town like Worcester, with its fifteen hundred inhabitants. His great-grandson Charles Francis Adams, Jr., reconstructed that life with an eye for dreary detail that, if it reflected the pessimism of a later generation of Adamses, nevertheless makes a convincing picture. In the houses of farmers of Deacon Adams's class "a huge stack of brick chimneys was the central idea, as well as fact." The house "was one room only in depth, and two stories in height." John Adams could look forward to boarding in Worcester at homes comparable to the relatively opulent seats of such local Braintree worthies as the Quincys and Sewalls. But in the best houses: "The cold of the sitting-rooms was tempered by huge wood fires, which roasted one half of the person while the other half was exposed to chilling drafts. The women sat at table in shawls, and the men in overcoats. Writing on the 'Lord's Day, January 15th, 1716,' Judge Sewall notes, . . . 'Bread was frozen at the Lord's Table. . . . At six o'clock my ink freezes so I can hardly write by a good fire in my Wive's Chamber.' " A visitor of the next century to one of the towns that held these homes "would find no newspapers, no mails, no travellers, few books, and those to

11. *Diary and Autobiography*, III, 262; Charles Francis Adams, ed., *The Works of John Adams, Second President of the United States: With a Life of the Author, Notes and Illustrations, by His Grandson Charles Francis Adams* (Boston, 1850–1856), I, 35, hereafter cited as *Works of John Adams; Diary and Autobiography*, I, 43, III, 263. On the legal profession at the time see Adams to Vanderkemp, Sept. 3, 1815, Vanderkemp Papers, and Gerard W. Gawalt, "Sources of Anti-Lawyer Sentiment in Massachusetts, 1740–1840," *American Journal of Legal History*, XIV (1970), 285, 301. If Adams's enemy Peter Oliver is to be believed, Adams showed his ambitiousness by choosing the law since "this Employment [school-master] is generally the Porch of Introduction to the sacred office, in *New England*." Douglass Adair and John A. Schutz, eds., *Peter Oliver's Origin and Progress of the American Revolution: A Tory View* (San Marino, Calif., 1961), 83 (italics in original). F. W. Grinnell has 25 members at the Massachusetts bar before the Revolution. "The Bench and Bar in Colony and Province (1630–1776)," chap. 6 of Albert Bushnell Hart, ed., *The Commonwealth History of Massachusetts*, II (New York, 1928), 173.

him wholly unreadable, Sunday the sole holiday, and the church, the tavern and the village store the only places of resort or amusement."[12]

Such was the life that John Adams returned to from Harvard College. Without a library, with little intellectual stimulation and few comforts, the single young man earnestly seeking his calling needed both physical and spiritual toughness to survive. And yet, beneath the surface—so little changed from the seventeenth century—a great transition was taking place from Puritan to Yankee attitudes. John Adams's defiance of his father was representative of a gradual erosion of parental authority in eighteenth-century New England. And the fiery independence that marked his life well expressed the atmosphere of freedom generated by a universal drift away from seventeenth-century Puritanism. The Yankee tended to express his anxieties not by suffering guilt like his forebears but through conflict with others—something that needs to be remembered in the case of John Adams's lifelong contentiousness.[13] At the same time, those Yankees who continued to feel the old prohibition against worldly gain were able to discharge their guilt in public benefices and public service rather than through self-denial.

But it was here that Adams differed. His aspiration for personal greatness was not in the main worldly. Indeed, it resembled the state of grace sought after by his ancestors, and it involved him in doubts and guilts far more like theirs than the misgivings of the successful merchants and professional men among whom he began to make his way. The Adamses, with their ministers who had aspired to and achieved only modest success of a worldly kind, left Adams a tradition of required public service different from the obligations of wealth handed down to his neighbors Samuel and Edmund Quincy, who also went on to public life. Adams's father served under theirs in the

12. Charles Francis Adams, Jr., *Three Episodes of Massachusetts History: The Settlement of Boston Bay; The Antinomian Controversy; A Study of Church and Town Government* (Boston and New York, 1892), II, 683, 682, 803 (my ellipsis, then C. F. Adams's). Also see Caleb Wall, *Reminiscences of Worcester* (Worcester, Mass., 1877), 175.

13. See Richard L. Bushman, *From Puritan to Yankee: Character and the Social Order in Connecticut, 1690–1765* (Cambridge, Mass., 1967), 288.

local militia, where an instance of the lieutenant's loyalty to his superior officer pointed up the difference. When a rival succeeded in replacing Josiah Quincy as colonel of the regiment, Deacon Adams refused "with disdain" the offer of a captaincy to serve under him. John Adams recalled the incident, which took place when he was ten, seventy-five years later. The deacon's great-grandson and great-great-grandson both showed pride in his gesture, too, the latter treating it as an instance of "yeoman" loyalty to a superior officer of the "gentry" class. The lesson was not lost on any of these descendants that the distinction of being an Adams involved not so much rising in the world as satisfying one's own standards of duty.[14]

Adams recalled this family tradition in a letter written while he was vice-president: "I am the first who has degenerated from the virtues of the house so far as not to have been an officer in the militia or a deacon"—this even though he had far surpassed the high provincial offices held by Colonel Quincy and had followed in his own family's footsteps better than he indicated. "My father," he went on, "was an honest man a lover of his Country and an independent spirit and the example of that father inspired me with the greatest pride of my life" (i.e., not election to high office but the uncompromising behavior that preceded it).[15] Typically the Adams pride expressed itself in acts of self-denial like the deacon's sacrifices to send his son to college, support the poor, and stand by his colonel. In his diary Adams translated such gestures into personal terms, performing exercises in restraint that prepared him to continue the family tradition where his father had left off. His defiances of his father, meanwhile, perpetuated the family trait of stubborn independence. But Adams owed his father a debt for having

14. Charles Francis Adams reprinted Adams's Oct. 27, 1820, letter to Jonathan Mason, here quoted from Adams Papers, Reel 124, in *Works of John Adams*, II, 93n-94n; Charles Francis, Jr., quoted from it in *Three Episodes of Massachusetts History*, II, 712, where he used the terms "gentry" and "yeoman." Samuel (1735–1789), the lawyer and loyalist, and Edmund (1733–1768), called "Ned," were sons of Col. Josiah Quincy, the Braintree justice and moderator of the town meeting, whom Adams referred to as "Coll. Quincy."

15. Adams to John Trumbull, Mar. 9, 1790, Adams Papers, Reel 115. Adams did serve briefly in the militia but apparently discounted this since it was in Boston. See Adams to James Tudor, May 10, 1817, *ibid.*, Reel 123.

launched him out of the Braintree orbit without preventing him from choosing his own way. He planned to pay him back by conducting his professional life in an exemplary manner.

Adams began in Worcester in 1755. Here, separated from family and friends, he first kept his diary with regularity, developing it into something more than a college lecture note-book and commonplace book. He continued his college prac-tice of observing the day's weather, but to this he now added a notation of who had fed and lodged him, in keeping with the terms of his employment, and who had invited him to tea. He began a separate book for copying and translating passages from his reading. Its emphasis on political writers and secular moralists indicated his proclivity for the law, though his formal decision still lay over a year away.

Adams started his diary on January 14, 1756, five months after coming to Worcester. A month of brief notations led to a generalization—characteristically an expression of dissatisfac-tion with himself:

11 WEDNESDAY.
Serene weather, but somewhat cool. I am constantly forming, but never executing good resolutions.[16]

Adams had begun a process of self-improvement both traced and spurred to execution by his diary. Actually he kept his prom-ises better than he would admit. Early in the morning and late at night he read the ancients and the most improving modern works. During the school day "he used to sit at his Desk . . . nearly all his time, engaged in writing. . . . He seemed, when not actually writing, absorbed in profound thought, and ab-stracted from anything about him—and he kept the School along, by setting one Schollar to teach another."[17]

Before dinner at the house where he was boarding, Adams often was invited to tea. No more satisfied with himself in

16. *Diary and Autobiography*, I, 6. Adams returned to his college weather habit in Europe in 1779–1780, again two years after that, and in 1796 just before becoming president. See Adams Papers, Reel 352, and chap. 9 below.

17. Quoted by Clifford K. Shipton, *Sibley's Harvard Graduates: Biographical Sketches of Those Who Attended Harvard College . . .* , XIII (Cambridge, Mass., 1965), 514–515.

society than in solitude, on returning home he pronounced himself "guilty" of "a childish Affectation of Wit and Gaiety" —"to a very heinous Degree." He kept reminding himself that above all he should not direct his wit too pointedly at highly placed local fools. The best he could manage, however, were fresh resolutions, which left fresh records of his social abandon. Whenever his naturally high spirits emerged, it seems, they carried to the surface opinions better left unexpressed. Too young, well-educated, and self-aware to be the town crank—a position already filled, anyway—Adams's manner expressed the impatience of his youthful perfectionism: "When in Company with Persons much superior to my self in Years and Place, I have talked to shew my Learning. I have been too bold with great men, which Boldness will no doubt be called Self Conceit. I have made ill natured Remarks upon the Intellectuals [i.e., intellectual credentials], manners, Practice &c. of other People."

Although this behavior seems not to have annoyed anyone in society—he continued being welcome in the best houses—Adams worried over his "unhappy Fate" of ever ruining his own chances in life. He kept promising to curb himself, but his terms suggested that his eye for sham was too sharp to be blunted by an enforced, pious respect: "I now resolve for the future, never to say an ill naturd Thing, concerning Ministers or the ministerial Profession, never to say an envious Thing concerning Governers, Judges, Ministers, Clerks, Sheriffs, Lawyers, or any other honorable or Lucrative offices or officers, never to affect Wit upon laced Wastecoats or large Estates or their Possessors, never to shew my own Importance or Superiority, by remarking the Foibles, Vices, or Inferiority of others."[18] What appears as calculated self-interest in such entries in Adams's diary is belied by the behavior they chronicle. Adams admonished himself like a wily politician while continuing to risk alienating the lawyers and ministers with whom he soon would be dealing as a fellow professional. (Having

18. *Diary and Autobiography*, I, 37.

stopped considering medicine as a possible career, he insulted no doctors.)

As long as he conceived of behavior in terms of conceit and utility, Adams would remain uncomfortable with his own wit. Yet, even in coming home to his diary in a paroxysm of remorse for his bold remarks in company, he called those he had attacked "superior . . . in Years and Place" but not in ability. Thus he implied that his fault lay not in "Self Conceit," which involved a false valuation of one's own worth, but in failing to observe the social amenities. At this period Adams entertained doubts not about his own superiority but about how to behave with it.

Later in life he suffered over the question whether he was vain. He ignored the useful distinction between vanity and pride that states, "A man is *proud* who values himself on the possession" of his "talent," "acquirements," or "superiority"; in contrast, "he is *vain* of his person, his dress, his walk, or anything that is frivolous." After nearly a lifetime of self-recrimination for being vain Adams finally made this distinction, only to return to a conviction of his vanity. In the meantime, aware of the contradiction between his sharp-tongued table talk and his imminent obligation to put on a laced waistcoat of his own, he resolved "to take Notice chiefly of the amiable Qualities of other People, to put the most favourable Construction upon the Weaknesses, Bigotry, and Errors of others . . . and to labour more for an inoffensive and amiable than for a shining and invidious Character."[19] Still, much as he sought the universal admiration that he felt he deserved, he never could put himself out to be popular. The truth was that from the beginning he courted not popularity but unpopularity as a mark of distinction. Outside of his own family there were only a few men whose approbation he could bear.

Living in Worcester with the express purpose of deciding on a profession, Adams dutifully wrote out religious exercises that

19. George Crabb, *English Synonyms Explained, in Alphabetical Order, with Copious Illustrations and Examples Drawn from the Best Writers* . . . , new ed., s.v. "pride"; *Diary and Autobiography*, I, 37.

suggest the outlines of practice sermons. Concerned with appreciating the majesty of "the Creator" through the "amazing harmony" and "Stupendous Plan of operation" of his universe, these essays made good Enlightenment religious doctrine but promised only trouble if they should be uttered in public. Much more in the spirit of the times, or at least of the town, were the sermons of "Mr. Maccarty," the man who had hired Adams: "You who are sinners, are in continual Danger of being swallowed up quick and born away by the mighty Torrent of Gods wrath and Justice. It is now as it were restrained and banked up by his Goodness. But he will by and by, unless Repentance prevent, let it out in full Fury upon you." Adams dutifully took this down, but he was too sophisticated in his religious views to be drawn toward exercising his collegiate dramatic talent in hell-fire sermons. Furthermore, he was keenly aware of the political and intellectual turmoil of the age. "The Years of my Youth are marked by divine Providence with various and with great Events," he wrote in his diary in 1756, and he went on to mention the opening battles in the Seven Years' War. "The greatest Part of Europe and the greatest Part of America, has been in violent Convulsions," he concluded.[20]

In such a time the most startling political and religious ideas were discussed freely even in Worcester, Massachusetts: "perfect Equality of Suffrage" (not advocated later by even the most radical figures of the American and French revolutions) and the various Protestant apostasies of the day—Arianism, Deism, and even atheism ("that all Religion was a cheat, a cunning invention of Priests and Politicians"). Yet, for all the turmoil religious dissent was not tolerated. The ecclesiastical council that met while Adams was in college examined the local minister "partly on Account of his Principles which were called Arminian."[21]

Adams, too, held "Opinion[s] concerning some disputed Points." His belief in the efficacy of an ethical life and his

---

20. *Diary and Autobiography*, I, 24, 31, 35, 36. "Mr. Maccarty," as Adams commonly referred to him, was the Rev. Thaddeus Maccarty (1721–1784).

21. *Ibid.*, III, 265, 264, 262.

instinct for toleration were both essentially "Arminian." Such a theology would have involved him in a life of unproductive controversy in any of the New England towns where he might have expected to begin as a minister. On the other hand, the same argumentativeness that precluded the ministry, suited the law. During court week in Worcester, Adams was bemused. He "neither read or wrote any Thing worth mentioning" and had "not one new Idea." On Wednesday his only diary entry read: "Rambled about all Day, gaping and gazing." He recalled in his autobiography that "the Law attracted my Attention more and more, and Attending the Courts of Justice, where I heard Worthington, Hawley, Trowbridge, Putnam and others, I felt myself irresistably impelled to make some Effort to accomplish my Wishes." Among the lawyers he found "a noble air and gallant achievements"; among the clergy, the "pretended sanctity of some absolute dunces."[22] Everything continued to point toward Adams's eventually becoming a lawyer, but he needed to go through the motions of soberly considering the matter both practically and philosophically before declaring himself.

The process became a familiar one in Adams's life. He commonly began with a desire accompanied by a scruple over the purity of his motive, and this delayed his decision. As he put it in his autobiography: "My Inclination was soon fixed upon the Law: But my Judgment was not so easily determined." His choice frequently lay between obscurity (demonstrated in this case by the lives of the previous Adams family ministers) and prominence (demonstrated by James Putnam, the young Worcester lawyer well connected with the leading men of the province). Always attracted to prominence, as in his growing friendship with Putnam, Adams would subject himself to a period of atoning preparation before approaching it. (His Puritan forebears had prepared themselves in their diaries for the glorious choice of Christ by a similar humbling process.) To convince himself that his choice was justified Adams had to

22. *Ibid.*, I, 43, 27, 26, III, 264; Adams to Charles Cushing, Oct. 19, 1756, Adams Papers, Reel 114. The legal figures mentioned were John Worthington, Joseph Hawley, Edmund Trowbridge, and James Putnam.

find difficulty and personal disadvantage in it. With the law, though "indeed an avenue to the more important offices of the State," he would be at a disadvantage for lack of "birth and fortune." On the other hand, "the more danger the greater glory" in success.[23] In the end Adams would take a sudden step toward gaining public acclaim (later without the ingenuous admission that he sought glory). Apparently precipitous, his final decision signified that his preparation was complete, the choice itself having been clear for some time.

During the crucial few months that led to announcing for the law Adams reported evenings spent "gaily" and "very sociably" with the ladies and gentlemen of the town. College friends occasionally came to visit, and during school vacations he traveled home to Braintree, visiting relatives on the way there and back. At times the provincial society of Worcester overwhelmed him: "I have no Books, no Time, no Friends. I must therefore be contented to live and die an ignorant, obscure fellow." He continued as schoolmaster in his "school of affliction," applied himself to his diary, took lonely walks, and sat ruminating in the woods. He courted stoic acceptance, but his rage to succeed broke through: "The Scituation that I am in, and the Advantages that I enjoy, are thought to be the best for me by him who alone is a competent Judge of Fitness and Propriety. Shall I then complain? Oh Madness, Pride, Impiety." It was *madness* to entertain thoughts of glory in the hamlet of Worcester, and it was an *impiety* to do so when it was evidently God's will that Adams be assigned the small but respectable station that he held there. But *pride* urged him on, as he guiltily recognized. It led to his jaunty public behavior, his desire to transcend Worcester society, and finally, a week after his outburst, to his decision to become a lawyer. He went to James Putnam after court week and arranged to study and board with him for two years. In order to pay his board and fee he was

23. *Diary and Autobiography*, III, 263; Adams to Cushing, Apr. 1, 1756, and Oct. 18, 1756, Adams Papers, Reel 114. For the lives of two previous family ministers, Adams's uncles Joseph and Ebenezer, see Shipton, *Sibley's Harvard Graduates*, V, 502, XII, 103.

"condemned" to continue keeping school.[24] No sooner had he made these arrangements than he lengthily summarized in his diary the week's sermon, not for his usual purpose of studying the minister's habits of address but rather in briefly remorseful expiation for his choice.

Since Adams's estimate of his own abilities was justified, it may appear strange that he should have found it so difficult, even in a diary, to admit the innocent desire to attain some place in the world through the law. In contrast, he frankly admitted a "Passion" for fame when writing to his classmates. He asked his friend John Wentworth to "redouble" his letters because they so fired him with ambition. But Adams merely discussed fame in letters. He prepared himself for it in his diary—not by stimulating his desire but by damping it. In his Worcester diary he launched a lifelong, secret struggle with pride calculated to make him worthy of success. He attempted to achieve humility both in social behavior and in his heart of hearts: "Oh! that I could wear out of my mind every mean and base affectation, conquer my natural Pride and Self Conceit, expect no more defference from my fellows than I deserve, acquire that meekness, and humility, which are the sure marks and Characters of a great and generous Soul."[25] Of course, Adams never could become a humble man; at most he might restrain himself in some situations. Indeed, the very form in which the idea of humility cast itself in his mind revealed that he really wanted justice (that "defference . . . I deserve") and greatness ("a great and generous Soul"). As he went on to say, if he could "subdue every unworthy Passion" he would be assured "a happy immortality."

But why call the passion to succeed in the world "unworthy"? Cannot a man have idealistic ambitions? Is all strong

24. *Diary and Autobiography*, I, 5, 22, 27; *Works of John Adams*, I, 28; *Diary and Autobiography*, I, 42; *Works of John Adams*, I, 32. Also see slightly later recollections, *Diary and Autobiography*, I, 98, II, 19.

25. Butterfield *et al*., eds., *Earliest Diary*, 64–65; *Diary and Autobiography*, I, 7–8. Wentworth (1737–1820), eventually a loyalist and the last royal governor of New Hampshire, was a good friend until the Revolution came between Adams and him.

feeling unworthy? Adams would have said that in planning to achieve the most selfless aim, one logically has to wish oneself a measure of personal success in the process. Once having done so, he would have insisted, one no longer can trust the motive urging toward this success. "If Virtue was to be rewarded with Wealth," he wrote years later, "it would not be Virtue. If Virtue was to be rewarded with Fame, it would not be Virtue of the sublimest Kind."[26]

What Adams knew in his letters, then—that greatness comes not from subduing but from igniting the passion in one's soul—he could not accept in his diary. A diary, the very keeping of which was an act that retained moral overtones from the Puritan period, raised problems that a letter, subject to ordinary standards of behavior, did not. If, like John Winthrop and others before him, Adams made of his diary the instrument —he called it an "Apparatus"—of his ambition, it was an instrument of restraint as well. Self-improvement through self-denial was the Adams way, with no provision for recognizing the desired end any more than a Puritan, obsessed with his salvation, was allowed to regard as efficacious his acts aimed toward achieving it. Furthermore, unlike salvation fame presented an unresolvable conundrum.[27] Without genius there was no desirable fame, while "men of the most exalted Genius and active minds, are generally perfect slaves to the Love of Fame."

Adams began to work out a psychological system with the puzzle of fame at its center. How was it, to begin with, that the same overweening desire for fame afflicted both the "Phylosopher" and the "gay Gentleman"? "Is this perfection," Adams asked himself (that is, is this the way God intended it to be?), or is it "downright madness and distraction?" "—A cold day," he concluded on this occasion, having for the first time omitted to begin a diary entry with a weather notation.

26. *Diary and Autobiography*, I, 8; Adams to Abigail Adams, Dec. 2, 1778, *Adams Family Correspondence*, III, 125.

27. *Diary and Autobiography*, I, 352, 8. The phrase "instrument for ambition" and the comparison with John Winthrop appear in Steven Earl Kagle, "Instrument for Ambition: The Personal and Artistic Significance of the Diary of John Adams" (Ph.D. diss., University of Michigan, 1967).

Where genius was not in question the desire to excel could be put to use by society. "I find by repeated experiment and observation, in my School," Adams wrote in a rare mention of his occupation, "that human nature is more easily wrought upon and governed, by promises and incouragement and praise than by punishment, and threatning and Blame." With his students, he went on, at once recalling his father's approach with him and anticipating the central thesis of his "Discourses on Davila" thirty-five years later, "corporal as well as disgraceful punishments, depress the spirits, but commendation enlivens and stimulates them to a noble ardor and emulation." Exalted geniuses, on the other hand, "sometimes descend to as mean tricks and artifices, in pursuit of Honour or Reputation, as the Miser descends to, in pursuit of Gold." Thus the man who succumbs to a "Love of Glory will make a General sacrifice [of] the Interest of his Nation, to his own Fame." Finally, "the greatest men have been the most envious, malicious, and revengeful." In this part of his theory, clearly meant for himself, Adams was much less charitable than with his students and indeed the rest of mankind. He fell back on the moral absolutism of his impossible struggle for humility and pronounced, "He is not a wise man and is unfit to fill any important Station in Society, that has left one Passion in his Soul unsubdued."[28]

Adams located both the highest and the lowest expressions of man's nature in the desire for fame. But his chief interest in the problem, except for his own case, was not moral but political: he explored the implications of ambition for a well-ordered polity. He concluded that society needed to stimulate ordinary men to "emulation"—the desire to shine in the eyes of one's fellows. The great ones, rather than being exhorted to humility, needed to have their desire to excel directed toward socially useful ends. The question of how to control the latter group eventually became the central concern of Adams's theoretical works.

The theory that man is moved by the love of praise was a

28. *Ibid.*, 9, 8, 33. See chap. 8 below for a discussion of Adams's theory of emulation.

philosophical commonplace of the seventeenth and eighteenth centuries. Adams adopted it with special fervor but exempted himself from its permission to be ambitious. He distrusted the pride certain to accompany his success, even though the theory allowed the kind of pride that followed on honorable means. Others he judged by their acts, himself by his thoughts. But a man who deals harshly with himself may not take easily to the criticism of others. Once having pronounced, "Vanity I am sensible, is my cardinal Vice and cardinal Folly," Adams rejected the same imputation by the burghers of Worcester.[29] He resisted criticism because he faced the world exonerated, or at least already mortified. Not surprisingly, few of his fellow townsmen understood the peculiar combination of diffidence and certainty in his manner—the result of private criticism stronger than their own sometimes showing through and sometimes producing an aftermath of self-righteousness.

Adams defined his character when he wrote, "Honesty, Sincerity and openness, I esteem essential marks of a good mind." He eventually evolved a severe, controlled manner that history has remembered better than the enthusiasm it masked. But while he lived in Worcester he remained ingenuous. John Quincy Adams wrote of him: "A deeply conscientious moral sense, combining with an open disposition, averse to all disguise or concealment," combined with his "quickness of temper, produced in after life an occasional irritability which he was not always able to suppress." If, from the point of view of his son, John Adams lacked control, nevertheless he behaved with more circumspection than his father the deacon, who could be drawn into family spats and who told off-color stories in company. Worcester conversation, Adams reported with sophisticated contempt, "is dry disputes upon politics, and rural obscene wit." Still, John Quincy was right. Whatever the social checks Adams thought it necessary to impose upon himself he could not hold himself back in a controversy. "I

29. *Diary and Autobiography*, I, 25. On 17th– and 18th–century theories see Arthur O. Lovejoy, *Reflections on Human Nature* (Baltimore, 1961), 131.

am . . . of opinion," he wrote, "that men ought . . . to avow their Opinions and defend them with boldness."[30] This he did through life, although when he was older few recognized in his opinionated outbursts the sparks of his youthful openness.

Adams's conviction was the product of an accumulation of righteousness built up in his diary. The Puritan diarists before him had undergone a similar daily introspection aimed at "softening" the heart to make it ready for salvation. For Adams it was pride that had to be broken down ("Oh! that I could *wear out* of my mind every mean and base affectation") in order to make him ready for his secular destiny. His lonely struggle with ambition was attended with as many doubts as the theological struggles of the Puritan diarists, who daily measured their progress toward the great community in heaven. Furthermore, his notations of study habits and expenses along with his progress in virtue reflected a notion of accountability similar to that of the Puritans, who aimed in their diaries to keep accurate spiritual records.[31]

Just as every act or thought of the Puritan adumbrated salvation, so for Adams any habit might predict his future. He was as dissatisfied with himself when he failed to rise at the hour before sunrise that he had assigned himself—"Rose not till 7 o clock. This is the usual Fate of my Resolutions!"—as when he could not adjust his social disposition to a balanced norm—"I find my self very much inclin'd to an unreasonable absence of mind, and to a morose, unsociable disposition. Let it therefore be my constant endeavour to reform these great faults." And he was as upset when he "smoaked, chatted, trifled, loitered away this whole day almost," as when he felt hints of his besetting sin of pride.[32] For the secularized Adams as for the religious Puritan the scrutiny of the self-examiner proved to be more severe than that of any putative future judge.

30. *Diary and Autobiography*, I, 12; *Works of John Adams*, I, 31, 28.

31. *Diary and Autobiography*, I, 7–8 (italics added). See Norman Pettit, *The Heart Prepared: Grace and Conversion in Puritan Spiritual Life* (New Haven, Conn., 1966), and Cynthia G. Wolff, "Literary Reflections of Puritanism," *Journal of the History of Ideas*, XXIX (1968), 13–32.

32. *Diary and Autobiography*, I, 35, 10, 45.

Adams found irresistible the opportunities in eighteenth-century America for attaining worldly fame, while at the same time retaining a version of the Puritans' striving for a perfect soul. As with the Puritans, purity of motive continued to be essential to his sense of personal integrity. Whereas Benjamin Franklin is often cited as the typical Puritan manqué, he was much further from the original character because his concern was all with practical external results. Adams's preoccupation with his interior, despite his secular ambitions, was much truer to the Puritan type.

Later Adamses regarded John Adams as a typical product of his time and place. As his grandson Charles Francis put it, the history of the Adamses "may stand for the history, not of one, but of most of the families spread over the territory of New England during the colonial period, whose hard labor and persevering, but unobtrusive virtues, made it what it is." Adams himself viewed the rise of the family in Braintree, a place that ever retained its "Strange Attraction . . . [with] my Heart," as a representative phenomenon, writing in 1813 that he could "give . . . a History of this Village . . . which would be an Epitomy of the History of the United States."[33] When that history culminated in resistance to Great Britain it drew in large part on the moral capital of Puritanism. It was this capital that prepared Adams for revolution and that produced the righteousness, as he put it, of "three mortals, Hancock and two Adams's" who "set the World in a blaze."

33. *Works of John Adams*, I, 12n; Adams to Thomas McKean, Sept. 19, 1813, Vanderkemp Papers.

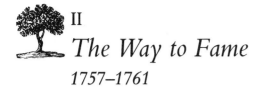

II
The Way to Fame
1757–1761

A week after beginning to study law with James Putnam, Adams stopped keeping his diary. He could dispense for the time being with its rigors because he had begun a period of exhaustive application to a task uncomplicated by doubt. (He did not leave off, however, without a final self-criticism; his last entry reported: "Came to Mr. Putnams and began Law. And studied not very closely this Week." Adams "trimm'd the Midnight Lamp" during his remaining two years in Worcester. Continuing as schoolmaster, he studied at night in books obtained by Putnam from London. When he was finished his preparation exceeded that "of any other law student of the time."[1]

James Putnam, then twenty-eight, had just married a second, "beautifull" wife. At his table the two young men disputed politics and religion before her, with Putnam showing that he was no old fogey by taking up daring positions just short of heresy. In defiance of his "master" Adams expounded traditional religious positions despite his own apostate tendencies. Putnam's behavior suggested a fear of Adams as a potential rival in the law. Unaware of Putnam's hostility, Adams suffered under his "satirical and contemptuous smiles" and his assumed air of sternness. Later he "learned with Design to

---

1. *Diary and Autobiography*, I, 44, II, 228; L. Kinvin Wroth and Hiller B. Zobel, eds., *Legal Papers of John Adams* (Cambridge, Mass., 1965), I, lvi n.

imitate Put's Sneer, his sly look, and his look of Contempt."[2]

It was at this period that Adams immersed himself in the religious and political controversies of the day. These were argued in the disputatious style of Massachusetts society. For all its openness to controversial subjects, that society radiated innocence. The gentlemen smoked and drank prodigiously, and they discussed hunting, debauchery, and vice. But there were few, if any, lechers among them, and none so far gone as to champion vice or make insinuations about women. When Adams imagined "Pleasure" and "delight" in his diary he thought of friendship, or of "the Fields of Nature. . . . the Flower, . . . the Prospect of Forrests and Meadows." As for "Pleasure hunting young fellows of the Town," they were guilty of no worse dissipations than "Songs and Girls, . . . flutes, fiddles, Concerts and Card Tables." A flirtatious girl alluded to sex by asking domestic questions: "How shall a [married] Pair avoid falling into Passion or out of humour, upon some Occasions, and treating each other unkindly"? With older men an evening commonly was spent drinking tea and discussing "original sin, Origin of Evil, the Plan of the Universe."[3]

Putnam, whether out of calculation, or as Adams saw it, simple "Insociability, and neglect of me," failed to provide his pupil with letters of recommendation to pave his way. Ignorant of this and other practical omissions in his preparation, in 1758 Adams returned to his parents' house in Braintree ready to commence practice as a lawyer. To arrange admittance to the bar he rode to Boston and presented himself to some of the lawyers Putnam should have contacted. The famous Jeremiah Gridley was impressed by Adams's preparation. He recommended that Adams abandon authors too advanced for him, notably Vinnius, and certainly stop studying Greek, "a meer Curiosity." About two weeks later Gridley spoke up for Adams

2. *Diary and Autobiography*, III, 270, 264–265; Adams to Josiah Quincy, Feb. 9, 1811, *Works of John Adams*, IX, 630; *Diary and Autobiography*, I, 83, 84. Putnam had married Elizabeth Chandler.

3. *Diary and Autobiography*, I, 43, 47, 67, 55. See also Butterfield *et al.*, eds., *Earliest Diary*, 99. These examples are taken from Braintree and Boston, 1758.

at the bar's swearing-in session, saying, "He has made a very considerable, a very great Proficiency in the Principles of the Law."[4]

In the course of his study Adams had grown self-confident, as his decision to practice in Braintree made apparent. Two leading citizens of Worcester had offered him a sinecure as town register of deeds if he would set up as their second lawyer (besides Putnam). In his autobiography Adams gave several reasons for refusing the offer, just as he did for his decision to become a lawyer, for again he was unaware of his deepest motive. He spoke of his reluctance to go into competition with his benefactor, and especially of his positive attraction to Braintree, where, in addition to enjoying the pleasures of the setting, he would be the only lawyer in the town. What he did not mention, however, was that the Braintree district included Boston and hence the best lawyers in the province. This challenge was what attracted Adams, though in his autobiographical account he made the one "decisive" motive for his move an excuse he frequently had recourse to—bad air. In this case it was Worcester's "want of the Breezes from the Sea and the pure Zephirs from the rocky mountains of my native Town."[5] He was not seeking repose, though, when he chose to walk first into the office of the leading lawyer of his time, Gridley, to be examined for the bar, nor did he show concern about his health when he chose to compete with Gridley and others of his caliber instead of Putnam.

Gridley advised Adams at the end of their interview "to pursue the Study of the Law rather than the Gain of it," a formula that permitted one to aim at becoming a great lawyer without having to look directly at success itself. But Adams already was reading books of the philosophical sort recommended by Gridley. In fact, a few days before the interview Adams had criticized his relative Dr. Elisha Savil in terms that anticipated Gridley's advice: "He is negligent of the Theory of

4. *Diary and Autobiography*, I, 63, 55, 58. On Vinnius see *ibid.*, III, 271. Jeremiah Gridley (1702–1767) was probably the leading member of the Massachusetts bar.

5. *Ibid.*, III, 270.

his Profession, and will live and die unknown.—These driveling souls, oh! He aims not at fame, only at a Living and a fortune!"[6] His two years with Putnam had reconciled Adams, at least for the time being, to the idea that the pursuit of fame logically required the pursuit of personal distinction—and he now could say so in his diary. His friends Robert Treat Paine and Samuel Quincy, the one recently admitted to practice, the other soon to be sworn in along with Adams, disappointed him with their lack of ambition. Quincy lacked "Courage enough to harbour a Thought of acquiring a great Character," while none of the other young lawyers of the district had "a foundation that will support them." In contrast, his own extensive knowledge of the law, if he could make it known, would "draw upon me the Esteem and perhaps Admiration, (tho possibly the Envy too) of the Judges, . . . Lawyers and of Juries, who will spread my Fame thro the Province."[7]

Adams's question no longer was what kind of ambition could be accepted but how to go about securing fame. He feared that among the other lawyers "Envy, Jealousy, and self Intrest, will not suffer them to give a young fellow a free generous Character, especially me." And so he looked to "take one bold determined Leap into the Midst of some Cash and Business," to start some "new, grand, wild, yet regular Thought that may raise me at once to fame." Whatever his dreams Adams accepted as the immediate term of his getting ahead the establishment of a successful law practice. "Reputation," he wrote, "ought to be the perpetual subject of my Thoughts, and Aim of my Behaviour."

Despite his acceptance of ambition, however, Adams continued to be insulted when anyone alluded to his high aspirations. Unfortunately, this was just the charge that he laid himself open to when he accused his friends of aiming too low:

6. *Ibid.*, I, 55, 53. Savil, married to a niece of Adams's parents, rented a next-door cottage from Deacon Adams.

7. *Ibid.*, 51, 52; Butterfield *et al.*, eds., *Earliest Diary*, 77. Robert Treat Paine (1731–1814), one of Adams's contemporaries at the bar, remained bitterly envious of Adams throughout their service together at the Continental Congresses. Samuel Quincy remained Adams's rival at the bar. A loyalist, he eventually went to live in England.

Paine (to me). You dont intend to be a Sage, I suppose. Oh! P. has not Penetration to reach the Bottom of my mind. He dont know me. Next time I will answer him, A Sage, no. Knowledge eno' to keep out of fire and Water, is all that I aim at.[8]

Paine could not distinguish between aspiring to the reputation of being a sage and aspiring toward wisdom itself, so Adams was forced to deny that he harbored any aspiration to either. Privately, though, Adams grew not only tolerant of ambition but intolerant of those who lacked it. Paine's and Quincy's willingness to live conventional lives struck him as evidence that each lacked spirit. Similarly, Parson Anthony Wibird, who confessed to Adams that he was attracted to Quincy's sister Hannah, but had "not Resolution enough to court a Woman," he judged to be "benevolent, sociable, friendly," and to have "a pretty Imagination, Wit, some Humour but little grandeur, Strength, Penetration of mind. In short, he has an amiable and elegant, not a great mind."[9] The men around him now had to measure up to his own hopes of greatness.

Characteristically, Adams could not keep his judgments to himself. He began to espouse his idealism with boyish pomposity: "I talk to Mr. Wibirt about the Decline of Learning, tell him, I know no young fellow who promises to make a figure." Parson Wibird was intimidated by this talk into confessing his own weaknesses, but Adams's young friends gave him the measure of scorn that youth reserves for idealistic youth: "I talk to Paine about Greek, that makes him laugh. I talk to Sam Quincy about Resolution, and being a great Man, and study and improving Time, which makes him laugh. I talk to Ned [Quincy], about the Folly of affecting to be a Heretick, which makes him mad. I talk to Hannah [Quincy] and Easther [her cousin] about the folly of Love, about despizing it, about being above it, pretend to be insensible of tender Passions, which makes them laugh."[10]

8. *Diary and Autobiography*, I, 78, 95, 78, 52.
9. *Ibid.*, 74. Rev. Anthony Wibird (1729–1800) remained in Braintree, then Quincy, all his life without marrying, always on cordial terms with the Adamses.
10. *Ibid.*, 68, 67-68. Hannah Quincy (1736–1826), daughter of Col. Josiah Quincy, married twice, the first time badly. She and Adams met and recalled their early flirtation when both were in their eighties.

Adams blamed himself, first, for not having "conversed enough with the World, to behave rightly" and, second, as he had in Worcester, for "Affectation and Ostentation" in advertising his indifference to worldly success: " 'Tis Affectation of Learning, and Virtue and Wisdom, which I have not, and it is a weak fondness to shew all that I have, and to be thot to have more than I have." Once again, though, he justified himself at the same time as he criticized. For his diary's train of jumbled thoughts led to Hannah Quincy, who, unlike himself, practiced "the Art of pleasing." The result: "Her face and Hart have no Correspondence."[11] By implication his own case was not one of affectation, since his private and public aspirations were, after all, identical.

Of all his attempts at self-control, Adams's rationality about love had the least chance of success in a stormy nature such as his. He recalled in his autobiography: "I was of an amorous disposition and very early from ten or eleven Years of Age, was very fond of the Society of females. I had my favorites among the young Women and spent many of my Evenings in their Company and this disposition although controlled for seven Years after my Entrance into College [that is, until his return to Braintree in 1758] returned and engaged me too much till I was married." He had advised his friend Richard Cranch to "conquer" his "Passion" for Hannah Quincy, but he very nearly proposed to her himself—only a fortuitous interruption saved him. This was Adams's period of "gallanting the Girls," and even after his balked offer he kept complaining that he could not work for "thinking on a Girl [Hannah]."[12]

Adams had time to make a fool of himself, because his law practice was not yet under way. The most dangerous periods of his life proved to be those without enough to occupy his ambitions. This time the result was no worse than wandering about his parents' house with his Cicero, then suffering in the loneliness of his room the urgings of a conscience that no

11. *Ibid.*, 67, 68.
12. *Ibid.*, III, 260; Adams to Charles Cushing, Oct. 18, 1756, Adams Papers, Reel 114; *Diary and Autobiography*, I, 57, 118.

amount of study could assuage. When he stepped out into society at the end of the day—feeling vaguely guilty for not being at his desk—he brought with him all the aspiration and nervous energy that his work-starved system had produced.

Adams found a more favorable testing ground once he had some legal work to occupy him. But here, too, he began awkwardly. The litigants in his first case were two local farmers, Luke Lambert and Joseph Field, feuding neighbors for years. The presiding justice of the peace was Hannah's father, Colonel Josiah Quincy, the opposing lawyer Samuel Quincy, the colonel's son who had failed Adams's standards of ambition. Two of Lambert's horses had broken into Field's pasture, and Field had taken them up, as the saying went, for the purpose of having them impounded until Lambert should be forced to pay damages for the trespass. Before Field could carry out his intention Lambert ran in and retrieved his horses, performing what was called a "rescous," or illegal removal of the animals from Field's declared legal custody. The case had begun just before Adams's admittance to the bar. He had attended its first round and pointed out the technicality that caused Field to lose. Now, approximately two months after his return to Braintree, Adams was engaged by Field to serve a second writ on Lambert. This time there were to be no slipups; one can presume that Field and Adams expected Justice Quincy to uphold any plausible new technicality that his son Samuel might offer in Lambert's defense.

At the time Field came to him, Adams was persisting in his abstruse studies, despite Gridley's advice, for he was working his way through Vinnius's notes on Justinian's *Institutes*—as he advertised to his friends to their annoyance. Robert Treat Paine, Adams noted, "asked me what Duch Commentator I meant? I said Vinnius.—Vinnius, says he, (with a flash of real Envy, but pretended Contempt,) you cant understand one Page of Vinnius." Of course Adams did know his Vinnius. What he did not know was how to draw up Field's writ. Of "the Province Law, and common Matters, . . . I know much less than I do of the Roman Law," he admitted a few months later. He did not want to take Field's case but was persuaded to "by the cruel Reproaches of my Mother [not his father], by the Importunity of Field, and by the fear of having it thought I was incapable of drawing the Writt." Adams worked for several nights to meet the deadline for filing cases in the coming court term. Then came afterthoughts. He realized that he had, indeed, made some technical errors, and he spent weeks of worry and speculation over them. When Field's writ finally was dismissed, evidently because it omitted the name of the county, Adams brooded over the deficiencies that led him to lose his case—"Indiscretion, Inconsideration, Irresolution, and ill Luck."[13]

Adams might have drawn from his experience the lesson that reading Cicero and Vinnius led only to professional incompetence and the resentment of friends. For the character of a duly sworn lawyer, classicist, and Harvard graduate was not enough to command respect for a young man of twenty-three in Braintree. Lambert and Field both knew the law quite well—the one how to "take up" a strayed horse, the other the consequences of having let it break free and the relative risk of performing the further illegality of a rescous. It was not enough, either, to be accepted into the society of the wealthy Quincys, or even to be conducting a flirtation with the colonel's daughter, Hannah. Quite correctly, Adams feared that "an opinion will spread among the People, that I have not Cunning enough to cope with Lambert." He felt "a fluttering concern upon my mind" and on the following day was partly responsible for instigating the family quarrel about the serving girls. Yet, despite temptation to forsake his high-minded approach, Adams contrived to improve his reputation on his own terms. His conception of what would aid him remained lofty, for his question was not, How shall I grow wealthy? (he never did) but "How shall I Spread an Opinion of myself as a Lawyer of distinguished Genius, Learning, and Virtue"? Years later he advised a law student not to worry over learning to draw writs but to master the study of the law.[14]

13. *Diary and Autobiography*, I, 59, 78, 64.
14. *Ibid.*, 65, 66, 78. For Adams's advice to a young lawyer see Adams to Jonathan Mason, July 18, 1776, *Works of John Adams*, IX, 423.

In this spirit Adams plunged into a study of the minutiae of the local law. On point after point of practice he questioned the lawyers with whom he came in contact (Gridley among them), while by letter he posed other legal questions for former classmates. Incessantly he admonished himself to learn his business: "Let me inquire of the next Master of a Ship that I see, what is a Bill of Lading, what the Pursers Book. What Invoices they keep. What Account they keep of Goods. . . ."[15] Adams had begun a process of omnivorous questioning by which he would prepare himself for each challenge in his life. Within a few years he became one of the leading lawyers in the province.

Adams's diary now reflected his development from pursuing a vague program of self-improvement in Worcester to a more organized effort to master the world. Although he continued to lament his social crudities, he also admonished himself to "make Observations" of his neighbors. Like his Puritan forebears he made a natural transition from remorseless self-scrutiny to moral evaluation of others. In the process he left memorable character sketches: Parson Wibird "is crooked, his Head bends forwards, his shoulders are round and his Body is writhed. . . . His Mouth is large, and irregular, his Teeth black and foul, and craggy. . . . his Visage is long, and lank, his Complexion wan, his Cheeks are fallen. . . . When he Walks, he heaves away, and swaggs on one side, and steps almost twice as far with one foot, as with the other. . . . Sometimes throws him self, over the back of his Chair, and scratches his Hed, Vibrates the foretop of his Wigg, thrusts his Hand up under his Wigg." Yet, concluded Adams, thinking of the parson's popularity (and, possibly, his consequent attractiveness to Hannah Quincy), "he is a Genius" at being popular.[16] "Coll. Quincy" affected a high tone in society, never losing the chance to puff up himself and his son Samuel (he praised Adams also, but whether as a test of his vanity Adams could not tell). When the colonel showed his familiar side Adams witheringly detailed his foibles and weaknesses—down to his being seasick

15. *Diary and Autobiography*, I, 53.
16. *Ibid.*, 134, 92–93.

during a boat outing in the bay. Yet, whoever, like the parson and the colonel, knew how to make himself popular, drew Adams's grudging admiration.

In his character sketches Adams was concentrating on the mystery of popularity—one that obsessed him through life. "What is it, that Settles Men's opinions of others?" he asked himself, and he answered, "It is Avidity, Envy, Revenge, Interest [i.e., self-interest]." Here lay the germ of his later theory of social relations as expressed in his "Discourses on Davila," though without that work's disillusionment. Men admired and promoted those who bore marks of success, like Colonel Quincy's house and equipage, for these somehow seemed to promise success to their admirers as well as their possessors. Popularity was decided by the passions, not by sober evaluation of other men's accomplishments or by actual self-interest. All of this was obviously unfair, as Adams's pen portraits implied. Yet, even though the inequity was especially to his own disadvantage, Adams welcomed it as a challenge at least as much as he resented it on philosophical grounds. Thus when he called Andrew Oliver, who could decipher codes, "a very sagacious Trifler" and observed, "but this is his Way to fame," he did so without rancor.[17] Adams had charted his own way to fame, and if he was disturbed by the vagaries of fortune in Braintree, he remained willing to chance them.

In contrast to Andrew Oliver's trifling, Colonel Quincy's self-aggrandizement, and Parson Wibird's courting of popularity by playing with children and asking their mothers questions about them, Adams planned to take the high road to fame—as he quickly let everyone know. "I talk to Parson Smith about despising gay Dress, grand Buildings, great Estates, fame &c.," he wrote, again admonishing himself for expressing his idealism in public. Although he feared that he was only boasting to Parson Smith (his future father-in-law),

---

17. *Ibid.*, 93, 66. Andrew Oliver (1706–1774), a loyalist, became a stamp tax official, with the result that his house was mobbed. He died while he was lieutenant governor, on the eve of the first Continental Congress.

what he told him nevertheless once again agreed with his diary, in which he advised himself, "Tis in vain to expect felicity, without an habitual Contempt of Fortune, Fame, Beauty, Praise, and all such Things."[18]

At about the same time, however, Adams wrote out a Latin tag and its translation on a blank page in his college diary: "Contemptu Famae, contemni Virtutem. A Contempt of Fame generally begets or accompanies a Contempt of Virtue." He went on to observe: "Iago makes the Reflection, that Fame is but breath, but vibrated Air, an empty sound. And I believe Persons of his Character, are most inclined to feel and express such an Indifference about fame."[19] In one place contempt of fame and in the other distrust of those professing that contempt —the two entries together expressed Adams's conundrum.

The phrase *contemptu famae, contemni virtutem* came from Tacitus. The emperor Tiberius, accused of unbecoming pride for planning to erect a temple to honor his mother and himself, bows to popular pressure and repudiates the temple. In his speech Tiberius courts favor by professing contempt of fame. Tacitus, however, makes the remark quoted by Adams: that to hold fame in contempt is to scorn merit as well. Adams agreed with Tacitus's implied disapproval and extended the critique to all wily Tiberius- and Iago-like politicians. Tiberius, Iago, and Richard III represented three kinds of dissembling about fame: false humility, pretended contempt, and ambition excused in the name of human frailty.

Of the three, ostentatious contempt of fame was the most insidious. A virtuous man held the "Phantom" of fame in "contempt" in the sense of refusing to stoop to gain it, but he maintained "a strong affection for the approbation of the wise and good." As Adams put it when he was fifty-five: "Contemptu famae fama augebatur [to act as though contemptuous of fame is to increase one's fame]. This tyrants and villains

18. *Ibid.*, 68, 82. Rev. William Smith (1707–1783) was the father of Abigail Smith. Adams's marriage to her connected him, through Rev. Smith's wife, with the locally influential Quincy family.

19. Butterfield *et al.*, eds., *Earliest Diary*, 91.

always knew."[20] In contrast, the ethical man instead admitted his ambition, then elevated it to the highest moral plane. This Adams did, although without achieving the inner harmony that such a decision seemed to promise. Instead his lifelong pursuit of fame was punctuated by a series of impulsive acts calculated to demonstrate his genuine contempt of it.

On the practical level, within six months of his return to Braintree, Adams sank into another period of inactivity in the spring of 1759. After representing Field and arguing a few other minor cases he had little to do until his practice began to quicken a year later. In March he felt "vexed, fretted, chafed, the Thought of no Business mortifies, stings me." To fill up his time he continued to visit often at the Quincys', less often at Parson Smith's, where he found the two Smith sisters (one of whom, Abigail, he was to marry four years later), less warm and exciting than the Quincys: the Smith girls were "not fond, not frank, not candid."[21]

Adams stopped regularly keeping his diary. He entered his observations, legal jottings, and drafts of letters without dates or order, and some time during the summer broke off completely for nearly a year. Before doing so he observed that he was "liable to absence and Inattention, stupidity," and that he had "behaved with too much Reserve to some and with too stiff a face and air, and with a face and Air and Tone of Voice of pale Timidity." He alluded to a growing impression that he was stern by remarking, "A Young fellow of fond amorous Passions, may appear quite cold and insensible." He was describing the effects of self-control over his passion for Hannah Quincy. Marrying her would have solved his immediate problem and at the same time would have elevated him to the gentry. But Gridley had warned that early marriage spelled intellectual ruin to a young lawyer, and Adams was resolved to complete his regime of legal study. Nevertheless: "I found a

---

20. Adams to Jonathan Sewall, Feb. 17, 1760, and to Benjamin Rush, Apr. 4, 1790, Adams Papers, Reels 114, 115. The source in Tacitus was located by my colleague Alice Wilson.

21. *Diary and Autobiography*, I, 80, 109.

Passion [for Hannah] growing in my heart and a consequent Habit of thinking, forming and strengthening in my Mind, that would have eat out every seed of ambition, in the first, and every wise Design or Plan in the last." After nearly proposing to Hannah, Adams was stunned; he had nearly abandoned his dreams in favor of amorousness and cupidity. But his will had proved triumphant. His nature, after all, was to deny, not to seize, pleasure. "The Thing is ended," he exclaimed. "A tender scene! a great sacrifice to Reason!"[22]

In Braintree, Adams eventually replaced his Worcester guilt for desiring fame with a regret for the psychic costs that he was now paying in its pursuit. He felt that he had given up much and began to think of a commensurate reward as justly his. "Ile have some Boon, in Return, Exchange," he wrote when he realized that in addition to Hannah he had given up the "Pleasure" of the outdoors: "fame, fortune, or something." While waiting for his reward, he sustained himself with casting his great sacrifice to reason in a heroic light—that of "the Choice of Hercules," a conventional artistic subject. He sketched a "Fable" adapting the story to "my own Case." "Let Virtue address me—'Which, dear Youth, will you prefer? a Life of Effeminacy, Indolence and obscurity, or a Life of Industry, Temperance and Honour? Take my Advice, rise and mount your Horse, by the Mornings dawn, and shake away amidst the great and beautiful scenes of Nature . . . all the Crudities that are left in your stomach, and all the obstructions that are left in your Brains. Then return to your Study, and bend your whole soul to the Institutes of the Law, and the Reports of Cases.' " How characteristic that when he invented a goddess she should come to him with advice about his digestion, and should concentrate not so much on virtue's "glorious Promises of Fame, Immortality, and a good Conscience," as on the details of work required to attain them.[23]

22. *Ibid.*, 109, 118, 87.
23. *Ibid.*, 73, 72, 73. On the 17th– and 18th–century tradition of gentlemen writing fables about such choices see Edwin T. Bowden, "Benjamin Church's *Choice* and American Colonial Poetry," *New England Quarterly*, XXXII (1959), 170–184.

Within two days of inventing his fable Adams decided that he had let himself be "seduced into the Course of unmanly Pleasures, that Vice describes to Hercules." The innocence of these sinful pleasures—"trifling Diversion or amuzement or Company," . . . girl, gun, cards, flutes, violin, dress, tobacco, laziness, languor, inattention, pipe, poem, love letter—testifies to the extremity of his program of self-denial. Adams truly believed that his choice lay between dissipated indolence and stern self-discipline. And he believed that the road not taken represented pleasure while his own choice would eventuate in a diminution of his vital spirits. Describing the spartan atmosphere of his study to his friend John Wentworth soon after setting up in Braintree, Adams called it a place of "ample Provision . . . for lasting Felicity" but added, "The only Thing I fear is, that all my Passions . . . will go down into an everlasting Calm." Nothing could have been less likely. Adams never lost the passion in his makeup; he only redirected it—first into study, then the law, and finally into politics. Nor did these pursuits exhaust his vitality, for all the energy he gave them; his marriage proved to be a passionate one, and his ardent friendships, love for the land, and burning for recognition lasted through life. What Adams really sensed was the violence to his spirit that resulted from imposing on it an ever-narrowing focus of attention. "Let me Remember to keep my Chamber, not run Abroad," he wrote; "Law and not Poetry, is to be the Business of my Life."[24] Yet, however relentlessly he worked at cropping away the rough edges of his spirit, he could not make himself a serenely stoic, single-minded man.

When he looked back on his Worcester days a few years later, Adams recalled that in his school "the Mischievous Tricks, the perpetual invincible Prate, and the stupid Dulness of my scholars, roused my Passions, and with them my Views and Impatience of Ambition." Passion remained the hallmark of his spirit. It led him to youthful revolt against his father, his tutors, his best friends' advice that he become a minister, and the

24. *Diary and Autobiography*, I, 73 (the list of trifling diversions is adapted from *ibid.*, 72); Butterfield *et al.*, eds., *Earliest Diary*, 64; *Diary and Autobiography*, I, 133.

constrictions of provincial society; later in life it led him to revolution—though always in the characteristic Adams family manner of assuming rather than rejecting responsibilities. Yet, throughout, whether in company, teaching school, or at the bar of his own judgment while writing his diary, Adams believed that the conditions of his life called for the suppression of his passionate spirit. Later in life he would be tempted to deny himself the great objects of his ambition and would devise a political philosophy calling on each class of men to be restrained by self-doubt and self-denial similar to his own. For the time being he advocated a reduction in the number of taverns in Braintree, no doubt expecting the public's gratitude for showing it the way to restraint.

While still studying in Worcester, Adams had begun to show physical signs of the overwork and mental strain to which he often subjected himself. Two doctors prescribed Dr. George Cheyne's milk diet, and for eighteen months Adams "*renounced* all Meat and Spirits and lived upon Bread and milk, Vegetables and Water." Deacon Adams, apparently familiar with an enthusiasm that conceived even self-control in terms of excess, "at last by his tender Advice at sometimes and a little good humoured ridicule at others converted me again to the Use of a little meat and more comforting Drink." Adams had again defied authority by carrying its demands further than they were intended. In his autobiography he recaptured the spirit in which he had done so by remarking that the local doctors were "unqualified Admirers of Cheyne's in Theory, though not in their own practice." (For at least sixty years Adams commonly reverted to the stringencies of Cheyne's diet when he felt unwell.) Adams had mastered Vinnius in the same spirit after Gridley warned him away from that author with "the benignity of a parent in his countenance." After Gridley's death Adams remarked that he had been "a buyer, but not a reader of books."[25] Later, when as a revolutionary Adams came to defy

25. *Diary and Autobiography*, I, 133, III, 269, 272; *Works of John Adams*, II, 313. On his reversions to Cheyne's diet see Adams to Francis Adrian Vanderkemp, July 5, 1814, Vanderkemp Papers, Pa. Hist. Soc., and to Vine Utley, Sept. 10, 1819, Adams Papers, Reel 124. See also chap. 12 below.

the paternal authority of the crown, he similarly regarded himself as a better upholder of the British constitution than the king.

If Adams remained in Braintree an idealist painfully aware of appearing absurd to his friends, he came to terms with his high aspirations. Among the Puritans, it has been observed, "private self-examination" amounted to "nothing less than public self-justification." His self-examination all but complete, Adams was ready to appear in a righteous public role. If it had been characteristic for him self-effacingly to cry "Oh Madness, Pride, Impiety" at his aspirations during his Worcester period, in Braintree he invoked ambition, writing "Oh Genius! Oh Learning! Oh Eloquence!" He crossed out the prideful word "Genius" and hastened to doubt whether he could "dare to think I have [it]," but he believed that he did and felt confident that it would bring him success.[26]

26. Sacvan Bercovitch, *Horologicals to Chronometricals: The Rhetoric of the Jeremiad*, in Eric Rothstein, ed., *Literary Monographs*, III (Madison, Wis., 1970), 35; Butterfield *et al.*, eds., *Earliest Diary*, 77, 82n.

 III
Farewell Politicks
1761–1773

When he thought of fame, Adams usually imagined him-
self catapulted into public recognition by a single stroke of
genius. But opportunities for the display of eloquence were rare
for a Massachusetts circuit-riding lawyer whose cases often
resembled the Field-Lambert trespass. When Adams tried to
broach larger issues one judge interrupted him, saying, "Keep
to the Evidence. . . . dont ramble all over the World to ecclesiastical Councils." Nevertheless, Adams steadily increased his
business in the early 1760s by persistence in following up many
writs for small fees. In 1761 he wrote in his diary: "I see several
Inadvertent Mistakes, and omissions [in the handling of cases].
But I grow more expert, less diffident &c. I feel my own
strength." He once filibustered before a jury for five hours to
keep a case open while his client rode home to fetch a document. The opposition had hoped to win on a technicality by
insisting that the inconsequential paper be produced. Adams
recalled the performance as a response to unethical tactics, but it
spoke as well for his tenacity.[1]

By 1763 Adams was in a position to marry. He had been left a
free choice in this by his father, and he proceeded to make it a
responsible one. Like Deacon Adams, who had married into
"one of the richest families in the Massachusetts for above an
hundred years," John Adams chose someone above his own
station in life, the daughter of "the richest Clergyman in the

1. *Diary and Autobiography*, I, 335, 193. For a sketch of the Massachusetts bar at this
period see Wroth and Zobel, eds., *Legal Papers*, xxxviii–lii. Adams described his filibuster
in a letter to Francis Adrian Vanderkemp, June 15, 1812, Adams Papers, Reel 118.

Province."[2] The modest seriousness of Abigail Smith of nearby Weymouth contrasted with Hannah Quincy's playfulness, but Adams's affections did not shift entirely in the direction of sobriety. In the Smith house he was attracted by "Spirit" as well as "Taste and Sense."[3] The names taken from their classical reading with which John and Abigail signed their courting letters —in keeping with the local fashion of their contemporaries— were "Lysander" and "Diana." She did resemble the goddess of light in her effect on those around her, especially in acting as a protectress of the young—a healer and watcher. Her demeanor, too, recalled Diana in its chaste modesty. As for Adams, who- ever chose the Spartan general Lysander, also a diplomatist and republican, understood how well that figure expressed his public aspirations.

When he gave up Hannah Quincy in 1759 Adams had antici- pated a political benefit. "Let Love and Vanity be extinguished," he had written, "and the great Passions of Ambition, Patriotism break out and burn." In Abigail Smith he found someone to purify this aspiration: "You who have always softened and warmed my Heart, shall restore my Benevolence as well as my Health and Tranquility of mind. You shall polish and refine my sentiments of Life and Manners, banish all the unsocial and ill natured Particles in my Composition, and form me to that happy Temper, that can reconcile a quick Discernment with a perfect Candour." Instead of the need inspired by Hannah Quincy to extinguish his fire, Abigail Smith stood for the controlled release of all that was best in Adams. "A Wonder," he wrote to her not long before they were married, "if the Fires of Patriotism, do not soon begin to burn!"[4]

2. Adams to John Trumbull, Mar. 9, 1790, and to Benjamin Rush, Aug. 25, 1811, Adams Papers, Reels 115, 118. For his father's permissiveness see *Diary and Autobiography*, I, 115. A late remark on hasty, passionate, youthful marriage suggests that in abandoning Hannah Quincy, Adams could have been satisfying his father's unspoken wish. Writing in 1813, Adams denounced "that capricious, inconsiderate, wild, mad passion of Love, which never looks forward to Posterity, nor backward to Parents or ancestors." Adams to Thomas McKean, Oct. 9, 1813, Vanderkemp Papers, Pa. Hist. Soc.

3. Adams to Abigail Smith, Feb. 14, 1763, *Adams Family Correspondence*, I, 3.

4. *Diary and Autobiography*, I, 87; Adams to Abigail Smith, Sept. 30, 1764, and Apr. 20, 1763, *Adams Family Correspondence*, I, 87, 49, 5.

Adams's patriotism had been awakened in 1761 by the revolutionary implications of James Otis's stirring constitutional argument in the Writs of Assistance case. Later in the same year, with his father's death, Adams gained a place in the Braintree town meeting. It was here that his political career began, for in practical terms the immediate issues of Adams's life were local. Beginning with his first case as a lawyer, his chief annoyance lay in the complications caused by nonprofessional drafters of writs. The Field case, after all, had turned on a writ no doubt originally drawn by one of them. Perhaps because at the outset of his career he had been embarrassed by ignorance equal to theirs, Adams took special pains to best the amateurs. He lectured the judges on the costliness of allowing them to continue to perplex the affairs of accredited members of the bar. His repeated triumphs in court over the amateurs, whom he called "Petty foggers," had given him the sense of "strength" as a lawyer that he had remarked early in 1761. When he took his place in the town meeting he began a formal campaign to have them excluded from legal business.

Adams first secured the election of his brother to the office of deputy sheriff, the strategic position for soliciting writs, at the time held by one of the leading pettifoggers. At first he reassured himself that he was "unpractised in Intrigues for Power." But on succeeding he admitted, "I began to feel the Passions of the World," and he hastened to warn himself that "Ambition, Avarice, Intrigue, Party, all must be guarded." These doubts initiated the pattern of the 1760s for Adams. First a public issue would demand his attention. Once involved in it he became an implacable crusader. He opposed the pettifoggers with the righteousness of a Puritan carrying out the will of his Old Testament God. "I see the complacent [i.e., approving] Countenances of the Crowd [in court]," he wrote, "and I see the respectful face of the Justice, and the fearful faces of the Petty foggers, more than I did."[5]

Adams often assumed that his opponents were motivated by

5. *Diary and Autobiography*, I, 217, 193.

envy—in this case of his superior education and position at the bar. One of them, he believed, "set himself to work to destroy my Reputation and prevent my getting Business, by such stratagems as no honest Mind can think of without Horror." Adams planned to announce this in court, and to add: "Such stratagems I always will resent, and never will forgive [him] till he has made Attonement by his future Repentance and Reformation."[6] In the end he thought better of making such a statement, but he did not overcome the tendency to view himself as the impersonal agent of a higher authority.

When victory came Adams typically experienced not elation but fresh doubts about his own purity of motives. Within a few days of securing the election of his brother in June 1761, for example, he retired to his study. "I have been latterly too much in the World," he told himself, "and too little in this Retreat. Abroad, my Appetites are solicited, my Passions inflamed, and my Understanding too much perverted, to judge wisely of Men or Things." Thus the initial flaming out of patriotic feeling calculated to recompense him for giving up Hannah Quincy led to fresh self-denial in the form of retreat from politics. Worldly success, it seemed, had to be followed by an equal and opposite reaction of unworldliness. Nor did it matter that Adams had chosen a virtuous cause. For "Virtues, Ambition, Generosity, indulged to excess degenerate in Extravagance which plunges headlong into Villany and folly."[7]

It was clear that Adams had not really solved the problem of ambition. In an unpublished essay he wrote: "It must be confessed, that the most refined Patriotism to which human Nature can be wrought, has in it an alloy of Ambition, of Pride and avarice that debases the Composition, and produces mischievous Effects." Two years later, in 1763, he went even further in his essay "On Self-Delusion." Referring to his own type of high-minded public servant, he warned of the dangers of "passions" like "ambition," which "are continually buzzing in the world" so that "the greatest genius, united to the best

6. *Ibid.*, 137.
7. *Ibid.*, 218, 181.

disposition, will find it hard to hearken to the voice of reason, or even to be certain of the purity of his own intentions."[8] The only way to convince himself that he had not acted in the hope of personal advancement was to retire from politics.

And yet, Adams could justify involving himself in the politics of the town on the ground that here he continued a family tradition of service. Accordingly he concentrated his public energies for several years on committee work in Braintree. When he was appointed to onerous local offices, he grumblingly but diligently carried out his tasks. Thus, as surveyor, he improved both the local roads and, after studying neighboring systems, the method of raising revenue to maintain them.[9] In due course he reached the highest local office—that of selectman—which his father had held for nine annual terms. After serving in it for only two years he received an unprecedented formal vote of thanks for his services. In his rise to local prominence Adams followed his father, who had advanced "by his Industry and Enterprize," become "a Select Man," and "for 20 Years together," had managed "almost all the Business of the Town."[10] But, where he was originally expected to take a single step in the church beyond his father's office of deacon, Adams fitted himself for a far wider horizon of service. Beginning in 1761, he began to justify his presumption.

Until this year Adams had not shown his full powers. Revealingly, on the page of his autobiography describing his transition "from a Boy . . . Spectator" to an adult "Member" of the town meeting, he mistakenly made 1761, when his father died, the year of two achievements that led to recognition of his talents. The first involved his being brought to the attention of Jonathan Sewall, an older lawyer, through "some juvenile

8. *Ibid.*, 222; *Works of John Adams*, III, 435. The essay was entered as a draft in Adams's diary.

9. See *Diary and Autobiography*, III, 278. According to Michael Walzer, "In Puritan writings, political activity was described as a form of work: it required systematic application, attention to detail, sustained interest and labor." Walzer, "Puritanism as a Revolutionary Ideology," *History and Theory*, III (1963), 59–90, 85.

10. *Diary and Autobiography*, III, 256, I, 1n. Charles Francis Adams, Jr., noted that John Adams's services must "have been of peculiar value" for him to have received the first such vote in the town records. *Three Episodes of Massachusetts History*, II, 846.

Letters of mine of no consequence" (this had occurred in 1759). The second was his election as surveyor of local highways, listed in the "usually reliable" town records as occurring in 1765.[11] Adams may have been nominated surveyor in 1761 by his friend Elisha Savil's maneuver to keep him from the worse job of constable—newcomers to town meetings were often elected to unwanted offices and left either to execute them or to pay fines of five pounds, from which the town realized considerable revenue. But the earliest record of Adams's connection with roads is his service on a road committee in 1763. Significantly, too, Deacon John Adams had been saddled with an unwanted office in the same manner that Adams, by his description, was drafted to be surveyor; thus his misdating may have resulted not only from association with the year of his father's death but also from identification with his father's experience.

One other year, 1745, loomed in Adams's memory of his father. He assigned to it the struggle over his going to school; his father's spurning the offer of a captaincy under Colonel Joseph Gooch, who had replaced Colonel Quincy; the beginnings of his own interest in public affairs, which he credited to the influence of his father, "who had a public soul" and who encouraged his political awareness; and his first attempt to keep a diary. This was also the year of two events momentous in American eyes: the insurrection in Britain led by Prince Charles Edward, the Young Pretender, and the victory at Louisbourg, Nova Scotia, by New England troops against the French—two exercises that demonstrated the capacity of British provincials to sustain a revolution. In 1820 Adams recalled that he had listened "with eagerness to his [father's] conversation with his

11. *Diary and Autobiography*, III, 278–279, I, 201n; C. F. Adams, Jr., *Three Episodes of Massachusetts History*, II, 675. Less significantly, Adams consistently misdated his 1762 elevation to Massachusetts Supreme Court barrister, which conferred the wearing of a robe, to 1761. See *Diary and Autobiography*, III, 276. See also John A. Schutz and Douglass Adair, eds., *The Spur of Fame: Dialogues of John Adams and Benjamin Rush, 1805–1813* (San Marino, Calif., 1966), 188, and Adams to William Tudor, May 30, 1819, Adams Papers, Reel 123. K. R. Eissler discusses the effects of fathers' deaths on sons and misdating in *Goethe: A Psychoanalytic Study, 1775–1786* (Detroit, 1963). D. H. Lawrence observes of a character in *Women in Love*: "Whilst his father lived Gerald was not responsible for the world."

friends during the whole expedition to Cape Breton, in 1745, and I have received very grievous impressions of the injustice and ingratitude of Great Britain towards New England in that whole transaction." Whether or not all of these personal episodes and events actually occurred when Adams was ten, they formed an association in his mind of self-improvement through study, sacrifice to principle, and politics.[12]

Adams's emulation of his father's career of service permitted him to go forward but did not resolve his anxieties about public life. For his conception of selflessness prevented him from actively seeking advancement. Throughout his life he had to wait for the public's call: he never sought nomination or, once nominated, ever campaigned for an office. This meant that, except for Braintree committees, he had no choice, in between the crises of the 1760s, but to devote himself to business. At such times Adams returned to the dissatisfaction of his Worcester days. The youth who invoked the choice of Hercules and then acted out the self-denial of his fable craved some "boon" in compensation, and he came to imagine that politics would provide it. Afterward, when his own reservations temporarily kept him from seeking the prize, he grew resentful.

His awkward turns of behavior in company began to settle into an unbending sternness. Abigail Smith complained of Adams's oak-like presence after he became her fiancé: neither she nor her friends felt "on a level" with him. (She did not know that he was imitating Putnam's assumed gravity.) But when she asked herself if there really was anything severe, "any

12. Adams always credited his father with stimulating his interest in "public affairs" when he was a boy by giving him newspapers to read. Adams to Skelton Jones, Mar. 11, 1809, *Works of John Adams*, IX, 611, and to Jonathan Mason, Oct. 27, 1820, Adams Papers, Reel 124. In France in 1782 Adams pointed to the Louisburg victory as an instance of New England's history of fighting to preserve the ocean fishery, which he had set himself intrepidly to defend. The Gooch episode was an example of patronage abuse much like those complained of by the patriot leaders in the American Revolution, and one of the abuses that most exercised Adams.

Adams said he burned the diary he had begun at the age of ten and that it filled two volumes. See A. B. Muzzey, *Prime Movers of the Revolution Known by the Writer: Being Reminiscences and Memorials of Men of the Revolution and Their Families*, 2d ed. (Boston, 1891), 48–49. Adams also recalled, of course, being "of an amorous disposition" from "ten or eleven years of age." Clearly this was his age of awakening.

thing austere in your countanance," she had to conclude that there was not. "As to the charge of Haughtiness," she decided, "I am certain that is a mistake, for if I know any thing of Lysander, he has as little of that in his disposition, as he has of Ill nature." Nevertheless, he had "an intolerable forbiding expecting Silence, which lays such a restraint upon but moderate Modesty that tis imposible for a Stranger to be tranquil in your presence." As a result, she wrote, "I feel a greater restraint in your Company, than in that of allmost any other person on Earth."[13]

Abigail Smith was able to recognize the tenderness and enthusiasm behind the mask. But she could not plumb Adams's frequent irritability any better than he could himself. Quite simply, he lacked a great political challenge. Within a year of his marriage at the age of twenty-eight this came, and 1765 proved to be an *annus mirabilis* for him. With no great public objects in view during 1763 he had stopped keeping his diary. Then, two years later, aged thirty and a father, he took it up again to record "the most remarkable Year of my Life." A man newly formed in decisiveness and permanently wedded to politics paused to comment on the great events of 1765: "That enormous Engine, fabricated by the british Parliament, for battering down all the Rights and Liberties of America, I mean the Stamp Act, has raised and spread, thro the whole Continent, a Spirit that will be recorded to our Honour, with all future Generations."[14]

Adams had begun the year by publishing newspaper installments of his "Dissertation on Canon and Feudal Law." News of the Stamp Act came before he had finished, and because he regarded it as a contemporary example of the "system of sacerdotal [and feudal] Guile" that he was describing, he dealt with

13. Abigail Smith to Adams, Apr. 30, 1764, *Adams Family Correspondence*, I, 42. Adams wrote to Jonathan Sewall: "I felt your reproof very sensibly for being ceremonious." Adams to Sewall, Feb. 7, 1760, Adams Papers, Reel 114.

14. *Diary and Autobiography*, I, 263. Adams made some odd jottings between 1763 and 1765 and used his diary book during 1765 for drafts of political writings and notes on the sodality, or lawyers' discussion group, that he had joined. But this is the first true diary entry. His daughter Abigail was born in July 1765.

it in his final installment. In the meantime he had drawn up the Braintree Instructions, a document setting forth the town's grounds of opposition to the Stamp Act. Then, in December, Adams went before the governor with his heroes, Otis and Gridley, to argue on behalf of the town of Boston on a question raised by the act.[15] Even the exchange of literary, pastoral letters in a newspaper, which he had been conducting with himself under two pseudonyms, began in the course of this year to take up opposition to the Stamp Act.

In the "Dissertation on Canon and Feudal Law" Adams was inspired to eloquence. "Let us dare to read, think, speak, and write," he declared, carrying his own studiousness into the fray. "Let every order and degree among the people rouse their attention and animate their resolution. . . . Let us study the law of nature; search into the spirit of the British constitution; read the histories of ancient ages; contemplate the great examples of Greece and Rome."[16] In the Braintree Instructions, a legal-style brief defending the town meeting's noncompliance with the Stamp Act, Adams expressed his sense of the historical moment. Addressed to "Ebenezer Thayer, Esq.," Braintree's representative, the instructions told him what to say at the General Court (the provincial assembly). They proclaimed: "We further recommend the most clear and explicit assertion and vindication of our rights and liberties to be entered on the public records, that the world may know, in the present and all future generations, that we have a clear knowledge and a just sense of them, and, with submission to Divine Providence, that we never can be slaves."[17]

Thus did the year 1765 raise up Adams's resentments, purify his enthusiasms, and heighten his prose. The fires of patriotism had indeed been ignited, as he suggested when he wrote in the

15. *Ibid.*, 200. The courts had been closed because many judges would not use the required stamps on their court documents. The three lawyers argued, unsuccessfully, "in Support of . . . [Boston's] Memorial, praying that the Courts of Law in this Province may be opened." *Ibid.*, 265.

16. *Works of John Adams*, III, 462.

17. *Ibid.*, 467. Charles Francis Adams singled out this passage in his biography of John Adams.

"Dissertation on Canon and Feudal Law": "These are not the vapors of a melancholy mind, nor the effusions of envy, [or] disappointed ambition . . . but the emanations of a heart that burns for its country's welfare."[18] That Adams did not sign his own name made his closing avowal of disinterestedness no less personally revealing, but rather more so. For anonymity permitted him to give voice to a pent-up idealism hardly expressed even in his private diary.

Adams never again found a form so well suited to him as the revolutionary newspaper essay. In it one subscribed oneself with a letter of the alphabet, with the name of an ancient or modern politician, or with an invented title. At the same time, one acted as the advocate of a cause just as a lawyer acts as the advocate of his client. The role-playing called forth Adams's literary bent (his style was vigorous if ponderous), while the legal aspect perfectly suited his philosophical approach to the law. (All his reading in Coke, Justinian, and Vinnius now came very much to the point.) Part of the newspaper essayist's assignment was to argue a just cause. For Adams this meant an opportunity to act as the man of selfless public virtue whom he had posited in his diary. Within his tracts the characters through whom he spoke played out an ethical drama turning on his own purity of motives.

Writing as "Clarendon" in his last tract of 1765 he addressed his newspaper antagonist, "Pym," as though both really were English statesmen of the preceding century. "You very well remember the surprizing Anecdote relative to my father and me," Clarendon writes: "I see the good old Gentleman even at this Distance of Time. I see in his aged venerable Countenance that ardent parental affection to me, that Zeal for the Laws of his Country, that fervent Love of his Country, and that exalted Piety to God and good Will to all Mankind, which constituted his Character." Here, in effect, was Deacon Adams as his son thought of him: a figure representing both love of his son and love of country. Appropriately, this father in effect pronounces

18. *Ibid.*, 464.

that his son has taken the right path and predicts that he will go on to excel him in public service. The scene ends with Adams assuming the mantle of his father's unimpeachable public character (as he had already begun to do in actuality).

Give me Leave [the father continues] to warn you, against that Ambition which I have often observed in Men of your Profession, which will sacrifice all to their own Advancement. And I charge you, on my Blessing, never to forget this Nation, but to stand by the Law, the Constitution, and the real Welfare and Freedom of this Nation vs. all Temptations, &c.—The Words were scarcely pronounced before his Zeal and Conscience [i.e., intense feeling of the significance of his words] were too great for his strength and he fell dead before my Eyes. His Words sunk deep into my Heart, and no Temptation, no Byass or Prejudice could ever obliterate them.

Never having written about his father's death in either his diary or letters, Adams paid tribute to him in "Clarendon." In twice using the word "zeal" to describe Clarendon's father he chose a term often used by himself and others to describe his own political involvement. In his career Adams perpetuated his father's best qualities. And he conducted himself according to a concept of public service—the avoidance of ambition through self-sacrifice—that he identified with his father.

The invented fatherly benediction in "Clarendon" was justified, then. Indeed, Adams's emergence as a public figure during 1765 could easily be thought of as an extension of Deacon Adams's career: the Braintree Instructions, after all, represented a local as well as a provincial service. On the evidence of the Instructions the deacon might well predict, with the elder Clarendon, that his son was destined for involvement in "the great Concerns of . . . [the] nation."[19] And, taken together, John Adams's Stamp Act activities justified his imagining for himself a place like Clarendon's in the history of mankind.

19. *Diary and Autobiography*, I, 276, Adams's draft. The printed version was somewhat more formal in tone. Lord Clarendon himself had in fact dwelt upon the death of his father, but without mentioning final advice and with only a hint of the scene described by Adams. In his autobiography Clarendon had written of his father that he "had the image of death so constantly before him . . . that for many years before his death he always parted with his son as to see him no more." *The Life of Edward Earl of Clarendon, Lord High Chancellor of England, and Chancellor of the University of Oxford . . . Written by Himself*

Ironically, though, his efforts did not ensure Adams recognition in Braintree. Retiring to his study at the end of 1765 he began to suffer not self-doubt but doubt about the public. Thus, on the same night on which he took up his diary after two years to hail the spirit of the people for their opposition to the Stamp Act, he complained of being ruined by the consequent closing of the courts. "Thirty Years of my Life are passed in Preparation for Business. I have had Poverty to struggle with—Envy and Jealousy and Malice of Enemies to encounter —no Friends, or but few to assist me, so that I have groped in dark Obscurity, till of late, and had but just become known, and gained a small degree of Reputation, when this execrable Project was set on foot for my Ruin as well as that of America in General, and of Great Britain."[20] The terms "Obscurity" and "Reputation" were the keys to Adams's meaning. He listed his own ruin ahead of that of two countries, and he meant by "ruin" not financial loss but personal costs—sacrifices of a sort rarely recognized by the public.

John Quincy Adams rightly drew attention to this diary entry and its sequel. For on the day that Adams wrote it in Braintree he was being appointed in Boston to argue for the reopening of the courts. On learning of this coincidence he was filled with wonder and "Gratitude" to the Town of Boston for calling on him. But what of Braintree? In three months his

---

(Oxford, 1827), I, 19. Clarendon mentioned his father's request, not long before his death, that Clarendon accompany him to the town where he proposed to live in retirement. But Clarendon has no dramatic, final meeting there. In Adams's version the death scene occurs when "Clarendon" is visiting his father while "upon one of the Circuits, which lead [i.e., led] me down to my native Country." Adams himself, in fact, not Clarendon, rode the legal circuits. Charles Francis Adams remarked how much Adams had studied Clarendon, the man. *Works of John Adams*, III, 469.

Adams's choice of Clarendon, a Tory, as his persona for a whig argument has always seemed odd. It is not surprising, however, that Adams should have identified closely with the (presumably rare) intimate kindness of the relationship that Clarendon said he had with his father. See chaps. 8 and 9 below for further examples of Adams's taking tory and monarchical sides in debate and chap. 2 above for his taking a conservative position when arguing with James Putnam. Further hints of Adams's identification with Clarendon were his transcribing parts of his diary into the argument between "Pym" and "Clarendon" and his adding a confession of his youthful ambition in the final version. See *Works of John Adams*, III, 473.

20. *Diary and Autobiography*, I, 264–265.

town would make Adams a selectman on the strength of his position on the Stamp Act, but he was already looking higher than this. When he went into Boston he met Samuel Adams, who knew the sort of recognition he had in mind. Adams at first did not record their conversation—it too baldly concerned his own prospects. But two days later he wrote, "Mr. S. Adams . . . was in Hopes such a Distinction from Boston" (i.e., being chosen to argue for reopening the courts) would both benefit John Adams's business and "fix" on him the eyes of Braintree "next May"—at election time for the General Court. Adams could not deny the likelihood of a spur to his business, but he felt "sure" that he would not be elected.[21]

He was right. In May, Braintree reelected Ebenezer Thayer, the worst of the pettifoggers. In a crisis John Adams might be called on to write Thayer's instructions and might even be chosen selectman, but neither the conferring of such distinctions nor the successful outcome of the Stamp Act agitation could significantly alter the power relations of local politics. Adams complained in his diary that, while everywhere else the repeal of the Stamp Act was received with public demonstrations, "the Town of Braintree [was] insensible to the Common Joy!" He then went on to reveal how much he thirsted for public recognition: "I had also the mortification to see that while allmost all the zealous opposers of the Stamp Act were caressed by their Towns and chosen Representatives . . . I was like to be neglected my self and that all my friends in my own Town were like to be neglected too."[22]

These were the only significant lines ever crossed out by Adams in his diary. His editor comments, "In view of his habitual indiscretions in the Diary it is remarkable that . . . [he] felt impelled to obliterate this harmless expression of hurt pride." But Adams had suffered a great blow: his program of disinterested service had brought not recognition but neglect. The shock led him to reveal the lofting ambition underlying his

21. *Ibid.*, 274. Samuel Adams was a distant cousin.
22. *Ibid.*, 312, 312n–313n. The words "also" and "were caressed" were supplied by the editors. Note Adams's use of the word "zealous."

pose of indifference to politics. Since his psychic economy now depended on avoiding, circumventing, and denying an emotion freely confessed only a few years earlier, he heavily inked out the passage.[23] The term "election," it should be remembered, continued to mean the singling out of a person for eternal grace. The Puritan diarist, who, like Adams, examined himself for signs of deserving this apotheosis, culminated one phase of his preparation in a kind of town meeting, a convocation in the church, where his spiritual election was certified or rejected by his fellows. Whether aware of the parallels or not, in not being elected Adams had undergone something akin to spiritual failure in the Puritan scheme of grace.

In June 1766, a month after the General Court election, Adams wrote to Richard Cranch, now his brother-in-law: "I am amazingly changed. Since the Stamp Act is repealed . . . I am at perfect Ease about Politicks. I care not a shilling, who is in and who is out. I have no Point, that I wish carried." It was true that he joined neither the committees of correspondence, nor the caucus club, though he visited it, nor the Sons of Liberty, though he dined with them and made himself available for consultation on the three days of the week that he spent in Boston.[24] But if Adams believed that he had suppressed his desire for political distinction, his friends knew better. Judge John Cushing recognized his continuing disappointment a year after the 1766 General Court election. Commenting on James Otis's election in May 1767 he observed: "Happy is he whom other Mens Errors, render wise." Adams understood him to mean that "Otis by getting into the general Court, has lost his Business," and that Adams should not be so anxious to suffer the same deprivation.[25]

At first Adams confined his political passions to his diary, where he lashed out against Governor Francis Bernard and

---

23. *Ibid.*, 312n. Steven Kagle well describes Adams's rising need for achievement, demanding ever wider recognition for ever greater efforts. In my terms, he required increasing recognition for his growing sense of self-sacrifice. See "The Diary of John Adams and the Motive of 'Achievement,' " *Hartford Studies in Literature*, III (1971), 93–107.

24. Adams to Richard Cranch, June 29, 1766, *Adams Family Correspondence*, I, 52.

25. *Diary and Autobiography*, I, 337.

wrote unpublished essays against the newspaper writings of "Philanthrop," his old friend Jonathan Sewall. The title of one of these suppressed essays expressed the theory informing all of them: "A Dissertation Upon Seekers—of Elections, of Commissions from the Governour, of Commissions from the Crown." Adams believed, along with those patriot leaders who shared his inheritance of the Puritan ethic, that the chief danger of the English revenue acts lay in their encouraging the "Ambition and Avarice" of such men.[26]

Virtuously removed from politics himself, Adams informed this view with personal fervor in applying it to Philanthrop-Sewall. He attempted to plumb Sewall's psychology by inventing for him a monologue in which Sewall rationalized his duplicities. At the end of it Sewall cried out: "Oh the Pangs, the pungent, excruciating Pangs of Ambition, Avarice, and Hunger."[27] In this way, adapting the patriot party's view of the opposition to his own uses, Adams fitted ambition, the chief term for scrutinizing himself, into the leading theme of his political essays.

In the "Dissertation on Canon and Feudal Law" the passion called "ambition" in Adams's diary became "the desire of dominion," or "the love of power." In this political form it continued to have both benign and malevolent possibilities. It was "often the cause of slavery . . . [but] whenever freedom has existed, . . . the cause of freedom." Insofar as he came to accept his own impulse of ambition, Adams had done so by identifying it as of the benign type. Now, in the politics of opposition to the English revenue measures, he found in the governor and his followers examples of the villains in his diary—great men with lofting ambition. Identified in the political terms of his essay as the aristocracy, these men displayed

26. *Ibid.*, 277, written Dec. 1765 but of a piece with Adams's unpublished essays of Dec. 1766. Sewall (1728–1796), a lawyer, had married Esther Quincy in 1764. He had been a close friend of Adams's until the events leading to the Revolution separated them politically.

27. *Ibid.*, 331, and see *ibid.*, II, 53–54.

an "encroaching, grasping, restless, and ungovernable" passion for power.[28]

The grand design, or conspiracy, involved in the revenue acts, Adams agreed, was to subvert not only potential office seekers but the morals of all the people. Adams's contribution in his "Dissertation" was to lend this view a historical legitimacy. As he told it, the "great struggle" for liberty in the seventeenth century had "peopled America." "Our fathers," the Puritans, "transmitted to their posterity . . . a hereditary ardor for liberty and thirst for knowledge." Well read in the ancients, they had established and bequeathed a system of balanced government calculated to preserve liberty. The revenue acts were "the first step" in an intended "entire subversion of the whole system of our fathers," and had to be opposed by all lovers of "this once happy country."[29]

"The people," who inspired such powerful and opposed feelings in Adams, were central in his version of the prevailing whig political theory. "Ignorant . . . of arts and letters, they have seldom been able to frame and support a regular opposition." Nevertheless, they functioned in a mixed government of the English and American sort as a "balance, to the powers of the monarch and the priest [and the aristocracy]." Though gullible and slow to resist tyranny, the people of America benefited from an educational establishment that diffused knowledge through all ranks of society in a manner that Adams believed "has been unknown to any other people ancient or modern."[30] In the "Dissertation's" secular and political version of the Puritan conviction that America was a chosen land, Adams was able to give form to his attitudes toward his New England countrymen. He deleted the passage in which he pro-

---

28. *Works of John Adams*, III, 449, 448, 449. "These vices," Adams pointed out later in language that recalled his diary, "are so much the more dangerous and pernicious for the virtues with which they may be accompanied." *Ibid.*, 457. Merle Curti expands on Lovejoy's demonstration in *Reflections on Human Nature* that thinkers threw together different aspects of human nature under the rubrics of pride or ambition. *Human Nature in American Historical Thought* (Columbia, Mo., 1968), 47–48.

29. *Works of John Adams*, III, 451, 455, 464.

30. *Ibid.*, 449, 453, 456.

claimed with Puritan-like, millennial "Reverence and Wonder" that "the settlement of America" represented "the Opening of a grand scene and Design in Providence, for the Illumination of the Ignorant and the Emancipation of the slavish Part of Mankind all over the Earth." But after removing a similar passage from "Clarendon" he let stand: "If ever an infant country deserved to be cherished it is America. If ever any people merited honor and happiness they are her inhabitants. They are a people . . . with the high sentiments of Romans, in the most prosperous and virtuous times of that commonwealth."[31]

After the events that produced Adams's political essays in 1765 and his unpublished attacks on Sewall in 1766, political excitement in the colony subsided, and Adams devoted himself to his practice and Braintree politics. Once again he set aside his diary. He resumed it after another two-year break to express dissatisfaction with his "vagrant, vagabond Life" on the court circuits. Despite his withdrawal from politics he had failed to make himself rich, so that as of 1768 he lacked "Fame, Fortune, [or] Power." Hoping to make more money, Adams in April 1768 resigned as Braintree selectman and moved his family into Boston. Almost immediately, though, he took up the cause again, "roused," as he put it in the *Boston Gazette* in May, from a "long Lethargy."[32] In June he wrote Boston's Instructions to its representatives in the General Court, an attack on the vice-admiralty court. Next he undertook the defense in the case that had given rise to the Instructions: a British seizure of John Hancock's ship, the *Liberty*. In turn, the following year Adams drew up a second set of Boston Instructions by adapting the address he had made to the court on Hancock's behalf. It was widely printed and evidently carried enough political charge for the opposition to attempt silencing Adams by offering him the post of vice-admiralty court prosecutor, which he refused.

31. *Diary and Autobiography*, I, 257; *Works of John Adams*, III, 475. The deleted "Clarendon" passage appears in *Diary and Autobiography*, I, 282.

32. *Diary and Autobiography*, I, 338, 337; "Sui Juris" [John Adams], *Boston-Gazette, and Country Journal*, May 23, 1768, reprinted in Roger B. Barry, "John Adams: Two Further Contributions to the *Boston Gazette*, 1766–1768," *NEQ*, XXXI (1958), 96.

Once renewed, the disputes between England and its Massachusetts colony grew increasingly tangled. In fall 1768 British troops were quartered in Boston. But Adams continued to remain in the background for the most part and, what was more important, to feel himself out of the main track of politics. Events finally were beginning to involve him, however: "The roles of lawyer, public servant, publicist, and political philosopher" grew "inextricably mixed."[33]

Then came the Boston Massacre. British soldiers fired into a crowd in Boston on the night of March 5, 1770. On the following day, with the town aroused against the soldiers, Adams agreed to help defend them. The trials were put off till fall, but Adams later insisted that he suffered "the instantaneous loss of more than half my business." He said that he and his fellow counsel "heard our names execrated in the most opprobrious terms whenever we appeared in the streets of Boston."[34] After a successful defense in the fall, by which time passions had subsided, Adams could congratulate himself for "one of the most gallant, generous, manly and disinterested Actions of my whole Life, and one of the best Pieces of Service I ever rendered my Country. Judgment of Death against those Soldiers would have been as foul a Stain upon this Country as the Executions of the Quakers or Witches, anciently."[35] And yet, Adams did not fall out of favor with the patriot party, which secured his election to the General Court in the period between his taking the case and the trial—that is, before popular feelings against the soldiers had cooled. How the patriot leader, Samuel Adams, the loudest voice of outrage over the Massacre, could have remained on friendly personal and political terms with Adams and even engineered his election remains matter for speculation. It has suggested to some an exaggeration in Adams's later descriptions of his loss of business and popularity.

33. Wroth and Zobel, eds., *Legal Papers*, I, lxxxvi; Adams to Elkanah Watson, Aug. 10, 1812, Adams Papers, Reel 118.
34. Josiah Quincy, *Memoir of the Life of Josiah Quincy, Junior, of Massachusetts, 1744–1775*, 2d ed. (Boston, 1874), 29n, from an 1822 interview with John Adams. See also *Diary and Autobiography*, III, 293–294, and *Works of John Adams*, X, 201.
35. *Diary and Autobiography*, II, 79.

The explanation may simply be that Samuel Adams respected the disinterested morality of John Adams's decision, then quickly realized that a fair trial for the soldiers lent respectability to his cause. The two men held divergent political views that later separated them. But in 1770 they shared a passion for the "moral rejuvenation" of the people.[36] Brooks Adams later well described Samuel Adams as a kind of late Puritan fanatic on the model of John Endicott, the self-appointed scourge of sinful political opponents. Governor Hutchinson compared the two Adamses by describing John Adams as "in general . . . of stronger resentment upon any real or supposed personal neglect or injury than the other; but, in their resentment against such as opposed them in the cause in which they were engaged, it is difficult to say which exceeded."[37] John Adams, the choice of Samuel Adams for the General Court, proved himself there to be just such a moral terrorist of the shared enemy, Thomas Hutchinson, as Samuel Adams would have wished.

After his election Adams found himself in opposition to Hutchinson when the latter moved the General Court's meeting place to Cambridge in order "to punish the Town of Boston." Adams was placed on a committee to protest the change of venue, and for the rest of the year he worked without stint on a series of anti-Hutchinson committee assignments. In listing these Charles Francis Adams commented that "the committees specified, embrace all but one of those raised during the year upon questions of any public importance."[38] In what amounted to a massive campaign against Hutchinson, Adams continued the principle of service that had guided his rise in Braintree politics.

The model for Adams in these attacks undoubtedly was

36. Stephen E. Patterson, *Political Parties in Revolutionary Massachusetts* (Madison, Wis., 1973), 224.

37. Thomas Hutchinson, *The History of the Colony and Province of Massachusetts-Bay*, ed. Lawrence Shaw Mayo, III (Cambridge, Mass., 1936), 214. In 1772 Adams emphasized that he and Samuel Adams "concurred" that "the Liberties of this Country had more to fear from one Man the present Governor Hutchinson than from any other Man." *Diary and Autobiography*, II, 55.

38. *Diary and Autobiography*, III, 295; *Works of John Adams*, II, 235n.

James Otis, the stirring orator of the Writs of Assistance case and, since then, a leader of the Stamp Act agitation (in which Hutchinson also was involved). Judge Cushing's comparison of Adams to Otis proved to be well taken. For in the General Court, Adams followed in the footsteps of the Otis who had built his political career on violent opposition to Hutchinson, helping in the process to make suspicion of him an article of faith in the opposition party.[39]

James Otis must be regarded as the most important single influence on Adams as a political figure. James Putnam had held up the young lawyer as "by far the most able, manly and commanding Character of his Age at the Bar." Adams proceeded in 1758 to become Otis's "pupil" and "imitator." By 1770, as Otis completed nine years in the General Court and Adams replaced him for a single term, the parallels between the two were evident. Both were the sons of cordwainers. Plump, scholarly, yet fiery when aroused, both owed some of their prominence to advantageous marriages from which they pointedly refused to benefit in the way of influence. Each rarely lost the opportunity to emphasize his lost business, pleasure, and health in serving the public. In court both were at once caustic and academic, succeeding by force of conviction and intellect rather than charm. When Otis wavered in his opposition to the crown, Adams, whose own role lacked definition until 1770, denounced him with a vigor for which he never could forgive himself. At the General Court he paid Otis back in the coin of emulation.[40]

39. The special fury directed against Hutchinson has been remarked as excessive, especially by Shipton in his sketch of Hutchinson. *Sibley's Harvard Graduates*, VIII, 166. Bernard Bailyn relates this fury to conspiracy theories of the period. *The Ideological Origins of the American Revolution* (Cambridge, Mass., 1967), 121–122. For the Otis family's campaign against Hutchinson see Hugh F. Bell, " 'A Personal Challenge': The Otis-Hutchinson Currency Controversy, 1761–1762," Essex Institute, *Historical Collections*, CVI (1970), 297–323. John J. Waters points out that Otis and Gov. Bernard held conspiracy theories about each other. He traces such theories to the English whig tradition's "belief in conspiracy as a way of understanding the past" and to Harvard tutor Henry Flynt, the old man to whom Otis compared Adams when trying to shame him back into politics. *The Otis Family in Provincial and Revolutionary Massachusetts* (Chapel Hill, N.C., 1968), 135. See further on Adams and Hutchinson below in chaps. 4 and 12.

40. *Diary and Autobiography*, III, 275; Adams's "Preface" to "Novanglus," in *Works of*

Adams invested the Writs of Assistance case with seemingly excessive importance. In fact, he took it as a model and later treated it as a microcosm of his career. When, for example, he insisted that he had been drawn by circumstances into public affairs, he had in mind Otis's leap into prominence with this case. It is impossible to judge the accuracy of Adams's rendering of Otis's speech at the Writs case, but the words that he recorded attest to identification with his friend. "The only principles of public conduct that are worthy a gentleman, or a man," Adams quoted him, "are, to sacrifice estate, ease, health and applause, and even life itself to the sacred calls of his country. These manly sentiments in private life make the good citizen, in public life, the patriot and the hero." As for Otis's doctrine of unconstitutional parliamentary laws, Adams employed it in court cases and political writings from 1765 to 1776.[41]

In personal terms it was symbolically significant that in the Writs case Otis had enacted Adams's own paradoxical mixture of filial defiance and homage. For the lawyer against whom Otis had argued was his teacher and Adams's mentor, Jeremiah Gridley. "It was a moral spectacle," Adams later wrote, "more affecting to me than any I have since seen upon any stage, to see a pupil treating his master with all the deference, respect, esteem, and affection of a son to a father, and that without the least affectation; while he baffled and confounded all his authorities, and confuted all his arguments and reduced him to silence." Adams imagined such defiance as capable of producing nothing but paternal approval: "Mr. Gridley himself seemed to me to exult inwardly at the glory and triumph of his pupil."[42]

John Adams, IV, 6. For the parallels between Adams and Otis see Shipton, *Sibley's Harvard Graduates*, XI; *Dictionary of American Biography*, s.v. "Otis, James, Jr."; Katherine Anthony, *First Lady of the Revolution: The Life of Mercy Otis Warren* (New York, 1958), 46; Adams to William Tudor, Feb. 25, 1818, and Mar. 11, 1818, *Works of John Adams*, X, 290, 296.

41. Wroth and Zobel, eds., *Legal Papers*, II, 141. For Otis's influence on Adams's pleadings and political writings, see *ibid.*, 190, 200, and Zoltán Haraszti, *John Adams and the Prophets of Progress* (New York, 1952), 43, 44.

42. Adams to Tudor, July 9, 1818, and Aug. 11, 1818, *Works of John Adams*, X, 327, 343.

The influence of Otis did not entirely account for Adams's fervid opposition to Hutchinson at the General Court. A few months after the Court's last session, "Coll. Sparhawk of Kittery" said to Adams, "Now you are come away, they are become peaceable." "Laughing," the colonel told Adams, "You kept up a shocking Clamour while you was there." He also reported the gossip, which Adams denied, that "there is some private Pique between the Governor and you."[43] There was. When Bernard had been governor and Hutchinson chief justice, Adams had appeared with Otis in an important trial presided over by Hutchinson. *Rex* v. *Corbet* concerned the killing of a British officer as he was attempting to impress American seamen. Because the case raised the great question of parliamentary authority, the trial drew large crowds. Adams prepared a speech that might have rivaled Otis's at the Writs case. It showed the "total Ignorance" of Governor Bernard and, Otis-like (Otis himself was suffering one of his intervals of mental distraction), argued "unalienable Right . . . by the Law of Nature."[44] In order to prevent Adams from raising such matters Hutchinson interrupted him before he was fairly launched. Although the case was decided in favor of Adams's client, Adams later wrote: "Never in my whole life have I been so disappointed, so mortified, so humiliated as in that trial."[45]

Adams resented Hutchinson personally, then, but he cared also about the issues raised in the Corbet case. As he put it in

Otis and Gridley argued the Writs case before Hutchinson. Gridley had the habit of acting fatherly toward young men. Adams recorded at length a story of his attempting to exert paternal authority over his nephew, his being repulsed, and then expressing remorse for having exceeded his prerogative. *Diary and Autobiography*, I, 345–346.

43. *Diary and Autobiography*, II, 42.

44. Wroth and Zobel, eds., *Legal Papers*, II, 333, 326. See also Adams to Jedidiah Morse, Jan. 20, 1816, *Works of John Adams*, X, 204–210.

45. Adams to Tudor, Dec. 30, 1816, Adams Papers, Reel 123. For the significance of Adams's use of the word "mortified," see chap. 12 below. Clifford K. Shipton traces Adams's hatred of Hutchinson to this one incident, commenting: "Upon such accidents of outraged vanity are revolutions fed." *Sibley's Harvard Graduates*, VIII, 166. In addition to his identification with Otis, Adams had personal causes for resentment. Hutchinson, in charge of Adams's county, caused him to lose business during the court closing period by keeping the courts under his jurisdiction strictly inoperative while other Massachusetts counties continued to sit. Janet Whitney, *Abigail Adams* (Boston, 1947), 42.

another recollection, Hutchinson's "Secret motives were two. 1st To prevent me from reaping an harvest of glory; 2d To avoid a publick exhibition of the law in all its details before the people." Adams carried this combination of personal resentment and concern for the issues into his works on government, especially where Hutchinson was concerned. His acerbity toward Jonathan Sewall as "Philanthrop" stemmed from a conviction that Hutchinson, "that awful Jesuit," had "seduced [him] from my Bosom," as well as having "destroyed" James Otis.[46] But Adams was equally convinced that Hutchinson was subverting the Colony in the same manner. "All the great Kingdoms of Europe" had "once been free," he wrote, until each, like ancient Greece and Rome, was brought down by a man of ambition. In Massachusetts, manifestly, that man was Thomas Hutchinson.[47]

If Adams directed an unmatched personal fury against Hutchinson, no doubt seeing in "his unbounded Ambition and his unbounded Popularity" a nightmare version of his own passion, in doing so he expressed a general conviction and a general emotion. Indeed, it has been said that his chief contribution as a political writer at this period lay not in any originality of ideas but in acting as a "director" of received opinion and emotions.[48] Just as Adams admired the "zealous . . . stanch and stiff and strict and rigid and inflexible" Samuel Adams and sympathized with Otis's "Excess of Zeal," the public accepted his own denunciatory rages.[49]

Thus eruptions of anger, usually omitted from his diary

46. Adams to John Quincy Adams, Jan. 8, 1808, and to Tudor, Nov. 16, 1816, Adams Papers, Reels 118, 123; *Diary and Autobiography*, II, 55. Adams always believed that Hutchinson, practicing "all his Arts upon me," lay behind Sewall's coming to him with the vice-admiralty court offer.

47. *Diary and Autobiography*, II, 59. For similar allusions to Hutchinson, see *Works of John Adams*, III, 457, and *Diary and Autobiography*, I, 349, 365.

48. *Diary and Autobiography*, II, 55. See Michael Kammen, "The Meaning of Colonization in American Revolutionary Thought," *Journal of the History of Ideas*, XXXI (1970), 348, for Adams as a director of received opinion. See Edwin G. Barrows and Michael Wallace, "The American Revolution: The Ideology and Psychology of National Liberation," *Perspectives in American History*, VI (1972), 293, for his role in expressing usually suppressed general resentment.

49. *Diary and Autobiography*, I, 271.

unlike the youthful enthusiasm out of which they grew, punctuated Adams's career without hurting it in Massachusetts. In his very first, abortive attempt to involve himself in politics, a campaign in 1760 against the proliferation of taverns, he had "discharged my Venom to Billy Veasey" in his disappointment. In the "wild sally" against Otis for which he never forgave himself, Adams recalled having said: "Otis is a mastiff that will bark and roar like a lion one hour, and the next, if a sop is thrown in his way, will creep like a spaniel." In court, when not arguing fundamental rights or discussing ecclesiastical councils, Adams apparently used a similar intensity against his opponents. The manner was familiar enough to New Englanders, who merely called him "saucy."[50]

But Adams was a man consumed by that which nourished him. If Colonel Sparhawk and others were amused by his "shocking clamor" in the General Court, he could not sustain it. Early in 1771 he suffered a collapse. His thirty-fifth year had proved to be the most demanding one of his life. (In addition to attending the General Court, he served as clerk of the Suffolk County Bar Association, maintained his growing practice, and participated until December in the continuing Boston Massacre trials.) In February 1771 he underwent an unexplained night of "great Anxiety and distress" ("never in more misery, in my whole Life—God grant, I may never see such another Night)." Then, in April, at the end of his legislative term, he moved his family back from Boston to Braintree—"still, calm, happy Braintree"—in an attempt to regain his health. His accompanying resolve to "divide my Time between . . . Law And Husbandry" implied the cause of his illness, for it concluded with the resolution, "Farewell Politicks."[51]

Adams took up his diary, suspended since the day after his attack of anxiety in February, with his move to Braintree. The first entries indicate a plan of recording his success in keeping away from politics—by burying himself in work and, it would

50. *Ibid.*, 132; Adams to Tudor, Mar. 11, 1818, *Works of John Adams*, X, 296; *Diary and Autobiography*, I, 140.

51. *Diary and Autobiography*, II, 6, 7.

seem, by spending more time with his farm and family. That his second entry mistakenly made the month February instead of April suggests the connection in his mind between retirement from politics and his mental suffering in February.

Although he appears to have enjoyed success at the General Court—short of driving Hutchinson out of office—Adams wrote of "the worthy People" of Boston: "My Wishes are impotent, my Endeavours fruitless and ineffectual, to them, and ruinous to myself." After years of wavering Adams had entered politics only to find it necessary to withdraw. Yet, politics had taken over the rhythm of his inner life. Beginning in 1765 he normally resumed his diary, after intervals of neglect, in response not to personal but to political matters.[52]

Politics had become the field for the resolution of his ambition quandary, only to provide no greater certainty than self-examination. His state of anxious uncertainty arising from self-examination constituted Adams's clearest inheritance from the Puritans. As a young man he translated the Puritan concern over salvation into the question of his worthiness for success. If a harsh judge of this unanswerable question, at least he was a fair one. But in politics the public judged worthiness. It could make a Hutchinson popular while ignoring or even insulting its true friends: the Boston Massacre case, Adams wrote, "procured me Anxiety, and Obloquy enough."[53]

The night of anxiety in February 1771 preceding Adams's farewell to politics had no apparent direct cause. But it resembled later reactions to strenuous political activity. Typically he suffered at the end or near the end of his exertions rather than at their peak: before succumbing to anxiety he had to complete his duties. Success, as in this case of his opposition to Hutchinson, tended to prostrate him more than failure—a not uncommon psychological pattern.[54]

52. *Ibid.*, 6, written on the day of his arrival in Braintree. Adams resumed his diary Aug. 10, 1769, the day copies of Bernard's incriminating letters arrived from England. *Ibid.*, I, 339–340n. Also see *ibid.*, II, 52, for another resumption, in response to Hutchinson, and below, chap. 4 at n. 2, for a resumption at the news of his selection for the Continental Congress.

53. *Ibid.*, 79.

54. See Freud's essay "Those Wrecked by Success" (1916), in James Strachey *et al.*, eds.

When he grew ill Adams tended to associate the air of the place in which he was exerting himself with his suffering. Earlier he had blamed Worcester, Massachusetts, and later it was Philadelphia, Amsterdam, and Washington. In 1771 it was "the Air of the Town of Boston which was not favourable to me who had been born and passed allmost all my life in the Country." Suffering from "a Pain in my Breast and a complaint in my Lung," symptoms that occurred after political crises until as late as 1798, Adams returned in 1771 to "the Air of my native Spot" and resolved to "mind my own Farm, and my own Office."[55]

His retirement in Braintree lasted only a few weeks. Ebenezer Thayer, with a great show of flattery, asked Adams to accept his son as a law clerk. The pettifogger's turnabout provided a "wretched Tryumph," and his bribing offer to step aside in Adams's favor at the coming General Court election could only rekindle a long-standing resentment against Braintree, which still insulted him by preferring Thayer. In the absence of proper expressions of gratitude from the town, Adams broke his resolve to keep out of politics "by a very small and feeble Exertion" to help elect Samuel Adams register of deeds of Suffolk County. When he could not gain even this, he lashed out in his diary: "I have acted my sentiments, with the Utmost Frankness, at Hazard of all, and the certain Loss of ten times more than it is in the Power of the People to give me, for the sake of the People, and now I reap nothing but Insult, Ridicule and Contempt for it, even from many of the People themselves."[56] In the election Samuel Adams had been a surrogate

---

and trans., *The Standard Edition of the Complete Psychological Works of Sigmund Freud*, XIV (London, 1957), 33. The common element among Adams's collapses may have been defiance of figures in authority. He grew sick in Worcester after beginning to study law in defiance of his father's wish that he become a minister. If Judge Peter Oliver is to be believed, when Adams was a young lawyer being taken advantage of by his elders at the bar, Hutchinson took a paternal interest in him, protecting him from them. Schutz and Adair, eds., *Peter Oliver's Origin and Progress*, 83. In any case, Hutchinson certainly was a figure of authority.

55. *Diary and Autobiography*, III, 296, II, 11. The pain, evidently in Adams's heart, returned after a crisis while he was vice-president and probably during his two breakdowns in Europe.

56. *Ibid.*, II, 10, 11.

for Adams himself. Just as after beginning to serve the town in 1761, Adams had supported his brother for deputy sheriff, in 1771 after his year at the General Court he supported his cousin Samuel Adams in indirect pursuit of recognition for his own services. And the Braintree people who had failed to advance him in the past failed him in this as well. As a result, after spending only a month in Braintree, on May 30, 1771, the day after Thayer won the General Court election, Adams sought a lonely cure at the Stafford mineral springs in Connecticut.

As ever his friends understood his emotions better than he. For, finding him still unwell on his return, Judge Trowbridge said: "You will never get your Health, till your Mind is at ease. If you tire yourself with Business, but especially with Politicks, you wont get well." Adams protested, "I have not wrote one Line in a Newspaper these two Years." But his diary showed that the judge was right. On his journey he had not forgotten about either politics or Hutchinson, who had become governor in March.[57]

Adams had hardly arrived at Stafford Springs when he confessed having begun to "grow weary of this idle, romantic Jaunt. . . . I want to hear the News, and Politicks of the Day." The next day he felt "guilty": "I feel as if I ought to be employed, for the Benefit of my fellow Men." On the day he returned home the news included "the cordial answer of the Council to the Governor's address to both houses at the opening of the session [of the General Court]" and the governor's "elegant Entertainment" that evening. Adams burst out with accumulated resentment: "If this wretched Journal should ever be read, by my own Family, let them know that there was upon the Scene of Action with Mr. Hutchinson, one determined Enemy to those Principles and that Political System to which alone he owes his own and his Family's late Advancement." As Adams saw it, a drama had been played out between himself and Hutchinson in which "with great Anxiety, and Hazard,

57. *Ibid.*, 38, 39. Hutchinson had been lieutenant governor, though acting governor, from 1769 to 1771. Edmund Trowbridge (1709–1793) was a justice of the Superior Court.

with continual Application to Business, with loss of Health, Reputation, Profit . . . I have for 10 Years together invariably opposed" Hutchinson's "System." The result was that "the People are now worshipping" the one side "and despizing, insulting, and abusing" the other. Adams ended his outburst by quoting lines that he remembered more than once during his life. "Edward and Alfred," he wrote, "closed their long Glories with a Sigh to find / th' unwilling Gratitude of base Mankind."[58]

An ambitious enemy, personal sacrifice and suffering, and an unappreciative public—all these might have been supportable had Adams not remained obscure. But he did, and his condition was impressed upon him as he returned to his circuit riding in July: "This has been the most flat, insipid, spiritless, tasteless Journey that ever I took. . . . I have neither had Business nor Amusement, nor Conversation. . . . I slumber, and moap, away the Day."[59] Soon after his "moaping" in Worcester, Adams had arranged to become a lawyer. Fifteen years later his dissatisfaction with family, farm, and profession poised him at another turning point.

Adams could not choose public life as long as he felt that his priorities should continue his father's: hard work to improve the family status, combined with a substantial contribution of time to the interests of the town. He now had two children, his daughter, Abigail, having been born in 1765, his son John Quincy in 1767, and he could expect more. If Deacon Adams had elevated his son above himself by sending him to Harvard, John Adams, in turn, bore the responsibility to earn enough to send all of his sons there. Up to now he had adapted inherited responsibilities to make them consistent with being first a lawyer and then a politician of sorts. But in the absence of any crisis in 1771 he could not deny his responsibility to return to a private life. This he did. But he remained for just a year and a half in Braintree, then took his family back to Boston. He was returning, in the fall of 1772, to the center of agitation.

Expectably, Adams planned to go "with a fixed Resolution,

58. *Ibid.*, 28, 30, 35n, 35, 34, 35.
59. *Ibid.*, 43.

to meddle not with public Affairs of Town or Province." The week before leaving he warned himself: "Above all Things I must avoid Politicks, Political Clubbs, Town Meetings, General Court, &C. &C. &C." But his friend Otis knew his man when he accused Adams of being "tired with one Years Service [in the General Court], . . . moaping about the Streets of this Town as hipped as Father Flynt at 90, and seemingly regardless of every Thing, but to get Money enough to carry you smoothly through this World." Inactivity and selfishness were stinging accusations to Adams. Yet, Otis's attack was as much a warning to stay away as to go back to politics. For Otis at this time had advanced into obvious mental disorder—in the throes of which he frequently raved at Hutchinson, and which Adams believed was the result of Otis's political "exertions."[60]

Nevertheless, within a week of settling in Boston, Adams's mind turned back to the forbidden subject. He singled out the comment of a visitor to his office to the effect that "Politicks are the finest Study and science in the World." "His Observation upon Politicks is just," wrote Adams; "they are the grandest, the Noblest, the most usefull and important Science, in the whole Circle."[61] He would have protested that his attachment to the *science* of politics differed from a daily involvement, but even that distinction did not remain long in effect.

Before giving way, though, Adams refused Samuel Adams's obviously calculated attempt to welcome him back to the cause in Boston, and he did so in revealing terms. When Samuel Adams called to invite him to deliver what had developed into the annual Boston Massacre oration, Adams refused on account of "the feeble State of my Health." But when pressed he added a string of "irresistable Syllogisms" showing why he could not speak. He had resolved "to avoid even thinking upon public Affairs." Speaking would "expose myself to the Lash of ignorant and malicious Tongues on both Sides of the Question."

---

60. *Ibid.*, 63, 67, 66; Adams to Francis Adrian Vanderkemp, Apr. 23, 1807, Adams Papers, Reel 118. Adams took Otis's case as a warning to himself by joking about politics with obvious reference to Otis: "That way madness lies." *Diary and Autobiography*, III, 291.

61. *Ibid.*, II, 68.

Finally, he claimed that he was "too old to make Declamations" —he was thirty-seven.[62]

Adams frequently offered a succession of excuses for his decisions, with his precarious health usually figuring among them. His protesting too much sometimes indicated that he was uneasy with his decision, sometimes that he could not admit his real motive. Unwillingness to admit ambition had marked his multiple explanations for choosing the law over the ministry and for choosing to practice in Braintree instead of Worcester. In the case of the Massacre oration the excuses reflected uneasiness with his decision. Obviously he was not happy with his announced resolution "to devote myself forever to private Life." Samuel Adams, biding his time, contented himself with inviting Adams to his house the next evening for some political conversation.

Soon afterward the *Boston News-Letter* printed General William Brattle's argument in favor of having the crown rather than the colony pay judges' salaries. Brattle had challenged any of the leading patriot lawyers to dispute the question with him, and "upon this," Adams wrote, "I determined to enter the Lists, and the General was very soon silenced." In this dispute Adams confined himself to citing "innumerable British legal authorities" supporting the judiciary's independence of the crown, a markedly pacific approach when compared with his earlier defiance of the authority of Parliament. But in company "the old Warmth, Heat, Violence, Acrimony, Bitterness, Sharpness of my Temper, and Expression, was not departed. I said there was no more Justice left in Britain than there was in Hell."[63] At about this time, too, according to a surviving anecdote, when the king was toasted at the home of a loyalist, Adams responded by organizing the patriot guests in a toast to "the Devil." His mildness in print and violence in company showed that Adams remained divided, a state of mind that he expressed by picturing himself on the one hand as devoted to

62. *Ibid.*, 73, 74.
63. *Ibid.*, 74, 78, 79n, 76.

private life and on the other as "stedfast and immoveable in the Cause . . . from the Year 1761."[64]

The political source of the division in Adams was his wavering, in common with many of his contemporaries, on the question of loyalty to England. When he was eighty-six he recalled that while living in Worcester he had so resented British conduct of the war with France between 1756 and 1758 that he longed for total independence for America. Then "in fifty eight and fifty nine . . . I again rejoiced in the name of Britain." As late as 1763 or 1764 he rejected Jean-Jacques Burlamaqui's revolutionary doctrine that the king forfeits his crown when he breaks the law,[65] and immediately after the success of the anti-Stamp Act agitation in 1765 he favored reconciliation.

One reason for Adams's mild position toward the crown in his dispute with Brattle was that the legalistic side of his politics drew him toward moderation. From the earliest calls by the patriots to argue for them as a lawyer, he took theoretically conservative positions in supporting defiance. Upholding "that most excellent monument of human art, the common law of England," he argued that with all due reverence to His Majesty, the Stamp Act was "utterly void, and of no binding Force upon us; for it is against our Rights as Men, and of our Priviledges as Englishmen."[66]

In this expression of divided loyalty Adams agreed with the sentiments of most of the opposition party, including Samuel Adams. The shared moralistic attitude of the two Adamses appears to have been more important than the few ideas about colonial rights that drew them together. As Adams argued the

64. Shipton, *Sibley's Harvard Graduates*, XII, 293; *Diary and Autobiography*, II, 55.
65. Adams to George A. Otis, Feb. 29, 1821, *New England Historical and Genealogical Register*, XXX (1876), 329. On Adams's 1765 favoring of reconciliation see *Diary and Autobiography*, I, 323, 325. On Adams's comments on Burlamaqui's *Principles of Natural and Political Law*, see Zoltán Haraszti, ed., "More Books from the Adams Library," *Boston Public Library Quarterly*, III (1951), 114.
66. *Works of John Adams*, III, 440; Edmund S. and Helen M. Morgan, *The Stamp Act Crisis: Prologue to Revolution* (Chapel Hill, N.C., 1953), 140. The argument represents another parallel with Otis, who preached natural law limitations on Parliament while upholding the king in similarly warm terms. See Bernard Bailyn, ed., *Pamphlets of the American Revolution, 1750–1776* (Cambridge, Mass., 1965), 206.

case, the colony's charter had been contracted with the king personally, not with Parliament. Hence, not the king but Parliament was being opposed, and on moral grounds at that. For Parliament's attempted usurpation of powers threatened the constitutional balance that sustained the king as much as it did his loyal colonists.

Near the end of the Stamp Act opposition Adams vehemently denied that "we are in a state of actual Rebellion. . . . Has any Man within the Province appeared in Arms, unless it was out of Attachment to his Majestys Person and Government? . . . Nay, I may go further and ask, has there been a disrespectful Speech uttered of his Majesty or his Government, thro the whole memorable Year 1765, even at Midnight? over the Bowl or the Bottle?—I believe not one." This claim, too, was consistent with an attitude discernible throughout the colonies, for there were few attacks on the king himself prior to Thomas Paine's *Common Sense* in 1776.[67]

In keeping with this underlying reverence for authority, Adams characterized his opposition to Parliament's laws as resistance to "innovation." He focused especially on Hutchinson, a son of New England and therefore the most dangerous innovator of all. The drama of the patriot cause had a local setting; it asked what effect each innovating revenue act and piece of supporting legislation, along with each response from the colonists, was likely to have on the moral fiber of the New England people.[68] It was not so surprising that the next development of 1773 raised an outcry against the governor more fierce than any against the king.

In March 1773 secret letters to England written by Hutchin-

67. *Diary and Autobiography*, I, 291, draft of "Clarendon." For the benign general attitude toward the king see Winthrop D. Jordan, "Familial Politics: Thomas Paine and the Killing of the King, 1776," *Journal of American History*, LX (1973), 294–308. The drama of the historical Clarendon's life had involved his tenacious loyalty to the king until he was forced to oppose him.

68. See Timothy H. Breen, "John Adams' Fight against Innovation in the New England Constitution: 1776," *NEQ*, XL (1967), 501–520. On the moral drama see Edmund S. Morgan, "The Puritan Ethic and the American Revolution," *William and Mary Quarterly*, 3d Ser., XXIV (1967), esp. 9. See chap. 12 below for Adams's later account of his revisions.

son and his supporters were released in Boston. One of Hutchinson's contained the notorious phrase, "There must be an Abridgment of what are called English Liberties." Adams was stunned. The letters soberingly confirmed his suspicions of conspiracy. He took up his diary to prepare himself in good Puritan style for the coming General Court election. He had waited to be called to public life as his ancestors waited for "a calling" to the ministry. When it came he was as determined as they to respond selflessly. "If I should be called in the Course of Providence," he wrote, "to take a Part in public Life, I shall Act a fearless, intrepid, undaunted Part, at all Hazards."[69] On the next day the lower house of the General Court elected him to the upper house, or Council (Council members were chosen both from the General Court and from the population at large). As Adams had expected, Governor Hutchinson exercised his constitutional negative to deny him his seat because of "the very conspicuous part Mr. Adams had taken in opposition."[70]

When Hutchinson sent the General Court a paper asserting Parliament's absolute authority over its colonies, however, Adams was asked by the Council to inspect the draft of a reply written by Samuel Adams. Instead of approving its outraged language, Adams substituted another of his studious recitals of the province's chartered privileges. "We humbly look up to his present Majesty . . . as children to a father," he wrote. Not the colonists but Hutchinson espoused unconstitutional doctrine, and not they but the governor reasoned so as to suggest that the colony was "independent." Adams had shifted the emotional issue from Parliament to the governor, going so far as to quote from Hutchinson's *History of Massachusetts-Bay* to trace charter privileges.

This displacement of anger onto the governor, which has appeared to many as a personal aberration by Otis and Adams, had profound implications for the Revolution. Rebellion in its

---

69. *Diary and Autobiography*, II, 80n, 82.
70. See *Works of John Adams*, II, 320n (Charles Francis Adams quoting Hutchinson's *History of Massachusetts-Bay*).

very nature, it has been written, amounts to "a public confession of the wish for power" with a resulting onset of guilt, followed by "aggression against society." In other revolutions these emotions have sometimes reflected a wish for "the destruction of patriarchal values."[71] The Massachusetts revolutionaries, regarding themselves as upholders of these values, directed their guilty emotions at the governor. The governors, deified in the seventeenth century instead of the far-off king, traditionally played this role in provincial politics. Nathaniel Hawthorne later made use of the patriot anger directed at Hutchinson in his story "My Kinsman, Major Molineux," which dealt with the parallel between revolution and the break with parental authority. ("Governor" was the Puritan term used for a father as ruler over his household, a usage reflected in Deacon Adams's insistence, during the family spat, on "his Right to govern.")[72] In Adams's case the traditional, contrasting attitudes toward governor and king were reflected in revolutionary rhetoric and conservative ideas.

In his first break with authority—his father's wish that he study for the ministry—Adams had experienced guilt followed by aggressive feelings directed against his neighbors and society in general. In addition, like a guilty rebel he displayed "aggression . . . against the self" in his diary. But then, as with Otis and in the Revolution itself, he legitimized his rebellion by upholding the principles of those he rejected. Samuel Adams expressed it well when confronted with the familiar accusation that the colonists were behaving as ungrateful children. They were children who had come of age, he answered, pursuing a

71. "Answer of the House of Representatives to the Speech of the Governor of sixth January" (Jan. 26, 1773), in Alden Bradford, ed., *Speeches of the Governors of Massachusetts, 1765 to 1775* (Boston, 1818), 349, 351–352, 363; Fred Weinstein and Gerald M. Platt, *The Wish to Be Free: Society, Psyche, and Value Change* (Berkeley and Los Angeles, 1969), 38, 59.

72. On the Puritan use of the word "governor," see Walzer, "Puritanism as a Revolutionary Ideology," *History and Theory*, III (1963), 85. Hawthorne enforced his point by citing examples of violence against colonial governors from Hutchinson's *History of Massachusetts-Bay*. For Adams's attacks on governors Shirley (for his "ambition"), Bernard, and Hutchinson, see Patterson, *Political Parties*, 49; *Diary and Autobiography*, I, 329, 325, II, 84.

natural assertion of independence by a child from its parents.[73]

John Adams, too, recognized the bid for power implicit in rebellion, justifying it by the people's virtue. Thus at the end of 1773 he welcomed the Boston Tea Party as "the most magnificent Movement of all" and "an Epocha in History," because of the virtuous "Dignity" of the patriots.[74] This view brought him close to Samuel Adams in sentiment, though not in approach: Adams's merely fellow-traveling relationship to the cause was implicit in his not having been privy to the planning for the Tea Party. Thoroughly committed as he was by the year 1773, Adams still held himself at an abstract, theoretical distance. All this changed in 1774, when his whole life was caught up in the Revolution.

73. Weinstein and Platt, *Wish to Be Free*, 38 (italics removed). For Samuel Adams's argument see Barrows and Wallace, "American Revolution," *Perspectives*, VI (1972), 193. Otis said as much in his *Rights of the British Colonies Asserted and Proved* (Boston, 1764), on which see Bailyn, ed., *Pamphlets*, 411–413. In 1765 Otis had written, "I am her most dutiful son." Barrows and Wallace, "American Revolution," *Perspectives*, VI (1972), 193. Adams followed Otis in employing the maternal analogy with regard to England, another indication that for him the important struggle was with the patriarchal governor. See *Works of John Adams*, IV, 43, 104, X, 282–283 (1818); Adams to Abigail Adams, July 7, 1775, *Adams Family Correspondence*, I, 241.

74. *Diary and Autobiography*, II, 85–86. Adams observed that the basic passion for dominance translates, in the case of the people, into the desire for political independence. *Works of John Adams*, III, 448. A similar analysis of Otis and patriarchy that came to my attention too late for inclusion in this discussion is John J. Waters, "James Otis, Jr.: Ambivalent Revolutionary," *History of Childhood Quarterly*, I (1973), 142–150.

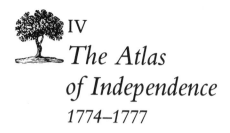

IV

The Atlas
of Independence
1774–1777

In May 1774 Adams was alone in Boston, suffering from a chronic cold, when news arrived of the act closing the port of Boston, the first of Parliament's "Coercive Acts" in retaliation for the dumping of the tea. He wrote ominously to his wife, then visiting her family at Weymouth, of the gravity of the situation. But he added: "Don't imagine from all this that I am in the Dumps. Far otherwise. I can truly say, that I have felt more Spirits and Activity, since the Arrival of this News, than I had done before for years."[1]

On May 25 Adams was elected to the Massachusetts Council, and again negatived, this time by General Thomas Gage, who replaced Hutchinson in order to impose martial law. Then, while on circuit in June, Adams learned that the General Court had elected him to a Continental Congress in Philadelphia. Initially he felt his "insufficiency" to represent Massachusetts at such a gathering of the leading men in America. He resolved to make himself "a scholar" of statesmanship and to "keep an exact Diary, of my Journey, as well as a Journal of the Proceedings of the Congress."[2] Within a few days, though, he

1. Adams to Abigail Adams, May 12, 1774, *Adams Family Correspondence*, I, 107.
2. Adams to James Warren, July 17, 1774, *Warren-Adams Letters: Being Chiefly a Correspondence among John Adams, Samuel Adams, and James Warren* (Massachusetts Historical Society, *Collections*, LXXII–LXXIII [Boston, 1917–1923]), I, 29, hereafter cited as *Warren-Adams Letters*; *Diary and Autobiography*, II, 96.

began to weigh the personal consequences of his election, for he could ill afford to give up his business.

Surveying his situation at the age of thirty-nine, after fourteen years of law practice, Adams found cause only for despair. "I had a pretty Estate from my Father, I have been assisted by your Father," he wrote to his wife, and "I have done the greatest Business in the Province. I have had the very richest Clients in the Province: Yet I am Poor in Comparison of others." How had this come about? He had squandered money on books in pursuit of Gridley's philosophical approach to the law. And he had spent "indiscreetly" on a few luxuries: "a Lighter [a boat] . . . a Pew . . . an House in Boston."[3] He complained that while he had wasted his time in politics, "Blockheads" had forged ahead of him and now lived in splendor like noblemen. His account books reveal that though he truly commanded the largest practice in Massachusetts, he made all of his money in small fees, never garnering the retainers, even from the wealthy John Hancock, that make a lawyer rich.[4] Despite much "pondering and Anxiety" over his career, Adams had never answered his old question: "Am I planning the Illustration [i.e., making illustrious] of my Family or the Welfare of my Country?"[5] As a result he faced going to Philadelphia with the feeling of having achieved neither.

It was in this state of mind that Adams took the case of the loyalist Richard King, victimized by a patriot mob in 1766 and still seeking damages. In distant Falmouth, Maine, where he had ridden his circuit on horseback, Adams delivered a stunning address to the jury in this now forgotten case. Summoning the terrors of a mob breaking in on the peacefully sleeping King and his wife and children, Adams raised the question of damages to a constitutional level. Once again echoing Otis's words at the Writs of Assistance case, he declared:

3. Adams to Abigail Adams, June 29, 1774, *Adams Family Correspondence*, I, 113–114.
4. *Ibid.*, 119, and see 114. See Wroth and Zobel, eds., *Legal Papers*, lvii–lxiv, for Adams's fees. On his expenses see Adams to James Warren, Sept. 26, 1775, *Warren-Adams Letters*, I, 117, and further in this chapter.
5. *Diary and Autobiography*, I, 352 (1770), 337 (1768).

"An Englishmans dwelling House is his Castle. The Law has erected a Fortification round it—and as every Man is Party to the Law, i.e. the Law is a Covenant of every Member of society with every other Member, therefore every Member of Society has entered into a solemn Covenant with every other that he shall enjoy in his own dwelling House as compleat a security, safety and Peace and Tranquility as if it was surrounded with Walls of Brass, with Ramparts and Palisadoes and defended with a Garrison and Artillery."[6]

The speech amounted to a grand gesture in defiance of the patriot side very much like Adams's defense of the soldiers in the Boston Massacre in 1770. It demonstrated his independence of any party and his adherence to fundamental rights above any cause. A few weeks later Adams made a similar gesture at a Boston town meeting. When "Thomas Boylston, a wealthy merchant of good standing, but not a favorite, attempted to speak against some proposition which the majority approved . . . the popular impatience broke out in efforts to stop him with noise." Adams stunned the meeting into silence by reciting lines from John Milton that he more than once remembered when feeling misused by the public: "I did but prompt the age to quit their clogs / By the known rules of ancient liberty, / When straight a barbarous noise environs me / Of *owls and cuckoos, asses, apes, and dogs.*"[7]

During the King case in Falmouth, Adams parted from his old friend and recent newspaper antagonist, Jonathan Sewall. Sewall had been his confidant when Adams, in Worcester, was

6. Wroth and Zobel, eds., *Legal Papers*, I, 137. In the Writs case Otis had spoken of the "privilege of house" rendering every Englishman "as secure in his house as a prince in his castle." Bailyn, ed., *Pamphlets*, 411. Otis was on Adams's mind at the time. Adams to Abigail Adams, July 9, 1774, *Adams Family Correspondence*, I, 135. See also Joseph Williamson, "The Professional Tours of John Adams in Maine," Maine Historical Society, *Collections and Proceedings*, 2d Ser., I (1890), 301–308.

7. *Works of John Adams*, I, 146n–147n. Charles Francis Adams is passing along John Quincy Adams's transmission to him of a family tradition. Catherine Drinker Bowen places the incident at a different time, but John Adams's tone fits his state of mind at this period. See Bowen, *John Adams and the American Revolution* (New York, 1949), 632n. Adams is quoting, correctly, from Milton's Sonnet XII.

deciding on a profession. In 1768 Sewall had carried Hutchinson's offer to Adams of a position in the vice-admiralty court. Now about to become a loyalist exile, Sewall made a last effort to dissuade Adams from his patriot activities. (Possibly Sewall was encouraged in this by Adams's stand in the King case.) When Sewall recalled the meeting years later he acutely analyzed Adams's state of mind on the eve of the Continental Congress. He had, wrote Sewall, "an unbounded Ambition and an enthusiastic Zeal for the imagined, or real, glory and welfare of his Country, (the ofspring perhaps, in part, tho imperceptible to himself, of disappointed Ambition)."[8] Sewall presumably did not realize that Adams's disappointment arose from a series of withdrawals from public life—from *suppression* of ambition. Nevertheless, "disappointed Ambition," all the more sharp for being self-created, was what he suffered.[9]

Adams's opponents were less likely than Sewall to appreciate the causes of Adams's style of "Passion and personal Altercation," as he himself described it. But they agreed in attributing it to an "ambition without bounds."[10] Both Judge Peter Oliver, whose impeachment Adams arranged, and Governor Hutchinson reported that in an "unguarded" moment Adams had revealed that "he could not look with complacency upon any man who was in possession of more wealth, more honours, or more knowledge than himself"—a characteristic confession.[11] The manner called "saucy" by Adams's sympathizers, and judiciously described by Sewall as "perhaps rather implacable to those whom he thinks his enemies," was called by Oliver an "Acrimony [that] settled into Rancor and Malignity."[12] The terms of these criticisms recall Adams's own published attacks

8. Jonathan Sewall to Joseph Lee, Sept. 21, 1787, *Adams Family Correspondence*, I, 137n.

9. Adams's resentment at being on circuit when he might have been conferring about the Congress may have been evident to Sewall. See Adams to Abigail Adams, June 30, 1774, *ibid.*, 115.

10. Adams to Abigail Adams, July 4, 1774, *ibid.*, 123; Hutchinson, *History of Massachusetts-Bay*, ed. Mayo, III, 214.

11. Adair and Schutz, eds., *Peter Oliver's Origin and Progress*, 83; Hutchinson, *History of Massachusetts-Bay*, ed. Mayo, III, 214.

12. Sewall to Lee, Sept. 21, 1787, *Adams Family Correspondence*, I, 137n; Adair and Schutz, eds., *Peter Oliver's Origin and Progress*, 83.

on Hutchinson and Sewall, as well as loyalist attacks on Otis. The same crude terminology, expressed with bluntness even among friends, tended to reduce motives to either pride or ambition, behavior to either deceit or honesty. "Warren told me," Adams wrote in his diary in 1773, "that Pemberton said I was the proudest and cunningest Fellow, he ever knew." Warren knew better. He told Pemberton that he thought Adams "rather a cautious Man, but . . . he could not say I ever trimmed. When I spoke at all I always spoke my sentiments."[13]

As he prepared to leave for the Continental Congress, Adams understood at least one thing about himself: his personal disappointment lay at the root of his public temper. He "determined," therefore, despite the "Torments" in his mind, "to be cool."[14] Yet, he confessed, "I have a Zeal at my Heart, for my Country and her Friends, which I cannot smother or conceal: it will burn out at Times and in Companies where it ought to be latent in my Breast. This Zeal will prove fatal to the Fortune and Felicity of my Family, if it is not regulated by a cooler Judgment than mine has hitherto been. Coll. Otis's Phrase is 'The Zeal-Pot boils over.' "[15]

A month later, in August 1774, mollifying himself with the promise that he would quickly return to private life, Adams set out for the Congress with the other Massachusetts delegates, Samuel Adams, Robert Treat Paine, and Thomas Cushing. Although Adams did not reveal it, "They made a very respectable parade, in Sight of five of the Regiments encamped on the Common, being in a coach of four, preceeded by two white servants well mounted and armed, with four blacks behind in Livery, two on horseback and two footmen."[16]

---

13. *Diary and Autobiography*, II, 77. In 1766 Adams wrote in his diary: "Brother tells me, that Wm. Vesey Jur. tells him, he has but one Objection against Jona. Bass [in the election], and that is, Bass is too forward.—When a Man is forward, We may conclude he has some selfish View." Mar. 1, 1766, *ibid.*, I, 301. For attacks on Otis in such terms see *ibid.*, 301n.

14. Adams to Abigail Adams, July 1, 1774, *Adams Family Correspondence*, I, 119.

15. Adams to Abigail Adams, July 9, 1774, *ibid.*, 135.

16. Shipton, *Sibley's Harvard Graduates*, XII, 471–472. As an old man, Adams grew angry at his grandson Charles Francis for questioning the panoply of the Congress delegates when the boy found it described in an old newspaper. *The Adamses on the Reading, Making, and Collecting of Books; the Place of Scholarship in a Republic; and Kindred*

For nineteen triumphal days the delegates were greeted by the leading men at each town and city on their way to Philadelphia. Adams conveyed his excitement in a revivified diary, in which he exuberantly described landscapes, analyzed characters, and listed the ingredients of dishes at banquets.

His observations had the purpose of preparing him for the Congress. As once he had questioned everyone he could about legal writs, he now asked at each town for information about the characters of the delegates and the factions they were likely to form. In New York City he noted: "Mr. Livingston is a down right strait forward Man. Mr. Alsop is a soft sweet Man. Mr. Duane has a sly, surveying Eye, a little squint Eyed— between 40 and 45 I should guess—very sensible I think and very artfull."[17]

Adams's first reaction to the news of a Congress had been to question whether the colonies should petition, vote "Spirited Resolves," or take "bolder Councils." By the time he left Massachusetts he felt that trade restrictions, the utmost of which a Congress was capable, would not go nearly far enough. On the way, in Connecticut, the strongest talk was of "a total Stoppage of Trade to Europe and the West Indies." Further on, though, there was fear "least the levelling Spirit of the New England Colonies should propagate itself into N. York." Outside of Philadelphia a friendly delegation from the city warned that the Massachusetts men had the reputation of desperadoes bent on independence.[18] This gave them "a delicate Course to steer,"

Topics: A Tribute to Thomas James Wilson (Cambridge, Mass., 1967), 21–22. John Adams described the scene to Timothy Pickering, Aug. 6, 1822: the delegates, "all destitute of fortune, four poor pilgrims, proceeded in one coach." *Works of John Adams*, II, 512n. See further in this chapter for travel to subsequent Congresses.

17. *Diary and Autobiography*, II, 106–107. Also see *ibid.*, 115, 121. Rush wrote in his autobiography that, outside Philadelphia, Adams asked him "many questions." Quoted, *ibid.*, 115n. Philip Livingston, John Alsop, and James Duane were New York delegates to the Congress.

18. *Ibid.*, 96, 99, 106. Also Adams to James Warren, July 25, 1774, *Warren-Adams Letters*, I, 29, 32, and to Timothy Pickering, Aug. 6, 1822, *Works of John Adams*, II, 512n–513n. John Trumbull, Adams's law clerk, reported a conversation in Adams's law office with Samuel Adams, just before the Congress, in which John Adams is supposed to have said: "I suppose we must go to Philadelphia, and enter into non-importation, non-consumption, and non-exportation agreements; but they will be of no avail; we shall have to resist by

Adams subsequently explained, "between too much Activity and too much Insensibility, in our critical interested situation." As he put it at the time: "We have been obliged to act with great delicacy and caution. We have been obliged to keep ourselves out of sight, and to feel pulses, and to sound the depths; to insinuate our sentiments, designs, and desires, by means of other persons, sometimes of one province, and sometimes of another."[19]

At first Adams found Congress "a Collection of the greatest Men upon this Continent." He spoke infrequently, and then mostly on technical points (his first words were a question), contenting himself with recording the speeches of others, as he had resolved to do. The universal concern for the plight of Boston brought him to tears.[20] Within a month, however, he grew weary of the debates, at which every man felt compelled to display his brilliance. His character sketches grew more caustic, and the language of his draft of a petition to the king had to be toned down.[21] At the end of September he complained: "We hear perpetually the most figurative penegyrics upon our wisdom, fortitude, and temperance; the most fervent exhortations to perseverance; but nothing more is done."[22]

The something more that he wished for but could not ask

---

force." Reported in Timothy Pitkin, *A Political and Civil History of the United States of America, from the Year 1763 to the Close of the Administration of President Washington . . .* , I (New Haven, Conn., 1828), 277.

19. Adams to Abigail Adams, Sept. 18, 1774, *Adams Family Correspondence*, I, 158; *Works of John Adams*, IX, 348.

20. Adams to Abigail Adams, Sept. 8, 1774, *Adams Family Correspondence*, I, 150. Technically, Adams's question came the day before Congress officially convened. See Julian P. Boyd *et al.*, eds., *The Papers of Thomas Jefferson* (Princeton, N.J., 1950–), I, 325. On Adams's talking in Congress, see *Diary and Autobiography*, III, 317; on his tears, see Adams to Abigail Adams, Sept. 18, 1774, *Adams Family Correspondence*, I, 159.

21. See *Diary and Autobiography*, II, 151n. Bernhard Knollenberg has observed evidences of Adams's temper in Congress, especially toward John Dickinson. See his "John Dickinson vs. John Adams: 1774–1776," American Philosophical Society, *Proceedings*, CVII (1963), 138–144, esp. 140. Adams tended to blend together the Congresses in his recollections. At the first Congress, he wrote, "I had not in my nature prudence and caution enough" to keep from "muttering" against Great Britain—with the result that he gained a reputation of being for independence. Adams to Francis Adrian Vanderkemp, Mar. 8, 1813, Vanderkemp Papers, Pa. Hist. Soc. See further in this chapter on his temper at later Congresses.

22. Adams to William Tudor, Sept. 29, 1774, *Works of John Adams*, IX, 347.

directly was military help for Boston. Short of this, he supported nonimportation, nonconsumption, and nonexportation, a vigorous declaration of rights, and an assumption of provincial government by the General Court under the old Massachusetts charter. Adams was pleased when the majority shared his opinion that Britain should be accorded only one kind of power over the colonies, that of regulating external trade. Since the Congress's nonimportation agreement in effect usurped this power, the colonies might be said to have asserted their independence. But Adams and his colleagues regarded independence as involving a series of steps: the assumption of governmental power by the provincial governments, the raising of a Continental army, and finally a formal renunciation of the king's prerogative.

For two months after he returned from Congress in October 1774, Adams served in the General Court. Then, in December, the adjournment of that body coincided with the appearance of a series of loyalist newspaper essays signed "Massachusettensis." In the leisure allowed him until the next Continental Congress, to which he was elected in December, he answered Massachusettensis in a series of essays signed "Novanglus." (With the courts closed, there was no legal business to be done.) "Novanglus" offered an "exuberance of proof" that Parliament had no power whatsoever over the colonies except what they freely granted by "*compact* and *consent*," namely, the regulation of external trade.[23] The legal basis of this position Adams established by the fullest tracing yet by any patriot theoretician of the history of charter rights.

But, mistakenly believing that Massachusettensis was his old friend and newspaper antagonist, Jonathan Sewall, Adams erected his structure of proof on an emotional base.[24] Because of this, and because the "Novanglus" essays embodied Adams's peculiarities as a writer, they obscured nearly as much as they clarified. That Novanglus went as far as anyone yet had in

23. *Ibid.*, IV, 162, 100 (italics in original).
24. The real author, Adams learned near the end of his life, was another friend, Daniel Leonard.

asserting the rights of the colonies, no one could doubt. But just what result the author envisioned from an assertion of those rights remains problematic. Whereas the "Dissertation on Canon and Feudal Law" had begun as an organized effort and had then been adapted to the exigencies of the Stamp Act agitation, "Novanglus" set the pattern for the rest of Adams's extended political writings by both beginning and ending in disorganized response to developing events. Adams refuted Massachusettensis, strayed into and out of historical narrative, shifted to an attack on a pamphlet by Joseph Galloway, returned to a point-by-point refutation of Massachusettensis, and finally "rambled" through every English statute bearing on the rights of the colonies, including the laws relating to the separated parts of the dominion (Ireland, Wales, Jersey, Guernsey), "however unentertaining it may be."[25] The battle of Lexington on April 19, 1775, ended the series after thirteen installments.

Novanglus's legal argument was accompanied by a moral one. Here Adams recounted in greater detail than in the "Dissertation" the history of conspiracy by the governors of Massachusetts since Bernard. Hutchinson came in for a predictable measure of denunciation, as well as for an attempted characterological and psychological analysis in terms of vanity and ambition.[26] As he recounted the sins of the opposition in response to Massachusettensis's questioning of the probity of the patriots, Adams grew angry. He rose to impassioned praise of "the whigs" and their "grievously oppressed" nation, abandoning in the process his promise not to "revile" his opponent.[27]

Massachusettensis was right that the whigs, being human, possessed ambition. "But this writer cannot name a set of men, in the whole British empire, who have sacrificed their private

25. *Works of John Adams*, IV, 158, 133. For other confessions of disarray and dullness, see *ibid.*, 155–156, 170. See Moses Coit Tyler, *The Literary History of the American Revolution, 1763–1783* (New York, 1897), 391–392, for a literary assessment.

26. Once again Hutchinson appeared as Adams's alter ego, this time in being a man whose "industry was prodigious" and who had as his chief distinction a "remarkable . . . degree" of susceptibility to flattery—the very reputation that Adams went on to create for himself. *Works of John Adams*, IV, 68. In the end, Adams decided that Hutchinson's "reason was manifestly overpowered." *Ibid.*, 120.

27. *Ibid.*, 165, 11.

interest to their nation's honor and the public good in so remarkable a manner, as the leading whigs have done in the two last administrations." (The sacrifices were Adams's own, of course, transferred to a party.) The people at large, too, had exhibited virtuous behavior—while suffering "in a state of nature . . . as the history of mankind cannot parallel." It was a commonplace, most eloquently expressed in Patrick Henry's opening speech in the Continental Congress, that the suspension of government returned the people to a state of nature. Adams believed that by going on in much the same way as they had before, the Massachusetts people had demonstrated the viability of democracy. A tory junto and the English had attempted to take away from them the charter "which nature dictated." Novanglus could only ask why "the great and necessary virtues of simplicity, frugality, and economy cannot live in England . . . as well as America?"[28]

Adopting a terminology then still common in New England pulpits, Adams rose once again to religious enthusiasm. The revolutionary struggle presented itself as an opposition between good and evil. The whigs were put upon like the magnanimous Joseph; their sufferings were providential.[29] If worse should come down upon them, "the world will see that their fortitude, patience, and magnanimity will rise in proportion." Their committees of correspondence were "intended by Providence to accomplish great events," while the remarkable unanimity of votes in the Continental Congress "cannot be considered in any other light than as the happiest omens, indeed as providential dispensations," demonstrating the "indissoluble union of the colonies." The rhetoric of a sermon's closing affirmation was reserved for these people. "*They know*," Adams intoned, "upon what hinge the whole dispute turns. . . . *they know* that . . . parliament has no authority over them. . . . *They know* that all America is united in sentiment."[30]

28. *Ibid.*, 75, 31, 99, 46, and see esp. 54, on "depraved" England.

29. *Ibid.*, 45. See Parson Wibird's sermon on America as Joseph, *Diary and Autobiography*, I, 316. Compare Adams's use of Jeremiah, *ibid.*, 233–234; also Boston suffering "like Zion in distress," in Adams to Edward Biddle, Dec. 12, 1774, *Works of John Adams*, IX, 350.

30. *Works of John Adams*, IV, 92, 95, 35, 32, 33 (italics added). On sermon form see Alfred

Both of the traditions inspiring this faith, however, offered sobering reflections. From the Calvinist point of view, the very evils of the tories, Americans themselves, demonstrated the ineluctably fallen state of man. On the other hand, whig theory taught that the tories' opposites, the people, *had* to be virtuous to sustain a popular government. But their virtue was as likely to dissipate as the power that sustained monarchy or the honor that sustained aristocracies.[31] The people were corruptible, Adams had learned, especially "the lowest and meanest." They "were not so virtuous or so happy," for example, as to have abstained from buying English tea.[32] The vigor of Adams's prose tended to obscure this inherited pessimism about human nature, but it came out in his legal argument.

That argument rested, still, on the assertion that the colonists wished no more than to protect their charter privileges. With these secured, their governments represented "little models of the English constitution." But here lay the conservatism implicit in Adams's approach. For the English system included a king and an aristocracy as well as a House of Commons (itself not a popular body even in the "greater purity and perfection" that the English system had reached in America). Once Adams claimed to be fighting to preserve this system, he was led to deny a republican spirit among the patriots. Even as he celebrated the rise of democracy and breathed enthusiasm for the spirit of antimonarchy and regicide, he protested his fealty to His Majesty, "whom God preserve."[33]

Habegger, "Preparing the Soul for Christ: The Contrasting Sermon Forms of John Cotton and Thomas Hooker," *American Literature*, XLI (1969–1970), 342–351.

31. See Lovejoy, *Reflections on Human Nature*, 195–196, and Curti, *Human Nature in American Historical Thought*, 10–23. Adams tended toward both greater optimism and pessimism than the philosophers and moralists on whom he drew. Thus in the same letter he could declare that ambition "in a Republic . . . is but another Name for public Virtue, and public Spirit," then add that "we, in America, are . . . contaminated with the Selfish Principles of Monarchy." Adams to [James Warren?], Apr. 27, 1777, Adams Papers, Reel 91.

32. *Works of John Adams*, IV, 61, 90. See Morgan, "Puritan Ethic and the American Revolution," *WMQ*, 3d Ser., XXIV (1967), for the importance accorded to the populace's capacity to deny itself the tea—an almost religious test.

33. *Works of John Adams*, IV, 117, 114. See also *ibid.*, 68, 131. For flirtations with regicide see *ibid.*, 17–18, 29. Adams regarded the English constitution as "nothing more nor less

By the same contradictory logic, although the Continental Congress had forged an indissoluble union and implicitly asserted self-rule, it was "wicked" to suggest that the patriots contemplated independence. Carried away in this manner, Adams granted concessions against which he had argued in Congress. He offered to pay the taxes that had been levied by Parliament, once compulsions were removed.[34] He allowed two exceptions, besides trade regulation, to his denial of parliamentary authority: "Such matters as concerned all the colonies together" and management of the post office. As for Massachusettensis's argument that by the patriots' logic they should accord George III titles as king of each colony separately ("King of Massachusetts, &c."), Adams declared: "I have no objection at all; I wish he would be graciously pleased to assume them."[35]

Eventually Adams was driven into an ambiguity resembling that in Otis's *Rights of the British Colonies Asserted and Proved* (1764), which had argued both defiance of and obedience to Parliament. "An absolute independence on parliament," Adams wrote, " . . . is very compatible with an absolute dependence on it." He referred to dependence on British regulation of America's external trade, independence with regard to American internal concerns. But the Congress had already usurped power over both. "It is honestly confessed," Adams confusingly wrote in an unacknowledged threat of independence, "rather than become subject to the absolute authority of parliament in all cases of taxation and internal polity," the patriots "will be driven to throw off that of regulating trade."[36]

"Novanglus" showed that Adams was both for and against independence after the first Continental Congress. In common

than a republic, in which the king is first magistrate." *Ibid.*, 106. But he denied any specially republican spirit among the patriots.

34. *Ibid.*, 52, and on taxes, 131. See also *ibid.*, 46–47, 106, and for his opposite opinion against paying taxes under any circumstances, see his letter to Gen. Joseph Palmer, Sept. 26, 1774, *ibid.*, I, 155.

35. *Ibid.*, IV, 49, 114n, 115. Adams's concession on the post office came in response to Massachusettensis's quibble that the colonies had always accepted British control of the postal service. *Ibid.*, 49n.

36. *Ibid.*, 130, 131. Note Adams's rare use of an indirect grammatical construction. For an analysis of Otis's ambiguity see Bailyn, ed., *Pamphlets*, 415.

with others who had taken up Otis's use of Lord Coke's doctrine in Bonham's Case—that an act of Parliament in conflict with natural rights was void—he had been propelled toward revolution by the logic of his position as much as by personal inclination. He could honestly denounce as a "slander" the suggestion that any of the patriots "pant after 'independence,' " even as he built a structure of logic showing the colonies already independent. In the same way, he inveighed against "innovation" even as he posited a system of colonial self-government that implied democratization.[37] Adams was a radical in spite of himself, although not until years later did he suffer attacks such as Otis had suffered when *his* ambivalence was perceived.

On April 15, 1775, Adams expressed the wish to "avoid public life," but four days later his political uncertainties were once again solved by the march of events. The fighting at Concord and Lexington convinced him that reconciliation with the mother country had become an impossibility.[38] Breaking off the "Novanglus" essays, he surveyed the battlefield at Lexington and the American force in Cambridge, coming away deeply concerned over the general confusion and lack of supplies. A few days later he left for the Continental Congress, absorbed in the military necessities of the crisis: above all he was convinced that the American army of irregulars outside Boston had to be adopted by Congress. "The Colonies" ought to declare themselves "free, Sovereign and independent States, and then to inform Great Britain" that they "were willing to enter into Negotiations . . . for the redress of all Grievances,

37. *Works of John Adams*, IV, 131. Merrill Jensen has shown how the removal of crown influence gave a new balance of power to the lower houses throughout the colonies, irrespective of anyone's conservative or radical desires. See "Democracy and the American Revolution," *Huntington Library Quarterly*, XX (1957), 321–341. Adams showed his awareness of this tendency in a proclamation written for the General Court session of November-December 1775. "The present generation," he wrote, " . . . may be congratulated on the acquisition of a form of government more immediately in all its branches under the influence and control of the people, and therefore, more free and happy than was enjoyed by their ancestors." *Works of John Adams*, I, 195.

38. *Works of John Adams*, IX, 355. Braintree had again not elected Adams to the General Court, although it made him selectman, Mar. 6, 1775. *Diary and Autobiography*, II, 161n.

and a restoration of Harmony between the two Countries, upon permanent Principles." Thus Adams left for the second Continental Congress theoretically in favor of reconciliation but practically in favor of independence.[39]

The march of events was carrying not only his opinions but all of the colonies into armed conflict and independence (the battle of Bunker Hill took place on June 11, 1775). At the second session of Congress, beginning in May 1775, Adams found more sympathy for Boston and a greater willingness to take military steps, but also a lingering desire to solve the crisis short of assuming independence. For the sake of union he was willing to allow such "Whims," but he grew critical as the noble sentiments of the first Congress dissipated. His own life was complicated by illness, personality clashes within the Massachusetts delegation, a political struggle between moderates and radicals at home, and other causes of "anxiety." And now the moderates in Congress grew angry with Adams, and he with them. Not since his birth, he wrote, had he been "so compleatly miserable."[40]

John Dickinson, the leader of the reconciliation forces pressing for yet another petition to the king, now became Adams's chief antagonist. Yet, when Dickinson angrily accosted him outside Congress, he was, Adams wrote in his autobiography, "in a very happy temper," and "answered him very coolly."[41] Hereafter, with only one exception, he treated Dickinson's undiminished attacks, both public and private, in the same controlled manner. This was characteristic. Adams suffered from a constantly rising temper at *anticipated* enmity. But when attacked directly he rarely took offence. After years of nearly hysterical resentment he responded with equanimity when

39. *Diary and Autobiography*, III, 315 (autobiography). Adams's autobiographical recollections tend to advance the dates of his views, but this one is connected to such vivid recollection of the days after the battle of Lexington and suits so well with his contemporary letters as to appear accurate.

40. "Whims," "miserable": Adams to James Warren, July 6, 1775, and July 23, 1775, *Warren-Adams Letters*, I, 74, 87; "anxiety," over differences with the aristocratic southerners concerning organization of the army: Adams to Elbridge Gerry, June 18, 1775, *Works of John Adams*, IX, 358.

41. *Diary and Autobiography*, III, 318 (autobiography).

Hutchinson negatived his election to the Massachusetts Council. "Good Treatment," he wrote in his diary in 1759, "makes me think I am admired, beloved, and my own Vanity will be indulged in me. So I dismiss my Gard and grow weak, silly, vain, conceited, ostentatious. But a Check, a frown, a sneer, a Sarcasm . . . makes me more careful and considerate."[42]

If he did not take offense on his own account, Adams nevertheless felt every delay as a blow against the suffering city of Boston. He had anticipated, as far back as 1771, "War and Desolation" and had speculated that "out of such Desolations, Glory and Power, and Wonders may arise, to carry on the Designs of Providence." Such a vision recalled the Puritans' characteristic welcoming of calamities as signs of the Lord's involvement in their destiny. For Adams, Boston's struggle, "a Cause which interests the whole Globe," remained like the religious crises of the Puritans' "city on a hill." He accepted, even welcomed, what he repeatedly called "the Furnace of Affliction" calculated to "refine" the people.[43] In such a crisis Adams knew his course. Suspending his diary, he plunged into the work of drafting resolutions and, especially, organizing the army as a Continental force.

During this period Adams had two confidants, his wife and James Warren. He wrote to them circumspectly at first, then gradually expressed his hopes and frustrations. In June he outlined to each his program for independence and complained to Warren of "a certain great Fortune and piddling Genius," obviously John Dickinson.[44]

Adams's letters were the more free since they were being privately carried to Boston. The British searched the ship on which the courier was traveling; he failed to destroy them, and

42. *Ibid.*, I, 69. "It may in short be made a Question," Adams continued, " . . . whether Smiles, kind Words, respectful Actions, dont betray me into Weaknesses and Littlenesses, that frowns, Satirical Speeches and contemptuous Behaviour, make me avoid."

43. Adams to Isaac Smith, Jr., [Sept. 1771?], and to Abigail Adams, May 2, 1775, *Adams Family Correspondence*, I, 82, 192. See also Adams to Abigail Adams, July 5, 1774, *ibid.*, 124–125, and for another source of his prophetic, apocalyptic language, see sermons on the prophets attended by Adams, in his letters to Abigail Adams, June 11, 1775, and Feb. 11, 1776, *ibid.*, 215, 345.

44. *Diary and Autobiography*, II, 174n.

they were taken and published. As a result, when Adams returned to Congress in September 1775, after a short August recess, he met a cold reception. His intercepted letters provided the basis for versified ridicule in the newspapers and for social ostracism led by Dickinson, who snubbed Adams when they passed each other. Benjamin Rush recalled seeing Adams "walk our streets alone, . . . an object of nearly universal detestation." Identified as having a radical bent on the question of independence, Adams along with the other Massachusetts delegates ceased to receive appointments to committees.[45]

Charles Francis Adams treated this period portentously but justifiably as the second great moral trial of Adams's life (he made the challenge of the Boston Massacre trials the first). The military news from Boston continued ominous. A dysentery epidemic swept Massachusetts, taking the lives of Adams's mother-in-law and a servant in his house while infecting his wife, his son Thomas, and two other servants. He was both drawn toward his defenseless home and repelled by Philadelphia and the Congress.[46] Nevertheless, a week after Dickinson's snub, which he mentioned without rancor in his diary, and after receiving the first hints of illness at home, Adams wrote to his wife: "I have enjoyed better Health, this session than the last, and have suffered less from certain Fidgets, Pidlings, and Irritabilities which have become so famous. A more serious Spirit prevails [here] than heretofore." The "famous" symptoms were those usually accompanying his nervous illnesses, which he tried to deprecate by calling them piddling, his term for Dickinson. His actual illnesses were less serious than the long periods of anxiety leading up to them. As soon as he had to deal with

45. George W. Corner, ed., *The Autobiography of Benjamin Rush: His "Travels Through Life" Together with his Commonplace Book for 1789–1813* (Princeton, N.J., 1948), 142. For the effects of the intercepted letters see *Works of John Adams*, I, 183; Cornelia Meigs, *The Violent Men: A Study of Human Relations in the First American Congress* (New York, 1949); Warren Hasty Carroll, "John Adams, Puritan Revolutionist: A Study of His Part in Making the American Revolution, 1764–1776" (Ph.D. diss., Columbia University, 1959), 291–292.

46. Carroll, "John Adams: Puritan Revolutionist," 295, suggests that Adams's strain is visible in the shaken handwriting of his Oct. 7, 1775, letter to William Tudor on Abigail Adams's illness.

physical symptoms alone, Adams tended to improve, especially if he could find hopeful signs for his cause.[47]

Adams plunged into work. His letters grew full of the details of military necessities, especially "the *Unum Necessarium*," salt-peter. Obviously reminded of Dickinson when a friend complained of a social insult, Adams wrote: "These Little things are below the Dignity of our glorious Cause, which is the best and greatest that ever engaged the human Mind."[48] He now felt free to press for the aims he had revealed in his intercepted letters: the assumption of all functions of government and the modeling of a constitution. Above all things, constitution-making absorbed him. The great question was whether the non-New England states would form governments sufficiently similar to the republican institutions of the North to make possible a viable union of all the states. Adams's short essay, *Thoughts on Government*, written in January 1776, was calculated to move the South toward republicanism.[49]

With an opening flourish suitable to the momentous undertaking of proposing a form of government, Adams invoked the English theorists of "the divine science of politics."[50] His ideal remained a government founded on its people's virtue—a republic. He advocated two legislative bodies, one popularly elected, along with a governor and an independent judiciary: in effect, the eighteenth-century charter government of Massa-

47. Adams to Abigail Adams, Sept. 26, 1775, *Adams Family Correspondence*, I, 285. Adams used the term "Pidling" to describe his nervous complaints: it appears in his correspondence some years later. That he had called Dickinson a "piddling Genius" and now revived the term for himself a few days after Dickinson's responding snub suggests the connection in his mind between his state of mind and his health.

48. Adams to James Warren, Sept. 26, 1775, *Warren-Adams Letters*, I, 115; Adams to Samuel Osgood, Nov. 15, 1775, Osgood Papers, New-York Historical Society, New York City.

49. Both of Adams's intercepted letters refer to "constitution" in the singular, whereas Adams's interest was in constitutions for all of the states. (See, as late as 1787, the same focus in his *Defence of the Constitutions*.) The letters may have been altered in this respect, or Adams may have been referring to the Articles of Confederation, in which his role was minor. For the various letters written by Adams from Nov. 1775 to Jan. 1776, see *Works of John Adams*, IV, 185–209 *passim*. These are treated here as one work since they amplify without contradicting one another, though only one of them was published as *Thoughts on Government*. Other versions are still being edited.

50. *Works of John Adams*, IV, 193.

chusetts and Connecticut. Adams never abandoned this system, but he viewed it with differing emphases at different times in his life.

In "Clarendon," Adams had professed himself interested not in the forms of government—"this is the Inquiry of the Founders of Empires"—but in liberty. During his fight against innovations in the 1760s and early 1770s, he had taken the Massachusetts form as given, putting his emphasis on the people's rights in a mixed government. As recently as 1774 he had written that governments achieved "happiness" only when they "leaned to the democratical branch," the lower house.[51] In *Thoughts on Government*, a work intended "for southern latitudes," Adams faced a different challenge. The southerners in Congress were aristocrats with "higher notions of . . . the distinction between them and the common people than we." They were coming around to more republican views but still held their own definitions of "the Words Liberty, Honour and Politeness."[52] Because they were free to choose any governments they wished, including hereditary monarchies, the best tactic was to defend the republican form as it had appeared in America, without suggesting too many of the liberalizations being looked for in the North.[53]

In the interest of stability Adams proposed direct election only of the lower house in such a government and gave the governor wide powers of veto and appointments ("unless you choose to have a government more popular"), until "affairs get into a more quiet course." If all of the states could set out with the same basic structure, the South could later move toward the greater republicanism of Massachusetts while Massachusetts

51. Draft of "Clarendon," *Diary and Autobiography*, I, 298; "Friendly Address to All Reasonable Americans" (1774), Adams Papers, Reel 343.

52. Adams to Francis Dana, Aug. 16, 1776, and to Joseph Hawley, Nov. 25, 1775, *Works of John Adams*, IX, 430, 367, and to Samuel Osgood, Nov. 15, 1775, Osgood Papers. See also Adams to Abigail Adams, Apr. 14, 1776, *Adams Family Correspondence*, I, 381.

53. For monarchical ideas in the air (both expressed with irony), see Adams to Mercy Otis Warren, Jan. 8, 1776, and to James Warren, Oct. 1775, *Warren-Adams Letters*, I, 201, 167. Abigail Adams wrote to her husband about "our Monarchy or Democracy or what ever is to take place." Nov. 27, 1775, *Adams Family Correspondence*, I, 330.

moved to Connecticut's popularly elected governor.[54] Adams soon afterward represented himself as having written *Thoughts on Government* as a corrective to the wildly egalitarian ideas of Thomas Paine's *Common Sense*. In fact, he wrote to overcome the "strong Aversion in . . . [southern] Patricians, to Common Sense" by offering a system calculated to lead them gradually into the democratic fold.[55]

If *Thoughts on Government* showed no change in Adams's democratic faith, its tactical requirements introduced a change in emphasis that began to give him the appearance of a conservative in Massachusetts. He predicted that "in New England, the *Thoughts on Government* will be disdained because they are not popular enough; in the Southern Colonies, they will be despised . . . because too popular."[56]

In Congress during the winter and spring of 1775 / 1776 Adams made "almost dayley exhortations to [i.e., in favor of] the Institutions of Governments in the States and a declaration of Independence."[57] When Benjamin Rush met him at the first Congress he observed of Adams that "this gentleman's dress and manners were at that time plain, and his conversation cold and reserved." Beginning with the second Congress, however,

54. *Works of John Adams*, IV, 198, and version in letter to Richard Henry Lee, Nov. 15, 1775, *ibid.*, 187. That Adams looked for liberalization in Massachusetts is evidenced by his regret that Congress did not in 1774 give the Massachusetts legislature the authority to carry out some of its "Sublime Conceptions." Draft of a letter, Dec. 12, 1774, Adams Papers, Reel 343, echoed in Adams to Edward Biddle, Dec. 12, 1774, *Works of John Adams*, IX, 349. While giving to the governor the power of militia appointments in *Thoughts on Government*, Adams supported the more democratic transfer of this power from the upper to the lower house when the issue arose in Massachusetts. Adams to James Otis, Sr., Nov. 23, 1775, in Edmund C. Burnett, ed., *Letters of Members of the Continental Congress* (Washington, D.C., 1921–1936), I, 258. In July 1776 Adams expressed pleasure when the southern states began to adopt constitutions more republican than his recommendations in *Thoughts on Government*. Adams to Abigail Adams, July 10, 1776, *Adams Family Correspondence*, II, 42. See also Adams to Patrick Henry, June 3, 1776, *Works of John Adams*, IX, 386.

55. Adams to Abigail Adams, Apr. 14, 1776, *Adams Family Correspondence*, I, 381. See Adams to Abigail Adams, Mar. 19, 1776, *ibid.*, 363, for the beginnings of Adams's change of mind about Paine.

56. Adams to James Warren, May 12, 1776, *Warren-Adams Letters*, I, 242.

57. *Diary and Autobiography*, III, 360 (autobiography). For other accounts by Adams of this period see Adams to Mercy Otis Warren, Aug. 17, 1807, "Correspondence between John Adams and Mercy Warren Relating to Her 'History of the American Revolution,' July–August, 1807," Massachusetts Historical Society, *Collections*, 5th Ser., IV (Boston, 1878), 465. Also, *Diary and Autobiography*, II, 232n, III, 383.

Rush recalled that "his replies to reflections upon himself, or upon the New England States, were replete with the most poignant humor or satyre." Rush was describing the reappearance of Adams's courtroom and General Court temper. "I have not and will not be restrained from a Freedom of Speech," Adams himself wrote in 1776, and years later he recalled that "my pertness was plentifully retorted upon me."[58] "Every member of Congress in 1776," Rush wrote, "acknowledged him to be the first man in the House."[59]

Some idea of Adams's labors is conveyed by his grandson's statement that he "was a member of ninety, and chairman of twenty-five committees"—an estimate that, as Adams's editors have noted, "hardly more than suggests the burden of committee and administrative work" that he "carried during his periods of service in the Continental Congress from September 1774 to November 1777." In addition Adams served between Congresses in the Massachusetts Provincial Congress, the renamed General Court, sometimes going straight there from Philadelphia. In that body "his work on committees was as intense as it had been in Congress."

He described his regimen in Philadelphia by way of apology for not writing home: "The whole Congress is taken up, almost[,] in different Committees from seven to Ten in the Morning—from Ten to four or sometimes five, we are in Congress and from six to Ten in Committees again." Beginning in June 1776 much of his time went to directing the Board of War and Ordnance, really a one-man committee serving as a war department that "handled the lion's share of Congress' routine work."[60]

The mounting crescendo of work and anxiety recalled Adams's term at the General Court in 1771, and so did his

<hr />

58. Corner, ed., *Autobiography of Rush*, 110, 140; Adams to James Warren, May 18, 1776, *Warren-Adams Letters*, I, 248; Adams to George Washington Adams, Mar. 10, 1822, Adams Papers, Reel 124.

59. Corner, ed., *Autobiography of Rush*, 140.

60. *Adams Family Correspondence*, I, 332n; *Diary and Autobiography*, II, 226n; Adams to Abigail Adams, Dec. 3, 1775, *Adams Family Correspondence*, I, 331; *Diary and Autobiography*, II, 262n. See *ibid.*, III, 342 *ff*, for Adams's later acccounts.

indefatigability. Without exercise, his usual diet, proper sleep, or "the bracing Quality of my Native Air," he suffered long hours of meetings in the unrelieved Philadelphia heat "providentially preserved" in health. He was embarrassed when charged with conflict of interest for holding office both in Congress and in Massachusetts, where in addition to sitting in the legislature he was appointed chief justice. Robert Treat Paine, his elder, took offense at being appointed a judge under him and, already at odds with Adams politically, angrily refused to serve.[61] Finally, as the agitation for independence reached a crescendo, Adams learned of a political crisis in Massachusetts. The western radicals put him under "fearful apprehension" by advocating the abolition of property qualifications for voting and of all executive offices.[62]

Adams's dismay stemmed not from conservative fears but from his concern that the southern colonies would be given new reasons for opposing independence. In Massachusetts the more conservative moderates did, in fact, sour on independence in reaction to the new democratic proposals—until they defeated the radicals in May 1776.[63] With the conservatives, Adams opposed abolishing executive offices and disapproved such a democratization as Pennsylvania's proposed single legislature. But, in a kind of addendum to *Thoughts on Government*,

61. Adams to Abigail Adams, July 11, 1776, *Adams Family Correspondence*, II, 44. For Adams's discomfort over the judgeship see his letter to Abigail Adams, Aug. 18, 1776, *ibid.*, 99. He eventually resigned the position (see below in this chapter). On Paine, see Shipton, *Sibley's Harvard Graduates*, XII, 474; *Adams Family Correspondence*, I, 351n.

62. Breen, "John Adams' Fight against Innovation," *NEQ*, XL (1967), 515–518. Breen posits "a period of trial for Adams" after which, beginning in July 1776, he had grown "older, slightly embittered." Breen documents Adams's receiving the information from Massachusetts. Patterson, *Political Parties*, 130–131, posits a similar crisis for Adams during 1775 over the question of which ancient charter to adopt in Massachusetts. On the other hand, Patterson shows that the 1776 crisis was over with the electoral defeat of the radicals in May. *Ibid.*, 144. Yet another crisis, in Europe, is posited by John R. Howe, Jr., *The Changing Political Thought of John Adams* (Princeton, N.J., 1966), 102–108 (discussed below in chap. 8). Howe finds a steadily increasing note of confidence on Adams's part during the 1770s in contrast to the 1760s. *Ibid.*, 57n. See n. 46 above for the crisis suggested by Carroll, "John Adams: Puritan Revolutionist." James H. Hutson, "John Adams' Titles Campaign," *NEQ*, XLI (1968), 38–39, also finds a disillusionment—in the 1790s. One can document Adams's dejection and apparent loss of faith at any of the fraught periods of his life, so consistently did he assume a generally apocalyptic and personally despairing tone.

63. Patterson, *Political Parties*, 141, 144.

he expressed his basic republicanism by arguing against changing property qualifications for voting *"at present."* After all, he correctly pointed out, "our people have never been very rigid in scrutinizing into the qualifications of voters, and I presume they will not now begin to be so."[64]

Moral questions, above all others, continued to absorb Adams. If "the Spirit of Commerce," so frequently denounced during the nonimportation of the 1760s, prevailed in Massachusetts, there was a "great Danger that a Republican Government would be very factious and turbulent there." It now became clear that Adams could not be regarded as a representative of either the western radical spirit or the eastern moderates in Massachusetts. He stood above party, still as ready as in 1763 to "quarrel with both parties and with every individual of each, before I would subjugate my understanding, or prostitute my tongue or pen to either." Samuel Adams, with whom he traveled to Congress, rather than joining with the radicals, joined him in deploring the party strife. Putting unity above hated "Party and division," Adams wrote that when it came to choosing a governor, "I confess, my Rule should be to vote for the Man upon whom the Majority run." The authority of such disinterest remained so strong in Massachusetts that, together with a few others, John and Samuel Adams, though "completely detached from the realities of Massachusetts politics," remained an effective force in the state amounting almost to a third party.[65]

64. Adams to James Sullivan, May 26, 1776, *Works of John Adams*, IX, 377 (italics added), treated as a tract on government by Gilbert Chinard, *Honest John Adams* (Boston, 1933), 92. See Robert E. Brown, *Middle-Class Democracy and the Revolution in Massachusetts, 1691-1790* (Ithaca, N.Y., 1955), 52–60, for support of Adams's view. Brown, it should be noted, has been challenged by revisionist scholars: see Jesse Lemisch, "The American Revolution as Seen from the Bottom Up," in Barton J. Bernstein, ed., *Towards a New Past: Dissenting Essays in American History* (New York, 1968), 3–45. Adams was somewhat taken aback by his wife's suggestion that women be given the right to vote, and by others who advocated universal suffrage, but he went no further than pointing out the inconvenience of their proposals. It was at this time that he welcomed the republicanism of the southern constitutions, which went further than what he had felt free to suggest in *Thoughts on Government*. See also his letter to Patrick Henry, June 3, 1776, on the spread of republicanism, in *Works of John Adams*, IX, 387. The struggle between radicals and conservatives in Massachusetts made itself felt at about this time, with Adams supporting the side of "innovation," as mentioned above and in n. 54. See also Patterson, *Political Parties*, 130-131.

65. Adams to Mercy Warren, Apr. 16, 1776, *Warren-Adams Letters*, I, 223; *Works of John*

Adams approached independence, with its overwhelmingly political implications, in much the same, unpolitical spirit. Independence, he declared in April 1776, "ought not to have been undertaken untill the Design of Providence by a Series of great Events had . . . plainly marked out the Necessity." Once undertaken, it became a practical matter, with Adams conducting a state-by-state letter-writing campaign that assured the votes for which he called in his speeches on the floor of Congress.[66]

In June and the first few days of July he repeatedly advocated a declaration of independence. Those in the Congress at the time later concurred in describing his contribution as something stupendous. Jefferson, who wrote that Adams had been "the pillar of [the Declaration's] support on the floor of Congress, it's ablest advocate and defender against the multifarious assaults it encountered," was reported also to have said in conversation: "John Adams was our Colossus on the floor. He was not graceful nor elegant, nor remarkably fluent but he came out occasionally with a power of thought and expression, that moved us from our seats." Two other delegates suggested the same kind of picture of strength when they independently called Adams the "Atlas" of independence.[67]

Unfortunately, there is no record of Adams's reputedly great speech on the resolution to declare independence—"almost the only one I ever made," he later wrote, "that I wish was literally preserved."[68] However, it is possible to reconstruct its argu-

Adams, III, 432; Adams to James Warren, May 12, 1776, *Warren-Adams Letters*, I, 243; Patterson, *Political Parties*, 145. Patterson calls this third party "the Adams group" and shows how John Adams and Samuel Adams joined in opposition to democratic reforms not out of conservative fear but in disapproval of the divisiveness of the reforms. *Ibid.*, 150, and see esp. 202–203.

66. Adams to James Warren, Apr. 22, 1776, *Warren-Adams Letters*, I, 233–234. See also Carroll, "John Adams: Puritan Revolutionist," 357–360.

67. John H. Hazelton, *The Declaration of Independence; Its History . . .* (New York, 1906), 162. Stockton and Lee were delegates. See *Works of John Adams*, III, 56n–57n, and Richard M. Gummere, "The Classical Politics of John Adams," *Boston Public Library Quarterly*, IX (1957), 167–182.

68. Adams to Mercy Warren, Aug. 17, 1807, "Correspondence between Adams and Mercy Warren," Mass. Hist. Soc., *Colls.*, 5th Ser., IV, 468. Adams called the debate "an idle mispence of time, for nothing was said but what had been repeated and hackneyed in that room before, a hundred times, for six months past." Adams to Samuel Chase, July 1, 1776, *Works of John Adams*, IX, 415. Jefferson's minutes of Adams's recent speeches, then, along

ments. Adams contended, "It is now universally acknowledged that we are, and must be, independent States"; it only remained to ask whether or not there should be "a declaration of it."[69] He proceeded to a lawyerly, point-by-point refutation of the arguments against publishing such a proclamation. It would not unite but divide England, where the populace would be enraged by the blundering of its government. The potential ally France, far from being frightened off, would not treat at all until, "consistent with European delicacy," a declaration existed. Above all, the states would be stimulated to form governments, pass laws, and raise armies and supplies. If the war went well, the Union would be the stronger for having declared itself; if it went badly, better already to have declared.

No one could stand before the torrent of Adams's insistent demonstrations that independence, which was virtual, should also be declared. The debate focused on a single question, and Adams's genius lay in seizing upon a central truth—in this case, that independence already existed—and, without fatigue to himself, advancing that truth over and over again through seemingly infinite, richly illustrated variations. On this occasion he seems utterly to have been carried out of himself— " 'carried out in Spirit' as Enthusiastic Preachers sometimes express themselves"—so as to act without internal restraint.[70] The conditions on the enervatingly hot days of early July called forth his physical stamina, while the numerousness of arguments on either side favored his ability to remember whole trains of reasoning and his skill at rebuttal. It has been suggested that a great man reaches his peak of psychobiological existence

---

with letters of June, July, and earlier, probably give a good account of the contents of the speech. See Boyd *et al.*, eds., *Jefferson Papers*, I, 311; Adams to Joseph Hawley, Mar. 23, 1776, Burnett, ed., *Letters of Continental Congress*, VII, 405–406. David Ramsey's *History of the American Revolution* has been suggested as a possible source. See also J. H. Powell, "Speech of John Dickinson Opposing the Declaration of Independence, 1 July, 1776," *Pennsylvania Magazine of History and Biography*, LXV (1941), 458–481. Powell concludes that Dickinson spoke first, although in rebuttal of past arguments. Dickinson mainly argued the uselessness of a declaration in gaining foreign aid.

69. Adams to John Winthrop, June 23, 1776, "Correspondence between John Adams and Prof. John Winthrop," Mass. Hist. Soc., *Colls.*, 5th Ser., IV, 308.

70. Boyd *et al.*, eds., *Jefferson Papers*, I, 311; Adams to Benjamin Rush, July 31, 1811, Adams Papers, Reel 118.

between the ages of forty-one and forty-four. John Adams's activities in 1776, when he was forty-one, represented just such a culmination.

As a matter of course Adams sat on the committee assigned to draw up a public declaration of independence. Continuing the policy of using Virginians to advance Massachusetts policy, he relinquished to Thomas Jefferson his usual function of preparing a first draft. But under any circumstances Adams would have been careless of the form. For him the preceding *resolution* of independence was the great event. When that resolution was adopted by Congress, Adams wrote the famous letter to his wife in which he predicted: "The Second Day of July 1776, will be the most memorable Epocha, in the History of America.—I am apt to believe that it will be celebrated, by succeeding Generations, as the great anniversary Festival."[71] In his old age, embittered by Jefferson's fame as the drafter of the famous document, he sometimes denigrated and sometimes claimed prior credit for it. "The Declaration of Independence I always considered as a theatrical show," he told Benjamin Rush. "Jefferson ran away with all the stage effect . . . and all the glory of it." On the other hand, he believed that he had anticipated Jefferson's "juvenile declamation" with his contribution to the 1774 congressional "Declaration of Rights."[72]

The great culmination of American independence left Adams exhausted and let down in the manner of earlier successful campaigns. He suffered inflammations of the eyes, "night sweats," and "tremulous" nerves. But, though he applied for leave right after the Declaration, he managed to survive

71. Adams to Abigail Adams, July 3, 1776, *Adams Family Correspondence*, II, 30.

72. Adams to Benjamin Rush, June 21, 1811, Adams Papers, Reel 118, and to Richard Rush, July 22, 1816, Vanderkemp Papers, Pa. Hist. Soc. In 1809, when a newspaper printed his prophecy of a break with England, written in a letter of 1755, Adams wrote: "It is demonstrative evidence that John Adams' Declaration of Independence was one and twenty years older than Thomas Jefferson's." Adams to William Cunningham, Sept. 27, 1809, *Correspondence between the Hon. John Adams, Late President of the United States, and the Late Wm. Cunningham, Esq. . . .* (Boston, 1823), 167 (italics removed and words all in capitals lowercased). For John Adams's 1774 Declaration of Rights see Worthington Chauncey Ford *et al.*, eds., *Journals of the Continental Congress, 1774–1789* (Washington, D.C., 1904–1937), I, 63–74, and *Diary and Autobiography*, III, 310.

through the treacherous Philadelphia summer. (Only in October when he returned home did he fall sick.)[73] From June 1776, acting virtually as a war department, he handled a daily, crushing burden of administrative details (clothing, supplies, troop movements, pay, promotions, appointments, decorations). Like his colleagues, he never lost his broad, classical perspective. He grandiloquently lectured the New England general Nathanael Greene on the Roman civil wars and, urging him to take the military initiative, likened "the Plains of Pharsalia" to "the Plains of Abraham" and "the Plains of Trenton and Princeton."[74]

The apocalyptic side of Adams's Puritan-biblical fervor continued to express itself as insistently as the enthusiastic. He called the smallpox epidemic among the soldiers "a Frown of Providence upon Us," and while he trusted that Providence would continue to preserve America, it gave him "inexpressible Grief that by our own Folly and Wickedness We should deserve it so very ill as We do." He saw the "New Jerusalem" but expected first "the Furnace of Affliction."[75]

These fears extended to the people. They were "extreamly addicted to Corruption and Venality, as well as the Great." Adams feared that "human nature will be found to be the same in America as it has been in Europe."[76] Up until the "No-

73. Adams to James Warren, July 27, 1776, *Works of John Adams*, IX, 42. See Adams to Abigail Adams, Oct. 1, 1776, *Adams Family Correspondence*, II, 132, for the "Miracle" of his health.

74. Adams to Gen. Greene, May 29, 1777, and Apr. 13, 1777, Adams Papers, Reel 91. The latter was "intended for G[eneral] Green but not Sent, Being too impolite." For parallels with the Peloponnesian War, Thebes, Demosthenes, etc., see Adams Papers, Reel 91 *passim*; Adams's letters to Edward Biddle, Dec. 12, 1774, *Works of John Adams*, IX, 349–350; to James Warren, July 17, 1774, *Warren-Adams Letters*, I, 29; to Abigail Adams, Aug. 20, 1777, *Adams Family Correspondence*, II, 320–321; and *Diary and Autobiography*, III, 439–449 *passim*. On the shared classical perspective of the delegates see Burnett, ed., *Letters of Continental Congress*, I, introduction.

75. Adams to Abigail Adams, July 3, 1776, *Adams Family Correspondence*, II, 30; to James Warren, May 18, 1776, *Warren-Adams Letters*, I, 248; to Archibald Bullock, July 1, 1776, Peter Force, comp., *American Archives . . .* , 4th Ser., VI (Washington, D.C., 1846), 1194; and to Abigail Adams, July 3, 1776, *Adams Family Correspondence*, II, 28.

76. Adams to Abigail Adams, July 3, 1776, *Adams Family Correspondence*, II, 28, and to Joseph Hawley, Aug. 21, 1776, *Works of John Adams*, IX, 434. At one point Adams said to his friend Benjamin Rush: "It would seem as if mankind were made to be slaves, and the sooner they fulfill their destiny the better." When reminded of the statement by Rush in

vanglus" essays he had taken a traditionally pessimistic view of the democratic polis. Yet, even when lamenting the ease with which the people could be corrupted, he maintained faith in the efficacy of the New England way of life to foster the virtues necessary to a successful government. In *Thoughts on Government* he transferred his faith almost imperceptibly from "institutions" like public education and local militia to the form of government. Meanwhile he warned his friend Warren against expecting too much from republican government: the Revolution might make Americans worse as well as better.[77]

Adams was not alone in losing some of his purer enthusiasm or in feeling a physical letdown after independence. July 1776 marked the beginning of seven years of drudgery for the members of Congress, who increasingly found it less illustrious to serve after the heady early days. Adams suggested a rotating panel of Massachusetts representatives but was simply left at his post until he took his own leave in October 1776. He returned in January to serve for eleven more months, during which he managed the affairs of the Continental army as Congress adjourned from town to town before advancing British troops. Cornwallis took Philadelphia in September, but Burgoyne surrendered at Saratoga in the middle of October, and Adams was able to return home in November 1777. Before he did he suffered over the defeats of New England troops and found much to criticize in still further "innovations" that were finding their way into the new state constitutions.

Adams expressed deep pessimism on both accounts, growing "ashamed" at being a New Englander and convinced that America was moving dangerously toward radical democracy. But his feelings were little different from those frequently occasioned by disappointment with himself. When he proposed as a national seal his favorite morality, the choice of Hercules

---

1805 the aged Adams regretted the second half. Schutz and Adair, eds., *Spur of Fame*, 28.

77. See Adams to James Warren, May 12, 1776, *Warren-Adams Letters*, I, 242–243; also Adams to Gen. Greene, Mar. 9, 1777, Adams Papers, Reel 91, and to Francis Dana, Aug. 16, 1776, *Works of John Adams*, IX, 429. For Adams's early pessimism about the people see his 1772 notes for an oration, *Diary and Autobiography*, II, 58, 60, and also his dispute with Brattle, *Works of John Adams*, III, 572.

between virtue and sloth, he revealed the continuing expectation behind his disappointment.[78] He did fear Pennsylvania's attempt to give total power to the people with its single legislature, for the control of men's passions by means of a balanced political constitution remained fundamental to his belief. Nevertheless, he maintained his own, mild republican principles, as he affirmed when *Thoughts on Government* was reprinted in June 1777. Expressing his opposition to innovations, he adhered to his initial willingness to let the people of each state choose whatever system they thought best.[79]

But nothing disturbed Adams so much as the charge that he had "been aiming at high Places" when he accepted the chief justiceship of Massachusetts, which he resigned in February 1777. Having achieved the prominence anticipated and brooded over in his diary, he disowned "the Cymballs of Popularity" and "the Butterflies of Fame," and again sounded his refrain of "farewell Politicks" and "farewell to great Affairs."[80] He would, as he expressed it in the convention of the times, "retreat like Cincinnatus, to my plough."[81] Decidedly, he meant what he said. For in November 1777 he took this farewell, returning to Braintree to begin a new law case for the first time in three years.

78. On New England see Adams's letters to Abigail Adams, Aug. 3, 1776, Jan. 14, 1777, Apr. 16, 1777, Apr. 26, 1777 (on his being "ashamed"), and May 6, 1777, *Adams Family Correspondence*, II, 76, 146, 211, 224, 233. Adams suffered especially over the "Cowardice of New England men" in the war but rallied to them on the ground that the successes of southern troops were better reported. *Ibid.*, 224; Adams to Gen. Greene, May 9, 1777, Adams Papers, Reel 91. On America see Adams's broadside, July 23, 1776, in Worthington Chauncey Ford, ed., *Broadsides, Ballads, Etc., Printed in Massachusetts, 1639–1800* (Mass. Hist. Soc., *Colls.*, LXXV [Boston, 1922]), no. 1973, facsimile opposite 272; Adams to [James Warren?], Feb. 27, 1777, Adams Papers, Reel 91; and to Abigail Adams, Sept. 22, 1776, and Oct. 8, 1776, *Adams Family Correspondence*, II, 131, 140. For the choice of Hercules see Adams to Abigail Adams, Aug. 14, 1776, *ibid.*, 97, and chap. 2 above.

79. On the reprint of *Thoughts on Government*: Adams to Abigail Adams, June 4, 1777, *Adams Family Correspondence*, II, 255–256. On the principle of free choice: Adams to Abigail Adams, June 2, 1777, *ibid.*, 253; to Francis Dana, Aug. 16, 1776, and to James Warren, Apr. 27, 1777, *Works of John Adams*, IX, 430, 463. Adams also supported religious freedom. Adams to James Warren, Feb. 3, 1777, *ibid.*, 451.

80. Adams to Abigail Adams, Aug. 18, 1776, and July 8, 1777, *Adams Family Correspondence*, II, 99, 277; to William Tudor, June 24, 1776, Adams Papers, Reel 89; and to Abigail Adams, June 16, 1777, *Adams Family Correspondence*, II, 267.

81. Adams to Tudor, June 24, 1776, Adams Papers, Reel 89. See Howard Mumford Jones, *O Strange New World. American Culture: The Formative Years* (New York, 1964), 247.

Adams had sacrificed much in serving for so long. Abigail Adams reported that other lawyers had made fortunes in his absence. After the plush trip to the first Congress, Adams went to the second in his father-in-law's "single horse chaise," while Hancock took Samuel Adams with him in his "Phaeton and pair."[82] Thereafter Adams traveled on horseback. In Philadelphia he shifted from one boardinghouse to another for the cheapest rates, choosing inexpensive drinks to serve to visitors.

Neither a lusting after fame nor any more than a temporary wish for retirement described Adams's motives in the Revolution. In effect, he sought recognition rather than fame. While fame can be undeserved, genuine achievement must precede recognition. As a young man Adams had grown angriest over the inequities of reputation, both when others successfully pretended to more knowledge than they possessed and when his friends unfairly questioned his own achieved competence in the law. Later he suffered more from lack of recognition by Braintree than he exulted at his fame in Boston. In Philadelphia he came to recognize the modesty of his desire. "Of that Ambition which has Power for its Object," he wrote, "I dont believe I have a Spark in my Heart." Instead, he vaguely concluded, he aimed at some sort of distinction—"Literary and Professional, I suppose."[83]

In the same spirit, whenever he looked back to the Continental Congresses, Adams attempted not to glorify himself but to allocate a just distribution of credit. He wrote on the day of his own speech advocating independence what he repeated

82. Andrew Oliver, ed., *The Journal of Samuel Curwen, Loyalist* (Salem, Mass., 1972), 8. See also *Diary and Autobiography*, II, 164n. Abigail Adams wrote: "One Gentleman of the Bar acknowledged that he had made a thousand pounds sterling since the opening of Business." To Adams, June 1, 1777, *Adams Family Correspondence*, II, 251. See Wroth and Zobel, eds., *Legal Papers*, I, lxxxi, on Adams's 1777 earnings. He normally earned £300 a year.

83. Adams to Abigail Adams, Mar. 16, 1777, *Adams Family Correspondence*, II, 176, 177n. Steven Kagle makes the distinction between recognition and fame in "Diary of John Adams," *Hartford Studies in Literature*, III (1971), 103. For a discussion of fame, recognition, and glory in the period see Douglass Adair, "Fame and the Founding Fathers," in Edmund P. Willis, ed., *Fame and the Founding Fathers* (Bethlehem, Pa., 1967), reprinted in Trevor Colbourn, ed., *Fame and the Founding Fathers: Essays by Douglass Adair* (New York, 1974), 3–26.

afterward; that it had only gone over old ground. This was his honest opinion of Jefferson's Declaration of Independence, too. His bitterness stemmed not so much from envy of a superior performance as from what he regarded as a false valuation of the importance of the document. For himself, he did not dream of becoming renowned as the "Atlas" or colossus of independence, though he could not forget John Jay's attempt to flatter him as "the first man" in the House. Instead he wished to be remembered as an early advocate of independence; as its champion on the floor; as the proponent of the formation of state governments, and a leading architect, through *Thoughts on Government*, of their constitutions; as a founder of the American navy; and as the originator of the foreign policy of no entangling alliances. Adams expected not wild applause but strict justice to his sacrifices and to these attainments. Within a few months of leaving Congress he began to learn that such justice was not to be his fate.

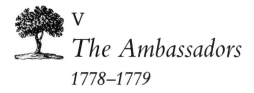

V
The Ambassadors
1778–1779

Adams returned from the Continental Congresses in November 1777 physically and emotionally spent. He had been sustained by association with an assembly that he ranked with the great lawmaking bodies of the ancients, but felt that he had served out his time. With a clear conscience he set out to make his fortune in the busy Admiralty courts.

Soon he was in Portsmouth, Maine, again, the furthest reach of his circuit. This time his fame made the scene more lively, as Ezra Stiles's diary record of dinner with the "Hon. John Adams Esq." shows. For the benefit of the company Adams detailed the proceedings in Congress. He delivered a judicious curriculum vitae of Henry Laurens, its new president, and he held forth on one of his old hobbyhorses: "the wisdom of our Ancestors," the New England Puritans. "Mr. Adams," Stiles noted respectfully, "does not desire a French or European War." Two days later, while he was speaking on a case in the Portsmouth Admiralty Court, word arrived that "Mr. Jno. Adams is appointed by Congress a Commissioner to joyn Dr. Franklin at the Court of Paris, in the Room of Mr. Deane."[1]

Despite the costs likely to result from this assignment, Adams accepted it almost immediately. He would be separated from his wife and three children for well over a year, at least. His clients would not wait for him a second time, so he would be abandoning his law practice for good. His family would

---

1. Franklin Bowditch Dexter, ed., *The Literary Diary of Ezra Stiles* (New York, 1901), II, 237. Adams was to replace Silas Deane on the commission.

have to manage on the income from their farm and what might be left over from the stipend paid to the diplomatic representative of an impoverished country. It being the end of December, he could look forward to a dangerous winter crossing of the Atlantic. British ships, no doubt already advised by spies of his appointment, would be on the lookout to capture and, if not hang him for treason, at the very least imprison him "in New Gate," since he could not expect "the honor of an Appartment in the Tower as a State Prisoner."[2] Lest they be captured, Congress had taken care until now to appoint four of its five diplomats (Franklin was the exception) from among Americans who were already in Europe when the fighting began.

While at Congress, Adams had discouraged his appointment to any diplomatic post, and he might well have done so again. But self-sacrifice amounted to a definition of his idea of public service. Furthermore, the call arrived at a time when he was professedly attending to his own gain, a circumstance that made him vulnerable, as it had when in 1772 James Otis had taunted him for avoiding his public duty in favor of making money. When letters accompanying Congress's appointment argued that his presence in France was needed to counter the effect of Silas Deane's peculations, Adams's favorable decision was all but sealed. Humbly protesting that he lacked diplomatic experience and sufficient knowledge of French, and complaining of the personal costs involved, Adams set sail for Europe in February 1778, declaring, "The honest Man is Seldom forsaken."[3]

Adams's crossing had the stuff of romance: the predicted pursuit by British frigates, two of which were outsailed, a third lost in the night; a hurricane that split the mainmast; capture of prize ships; coming under fire. The seas were so rough that Adams could hardly keep his diary, much less maintain the official tone—much like that of his setting out for the first Congress—with which he began when first aboard ship:

2. *Diary and Autobiography*, IV, 4.
3. Adams to Benjamin Rush, Feb. 8, 1778, Adams Papers, Reel 89. Complaints: Adams to James Lovell, Dec. 24, 1777, *Works of John Adams*, IX, 471.

1778 FEBRUARY 13, FRYDAY

Captain Samuel Tucker, Commander of the Frigate Boston, met me, at Mr. Norton Quincy's [on the water side of Braintree], where We dined, and after Dinner I sent my Baggage, and walked myself with Captain Tucker, Mr. Griffin a Midshipman, and my eldest Son, John Quincy Adams, between 10 and 11. Years of Age. . . . [4]

Years later Adams memorably told the story of his sea adventures in his autobiography and to his grandchildren—in 1804 he described how, during the hurricane, father and son had "clasped each other together in our Arms, and braced our feet against the bed boards and Bedsteads to prevent Us from having our Bodies dashed against the Plants and Timbers of the Ship."[5] At the time, however, such obvious drama seemed to him relatively unimportant to record, and he paused in his sketchy diary account only to remark that he had stood without fear above decks while the ship was fired on and that his son "Johnny" had borne up well. He regretted all the alarms as distractions from his French grammar. Only when, on March 30, he saw the coast of France was his imagination fired: "It gives me a pleasing Melancholly to see this Country. . . . Europe thou great Theatre of Arts, Sciences, Commerce, War, am I at last permitted to visit thy Territories.—May the Design of my Voyage be answered."[6]

Unfortunately, most of the design had already been answered, as he learned within a few hours of arriving. During the week before he set sail the French had agreed to a treaty with the United States. Adams had intended to begin his usual questioning as soon as he touched land—about the state of the war, the location of American shipping, and so forth—but the treaty now made it more important for him to tour Bordeaux as a visiting dignitary and to dine at its principal houses. In his diary he did not mention learning of the new treaty, but he

4. *Diary and Autobiography*, II, 269.

5. Adams to John Quincy Adams, Nov. 9, 1804, Adams Papers, Reel 403. See *Works of John Adams*, I, 277.

6. *Diary and Autobiography*, II, 292. Adams several times recalled his vertigo on this arrival. See his letter to John Adams Smith, Dec. 19, 1808, Adams Papers, Reel 118.

appeared "very much disappointed" and talked of turning around for home. When he narrated his disappointing arrival in his autobiography he recalled having feared at the outset that "all my Voyages and Negotiations" would amount to only "a Commedy."[7]

Rather than a comedy, however, Adams's experience of Europe had the quality of a fable. He regarded himself as a representative of American innocence faced with the duplicities of the Old World. In such a confrontation the American is by no means at a disadvantage, as Henry James showed in his international novels. Adams's arrival in Bordeaux recalled that of Lambert Strether in James's *The Ambassadors*. Another middle-aged New Englander sent out to right the excesses of a previous "ambassador," Strether confronts the sensuousness of Europe in the provincial city of Chatham, England, and then proceeds by stages to Paris. His stay is marked by an aura of mystery that he never quite penetrates, though he is able to master the situation in the end by a New England renunciation of all the European pleasures that he has come to love and admire. Adams's adventure paralleled Strether's, especially in that its most significant encounter took the form of a psychological struggle, not with a European, but with a sophisticated, Europeanized American—Benjamin Franklin.[8]

If Adams had been aware of his markedly sensuous nature in America, it can only have been in a limited way. He loved, at one time or another, the Braintree countryside, the company of young ladies, hard cider, porter, and beer, and even the sublimity of oratory like Otis's argument on the Writs of Assistance. But he found in Europe a civilization long practiced in satisfying all of the senses at once. A sumptuous dinner in Bordeaux followed sightseeing, an embrace "a la française" by the president of the city's parliament, chat at the coffee shop, and a

7. James H. Hutson, "John Adams and the Diplomacy of the American Revolution" (Ph.D. diss., Yale University, 1964), 24–25; *Diary and Autobiography*, IV, 7.

8. "My Evils here arise altogether from Americans," Adams wrote to Abigail Adams, Feb. 9, 1779, *Adams Family Correspondence*, III, 160. About to leave Europe, he wrote: "It was not Versailles, Paris, France . . . that made me unhappy, but my own *Countrymen*." Adams to Edmund Jenings, May 22, 1779, unsent, Adams Papers, Reel 93.

play by Molière. At table beautiful women exposed their bosoms and their morals. Adams was shocked—as much by his own enjoyment as by the dangers to republican morality posed by the French attention to luxury.

He was forty-three years old when he arrived in Bordeaux. The last four years of his life had described a widening initiation from Boston to New York, Philadelphia, and now Europe. At each stage in his sentimental education Adams continued to feel himself the provincial. In Boston, in 1766, invited to dinner with, among others, the city's comptroller of customs, he wrote: "An elegant Dinner indeed! Went over the House to view the Furniture, which alone cost a thousand Pounds sterling. . . . The Turkey Carpets, . . . the beautiful Chimny Clock, the Spacious Garden, are the most magnificent of any Thing I have ever seen." In Connecticut for his travel and rest cure in 1771 he was "absolutely charmed" during the Sunday afternoon service by "the finest Singing, that ever I heard in my Life." In 1774, on his way out of New England for the first time to attend the Continental Congress, "the Steeple of Weathersfield [Connecticut] Meeting House" afforded "the most grand and beautifull Prospect in the World, at least that I ever saw." In New York, which he found "vastly more . . . elegant" than Boston, while overlooking the Hudson from rural West Fortythird Street he had "toast and bread and butter in great Perfection" out of "a very large Silver Coffee Pott" and "a very large Silver Tea Pott"—all in all, "a more elegant Breakfast, I never saw." Downtown he had "the most splendid Dinner I ever saw."[9]

No wonder, then, that aboard a French cruiser in Bordeaux harbor for his first taste of French cooking he was impressed by "the Lights of a Calf, dressed one Way and the Liver another," and declared that dessert provided "the most delicate Raisins I ever saw." In Paris a private home provided "the superbest Gallery that I have yet seen," and Marly constituted "the most

9. *Diary and Autobiography*, I, 294, II, 31, 99, 103, 105, 111. See also *ibid.*, I, 54 (1758), for Adams in Boston in "the most Spacious and elegant room" he had ever seen and *ibid.*, II, 114 (1774), in Philadelphia at the "most genteel" tavern in America.

curious and beautifull Place I have yet seen."[10]

At dinner ashore in Bordeaux: "One of the most elegant Ladies at Table [a Madame de Texel], young and handsome, tho married to a Gentleman in the Company, was pleased to Address her discourse to me. . . . 'Mr. Adams, by your Name I conclude you are descended from the first Man and Woman, and probably in your family may be preserved the tradition which may resolve a difficulty which I could never explain. I never could understand how the first Couple found out the Art of lying together?' " Never having heard a woman speak in this way, Adams found the question "surprizing and shocking." "I believe at first I blushed," he recalled, but, speaking slowly through a translator, he replied: " 'There was a Physical quality in Us resembling the Power of Electricity or of the Magnet, by which when a Pair approached within a striking distance they flew together like the Needle to the Pole or like two Objects in electric Experiments.' " "When this Answer was explained to her," Adams wrote, "she replied 'Well I know not how it was, but this I know it is a very happy Shock.' "[11]

If not quite a happy shock for Adams, French society quickly touched his sensuous nature. He did not write from Bordeaux, where he was received with such enthusiasm that he avoided the streets for fear of being crushed by well-wishers. Then, almost two weeks after landing in that city, he admitted in his first letter to his wife that "the Delights of France are innumerable. The Politeness, the Elegance, the Softness, the Delicacy, is extreme. In short stern and hauty Republican as I am, I cannot help loving these People."[12] In Paris he learned that at Madame Brillon's, where Franklin took him to dinner, one sat at table with both the mistress of Monsieur Brillon and Madame's lover, yet he continued to dine there. Adams could not help but conceive himself faced with a series of choices between

10. *Ibid.*, 292, 313, 316. See also *ibid.*, 297, and Adams to Abigail Adams, Apr. 12, 1778, in Charles Francis Adams, ed., *Familiar Letters of John Adams and His Wife Abigail Adams, during the Revolution, with a Memoir of Mrs. Adams* (Boston, 1875), 329.

11. *Diary and Autobiography*, IV, 36, 37.

12. Adams to Abigail Adams, Apr. 12, 1778, *Adams Family Correspondence*, III, 9.

pleasure and duty. But in diplomacy dining out represented one's duty. He had to satisfy himself with pursuing his shipboard plan of gathering information and furthering his education. Accordingly he began to ask his prepared questions and to inquire at social gatherings about guidebooks to Paris, "the purest Writers of french" for him to study, and "the best Historian of France."[13]

In the past such a program, however naïve it might appear in the great world, had made a prelude to mastery and action. But now it had little apparent application. Adams might use his French to study the newspapers, but so uncertain were the mails that in the course of a year he would be able to manage only a single exchange of information with the committee on foreign affairs.

In the meantime he was faced with a serious personal and ideological split among the American agents in Europe, who warned him against one another. In addition he discovered that the commission's paperwork was in disarray. All three original members of the embassy to France—Franklin, Deane, and Arthur Lee—independently had bought arms and supplies for the Continental army, had given sailing orders to American ships in French ports, and had run up large personal accounts that they failed to distinguish from the public ones. If not earthshaking, these were serious problems and fit objects of Adams's attention while he waited to hear Congress's reaction to the signing of the French treaty.

To begin with, he determined not to make himself an added expense. Rather than rent a building of his own like Deane and Lee, he decided to accept Franklin's invitation to take some empty rooms in the house provided for him by a supposed French admirer in the suburb of Passy. Here Adams lived as parsimoniously on Congress's money as he had on court circuit or in Philadelphia. Rather than hire a carriage, for example, he made do with Franklin's on the rare occasions when it was free.

13. *Diary and Autobiography*, II, 315. But see Claude-Anne Lopez's version of the Madame Brillon incident in *Mon Cher Papa: Franklin and the Ladies of Paris* (New Haven, Conn., 1966), 42–43.

"I am told," he wrote a few months after arriving, "I am the first public Minister . . . without a Carriage."[14] Franklin took him into society to meet the luminaries of the age: Beaumarchais, Turgot, Abbé Condillac, and of course the king, of whom Adams, the third ambassador of a weak, client nation, observed in his diary, "His Reign has already been distinguished, by an Event that will reflect a Glory upon it, in future Ages I mean, the Treaty with America."[15] Very quickly, though, Adams began to refuse as many invitations as decorum allowed, in order to have time to study his French and to put the public papers in order.

Gathering up the commission's outstanding bills, he drafted a series of notes refusing payment without proper vouchers and authorizations; these he presented to Lee and Franklin for signature. Soon he was conducting all of the correspondence, presenting letters to his colleagues for signature. He began to remain at home out of what proved to be a justified fear of spies and because "here are a Thousand Things to do, and no Body else to do them. The extensive Correspondence We have with Congress, with the Court, with our Frigates, our Agents, and with Prisoners, and a thousand others, employs a vast deal of my Time in Writing." Finally, Adams took care of the copying as well as the drafting of letters since he had elected to keep no secretary, "altho every other Gentleman has constantly had two."[16]

Despite his attempts to make his dutiful and self-sacrificing labors seem significant—at a dinner he "maintained . . . that it was the Duty of a good Citizen to sacrifice all to his Country, in some Circumstances"—Adams knew himself to be a super-

14. Adams to Abigail Adams, Dec. 3, 1778, Adams Papers, Reel 95. See also Adams to Abigail Adams, Dec. 27, 1778, C. F. Adams, ed., *Familiar Letters*, 349, and May 14, 1777, *Adams Family Correspondence*, II, 238. Arthur Lee, M.D. (1740–1792), became an Adams supporter and Franklin opponent in Congress after the joint commission was dissolved.

15. *Diary and Autobiography*, II, 310.

16. Adams to Abigail Adams, Dec. 3, 1778, *Adams Family Correspondence*, III, 129. For six weeks, though, Adams did keep a secretary. See Adams to Treasury Board, Sept. 19, 1779, *Works of John Adams*, VII, 114. Still, nearly all of the records are in Adams's hand. See Abigail Adams to Mercy Warren, Dec. 10, 1778, *Warren-Adams Letters*, II, 79.

numerary.[17] He soon wrote to Samuel Adams, then in the Congress, suggesting that he be recalled and that Franklin be left sole commissioner. He added, however, that Franklin should be relieved of all routine consular duties, for "his mind [is] in such a constant State of Dissipation that if he is left alone here, the public Business will suffer in a degree beyond description."[18]

At the age of seventy-two Franklin certainly appeared unfit by both inclination and ability to attend to all the details of an embassy in time of war. Years later Adams recalled that "the Life of Dr. Franklin was a Scene of continual discipation," and he described a typical Franklin day as consisting of a late breakfast, a morning of receiving admirers, dressing for dinner abroad, an afternoon out in company or at "the Play," then tea, after which "the Evening was spent, in hearing the Ladies sing and play upon their Piano Fortes and other instruments of Musick, and in various Games as Cards, Chess, Backgammon, &c. &c. . . . he came home at all hours from Nine to twelve O Clock at night." Adams tried to confine his disapprobation to Franklin's unavailability for work (one often had to wait several days for him to sign a letter), but he was offended also by his manner, which recalled Parson Wibird's way to fame: "He has the most affectionate and insinuating Way of charming the Woman or the Man that he fixes on. It is the most silly and ridiculous Way imaginable, in the Sight of an American, but it succeeds, to admiration, fullsome and sickish as it is, in Europe."[19]

There was much in Franklin's life to disturb a stern and haughty republican. He had with him the illegitimate son of his own illegitimate son, he regularly kissed and was kissed by the ladies he met, the conversation surrounding him was full of sexual innuendo. But these matters were not what disturbed Adams most. He knew in advance about Franklin's supposedly

17. Adams to Abigail Adams, Sept. 23, 1778, *Adams Family Correspondence*, III, 91. See also *ibid.*, 163n.

18. Adams to James Warren, Dec. 5, 1778, *Warren-Adams Letters*, II, 74.

19. *Diary and Autobiography*, IV, 118, 119, II, 367.

deficient morals. If he disapproved of Franklin, he was not shocked: on the contrary, he recorded with a certain amused irony his risqué conversations and freedom with the ladies. On the other hand, Adams showed his uneasiness by crossing out several words in a letter to his wife about Franklin "bussing" the ladies. For the rest of his life Adams's written mentions of Franklin were accompanied by a remarkable series of emendations, slips of the pen, and other irregularities.[20] These blots on Adams's usually neat, unrevised sheets indicate that Franklin's behavior raised problems far more serious than social embarrassment. Eventually Franklin posed Adams with the deepest personal challenge of his life.

Adams's and Franklin's relationship in America held no portents of their difficulties in Europe. Indeed, it had been an example of Franklin's industry, his "Activity and Resolution," that had stimulated Adams to resume his diary in 1760. In 1773 Franklin had transmitted to the patriots Governor Hutchinson's secret letters from London, and Adams had defended him in print on this and other matters. In Congress both men supported independence and served together with Jefferson on the drafting committee for the Declaration. Although Adams disapproved of Pennsylvania's constitution supported by Franklin, they never quarreled, and he called Franklin "a great and good Man."[21] A charming scene recollected in Adams's autobi-

20. In a letter to his wife Adams quipped that his "venerable Colleague enjoys a Priviledge here, that is much to be envyd. Being seventy Years of Age, the Ladies not only allow him to embrace them as often as he pleases, but they are perpetually embracing him." Instead of "embrace them as often as he pleases," Adams's editors note, he had originally written "buss them as often as he p," which was crossed out; "buss" may have been written "kiss," but "this word is heavily scratched out." *Adams Family Correspondence*, III, 17, 17n. See also *Diary and Autobiography*, IV, 64, 87; memories dictated to Harriet Welsh, Adams Papers, Reel 327; William B. Evans, "John Adams's Opinion of Benjamin Franklin," *Pennsylvania Magazine of History and Biography*, XCII (1968), 220–238. Evans concludes that Adams's differences with Franklin were political, not personal.

Some further examples of flaws in Adams's manuscript when Franklin was mentioned: *Diary and Autobiography*, IV, 41 (sentence deficient in grammar); Adams's letters to Edmund Jenings, Sept. 16, 1782, Adams Papers, Reel 107 (crossings out); to John Jay, Apr. 13, 1785, *ibid.*, and to [Osgood?], Apr. 9, 1784, apparently not sent, *ibid.*, 362 (marginal interpolations); and to Abigail Adams, Feb. 13, 1779, *Adams Family Correspondence*, III, 170 ("Dr. J." for "Dr. F."). See also Adams to James Warren, Mar. 21, 1783, Adams Papers, Reel 108, printed in *Warren-Adams Letters*, II, 197.

21. *Diary and Autobiography*, I, 125; Adams to Abigail Adams, July 23, 1775, *Adams*

ography suggests their relationship. In 1776, traveling together from Philadelphia to Staten Island to confer with Lord Howe about a British offer of reconciliation, "at Brunswick, but one bed could be procured for Dr. Franklin and me." Adams consented to "run the risque of a cold" by leaving the window open in order to hear Franklin hold forth on the evils of vapors in closed rooms and the healthful properties of fresh air. The two philosophers then fell asleep discussing Franklin's "Theory of Colds."[22]

Adams was much taken with Franklin's electrical experiments (as he had shown by his answer to Madame de Texel in Bordeaux), and had an open mind about the quarrel among the commissioners. But he found himself confronted with a figure no longer suitable for his kind of emulation, or even respect. Franklin played when he should have been at work, showed levity where seriousness was prescribed, extravagance instead of thrift, laxity instead of responsibility. Despite these derelictions, or rather because of them, Adams soon discovered, Franklin was consistently covered with adulation and fame, while he was left to live in obscurity.

And yet, withal, Franklin still had charms to soothe what Adams called "the savage sachem in me." Adams enjoyed Franklin's parable jokes enough to write them down in his diary, profanity (slightly edited) included; but he did not think Franklin's stories were directed at himself any more than he ever came to suspect the disquisition on colds a kind of ruse to get the window opened (Franklin's story with the moral that a simple man should be content with his cabbage may have been pointed specially at him).[23] Much of Adams's conduct, beginning with his refusal to side with Franklin in the quarrel among

---

Family Correspondence, I, 253. For Adams's praise and defense of Franklin see "Novanglus," *Works of John Adams*, III, 19, and Adams's draft of a newspaper article on Franklin's examination before a government committee in London, Adams Papers, Reel 344 (Jan. 29, 1774).

22. *Diary and Autobiography*, III, 418.

23. Adams to Abigail Adams, Feb. 27, 1779, *Adams Family Correspondence*, III, 180. Adams more than once repeated Franklin's parable of the eagle (England) forced to drop its prey (America), using the tale even in his *Boston Patriot* attack on Franklin in 1811. *Works of John Adams*, IX, 269.

the American agents in Europe, implied criticism of Franklin. Adams, maintaining his antiparty orthodoxy, refused to align himself with either faction—"I must do my duty to the Public, let it give offence to whom it will"—and not surprisingly ended up estranging both. Later his spartan living arrangements and his handling of the commission's bills cast a perpetual reflection on Franklin's ease and neglect of his duties. Despite these irritations, the two representatives managed to live and work together (on the occasions when Franklin was available). Franklin took John Quincy Adams sightseeing along with his grandson and, when the great world was not watching, Adams and Franklin could sit down together to simple suppers of cheese and beer.[24]

Yet, Adams had sacrificed his career and risked his life to bring his probity and dependability to a negotiation that had gone through in a matter of hours once France realized that the colonies were capable of sustaining the war. He could indicate his contempt for the way things had been handled by writing in a private letter that it was "plain that there was not much Negociation or Discussion" of the treaty, yet he witnessed daily the triumphs of what he considered to be Franklin's now deplorable character.[25] Franklin seemed to have been put on the earth to taunt Adams with his easy successes. If his own drudgery had been really useful, Adams could have borne with this. With nothing to do but wait to be relieved by Congress, however, he began to suffer.

He was disgusted at the accolade given Franklin and Voltaire at the Academy of Sciences, where the audience clamored for them to embrace, and when Franklin's bust was brought on the stage of a theater, he is supposed to have "feigned sickness and

24. *Diary and Autobiography*, II, 305. On familiar relations with Franklin see John Quincy Adams to Abigail Adams, Apr. 31, 1778, Adams Papers, Reel 96; *Diary and Autobiography*, II, 297; and Adams to Franklin, Sept. 22, 1778, and Franklin to Adams, Sept. 26, 1778, Francis Wharton, ed., *The Revolutionary Diplomatic Correspondence of the United States* (Washington, D.C., 1889), II, 736, 746. Ralph Izard and Arthur Lee were Franklin's detractors before Adams's arrival. Izard (1742–1804), of South Carolina, held an unsuccessful commission from 1777 to 1779 to treat for recognition from the Grand Duchy of Tuscany.

25. Adams to James Warren, Dec. 5, 1778, *Warren-Adams Letters*, II, 77.

left the performance."[26] What Adams could not abide was the undeserved part of Franklin's reputation. That a dissipated, "indolent," and scheming old man, though he had once been great, should continue to take credit while doing so little, while his own services and genius went unappreciated, was more than Adams could bear. Appearance and reality had gone askew.

As Adams saw it, Franklin had a "real character" and an "artificial character." Franklin was highly sophisticated where he was believed simple: there was nothing about him that merited his fame as a "backwoods" philosopher. If anyone deserved that character it was John Adams. Still smarting in 1811 from the unfairness of the Franklin image, Adams referred to himself as "a poor man almost without a name, unknown in the European world, born and educated in the American wilderness, out of which he had never set his foot till 1778." Truly a more simple-mannered republican than Franklin, Adams suffered from being regarded as both exclusive and unpolished—neither one of nature's noblemen nor yet a courtier. It was a moral commonplace of the age, which Adams had applied to the divergence between Hannah Quincy's face and heart, that it was sinful to appear as other than one's true self. "Your double-tongued and double-minded men, your disguised folk, I detest most," Adams wrote in 1776, giving a portent of how he would react to Franklin in Europe.[27]

Where Franklin improved himself by adding to his experience and accomplishments, Adams employed self-denial. He pruned away from his handwriting, his public writing style, and his personal behavior alike, those flourishes upon which most men largely depend for their influence in the world. His was an entire dependence on the thing itself; he would have considered taking advantage of such accidental attributes of

26. *Diary and Autobiography*, IV, 95n. This story was told of Adams by a bitter enemy and calumniator.

27. *Works of John Adams*, I, 663; Adams to Samuel Chase, June 14, 1776, *ibid.*, IX, 396. On the age's disapproval of dissimulation, usually connected with pride, see Lovejoy, *Reflections on Human Nature*, 236.

the personality as charm to be a kind of cheating at life.

In contrast, Franklin had "a Passion for Reputation and Fame, as strong as you can imagine, and his Time and Thoughts are chiefly employed to obtain it." He was the very man that Adams had struggled not to become. Adams wryly told his friend James Warren (a man of genuine, if self-important, retiring modesty on Adams's own plan who often spurred Adams to speculations on fame): "Modesty is a Virtue, that can never thrive, in public. . . . a Man must be his own Trumpeter . . . [to] perpetuate his Fame. . . . You and I have had an ugly Modesty about Us, which has despoyld Us of almost all our Importance."[28]

Adams's rigid terminology has rendered his estimate of Franklin as obsolete as his estimate of Hutchinson, which in some ways it resembled. When he wrote in his diary that Franklin was "cunning," Adams may have recognized his tendency to assimilate Franklin into a personal demonology. He had lamented his own lack of cunning in his first legal case. Then, in 1760 he noted that "Cunning" was a word "that Milton applies to the Devil," and soon he began to use the same word to denounce Hutchinson and his newspaper antagonists "Pym" and Jonathan Sewall, among others. Now he had no sooner applied it to Franklin than he crossed it out, though this time he had more justification than he realized.[29]

Adams could not be sure what to think because he felt a generalized uneasiness over his anomalous role in France. As he waited to learn that Congress had ratified the French treaty, which logically would be followed by his own removal from the commission, he daily felt his uselessness to any important end. At first he expected to wait for two, three, or even four months for Congress's decision, but, in the event, he became

28. *Diary and Autobiography*, II, 367; Adams to James Warren, Dec. 2, 1778, *Warren-Adams Letters*, II, 71–72.

29. *Diary and Autobiography*, II, 346, I, 182. "Cunning" antagonists: *Works of John Adams*, III, 21 (Hutchinson, the junto), 470 ("Pym"); *Diary and Autobiography*, I, 336 (Charles Cushing). See the similar usage of Adams's opponent "Massachusettensis" in the *Massachusetts Gazette, and the Boston Post-Boy*, Jan. 9, 1775, in George A. Peek, Jr., ed., *The Political Writings of John Adams: Representative Selections* (Indianapolis and New York, 1954), 32.

the victim of a strange and still unexplained failure of Congress to act for over nine months.[30]

At the end of a year in France the first news to arrive from Congress was that Silas Deane, Adams's predecessor, had taken his case to the public in the form of a newspaper "Address." Henry Laurens, the president of Congress, thought the publication so serious an insult that he resigned his chair when the members failed to censure Deane. To Adams the fact that Deane was answering charges placed by his fellow commissioner Arthur Lee (whom Deane had attacked in turn), when combined with Franklin's public support of Deane, threatened to put the American commission in an embarrassingly divided posture before the French court. None of these opponents of Deane realized that he was in fact a British spy, and only Lee seems to have understood his business connections with Franklin. Deane's public defense was a blind that shielded his stealing and spying until years after the deaths of all involved.

In extreme agitation, Adams first told Franklin, "with great Freedom and perhaps with too much Warmth," that Deane's address "was one of the most wicked and abominable Productions that ever sprung from an human Heart." Next he decided that it was his "indispensable Duty" to inform Vergennes, the French minister of foreign affairs, that Lee was a man of probity, that Franklin was mistaken in his trust of Deane, and that despite the apparent dangers of the address, which was "the most astonishing Measure . . . that has ever happened, from the Year 1761," he did not "despair" of his "Commonwealth." This

30. The French treaty arrived in Congress in three months, on May 2, and was immediately ratified. Edmund Cody Burnett, *The Continental Congress* (New York, 1941), 330–331. It then took four more months before Franklin was appointed sole commissioner (on Sept. 14), and more than another month to draft Franklin's instructions and a letter to Adams (Oct. 28). More remarkable still, this letter failed to tell Adams what to do. He was assured only that Congress would "speedily" determine his case. *Ibid.*, 360. There followed a delay of nearly three more months, until Jan. 14, 1779, when a ship finally sailed carrying Franklin's instructions and this letter to Adams. During these three months no further message had been inserted for Adams. See Adams to Abigail Adams, Feb. 20, 1779, C. F. Adams, ed., *Familiar Letters*, 356. James Lovell wrote to Abigail Adams admitting that there was a "strange delay and something of Mystery" in Congress's failure to act. [Feb. ?] 1779, and Mar. 9, 1779, Adams Papers, Reel 350. See also Lovell to James Warren, probably shown to Adams on his return, referring to Adams's "very odd Situation." June 15, 1779, *Warren-Adams Letters*, II, 108.

proved to be a blunder that Adams had no way of anticipating. For the comte de Vergennes had been incorrectly informed by his minister in Philadelphia that, with Arthur Lee, Adams was part of a pro-English party in Congress. Vergennes took Adams's letter as proof of his collusion with Lee.[31] For four days Adams lived with his "Mind . . . in such a State . . . as it never was before." On the fifth day there arrived the long-awaited news of Franklin's sole appointment, which, as it removed the problem of a divided commission, provided "the greatest Relief to my Mind, that I have ever found since the Appearance of . . . [Deane's] Address."[32] But a web of intrigue began to gather about Adams. Feeling the effects but never privy to the causes, he grew confusedly suspicious.

From the end of November until a few days before news of Deane's address, Adams had not kept his diary, and he had resumed it only to keep a brief record of engagements. Then, in the four days of apparent crisis and in a burst of letter writing afterward (at which time he could write again as a private citizen), he explored his feelings about himself and his fellow commissioners, who, much in the manner of the Worcester and Braintree townsmen limned in his diary, projected exaggerated versions of his own foibles. Commenting on Arthur Lee and Ralph Izard, Adams correctly observed: "Virtue [Lee] is not always amiable. Integrity [Izard] is sometimes ruined by Prejudices and by Passions."[33]

But it was especially to Franklin that Adams's evaluating eye turned as he contemplated his situation in the light of Deane's address. His own openness, volubility, and candor, so apparent to him as he went from one acquaintance to another voicing his

31. *Diary and Autobiography*, II, 345, 352, 348. Deane's address, "To the Free and Virtuous Citizens of America," was published in the *Pennsylvania Packet* (Philadelphia), Dec. 5, 1778. *Ibid.*, 348n. The French minister was Charles Gravier, comte de Vergennes, born Dijon (1719–1787).

32. *Ibid.*, 353. See Sr. Mary Briant Foley, S.S.N.D., "The Triumph of Militia Diplomacy: John Adams in the Netherlands, 1780–1782" (Ph.D. diss., Loyola University of Chicago, 1968), 5; Hutson, "John Adams and Diplomacy," 65–66. Hutson points out that Adams went out of his way *not* to inform Lee that he had defended him.

33. *Diary and Autobiography*, II, 346. Izard was marking time in Paris until Tuscany might show interest in receiving him.

apprehensions, contrasted vividly with Franklin's reserve in a situation that concerned him personally, as a supporter of Deane, far more than it did Adams. Feeling particularly aware of his own insignificance because he could do so little to dispel the unfortunate effects of Deane's address, Adams now recorded how he had arrived in France reputed to be "le fameux Adams," the author of *Common Sense* (a double mistake for Samuel Adams and Thomas Paine); when he modestly explained that he was not the author, he quickly came to be regarded as "a Man of no Consequence—a Cypher."[34]

The news from Congress solved the Deane question but hardly assuaged Adams's growing resentment. Although he had recommended that Franklin be made sole ambassador, the dispatches revealed that Congress had removed him before receiving his letter. Adams began to suspect Deane's intrigues, partly directed at himself, but never learned the extent of them as long as he lived. In his anxiety he turned on Congress, which by not taking "the least Notice" of him, had left him "in a ridiculous situation" of excruciating uselessness. "The Scaffold is cutt away," he wrote to his wife, "and I am left kicking and Sprawling in the Mire, I think. It is hardly a State of Disgrace that I am in but rather of total Neglect and Contempt."[35] Adams betrayed a testiness rare in his letters to Abigail Adams, scolding her for complaining about lack of mail from him and for pestering him for descriptions of French life that he was in no mood to provide (she hardly deserved either rebuke). He told her that he had burned three letters to her one day: "This is the fourth . . . in one I was melancholy in another angry, and in the third merry."[36]

On the next day Adams repeated his characterizations of Lee and Izard, Deane and Franklin's accusers, in a letter to James

34. *Ibid.*, 351. In contrast, "on Dr. F. the Eyes of all Europe are fixed." *Ibid.*, 347.

35. Adams to Abigail Adams, Feb. 20, 1779, and Feb. 28, 1779, *Adams Family Correspondence*, III, 175, 180, 181. For Deane's activities, partly evident from his brother's machinations in England, see Hutson, "John Adams and Diplomacy," 39, 41.

36. Adams to Abigail Adams, Feb. 19, 1779, Adams Papers, Reel 350. The following day John Quincy Adams wrote to his mother echoing his father's resentment at her complaints. In a crossed-out sentence he warned her: "The result if all your letters are like this my Pappa will cease writing at all." Feb. 20, 1779, Adams Papers, Reel 96.

Lovell, his fellow Massachusettensian in charge of foreign affairs in the Continental Congress. He expressed his own resentment of Franklin under the guise of explaining theirs: "There was a monopoly of reputation here, and an indecency in displaying it, which did great injustice to the real merit of others, that I do not wonder was resented." In his new situation, with nothing to do but try to "guess" Congress's intentions, Adams felt himself growing into the ill-bred character that he seemed to pass for among both the French and the British. "I believe I am grown more austere, Severe, rigid, and miserable than ever I was," he wrote to his wife.[37]

For months Adams first had "expected, every moment . . . my recall" and then, after the disappointing letter from Congress, a prompt clarification. When none came he resolved to return home, yet he worried lest a commission arrive for him (Holland and Austria had been hinted at) after his departure. In this state of mind his old hobgoblins returned. He had seen, he now wrote, "so much Corruption . . . the virtuous few struggling against it, with so little success," that he feared an utter degradation of his countrymen.[38] Within three weeks of Franklin's appointment Adams took official leave of the French court, wound up his affairs, and left for the port of Nantes. Thus far he had suffered under the neglect of Congress in ways that had exposed but not altered his character. But now, from March until June 1779, he experienced an apparently coincidental series of delays that left him embittered.

At first, taking up quarters aboard the American frigate *Alliance*, he sailed among the ports of Brest, St. Nazaire, and Nantes in an attempt to make himself of some use to his

37. Adams to Lovell, Feb. 20, 1779, *Works of John Adams*, IX, 477, and to Abigail Adams, Feb. 28, 1779, first letter of day, Adams Papers, Reel 350. In contrast to earlier and later episodes of similar anxiety followed by success and then breakdown, this time Adams "enjoyed uncommon Health" throughout his frustrating service. See Adams to Abigail Adams, Nov. 6, 1778, Adams Papers, Reel 349, also in C. F. Adams, ed., *Familiar Letters*, 345. See also his letter to Abigail Adams, Feb. 13, 1779, *ibid.*, 355. During the Deane crisis he remarked, "Trouble is to you and me familiar, and I begin to think it necessary for my health." Adams to Samuel Adams, Feb. 14, 1779, Wharton, ed., *Diplomatic Correspondence*, III, 49. James Lovell (1747–1814) was secretary for foreign affairs until 1781.

38. Adams to Abigail Adams, Dec. 30, 1778, C. F. Adams, ed., *Familiar Letters*, 352, and to James Warren, Feb. 25, 1779, *Warren-Adams Letters*, II, 91.

country and speed his departure by clearing up such complications as prisoner exchanges. From March 12 to April 28 he lived in the "dull" confinement of a ship's cabin, attending to consular details and helping his son write translations of the classic orators. On April 28 a letter from Franklin directed him not to sail on the *Alliance* but to transfer to the French frigate *La Sensible*, on which he could cross the ocean with the new French ambassador to the United States, who was "to set off in a few Days." This news brought a "cruel Disappointment" that was simply "too much." The day after receiving it Adams wrote that he was "Suffering Tortures."[39] The Chevalier de La Luzerne, moreover, did not arrive in Lorient, where Adams sailed to meet him, until June 11, a week after which the *Sensible* finally left for the United States.

The months of waiting, like the similarly inexplicable wait for a reappointment from Congress, left Adams unable to "do any Thing, or contrive any Thing for the public." One day, in Nantes, he looked at himself "in the Glass." He thought that his features betrayed "a Feebleness and a Languor in my Nature." "The Times alone," he concluded, "have destined me to Fame —and even these have not been able to give me, much." Then, thinking apparently of his great moments—his battle against Hutchinson, perhaps; doubtless the Boston Massacre trials and his championing of American independence—he described himself: "By my Physical Constitution, I am but an ordinary Man. . . . Yet some great Events, some cutting Expressions, some mean Scandals [crossed out] Hypocrisies, have at Times, thrown this Assemblage of Sloth, Sleep and littleness into Rage a little like a Lion. Yet it is not like the Lion—there is Extravagance and Distraction in it, that still betrays the same Weakness." Adams had recognized the conditions of his genius. Unlike Franklin, who would have "cut a large figure in any age and on any continent," he had required the circumstances of

39. *Diary and Autobiography*, II, 362, 363, 363n; Adams to Edmund Jenings, Apr. 29, 1779, Adams Papers, Reel 350. Certain of his imminent departure, but perhaps depressed as well, Adams stopped writing home after leaving Paris. See *Adams Family Correspondence*, III, 183n, which also gives his itinerary.

revolution to reveal his talents. Without the spur of personal anger—"some cutting Expressions" (at the traducing of the public), "some mean Scandals, Hypocrisies"—he never would have come forth.[40] With his occupation gone, Adams felt empty.

In the absence of "some great Events" he set about cleaning up the affairs of the *Alliance*, in whose Captain Landais he found an exemplar of his weaknesses. Landais was above all "Jealous," a term that signified for Adams not envy but suspicion or fear about possible breaches of one's prerogatives. Captain Landais was "Jealous of every Body, of all his Officers, all his Passengers," and revealed this by warning that Adams was deceived by the ship's officers, who "never obey me, but when you are on deck."[41] In other words, Landais suspected his officers of concerting to show him lack of respect and obedience.

Adams commented, "I shall grow as jealous as any Body" and explained, "I am jealous that my Disappointment is owing to an Intrigue" (among Franklin, John Paul Jones, and the Frenchman, Chaumont). Franklin, Adams now suspected, was trying "to prevent me from going home, least I should tell some dangerous Truths," presumably about Franklin's conduct of his job. "Does the old Conjurer dread my Voice in Congress?" Adams wrote. "He has some Reason for he has often heard it there, a Terror to evil doers." A long-pent-up resentment is clear in these words, but not that "envy" with which Adams is usually credited. "Whatever may be Said of me, I certainly do not abound with Envy," he wrote with justice.[42]

40. *Diary and Autobiography*, II, 362–363. The comparison with Franklin is from Edmund S. Morgan's essay review of the Adams Papers, "John Adams and the Puritan Tradition," *NEQ*, XXXIV (1961), 529.

41. *Diary and Autobiography*, II, 368, 369. Crabb's *English Synonyms Explained*, new ed., defines "*jealousy*" as "a noble or an ignoble passion, according to the object; . . . *envy* is always a base passion." The *New English Dictionary* lists "suspicious, 1532," as a meaning of jealous. Adams's captain was Pierre Landais, who had accompanied Bougainville on his voyage of circumnavigation, 1766–1769.

42. Adams to Jenings, June 6, 1779 (unsent), Adams Papers, Reel 93. Carl Van Doren tells of dealings between Franklin and John Paul Jones, in *Benjamin Franklin* (New York, 1938), 602. Apparently Jones needed command of the *Alliance* to achieve a commodoreship. Yet, Jones eventually sailed with another ship. Hutson, "John Adams and Diplomacy," points

Instead his weak passion was jealousy, that is, suspicion, in the form of a gnawing uneasiness over the way that others, especially the public, regarded him.

Because he recognized this weakness, Adams partially suppressed it, with the result that his suspicion of Franklin, though it gave him a reputation for envy, never went so far as appearances justified. In fact, Franklin's intimates Silas Deane, Edward Bancroft, and William Carmichael, the commission secretary, were in the pay of the British secret service. Chaumont, who donated Franklin's house, was a partner with Franklin, along with Deane and Bancroft, in an old scheme to buy up western lands in America. In Nantes, Franklin's grandnephew, also a British spy, managed the privateering speculations in which Franklin, Deane, and Bancroft were involved. Arthur Lee had seen all this and had warned first Franklin and then Adams. But Adams, stifling his outrage, displaced his suspicions. He spoke of "indolence" where he was justified in a far more severe condemnation of Franklin's laxity with the commission papers, which reached the British secret service before they did the American Congress.[43]

There was good reason to distrust men as emotional as Izard and Lee. But Lee had been suspiciously detained by John Paul Jones in Lorient under similar circumstances, so that suspicion inevitably pointed at Jones's friend, Franklin. Doing his best to

out Adams's suspicions over the seaworthiness and fighting ability of the *Sensible* (the ship did leak seriously on his return voyage to Europe six months later). Presumably there was no danger in a capture for La Luzerne, an accredited diplomat.

Jacques Donatien Le Ray de Chaumont (1725–1803) was a capitalist and speculator in contracts for supplies for the Continental army and navy.

43. Cecil B. Currey, *Code Number 72 / Ben Franklin: Patriot or Spy?* (Englewood Cliffs, N.J., 1972), esp. 86, 96, 97, and appendix. Currey's bias against Franklin renders his conclusions questionable, but he writes in a scholarly format so that his facts, used here, can be checked. Lee's suspicions have been dismissed because of his cranky personality and his rivalry with Franklin dating from when the two represented rival land companies several years earlier in England. At that time Lee lost out to Franklin when both tried for the post of Massachusetts agent. Currey, *Code Number 72*, 43. For the speculators' monetary costs to the United States, see Thomas Perkins Abernethy, "The Origin of the Franklin-Lee Imbroglio," *North Carolina Historical Review*, XV (1938), 51–52. For Adams's passing suspicion of the double agent Edward Bancroft see *Diary and Autobiography*, IV, 71n–72n; for his fear of spies, see Adams to Abigail Adams, Feb. 20, 1779, *Adams Family Correspondence*, III, 174. Franklin's grandnephew was Jonathan Williams (1750–1815).

divert himself with his diary, Adams expressed himself through his continuing portrait of Captain Landais. As he had shown himself lacking in finesse compared to Franklin, Landais showed himself "incapable of all Art. He has no Address or Dexterity at all in managing men." Like Adams in his affected stiffness of bearing, Landais resorted to "Silence, Reserve, and a forbidding Air"—the very manner copied by Adams from lawyer Putnam. Alone in his ship's cabin, the disappointed Adams concluded: "I have arrived almost at 44 without any ['Art and Design']. I have less than L. and therefore shall do less Things than even he."[44] Ordinarily inaccurate about the motives of others, Adams brought to Landais's suffering—Landais later went mad—the insight of the aggrieved.

Despite his effort at self-control, Adams seems to have made his resentment against Franklin apparent. When the *Sensible* finally sailed, the Frenchmen aboard brought up Franklin's French, which by now Adams fancied to be no better than his own. (Characteristically, Franklin spoke ungrammatically and with poor pronunciation, but, it would seem, with greater ease than Adams, who was more correct.) Thinking of himself and Franklin, Adams, who realized that the Frenchmen were leading him on, feared that the deviousness of European diplomacy would "be too much for our hot, rash, fiery Ministers, and for our indolent, inattentive ones." Nevertheless, he felt it his duty to give his opinion of Franklin and his "great Faults."[45] In Adams's defense, it may be said that, as usual, he recorded his indiscretion with more thoroughness than he did his wisdom. But there is reason to believe that on this voyage he several times went too far. When he reached Braintree, Adams found new evidence of Congress's neglect. Continuing his indiscre-

44. *Diary and Autobiography*, II, 373, 368, 375. See also *Adams Family Correspondence*, III, 397n. On Franklin, Jones, and the detaining of Arthur Lee, see Shipton, *Sibley's Harvard Graduates*, XIII, 255.

45. *Diary and Autobiography*, II, 388, 392. On Franklin's French see *ibid.*, IV, 59–60. La Luzerne reported Adams's "displeasure" with Franklin but also observed favorably that "conduct touches him even more than praise"—and this to Vergennes, whom he knew already to be set against Adams. John E. Little, "John Adams and American Foreign Affairs" (Ph.D. diss., Princeton University, 1966), 273–274.

tion, he began to write letters anatomizing his colleagues and complaining about "the *Neglect* and *Contempt*" of Congress, which had "done the only thing that could dissolve the charm; that is, left one alone."[46]

A few days after he reached home, however, Adams was distracted from his complaints by his election to the Massachusetts constitutional convention. For this body he wrote his "monument as a political thinker," the Constitution of Massachusetts, a document that remains in force, though amended, to the present day.[47] In 1779 state governments, far from being regarded as unimportant compared to the central government, appeared as crucially important new sovereignties in the world. They posed the question of whether republican forms, previously successful only for short periods in the tiny city-states of the ancient world, could succeed in the vast territories of states like Massachusetts (which then included Maine), New York, and Virginia.

Other state constitutions already had been written, probably influenced by Adams's *Thoughts on Government*, but the voters of Massachusetts rejected the instrument proposed to them in 1778.[48] Adams set out to incorporate in his constitution the traditional principles of Massachusetts self-government. His plunging directly and abstractly into such a task told much about his relationship to American history. In the first place, he was being diverted from his own practical interest. He might have contacted his friends in Congress concerning the intrigue against him over which he had suffered bitterly and which he

46. Adams to William Whipple, Sept. 11, 1779, Adams Papers, Reel 350, and to Thomas McKean, Sept. 20, 1779, *Works of John Adams*, IX, 485. For Congress, Adams listed a "detail of disappointments," or delays, in leaving France. Adams to the president of Congress, Aug. 3, 1779, *ibid.*, VII, 98. James Lovell and Henry Laurens, the former president of Congress, apologized and explained, although Laurens waited until Adams had been offered another diplomatic mission before doing so. Lovell to Adams, Sept. 27, 1779, and Sept. 28, 1779, *Works of John Adams*, IX, 486–491; Laurens to Adams, Oct. 4, 1779, Burnett, ed., *Letters of Continental Congress*, 467. Adams resolved not to "whine to Congress." Adams to Lovell, Sept. 10, 1779, Adams Papers, Reel 93.

47. *Diary and Autobiography*, II, 401n.

48. See Jackson Turner Main, *The Upper House in Revolutionary America, 1763–1788* (Madison, Wis., 1967), 206, for the influence of *Thoughts on Government*.

considered a danger to American foreign policy. In the second place, he set to work with hardly a care for the partisanship threatening to defeat the second proposed constitution just as it had the first. Neither self-interest, in other words, nor party considerations touched Adams once he conceived his duty in a philosophical light.

To the constitutional convention Adams presented, in effect, his venerated charter of the Massachusetts Bay Colony with a few necessary changes and additions. Most of these liberalized the old system. They included a popularly elected governor, a bill of rights extending religious liberty, and a section on "the Encouragement of Literature, &c.," calling for inculcation of "the principles of humanity and general benevolence, public and private charity, industry and frugality, honesty and punctuality . . . sincerity, good humor, and all social affections and generous sentiments among the people."[49] This last section was adopted, but others, because they ignored the divisions of parties that had caused the first constitution to be rejected, were not.

The most remarkable proposal, given the history of the Revolutionary struggle in Massachusetts, was for a strong governor, to be called "His Excellency." In the battle over the first constitution, which Adams had watched neutrally but with interest from Philadelphia, the power of the governor, the "symbol of the old kind of government," had been a focus of debate. As the result of compromise, he was made a relatively weak executive. Ignoring this, Adams gave him an absolute negative on laws passed by the legislature as well as the power of militia appointments. After years of fighting the excesses of royal governors in possession of these powers, Adams returned them to the governor in his constitution. In common with his other revolts, once Adams had defeated an individual in au-

49. *Works of John Adams*, IV, 259. See Main, *Upper House*, on Adams's *reduction* of the property qualification for being a senator from £400 to £300, liberalizing the proposal of the previous draft constitution though accepting a generally illiberal departure from the old charter.

thority, he acted to legitimate the principles underlying his opponent's position.[50]

As he had missed the squabbles leading up to his being asked to draft the constitution, by being called away to Europe, in November 1779, he missed the debates on ratification. Thus he was spared by coincidence an episode of the kind of partisan struggle that he always abhorred, and as a result he gained confidence in an outmoded approach to politics. At the constitutional convention he, Samuel Adams, and a few others continued to represent a party above party: men of conscience representing no group or partisan ideology. On his departure the authority of this group appeared to be undiminished. In fact, it virtually had come to an end, as the revisions arrived at in the convention eventually demonstrated. Adams undertook his second diplomatic mission with the mistaken notion that he could continue to influence history largely on the strength of his personal authority. As it developed, for the next eight years his fate was to be at the mercy of the very partisanship he scorned.

50. Patterson, *Political Parties*, 232. See chap. 9 below for Adams's final restoration of even the governor's "prerogative," of which he wished to strip him until 1779. For Adams's recent positions on militia appointments and the negative, see the "Report of a Constitution, or Form of Government, for the Commonwealth of Massachusetts," in *Works of John Adams*, IV, 231, 249. Adams's section on representation, another disputed issue with the first constitution, was also rejected.

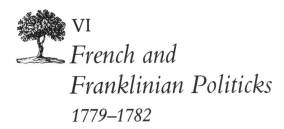

VI

French and Franklinian Politicks
1779–1782

During the four months he spent at home in 1779 Adams had much to do with politicians but little with politics. His friends in Congress—Samuel Adams, James Lovell, Elbridge Gerry—confined their correspondence with him to the Adams philosophical level. He lectured them as he did Congress at large, but he made no attempt to form a party that would resist the unnecessary "complaisancy" to France that he considered so dangerous. He advised appointing a minister to Holland and provided a list of prerequisites for the position that suggested his own talents, but he did not lobby in his own behalf, and when he did receive an invitation from Congress it was to return to Europe to treat for peace with England.

The appointment promised to renew the dangers of a winter Atlantic crossing, the unhappiness of separation, and the frustrations and longueurs of diplomatic marking time. Nevertheless, Adams again accepted immediately, for he could not refuse a challenge promising "the greatest labor and privation while offering few chances of success against many of failure." In urging him to accept, Henry Laurens, recently the president of Congress, emphasized the two considerations most certain to weigh with Adams: that serving represented his patriotic duty and that Congress intended by his appointment to "expiate" its previous neglect of him. The question of his honor influenced Adams throughout his second mission.[1]

Accepting the appointment with "the warmest sentiments of gratitude to Congress," and feeling "acquitted with . . . much splendor," Adams determined to prevent a repetition of his first mission. He anticipated "Vexations enough, as usual," but felt confident that he held all the strings of negotiation in his own hands.[2] Furthermore, since no one in Europe held a higher commission he saw no danger of compromising his country's interests or his own dignity in a required deference to its other representatives. Especially important to him was his discretionary power to decide the major issues likely to arise in a peace negotiation (the boundaries of the United States, treatment of the loyalists, and the uses of common waters between the United States and Canada). "My success may depend in very great degree," he told Samuel Huntington, the president of Congress, "on the punctuality with which several articles in my instructions [relating to these points] may be kept secret." What he did not realize, so tenuous were his ties to Congress, was that the French minister, Alexandre Gérard, not only had seen but "had had the largest part in framing" his instructions.[3] Before he left America the French doomed Adams's second embassy to sharper personal injuries than the first.

No longer could Adams ignore politics with impunity. Diplomatic instructions, as he was to learn, are not made in a vacuum, and are not irreversible. Had he been in closer touch with Congress he would have learned that Franklin had originally been proposed for his commission. He might have discovered, too, that Franklin's champion was Alexandre Gérard

---

1. *Adams Family Correspondence*, III, 233n; Henry Laurens to Adams, Oct. 4, 1779, Burnett, ed., *Letters of Continental Congress*, IV, 468.

2. Adams to the president of Congress, Nov. 4, 1779, and to James Lovell, Oct. 17, 1779, Wharton, ed., *Diplomatic Correspondence*, III, 400, 382; and to Abigail Adams, Nov. 13, 1779, *Adams Family Correspondence*, III, 224.

3. Adams to the president of Congress, Nov. 4, 1779, Wharton, ed., *Diplomatic Correspondence*, III, 400; *Diary and Autobiography*, IV, 246n. Some limitations were placed on Adams's discretion with respect to United States–Spanish boundaries.

1. John Adams, 1766 (age 31).

Pastel by Benjamin Blyth.
Courtesy of the Massachusetts Historical Society, Boston

2. John Adams, 1783 (age 48).

Oil by John Singleton Copley.
Courtesy of the Harvard University Portrait Collection,
Cambridge, Mass. Photo by James K. Ufford

3. John Adams, 1788 (age 53).

Oil by Mather Brown.
Courtesy of the Boston Athenaeum

4. John Adams, 1823 (age 88).

Oil by Gilbert Stuart.
Courtesy of Charles Francis Adams

and that Gérard had virtually run the foreign affairs of the Continental Congress since 1778.[4] But Adams planned simply to conduct himself as in the past: selflessly, dependably, and fearlessly performing his duty by undertaking prodigies of work.

Forced to put in at El Ferrol, Spain, because of a leaking ship, Adams set off with his party overland on donkeys as the quickest way to reach France. With him were his friend Francis Dana, Congress's appointee as secretary to the legation; Dana's servant; Adams's two sons, John Quincy (aged eleven) and Charles (aged eight); another boy, Samuel Cooper Johonnot, traveling in Adams's care; Adams's young secretary, John Thaxter; and Adams's servant.[5] The party advanced through the most primitive and arduous winter conditions imaginable. Most of its members grew listless, then took sick. But there could be no question of Adams's fortitude, though he suffered as many of the discomforts and more of the anxieties of the trip than the others. About the test of events—temptations, dangers, hardships—there never could be any question with him; uncertainties arose only in tests of his personality.

Adams had reached Europe a determined man: determined to patience until he could exercise his commission for peace; to prudence, "which I fear is not enough my Characteristick, but I flatter myself I am rather growing in this Grace"; and, judging from his first letters, to equanimity. To Franklin, writing from Spain, he was formal and correct, while to John Paul Jones, showing no trace of resentment over the delay of his return a year earlier, Adams wrote, "I have the Pleasure to congratulate you on your glorious success."[6] This was the frame of mind in

---

4. See Foley, "Triumph of Militia Diplomacy," 4–5, 37n. Conrad Alexandre Gérard (1729–1790) was the first French minister sent to the United States.

5. See Adams to Abigail Adams, Dec. 2, 1779, *Adams Family Correspondence*, III, 245, 246n. Johonnot (1768–1806), the grandson of Adams's Boston pastor, Rev. Samuel Cooper, was traveling to France for schooling. John Thaxter, Jr. (1755–1791), was a cousin of Abigail Adams. *Ibid.*, 236n. Another American from the ship, Jeremiah Allen, and his servant traveled with the Adams party.

6. Adams to Benjamin Rush, Nov. 4, 1779, and to John Paul Jones, Feb. 22, 1780, Adams

which he had set out for the first Continental Congress, where his temper had not taken long to erupt. But Adams's outbursts accompanied his actions without necessarily determining them. It was unnatural self-control that tended to play him false.

After settling in Paris early in 1780, this time in quarters of his own, a patriarchal cast crept into his letters home. When he thought about the temptations of Paris he recalled the choice of Hercules. This time Adams was thinking neither of his own development nor of the nation, but of the dangers to his children of "the syren songs of sloth." With little to do immediately after his arrival, he drove "about Paris, more than I did before." Feeling himself captivated by all that he saw, he needed once again to invent and act out his characteristic drama of renunciation, though now as the imagined progenitor of generations: "I must study Politicks and War that my sons may have liberty to study Mathematicks and Philosophy. My sons ought to study Mathematicks and Philosophy, Geography, natural History, Naval Architecture, navigation, Commerce and Agriculture, in order to give their Children a right to study Painting, Poetry, Musick, Architecture, Statuary, Tapestry and Porcelaine."[7] Thus, even this famous prediction of family history had its immediate context of self-denial as a means of preparing for a task.

Adams's efforts at self-control, needless to say, resulted in no diminution of energy. Despite the lack of amenities in Spain he kept a vigorous diary full of detailed descriptions of landscapes, furnishings, meals, and characters. At the same time, he furnished Congress with lengthy, suitably philosophical and informative reports on the political, economic, and social condition of Spain, the prospects for trade with her various provinces, and lists of goods that might be exchanged.

When he reached Paris in February 1780, Adams was pre-

Papers, Reels 93, 96. See Adams to Franklin, Dec. 8, 1779, from El Ferrol, Adams Papers, Reel 96. Adams wrote to his wife: "I dont expect before another Winter to have much to do in my present Capacity." Dec. 16, 1779, *Adams Family Correspondence*, III, 252.

7. Adams to Abigail Adams, [Apr.–May 1780] and [post May 12, 1780], *Adams Family Correspondence*, III, 333, 341–342.

sented at court. Then, three days after his arrival, he wrote asking the comte de Vergennes his "opinion and advice" on whether or not he should make public the two commissions given him by Congress—one to negotiate for peace, the other to make a subsequent treaty of commerce with England. Vergennes promised to mention Adams's peace mission in one of the newspapers under his control but asked him to keep his commerce commission secret. Adams bowed to Vergennes's advice and, contenting himself with a deft evasion of the minister's request to see his instructions, forwarded the exchange of letters to Congress. For the record Adams indicated his own preference for "a bolder plan" of communicating both of his powers directly to the British ministry.[8]

His pains were wasted. Adams realized that Vergennes, who should have been the one to propose announcing his arrival, wished to maintain the client status of the United States. But Adams did not realize that Congress, its leading men no longer in attendance, had put itself into French hands. Nor could he know that Vergennes, still acting on the false intelligence that Adams belonged to a pro-English party, doubly mistrusted his attempts to initiate peace and commerce talks with England. (In the circumstances, every word of Adams's innocent letter took on sinister overtones for the Frenchman.) Nevertheless, by deducing the self-interested basis of Vergennes's policy, Adams, anticipating his negative reply, at least secured a record of his desire to publicize his mission.[9]

During this exchange Adams initiated a policy of keeping aloof from Franklin, inadvisedly giving him a dose of his own medicine by not communicating his exact mission and

8. Adams to comte de Vergennes, Feb. 13, 1780, Wharton, ed., *Diplomatic Correspondence*, III, 494, and to the president of Congress, Mar. 30, 1780, *Works of John Adams*, VII, 138.

9. See Foley, "Triumph of Militia Diplomacy," 5–8. Gérard also misinformed Vergennes about Adams's instructions, leading him to believe that Adams was waiting for a new set. See further on French confusion about Adams, in Hutson, "John Adams and Diplomacy," 67–68. For Gérard's false report that Adams was a minor adherent of Samuel Adams's and Arthur Lee's English party see Henri Doniol, *Histoire de la participation de la France à l'établissement des États-Unis d'Amérique, correspondance diplomatique et documents*, IV (Paris, 1890), 4.

instructions. Fearing what he later called "French and Frank-linian Politicks," Adams isolated himself, suffering with special keenness the order not to announce his commerce commission at a time that appeared particularly ripe.[10] Soon the difference between planning to wait and actually having to do so, in a period when European events were at a "calm," began to tell on him. "A situation so idle and inactive," as he put it, "is not agreeable to my genius." By the middle of March, a month after his arrival, he was anticipating either his recall or his having to resign on the grounds that he was serving no useful purpose.[11]

Adams had found waiting in Paris a letter from James Warren sent during his previous mission. It warned of a movement in Congress to replace him out of "Envy." Warren alluded to his own unrewarded efforts compared to the undeserved riches of others, and as usual Adams responded to his terminology. "I have seen enough of Envy to know, that it will have its perfect Work. Let it," Adams wrote. And he added, "It is a Distemper, that I hope will never seize me." He had prepared himself too well to be envious of Franklin, but he remained obsessed with the *idea* of envy, just as when he presumed that the legal pettifoggers in Braintree were motivated by envy of his position at the bar. He wrote but did not send to James Lovell the speculation: "My Situation here, will naturally make all the Drs

10. Adams to Abigail Adams, Apr. 16, 1783, Adams Papers, Reel 360. For a discussion of Adams's failure to communicate with Franklin, who complained of being kept entirely in the dark even though he knew in general of Adams's business, see Hutson, "John Adams and Diplomacy," 49–51. Abigail Adams's letter to Mercy Warren, Feb. 28, 1780, undoubtedly echoed Adams's view of the Franklin circle. In it she mentioned the "party in France of worthless ambitious intrigueing Americans, who are disposed to ruin the reputation of every Man whose Views do not coinside with their selfish Schemes." *Adams Family Correspondence*, III, 288.

When Vergennes failed to arrange a newspaper paragraph announcing Adams's arrival and peace commission, Adams reminded him of his promise, had the partial satisfaction of seeing his name mentioned in an unofficial journal not taken by the British Foreign Office, and finally extracted the assurance to forward to Congress a statement that this mode of announcement was usual and correct, though manifestly it was not. See Wharton, ed., *Diplomatic Correspondence*, III, 580–581. Hutson, "John Adams and Diplomacy," 61–62, points out that Lord North in England had suggested that the Franco-American alliance gave France exclusive trade agreements. Announcement of the commission would have corrected this error.

11. Adams to Abigail Adams, Mar. 15, 1780, Adams Papers, Reel 351, and to James

Friends jealous [i.e., suspicious] of me, least I should be Set up as his Superior. I assure you, altho I have no Expectation of having any Thing to do, in Consequence of my present Powers, yet I have no ambition to be the Drs Superior.—it is a Plan of too much Envy."[12]

Adams at first studiously kept out of any affairs that might seem to lie within Franklin's province. He concentrated instead on propaganda articles in the French and English newspapers, and he continued the letters begun in Spain, with which he now "overwhelmed" Congress. He aimed gradually to accustom the English people, whom he addressed over the heads of their rulers in prototypical American diplomatic fashion, to the American alliance with France and to the idea of American independence. The English, he believed, sustained the war by encouraging their people and their armies by means of "falsehood and fiction," while "their enemies have no occasion for anything but the truth."[13]

Adams again took an opposite course from Franklin, who was willing to employ hoaxes in propaganda even as he entertained undercover activities in diplomacy. As Adams later put it to the secretary of foreign affairs: "All appearance of intrigue, and all the refinements of politics, have been as distant from my conduct as you know them to be from my natural and habitual character." Adams relied instead on a straightforward plethora

Lovell, Mar. 16, 1780, Wharton, ed., *Diplomatic Correspondence*, III, 551. On recall and resignation see *ibid.*, and Adams to R. H. Lee, Mar. 15, 1780, Adams Papers, Reel 96.

12. Adams to James Warren, Mar. 16, 1780, *Warren-Adams Letters*, II, 130, and to Lovell, Mar. 4, 1780, Adams Papers, Reel 96. Adams had written in his diary of one of the chief pettifoggers that he had set out "to destroy my Reputation." See above, chap. 3 at n. 6. For the other colonies' envy of Massachusetts see Adams to William Tudor, Mar. 22, 1777, *Works of John Adams*, IX, 460. On Franklin's envy see *Diary and Autobiography*, III, 305. Adams presumed that Franklin's envy stemmed partly from the likelihood that Adams, not he, would be appointed first American minister to England. Adams to Arthur Lee, Mar. 31, 1780, Adams Papers, Reel 96. Vergennes's letter to Adams assuming his appointment to England gives some color to Adams's suspicion. Vergennes to Adams, July 25, 1780, Wharton, ed., *Diplomatic Correspondence*, IV, 3. Furthermore, Franklin and Adams by now knew of the movement in Congress to replace Franklin, the result of which had been Adams's receiving the peace commission. See H. James Henderson, "Congressional Factionalism and the Attempt to Recall Benjamin Franklin," *WMQ*, 3d Ser., XXVII (1970), 246–247.

13. *Diary and Autobiography*, II, 58n; Adams to Edmé Jacques Genet, Apr. 15, 1780, Wharton, ed., *Diplomatic Correspondence*, III, 680.

of information, exhortation, and argument—in lengthy reports that contrasted with Franklin's little fables. Edmé Jacques Genet, the French publicist, was grateful to have his pages in the *Mercure de France* filled by Adams, but he soon had to beg that his supplier not fill so many, delicately explaining that the French preferred to read shorter essays.[14]

In the meanwhile Adams's letters to Congress—forty-six of them in his first two months—did not abate either. After four months, apologizing for neglecting his correspondence with friends (in his personal dejection he was by now writing fewer and shorter letters to his wife and none to his children at home), he complained that though he "put . . . [his] eyes out writing," he could count on few of his letters successfully crossing the Atlantic to reach Congress. "I have however Sworn," he declared, "and I will perform."[15]

The president of Congress occasionally sent Adams an apologetic note acknowledging batches of letters, which he referred to the committee on foreign affairs. The so-called committee, however, consisted only of James Lovell, its secretary, who contented himself with a line in July, to which he added postscripts in August, October, and December acknowledging Adams's first seventy-four letters. This neglect continued while Adams remained in Europe, despite his having specified before he left: "My Success . . . may depend in a very great degree, on Intelligence and Advices that I may receive from Congress."[16]

14. Adams to R. R. Livingston, Feb. 14, 1782, *Works of John Adams*, VII, 512. See also Genet to Adams, Wharton, ed., *Diplomatic Correspondence*, III, 685. For Franklin's false "British Indian atrocities" propaganda see Samuel Flagg Bemis, *The Diplomacy of the American Revolution* (Bloomington, Ind., 1965; orig. publ. 1935), 51. The elder Genet (1715–1781) from early 1776 to late 1779 had also edited *Affaires de l'Angleterre et de l'Amérique*, to which Adams contributed letters during his first mission to France. See *Diary and Autobiography*, II, 354n–355n, 434n.

15. Adams to Arthur Lee, May 25, 1780, Adams Papers, Reel 351, partly quoted from transcription in Wharton, ed., *Diplomatic Correspondence*, III, 701. See also Adams to the president of Congress, Apr. 17, 1780, *ibid.*, 619, and to Abigail Adams, May 12, 1780, Adams Papers, Reel 351. A month later Adams estimated that he had "written an hundred Letters to Congress, I believe almost." Adams to Lovell, June 24, 1780, Adams Papers, Reel 351. Seven months after his arrival he had "not a Line from Congress." After "almost 6 months" he had but one letter from Abigail Adams. Adams to Abigail Adams, June 17, 1780, and May 3, 1780, *Adams Family Correspondence*, III, 366, 337.

16. *Diary and Autobiography*, IV, 178. For Lovell's letters and postscripts to Adams see

But the floodtide had set, and nothing could stop it, not even the occasional depressions of Adams himself. For his labors over the next two years he would be criticized by the French, by Franklin, Congress, historians, his grandson-biographer, Charles Francis Adams, and, of course, himself. Virtually alone in Europe, and cut off from America except for occasional letters from a few Massachusetts friends, he conducted diplomacy in his own style. He was not always judicious, but he prevailed. His first step, though, inspired by chafing at inactivity, proved to be his most costly.

In June, Vergennes, possibly calculating that he could provoke Adams into a too vigorous defense of American policy, initiated a debate over Congress's devaluation of its paper money, much of which was held by French investors. Vergennes asked that French holders of American bills have them redeemed at the predevaluation rate. Adams pointed out that if this were done, the American holders would simply find Frenchmen to turn in their money for them. He asked Franklin to support him, while Vergennes asked that Franklin support the French case in Congress. Here it was that Franklin committed what Charles Francis Adams later called a "moral abandonment" of Congress and of Adams.[17]

Franklin avoided taking a position on the issue, agreeing only to Vergennes's request that he forward the letters to Congress. However, he did not inform Adams until months later that he had done so, and he went out of his way to tell Vergennes and then Congress that Adams was hostile to the Franco-American alliance and to suggest that other Americans held much different "Sentiments" toward France. When Franklin's letter to

---

Wharton, ed., *Diplomatic Correspondence*, VII, 343; also Burnett, ed., *Letters of Continental Congress*, V, 430n, 258.

17. *Works of John Adams*, I, 317n. The intrigues and complications of this exchange were numerous. James H. Hutson suggests that Adams maneuvered to keep Franklin out of the matter in order to demonstrate to Congress his own greater vigor and care for its interests. "John Adams and Diplomacy," 81–83. This is possible. Yet Adams, as Hutson shows, was inveigled into the controversy, initially through a conversation with Chaumont, the secret agent mentioned in chap. 5. Also see Foley, "Triumph of Militia Diplomacy," 13. Adams also argued that French speculators actually had profited from the devaluation through currency manipulation. Hutson, "John Adams and Diplomacy," 79–80.

Vergennes reached Congress, Lovell wrote to Abigail Adams, calling it "most unkind and stabbing."[18]

Like Franklin, Adams too sent his exchange with Vergennes to Congress, from whence he eventually received considerable support, though the devaluation itself eventually failed for lack of national stability. In the meantime, however, apparently taking to heart an assurance that he could "on every occasion" address the comte de Vergennes directly, he undiplomatically took the opportunity to begin a series of letters urging more vigorous French participation in the fighting against England. Vergennes was able to use Adams's lecturing tone in these as an excuse for administering a sharp diplomatic rebuff, which he then made the basis for a campaign in Congress against him. As with the paper money question, the issue here of diplomatic correctness (though not that of military urgency) remains debatable. What is certain is that, while Adams had sufficient justification for pressing Vergennes, he hurt himself by doing so. So great was French influence that Congress eventually sent Adams a rebuff for his urgings of Vergennes.[19]

Even as he had come to suspect a plot between Franklin and John Paul Jones in 1779, Adams came to believe in one between Vergennes and Franklin, based on Franklin's "sordid Envy" of

18. Franklin to comte de Vergennes, July 10, 1780, Albert Henry Smyth, ed., *The Writings of Benjamin Franklin*, VIII (New York, 1907), 118; Lovell to Abigail Adams, Sept. 15, 1781, Burnett, ed., *Letters of Continental Congress*, V, 219. Franklin also wrote to Congress that Adams had given "Offence to the Court here," adding that "he seems to have endeavoured to supply what he may suppose my Negociations defective in." Aug. 9, 1780, Smyth, ed., *Writings of Franklin*, VIII, 126, 127. But Franklin had complained in the same way about Arthur Lee, reporting that he was persona non grata with the French court. Shipton, *Sibley's Harvard Graduates*, XIII, 253–255.

19. Genet to Adams, Feb. 20, 1780, Wharton, ed., *Diplomatic Correspondence*, III, 509. Adams was supported on the paper money issue by James Lovell, James Duane, Oliver Wolcott, and Jesse Root. Burnett, ed., *Letters of Continental Congress*, V, 576, 478, 490, 497. For Congress's failure see *ibid.*, ix–x. At this time Adams had received only one letter from America—from Elbridge Gerry, asking him to urge the very measure at which Vergennes took offence. Gerry to Adams, May 5, 1780, Adams Papers, Reel 351. Charles Francis Adams called the last of Adams's letters to Vergennes "scarcely . . . prudent." *Works of John Adams*, I, 327. But the editors of the Adams Papers write that Adams argued "with cogency," and was proved right by subsequent military events. *Adams Family Correspondence*, III, 391n. It may be added that Cornwallis eventually was defeated with the help of just such a French blockade as Adams was calling for. It is significant that John Laurens was dispatched by the end of the year 1780 "to plead . . . for increased French naval assistance," among other things. *Ibid.*, IV, 63n.

his commissions. If he lacked conclusive evidence for his suspicions (which would seem less extravagant if expressed as a temporary coincidence of interests between Vergennes and Franklin), they eventually proved to have been justified. For the comte de Vergennes instructed his minister in Philadelphia to use his influence to have Adams recalled, and La Luzerne (Gérard's replacement) succeeded in having Adams's commerce commission lifted and his authority as peace commissioner diluted by joining with him Franklin, Henry Laurens, John Jay, and Thomas Jefferson in a new peace commission.[20]

Rather than being the product of a plot with Vergennes, Franklin's conduct stemmed from what a recent psychohistorical study of him calls "an aversion to contention." The pattern of his personal and political life shows numerous parallels with his behavior toward Adams. "Conflict" such as that posed by the choice between the urgings of Adams and Vergennes normally called forth a gesture of "conciliation" from Franklin, after which "he would try to prove his innocence," as in the letter to Congress. Once he became convinced that his dilemma had been caused by someone who threatened him, however, Franklin would in the end clandestinely attack that person. This he did to Adams when he waited two months to inform him that he had forwarded his letters to Congress (never reporting what he had said about him as a diplomat).[21]

Adams's towering resentment was personal, to be sure, but his attachment to his commissions derived from a consistently held theory of American foreign policy. The question came

20. Adams to Jenings, July 20, 1782, Adams Papers, Reel 357. See William Emmett O'Donnell, *The Chevalier de La Luzerne, French Minister to the United States, 1779–1784* (Bruges, 1938), 124; also *Secret Journals of the Acts and Proceedings of Congress, from the First Meeting Thereof to the Dissolution of the Confederation . . .* (Boston, 1820), II, 416, for La Luzerne's "several observations respecting the conduct of Mr. Adams." For a later version of Adams's suspicions see his correspondence in the *Boston Patriot*, May 15, 1811.

21. Richard L. Bushman, "On the Uses of Psychology: Conflict and Conciliation in Benjamin Franklin," *History and Theory*, V (1966), 230–231. For Franklin's letter, apparently not received for another two months (although Adams may, in turn, have delayed his answer), see *Works of John Adams*, I, 318n. For an earlier example of Franklin denying resentment yet taking revenge see Currey, *Code Number 72*, 5–6. Quite the opposite of Franklin in this respect among others, Adams had an almost pathological compulsion to forgive. See below, chaps. 10 and 12.

down to what kind of connection with France was necessary to the survival and growth of the United States. The key to greatness for the United States, Adams believed, lay in establishing equal and free trade with all nations. Having no need for conquest or fear of invasion once the present war ended, America was promised unbounded growth that only wasteful and unnecessary involvements in European politics could interrupt. So advantageous was trade with America for any European country that even France need not be bribed into support of the Revolution with anything further than an offer of trade. As for the English, with whom America had broken over questions of trade, it was imperative to announce to them that Adams held a commission to establish commercial relations as soon as peace should be settled, for the prospect of renewed trade with America constituted their sole motive for stopping the war.[22]

In 1776 Adams wrote the model treaty for use by American diplomats, especially those who should first attempt to establish an alliance with France. His draft proposed an offer of trade with France but sought no military support. Although more concessive than his draft, the model treaty that Congress eventually adopted still offered the French "astoundingly" little: only a guarantee, should England and France go to war, to refrain from taking advantage of the hostilities by aiding or coming to an understanding with England. Adams's forward-looking approach was "entirely alien to the spirit of the diplomatic practice of the time," and Vergennes was shocked by it when Franklin and his colleagues set the model treaty before him in 1777. Adams's dismay was understandable when Franklin proved willing further to compromise the terms and subsequently to favor closer involvement with France.[23]

22. *Works of John Adams*, I, 323. See also Randolph G. Adams, "John Adams as a Britannic Statesman," in *Political Ideas of the American Revolution: Britannic-American Contributions to the Problem of Imperial Organization, 1765 to 1775*, 3d ed. (New York, 1958), 123; Merrill Jensen, *The Founding of a Nation: A History of the American Revolution, 1763–1776* (New York, 1968), 503–504; John M. Head, *A Time to Rend: An Essay on the Decision for American Independence* (Madison, Wis., 1968), 105. "The majority of John Adams' cases in the Court of Vice Admiralty," it is worth noting, "involved . . . the British Acts of Trade." Wroth and Zobel, eds., *Legal Papers*, II, 98.

23. Felix Gilbert, *To the Farewell Address: Ideas of Early American Foreign Policy* (Princeton,

In his letter to Congress, Franklin contrasted his own, psychological approach to Adams's "boldness." "He thinks," wrote Franklin, "as he tells me himself, that America has been too free in Expressions of Gratitude to France." Franklin proposed instead to use "Decency and Delicacy" to "increase" the French king's "Pleasure" in his "generous Benevolence" toward the United States. Franklin depicted Adams as attempting to bully the French—"Mr. Adams . . . seems to think . . . Stoutness . . . Independance and Boldness in our Demands, will procure us more ample Assistance"—and he suggested that Congress had to choose between the two approaches.[24] Congress agreed with Franklin that a semiclient relationship with its only ally and creditor was necessary for survival. Accordingly, when Vergennes wanted Adams removed, it compromised by enlarging his peace commission and removing his commerce commission without reassigning it.

When he was seventy-six Adams reviewed Franklin's letter with undiminished outrage and took it upon himself to "explain [or, rather, denounce] this dark transaction to posterity." He pointed out that he agreed with the policy of flattering the king. Had he recalled it, he could have referred to his letter of March 1780 to Samuel Adams in which he contrasted his own approach to that of Ralph Izard, whose irascibility, perhaps because it reminded him of his own, brought out Adams's moderation. Where Izard advocated holding "an high Language to this Court," Adams, while he agreed that the French had made the alliance out of self-interest, opposed "the Style of Menace." He was for "Frankness," not "hardness."[25] Neither

N.J., 1961), 53–54. For the earliest expressions of Adams's purely commercial philosophy of diplomacy see his letter to John Winthrop, June 23, 1776, "Correspondence between Adams and John Winthrop," Mass. Hist. Soc., *Colls.*, 5th Ser., IV, 309; also *Diary and Autobiography*, II, 153n. Adams could not have known that Franklin told Vergennes that the draft treaty "had been worked out over his own objections." Currey, *Code Number 72*, 256.

24. Benjamin Franklin to Congress, Aug. 9, 1780, Smyth, ed., *Writings of Benjamin Franklin*, VIII, 127. Compare Wharton, ed., *Diplomatic Correspondence*, IV, 181, for remarkably similar language by Vergennes.

25. *Boston Patriot*, May 15, 1811; Adams to Samuel Adams, Mar. 4, 1780, Adams Papers, Reel 96. See also Adams on "Gaiety" and "Show" in diplomacy, Adams to Jenings, May

Franklin's flattery nor Izard's high-handedness, Adams seemed to be saying, but rather his own open honesty would succeed with the French. The verdicts of historians have sometimes favored Adams, more often Franklin, but the truth is that, as Adams remarked on numerous occasions, there was little that diplomats could do either way: only the success of American armies could secure the success of American diplomacy.

The style of flattery, however, carried with it a danger, Adams believed, and he warned Congress against it. No European nation, "not even Spain nor France, wishes to see America rise very fast to power. We ought, therefore, to be cautious. . . . Let us treat them with gratitude, but with dignity. . . . Let us, above all things, avoid, as much as possible, entangling ourselves with their wars or politics. Our business with them, and theirs with us, is commerce, not politics, much less war."[26]

During his arguments with Vergennes in July, Adams reminded himself of his principles by recalling his role in drafting the model treaty for the French alliance. In a letter to his one confidant in Europe, Edmund Jenings, Adams recalled his advocacy of purely commercial relations: "I never had the Honour to Support any Argument, in Speech or in Writing with more applause, than this was received with in Congress." While he was away from Congress, he recalled, the treaty had been amended to extend more advantages to France, but, he wrote, "If my Life should be Spared I am determined Posterity shall know which was my Treaty and which was other Peoples Treaty."[27] In lecturing Vergennes, then, on sending more frigates and on Congress's wisdom in the devaluation of the paper

26, 1780, Adams Papers, Reel 96. There was an irony in Adams's protestations of his own "frankness" compared to the devious Frank-lin. Adams insisted on the "Frankness that makes a Part of my Character." *Diary and Autobiography*, II, 389, and see 387. In responding to Franklin's charges of jealousy Adams called himself "frank." Adams to John Quincy Adams, Dec. 2, 1804, Adams Papers, Reel 403. And, at about the same time, he felt it incumbent on him to give his "frank Sentiments of a certain Minister"—Franklin.

26. Adams to the president of Congress, Apr. 18, 1780, Wharton, ed., *Diplomatic Correspondence*, III, 623. Note Adams's use of the word "entangling."

27. Adams to Jenings, July 18, 1780, Adams Papers, Reel 352. Edmund Jenings (1731–1819), nominally a lawyer, was an American who spent most of his life of leisure in Europe.

money, Adams showed a determination to sustain his own line in foreign policy.

Adams's commercial theory took its place with the rest of his solutions to psychological and political questions. It accepted as given the existence of a basic individual or national passion, in this case commercial greed, and attempted to harness it to good. The hated ambition of his diary he translated into the "virtue" of seeking eminence in a republic, the form of government he labored to install during the Revolution. Similarly, he took the morality-sapping, New England love of commerce, which he had denounced for years, and made of it a virtue in an international scheme of free trade. As always, self-interest was his ruling principle of action. If only he could be permitted to explain the matter, he could demonstrate that free trade with the United States represented the self-interest of the European nations. (Without a commercial treaty with the United States, the Dutch would "dwindle away to nothing.") The exception to Adams's theory of self-interest in human nature continued to be himself, the one man who acted naturally from ethical motives. Tacitus-like historians would assume "Ambition . . . and the Love of Glory" as his motives, but the truth was, he insisted, that he acted from "nothing but a Sense of duty."[28] In international relations Adams erected a self-interest theory with a similar exception, the United States of America, which now replaced New England in his system. This nation alone had no need of the armaments, conquests, or intrigues of Europe, since its inclination and destiny lay in peaceful economic development.

America, Adams further believed, found itself placed at a critical point in history as a kind of fulcrum of the European balance of powers. Its temptation lay in involving itself in the dynamics of that balance; its wisdom lay in "an abstentive neutrality" that would preserve the balance and result in an eventual peace.[29] The bearer of the new nation's prospective

28. Adams to Abigail Adams, May 22, 1781, *Adams Family Correspondence*, IV, 122, and to Dr. Gordon, May 26, 1780, Adams Papers, Reel 96.

29. Malbone W. Graham, *American Diplomacy and the International Community* (Baltimore,

commercial treaty with England was of course John Adams. When Franklin's letter to Congress and Vergennes's efforts eventually resulted in the revocation of that commission, Adams suffered a blow both to his *amour propre* and to his *amour patrie*. His resentment and suspicions, if not entirely justified, were at least understandable.

In the meantime Adams turned his attention to the Netherlands, where he felt that he could do more good than in France. If he succeeded in raising money there, the United States would not have to depend exclusively on France. At the same time, by starting commercial discussions with the Dutch, Adams hoped to encourage England to make peace. The English would read his attempt to secure another ally and trading partner as a sign that they might hope to regain a portion of their American trade, which they would realize was not wholly to be monopolized by the French ally. Consistent with Adams's theory of diplomacy, commerce thus would lead to peace. Adams left for the Netherlands with high hopes on July 27, two days before Vergennes's note telling him that his letters were no longer acceptable.[30] Rather than the few weeks that he expected to spend, he was beginning a stay of two years: his most difficult but ultimately most successful period as a diplomat.

Soon after he arrived Adams's prospects for raising money faded. In the face of a threat of war by England it became politically inadvisable for anyone in power to deal with him. News of recent American military losses and divisions in Congress made matters worse. Adams stayed on, nevertheless, in the belief that the Netherlands made a better propaganda base than France, and in the continued hope of borrowing money. Then, in October 1780 it was learned that Henry Laurens, recently sent by Congress to negotiate with the Dutch, had

1948), 16. See also Wharton, ed., *Diplomatic Correspondence*, IV, 213: "America is the very centre and axis of the whole."

30. For the chronology see *Adams Family Correspondence*, III, 391n–393n. For Adams's high spirits on the way and after arrival in the Netherlands see his letters to Abigail Adams, Sept. 4 and 15, 1780, *ibid.*, 410, 414. On Adams's commercial motives see Hutson, "John Adams and Diplomacy," 109–110.

been captured at sea by the British. They found among his papers a proposed Dutch-American treaty, which they used as a pretext for bullying the Dutch and then, in March 1781, for a declaration of war. By the end of 1780 Adams had grown despondent. In Amsterdam he was shunned by the diplomatic community (much as he had been by his fellow delegates in Philadelphia in 1775). His efforts to borrow money failed. He began to complain about his recurrent eye ailment. "Deeply troubled," he abandoned his diary and stopped writing home. "Things dont go to my Mind," he wrote to his wife after three months of silence, having in the meantime gone from praising to denouncing the Dutch. He wrote that he wished to leave Europe in order that he "might do something worthy of History."[31]

He soon realized, though, that the split between England and the Netherlands offered him an opening for a treaty with the Dutch. With his sons removed to school in Leyden (accompanied by his secretary, John Thaxter), he began alone the long process of gaining recognition—after which he could borrow money and negotiate for his treaty.

For the last time in his life a challenge proved congenial to Adams. The Dutch lived under a republic of sorts, and he was at his best in dealing with legislative bodies and public opinion, neither of which existed in France. The French minister in Amsterdam, La Vauguyon, had orders from Vergennes, who complained about Adams's "stubbornness," to keep him from pressing his case. La Vauguyon succccdcd for a while, but, being this time slightly out of French jurisdiction, Adams was able to defy him when he had to. Congress eventually accredited Adams as its official emissary to the Netherlands, with powers to borrow money and negotiate a treaty. Acting on the advice of Dutch friends, he published a philosophical memorial that broke "all diplomatic precedents" by addressing the na-

---

31. *Adams Family Correspondence*, IV, 90n; Adams to Abigail Adams, Mar. 28, 1781, *ibid.*, 108, and to James Warren, Dec. 9, 1780, *Warren-Adams Letters*, II, 155. Here and in other letters one has to allow for Adams's usual exaggeration with the Warrens. On the Dutch see Adams to Baron Van der Capellen, Dec. 9, 1780, *Works of John Adams*, VII, 340.

tion at large to explain the natural, largely commercial bases for alliance between the two peoples.[32] Thus, through his favorite channel of newspaper writing he put to work both his assiduity and his ability for making others accept his long-range vision.

To be sure, Adams had to suffer through a year of frustrating delay, during which he underwent "paroxysms of patriotic rage." But as always when he engaged himself whole-heartedly to a cause, his vigor returned and his mind raised itself above both doubts about his countrymen and petty concerns with individuals. "You will say nothing," he wrote to one of his agents in a marked revivification of his prose, "reflect well upon the times, and be prepared to answer me serious questions upon public affairs; nothing personal, nor selfish, nor little."[33]

Within a few months, though, Vergennes's agent in America succeeded in expanding Adams's peace commission to five members. Not yet knowing this, Vergennes had to summon Adams, still the only American empowered to discuss peace offers, to Paris to lay before him an Austrian-Russian offer to mediate between Great Britain and her colonies. (Congress's instructions to accept such an offer, dictated by Vergennes, were also on the way.) The key feature was a truce, something that Franklin had given signs of favoring but that Adams, despite his instructions, had peremptorily rejected on his arrival in Paris. He did so even though Vergennes withheld parts of the proposal (as Charles Francis Adams later put it: "Mr. Adams was permitted to see but a very small corner of the picture, nor had he much time to study even that"). Had Adams accepted the offer of mediation, with its chance for him finally to exercise his powers as American peace commissioner, the English

32. Comte de Vergennes to La Vauguyon, cited by Foley, "Triumph of Militia Diplomacy," 133; Chinard, *Honest John Adams*, 159. Adams dated his memorial Apr. 19, the anniversary of the battle of Lexington. Years later he began a section of his autobiography on the same date. Paul François de Quélen de Stuer de Caussade, duc de La Vauguyon (1746–1828), was French ambassador to the Dutch republic from 1776 to 1783.

33. Benjamin Waterhouse to Levi Woodberry, Feb. 20, 1835, cited in *Adams Family Correspondence*, IV, 33n; Adams to Alexandre Dumas, Mar. 1, 1781, *Works of John Adams*, VII, 372.

might have gained the key cities held by their armies in 1781, with territorial arrangements and the very matter of American independence left as open questions.[34]

Adams at first inclined not to stick over the point of etiquette, that is, prior recognition of independence by Great Britain. But as he thought the matter over while waiting for three days without an answer to his first, cautious letter to Vergennes, he grew suspicious. When Vergennes finally answered him by addressing a letter to "Mr. Adams, Agent [rather than representative] of the United States," he revised his view of etiquette, and he ended, in the last of four, typically long letters, by insisting that before appearing at a peace conference he would have to be accorded full diplomatic recognition, with "all the prerogatives of . . . a minister from a sovereign power."[35]

Franklin—with whom Adams apparently did not consult about the mediation even though he could have visited him outside Paris—had he been faced with the same offer, and had he seen through it as Adams did, might have written a short, temporizing note that would have left it to die a natural death. But Adams could bring to bear on almost any matter an arsenal of devastating logic and erudition without pausing, even when his first volley was decisive, till all his batteries were spent. Nevertheless, he had a right to the claim that his letters "defeated the profound and magnificent project of a Congress at Vienna, for the purpose of chicaning the United States out of their independence."[36] His grounds for rejecting the mediation

34. *Works of John Adams*, I, 337. For Congress's instructions see Wharton, ed., *Diplomatic Correspondence*, IV, 504; Adams's truce instructions are at 101. Foley, "Triumph of Militia Diplomacy," 167–168, 213n, gives the circumstances of Vergennes's complicity and reveals that John Sullivan, bribed by La Luzerne, maneuvered to secure Franklin's election to the commission.

35. Comte de Vergennes to Adams, July 18, 1781, *Works of John Adams*, VII, 444n (my translation); Adams to Vergennes, July 19, 1781, *ibid.*, 447–448. See also Adams to the president of Congress, July 15, 1781, *ibid.*, 440.

36. *Diary and Autobiography*, II, 458n, from Adams's *Boston Patriot* correspondence. Butterfield, *ibid.*, supports Adams's claim, as does Bemis, *Diplomacy of the American Revolution*, 187. See also the appendix to *Works of John Adams*, VII. The *uti possidetis* proposal of the mediation offer would have had the British evacuate New York City but hold "Georgia, East Florida, most of the Carolinas, and a great area in the north-west . . . while

offer, however—an insistence that the United States be treated with dignity through deference to him—intensified his identity with his country to a psychologically dangerous degree.

On his return to Amsterdam, Adams sent his ten-year-old son Charles, who had earlier in the year been too sick to attend school and now had grown homesick, back to America in the care of a friend. At about the same time, Francis Dana was ready to leave for Russia, and having no provision from Congress for a secretary, arranged to take John Quincy Adams with him in that capacity. Adams's second mission to Europe alternated between crises and lulls like the present one, which was intensified by separation from his sons and the diplomatic vacancies of August. In the letdown after besting Vergennes, all he could do was to mark time while waiting for some response to his request for Dutch recognition.

At this point he received a letter from Benjamin Franklin, who forwarded the news that the two had been joined by Congress in an expanded peace commission. The "powers" of an exclusive commissioner that meant so much to Adams, especially in relation to Franklin, were taken away. The blow was worsened not only by coming via Franklin but by Franklin's treating the new commission as a congressional vindication of his own conduct. In addition, when Franklin mentioned that he might not be able to continue paying Adams's bills he seemed to confirm Arthur Lee's warning that he would use his position as European dispenser of congressional money to cut off Adams as he had Lee. Moreover, Congress's announcement of the new commission came with an accompanying letter from the ambiguous James Lovell, written, as he put it, "in a half light" and partly in his confusing cipher. The letter hinted at Vergennes's role in expanding the peace commission: so much for Adams's recent triumph in Paris![37] On the following

Spain would have retained West Florida and extensive claims east of the Mississippi." Vincent T. Harlow, *The Founding of the Second British Empire, 1763–1793*, I (New York, 1952), 241.

37. Lovell to Adams, June 21, 1781, and July 21, 1781, Burnett, ed., *Letters of Continental Congress*, VI, 125, 125n, 151. Franklin's letter was sent Aug. 16, 1781, Adams Papers, Reel

day, August 25, 1781, Adams suffered the most severe breakdown of his life.

Adams called it a "nervous Fever." He associated it not with
the news about the expansion of his commission but as having
come "soon after my Return from Paris," actually a month
earlier, and as being the product of Amsterdam's damp air. The
bad air that threatened Adams whenever he ventured away
from the pure zephyrs of Braintree continued to explain his bad
health whenever its origin was psychological. He had remarked
his surprise in April at his good health despite the air (just as he
had during the hottest part of the summer in Philadelphia), and
from Paris in July he had been reported "in good health and
Spirits."[38] The connection in Adams's mind with Paris had to
do with what he termed the "Anxiety" caused by his trip there.
He had used the same word to describe his state of mind while
opposing Hutchinson in 1770: a struggle like the one with
Vergennes in Paris, with a similar aftermath of breakdown.
Years later he recurred to the word to explain this breakdown
in Amsterdam.[39]

When the fever "seized upon my head," Adams reported, he
lost consciousness and memory for "five or six days," during
which it was believed that he was near death, and afterward he
suffered for at least a year with memory loss and a "Weakness
and a Lameness that is new to me." He stopped writing for
almost two months, making a unique hiatus in his official and
personal correspondence, and then remarked that he was send-

355. Franklin had "resigned" to the scorn of Adams, Arthur Lee, and Abigail Adams,
although Adams never responded to the letter in which Franklin informed him of this
move. On Lee's warning to Adams about Franklin, see Hutson, "John Adams and
Diplomacy," 141–142. On Adams's difficulties with Lovell's cipher see "The Lovell
Cipher and Its Derivatives," appendix to *Adams Family Correspondence*, IV. Adams wrote to
Lovell, Feb. 7, 1809, Adams Papers, Reel 407, on his confusing style.

38. Adams to Abigail Adams, Oct. 9, 1781, *Adams Family Correspondence*, IV, 224; John
Thaxter to Abigail Adams, July 21, 1781, and to Adams, July 16, 1781, *ibid.*, 187, 180. See
also, on the "air," Adams to Abigail Adams, Apr. 28, 1781, Adams Papers, Reel 354, and to
the president of Congress, Oct. 15, 1781, Wharton, ed., *Diplomatic Correspondence*, IV, 780.

39. Adams to Abigail Adams, July 11, 1781, *Adams Family Correspondence*, IV, 170. For
his later use of the word "anxiety" in the *Boston Patriot* see *ibid.*, 225n.

ing his first letter, as he had his last before succumbing, to Franklin.[40]

At about the time that Adams recovered sufficiently to take up his correspondence, he received the news that his commerce commission, in some ways as important in his view as that for peace, and certainly closer to him personally, had been revoked outright. A few days later he resigned, but as Franklin had, left open the possibility of staying on: "My prospects both for the public and for myself are so dull, and the life I am likely to lead in Europe so gloomy and melancholy, and of so little use to the public, that I cannot but wish it may suit with the views of congress to recall me." Disturbed as he was, Adams could not long remain in such a state of mind. He solaced himself with the truth, which to his credit he had seen immediately, that an enlarged peace commission, representing each section of the country, would help secure congressional ratification of a treaty. By the end of 1781 he was telling Francis Dana that the changes "would nettle some men's feelings; but I am glad of them. They have removed the cause of envy, I had like to have said, but I fear I must retract that, since 18 [Adams] still stands before 17 [Franklin] in the commission," an allusion to his having been made senior member of the commission.[41]

Fall 1781 also brought favorable public developments and unfavorable personal ones, both calculated to rouse Adams back to his old self. In November came a new commission to negotiate a triple alliance with France and the Netherlands, along with the news of Cornwallis's defeat, which made it

40. Adams to Abigail Adams, Oct. 9, 1781, *Adams Family Correspondence*, IV, 224, and to Alexandre Dumas, Oct. 13, 1781, Adams Papers, Reel 102. On Adams's memory loss see *Adams Family Correspondence*, IV, 340. Adams wrote to Franklin that, since his last to him, "this is the first Time that I have taken a Pen in hand to write to any body." In fact, this letter was "actually in John Thaxter's hand and only signed by JA, as are the two or three other letters sent over his name during the preceeding six weeks." *Ibid.*, 225n, which quotes Adams to Franklin, Oct. 4, 1781. Thus Adams himself forced a connection between Franklin and his illness.

41. Adams to the president of Congress, Oct. 15, 1781, *Works of John Adams*, VII, 475, and to Francis Dana, Dec. 24, 1781, Dana Papers, Massachusetts Historical Society, Boston. When Adams transcribed this letter for his correspondence in the *Boston Patriot*, Apr. 29, 1810, he left an ellipsis after "I must retract that."

possible to insist on a Dutch decision about recognition. Next came the first of several hectoring letters, "probably stimulated by the French Minister in Philadelphia," from Robert R. Livingston—a "partizan of Dr. Franklin, and an enemy to Mr. Adams," as Arthur Lee put it.[42] Congress had put the franco-phile Livingston in charge of foreign affairs (choosing him over Arthur Lee) when it created a secretaryship to replace Lovell's one-man committee. Livingston's tone with Adams contrasted with his deference to Franklin. Even after the defeat of Cornwallis, Livingston criticized Adams for pressing the Dutch too hard for recognition. To others in Congress at this time, too, it seemed that "Mr. Adams has been harassing the pensionary of Holland . . . [and has] committed the dignity of America . . . against the opinion and advice of the Count de Vergennes."[43] But Adams was too caught up in the final steps necessary for recognition to be vulnerable to personal attack.

He wrote ruefully that he was "a Sheep . . . fleeced" of the peace commission, yet he rose to a spirited but balanced defense of his ministry in expectably gargantuan letters to Livingston. In these Adams had to face in public for the first time the charge of vanity with which he so regularly tortured himself in pri-vate. He admitted in an unsent letter to Jenings that he could be "perhaps sometimes too ardent" and that "I abound too much in my own Conceit." (Adams chose a word that suggested introspection as much as it did the modern meaning of con-ceitedness.) With Livingston, though, anticipating that he would be called vain for speaking so vigorously in self-defense, he dismissed the charge. "I have long since learned," Adams declared, "that a man may give offence and yet succeed."[44]

42. *Adams Family Correspondence*, III, xxvi; Arthur Lee to Francis Dana, July 16, 1782, Burnett, ed., *Letters of Continental Congress*, VI, 379.

43. Edmund Randolph to Thomas Jefferson, Oct. 9, 1781, Burnett, ed., *Letters of Continental Congress*, VI, 236, in a letter written just days before the defeat of Cornwallis. For the disinterested basis of Livingston's francophilia see George Dangerfield, *Chancellor Robert R. Livingston of New York, 1746–1813* (New York, 1960), 146–153.

44. Adams to James Searle, Dec. 26, 1781, and to Jenings, Nov. 29, 1781 (letter unsent), Adams Papers, Reels 102, 355; and to Livingston, Feb. 21, 1782, *Works of John Adams*, VII, 528.

Adams traveled the Netherlands stirring up support for recognition, filled the newspapers with articles favorable to America, and organized petitions by merchants in his favor. Finally, in April 1782, two years after reaching the Netherlands, he did succeed. He achieved what he considered to have been "the happiest Event, and the greatest action of my Life past or future": Dutch recognition of American independence.[45]

Adams felt elated not least because recognition vindicated his unorthodox diplomatic style. On the strength of his comparison between the unprofessional efforts of the first American diplomats and the tactics of a militia, the style has come to be known as "militia diplomacy." Franklin opposed the militia approach of breaking accepted practice by sending unwanted emissaries about Europe seeking recognition. He could point to John Jay's failure in Spain and to Francis Dana's in Russia, it was true. But Adams succeeded in the Netherlands, showing that not he but Franklin was restricted by diplomatic orthodoxy.

From the beginning Adams feared, though, that his "Tryumph" would "never appear in a Striking Light." This is exactly what happened. The flood of his letters to Congress continued to arrive in a long-delayed trickle, with his announcement of recognition taking six months despite his having sent it in several copies by different routes. "Nobody Seems to know any Thing about me," he complained in September.[46] Yet he was responsible for having neglected the friends in America who might have drawn attention to him. During both his three-month-long dejection after arriving in the Netherlands and his breakdown and long illness the summer before achieving recognition, he had lost contact with the Massachusetts delegates to Congress. If he ended by enjoying but a lonely triumph, the fault was partly his own.

45. Adams to Abigail Adams, Aug. 29–30, 1782, Adams Papers, Reel 357. For Adams's activities in stimulating recognition see Foley, "Triumph of Militia Diplomacy," 223, 240; also *Adams Family Correspondence*, IV, 304n–305n.

46. Adams to Edmund Jenings, June 1, 1782, and to James Warren, Sept. 6, 1782, Adams Papers, Reel 107.

Adams went through a familiar cycle of responses after his success. Starting with self-deprecating modesty (George Washington's victory at Yorktown deserved the credit), he moved to embarrassed pride, the conviction that his coup had altered the international balance of power so as to assure a century of peace for America, and finally to the fear that "Jealousy" and "Envy" would play down the achievement that he lacked the "Patience" or "Liesure" to advertise.[47] Received at court and no longer ostracized, Adams heard extravagant praise from the little circle of diplomats in the Netherlands. As with his success in the Continental Congress, he did not lean toward the dangers of corruption and power madness speculated about in his diary's sections on fame. Instead he worried again over receiving the proper degree of recognition and suffered from what he regarded as vanity for wanting to explain to the world what he had accomplished. "I disdain to Say or write a Word in my own Vindication," he wrote; he was not "dazzled with . . . Glory." Yet, he repeated everywhere the Spanish minister's praise—it "expressed but the litteral Truth"—only to add in a letter to his wife, "Pardon, a Vanity, which however is conscious of the Truth, and which has a right to boast."[48] In fact, Adams never learned the extent of French influence on his Dutch negotiation. He recognized La Vauguyon's delaying tactics at about the time that La Vauguyon shifted to temporary support; then he grew convinced that he had secured that support when, despite La Vauguyon's personal esteem, it had been withdrawn at the behest of Vergennes. Adams's later accounts of his two-year campaign in the Netherlands, which pitted his inexorable determination against an implacable rather than a changeable Vergennes, showed that he never recognized the shifts in French policy or their influence over him.

47. Adams to Abigail Adams, May 14, 1782, *Adams Family Correspondence*, IV, 324, and June 16, 1782, Adams Papers, Reel 357. See also Adams to James Warren, Dec. 15, 1782, *Warren-Adams Letters*, II, 187.

48. Adams to Jenings, Apr. 28, 1782, and to Abigail Adams, July 1, 1782, Adams Papers, Reels 356, 357. For Don Liano's praise see Adams to Benjamin Rush, Apr. 22, 1782, Alexander Biddle, ed., *Old Family Letters: Copied from the Originals for Alexander Biddle*, Series A, Letters from John Adams to Benjamin Rush (Philadelphia, 1892), 21–22. Here Adams mentioned "my known Character for Vanity."

From Adams's arrival in France, which coincided with French setbacks in fighting against England, until Dutch recognition, French military and financial problems affected his mission. Vergennes welcomed hostilities between England and the Netherlands as hurtful to both of France's rivals. He transmitted to Congress the proposal that it attempt to form an alliance with the Dutch only because he wished to keep both powers embroiled in war with England. Then, when Congress exceeded his recommendation by empowering Adams to form a *triple* alliance with the Netherlands and France, Vergennes cut off support of Adams just before he gained recognition.

Adams's daring memorial of April 1781 was the product of initial French interest in an alliance between the Americans and Dutch. His subsequent wait of a year for Dutch action was partly the result of Vergennes's instructions to La Vauguyon to withdraw his encouragement. In the opinion of an observer sympathetic to Adams, La Vauguyon "duped that honest patriot" into inaction for "more than a twelvemonth." As Adams never revealed, it was La Vauguyon, on new instructions from Vergennes, who suggested that he finally press for a reply. Vergennes quickly rescinded French support when he learned that a triple alliance might be its result. It was at this point that Adams, for the second time, daringly went further than La Vauguyon's advice by his demand for a categorical reply from the Dutch. The decision did him credit, but it hardly represented a policy of relentless pressure, as he believed.

Adams's demand was wholly in character, for it came as an expression of resentment over his enforced idleness. Finally enraged by the months of delay, "full-dressed even to his sword," he had marched dramatically past his sons and secretary to carry his demand to the Dutch. The drama, as he knew in his soberer moments, was located not in his personal gestures but on the battlefield at Yorktown. And yet, he had some justification for his belief that he had providentially been faced with a crisis in the alignment of nations and had administered a well-timed push in the right direction. His defiance of La Vauguyon's advice to go slow at the very least advanced the date of Dutch recognition—with the result of a subsequent Dutch loan in time to prevent a likely bankruptcy of the United States.[49]

Adams took little pleasure in his changed status after recognition. He did not enjoy dinner with a prince and princess, his official reception by the stadtholder, celebrations hosted by Dutch organizations, or the splendors of the house that he purchased as an American legation. He had been right in 1774 when he said that he was made for work alone. By June he came down with influenza; in July he wrote his wife that "your Friend . . . is much altered. He is half a Century older and feebler." "I sometimes think I Shall die a Martyr to the Dutch Alliance," he declared. Fatigued and lonelier than ever "in this horrid Solitude," he wrote to John Quincy Adams to return to him and repeatedly wished himself home with his wife or she with him in Holland. If he sent for her, though, he believed that they would run the risks of the Atlantic together on a return trip "in a Month or Six Weeks."[50]

Success turned Adams's thoughts not to what he had accomplished so much as to his loss of commissions, especially that for commerce. Had Congress "intended to make him resign"? If so, what should he do? For a while he was immobilized, then inevitably decided to stay on in order not to give the "Ennemies" of Congress "the compleat Tryumph which they wished for and sought but could not obtain." He sometimes believed that the "independent statesman . . . will be regarded . . . by posterity." But in the meanwhile, as after previous successes, he appealed for recognition of the several men who had aided him (substantially without pay) in what was really an expression of his own resentment: "It is high time, it is more than time, that a proper discernment of spirits

49. Benjamin Waterhouse to Levi Woodberry, Feb. 20, 1835, Woodberry Papers, XVI, 3–4, 5, Library of Congress. For Adams's pressing further than La Vauguyon advised see Foley, "Triumph of Militia Diplomacy," 243–244. Adams's first defiance of La Vauguyon had come exactly a year earlier when he insisted on submitting and publicizing his memorial.

50. Adams to Abigail Adams, July 1, 1782, to Jenings, June 1, 1782, to Abigail Adams, May 12, 1782, and to John Quincy Adams, May 13, 1782, all in Adams Papers, Reel 357.

and distinction of character were made." Then, in September, Adams let slip out the boast in writing to Livingston that "nothing but that well-hewn Harpoon Iron (thrown by a Cape Cod Whaleman) the Memorial of the 19 of April 1781" could have kept the Dutch from making a separate peace with England.[51]

Yet, Adams's extravagant figures of speech expressed above all that he was preparing himself, through a renewal of his private drama of independence, for the coming challenge of peace negotiations. In language that recalled his mortification at being left "dangling" by Congress during his first mission, he justified his independent action in Holland with an eye to the future: "If I had transmitted to Congress, the Advice and Exhortations and Remonstrances I rec[eive]d and asked their Instructions, I should have been forbidden to Stir, and should have been here Sprawling with Hands and feet in the Air pegged like Ariel in a rifted oak."[52]

It has been said that his characterization of his Dutch accomplishment as a "triumph of Stubborn Independence" would "serve well as a motto for Adams's conduct as a servant of his country." As he grew obsessed with the idea of his independence, however, he equated it, in effect, with stubbornness, thereby rendering it a political liability. His metaphors of helplessness and his old tendency to see himself in a morality of good versus evil pointed to the danger, for him, of a too rigid conception of his accomplishments—especially with peace talks nearing.[53]

51. Adams to Abigail Adams, July 1, 1782, *Adams Family Correspondence*, IV, 338; to James Warren, June 17, 1782, *Works of John Adams*, IX, 512; and to Livingston, May 16, 1782, *ibid.*, VII, 590–591, and Sept. 4, 1782, Adams Papers, Reel 106.

52. Adams to Francis Dana, Sept. 29, 1802, Adams Papers, Reel 107.

53. *Adams Family Correspondence*, III, xxviii. "What affects me most," Adams wrote, "is the Tryumph given to Wrong against Right, to Vice against Virtue, to Folly vs. Wisdom, to Servility against Independence, to base and vile Intrigue against inflexible Honour and Integrity." Adams to Abigail Adams, July 1, 1782, *ibid.*, IV, 338. Eight years earlier to the day Adams had written that he would not let "Knavery . . . get the better of Honesty, nor Ignorance of Knowledge, nor Folly of Wisdom, nor Vice of Virtue." To Abigail Adams, July 1, 1774, *ibid.*, I, 119. See above, in chap. 3. See also Adams to Livingston, May 16, 1782, *Works of John Adams*, VII, 591.

However agreeable in principle to several peace commissioners, Adams grew reluctant to act otherwise than independently. He recurred to his suspicion, not far from the truth, that the makeup of the commission had been calculated to leave him in a minority. John Jay, who joined Franklin in Paris in summer 1782, had been a political opponent of American independence in Congress, a confidant of the French minister, Gérard, and a friend of Silas Deane. Jay might have had reason to resent Adams since he lost out to him in the voting for peace commissioner. Also, Adams resented Jay's being given rank over him by the date of his appointment to Spain and, more recently, Jay's acquiescing in Franklin's appointment of his grandson William Temple Franklin as the peace commission secretary.[54] Although Adams maintained a polite correspondence while Jay was in Spain, he hardly imagined that this man was destined to become his ally.

The methods employed by Adams in Holland contrasted with Franklin's in gaining (along with Deane and Lee) French recognition, and their two philosophies, not to speak of their characters, promised to clash when they met again. Where Franklin had let events take their natural course, Adams had agitated incessantly to overcome Dutch "*vis inertia*." If Franklin's success seemed to justify and certainly confirm him in his easy geniality toward France, Adams's success suggested an opposite approach. "We must let them know that we are not to be moved from our purpose [recognition as a free and independent state], or all is undone," he wrote to Jay in Paris, and he consistently advocated unequivocally rejecting all English approaches that lacked explicit recognition of American independence.[55]

When at the end of May, Adams proposed this line to Franklin he received no reply throughout the summer—not even

54. Burnett, *Continental Congress*, 439. See Page Smith, *John Adams* (Garden City, N.Y., 1962), I, 448, 448n, and Gerald Stourzh, *Benjamin Franklin and American Foreign Policy* (Chicago, 1954), 168. In Congress in 1779 Jay voted against the recall of Franklin.

55. Adams to the president of Congress, June 5, 1781, Wharton, ed., *Diplomatic Correspondence*, IV, 469, and to John Jay, Aug. 13, 1782, *Works of John Adams*, VII, 610.

notification of the appointment in August of Lord Shelburne's man Alleyne Fitzherbert, whose commission involved an English offer to treat without recognizing American independence. Adams procured a copy of Fitzherbert's commission through public channels and sent it on to Congress; in the draft of an accompanying letter he thundered out against Franklin, especially for his renewal of unauthorized contacts with English emissaries, only to cross out much of what he had written. A sentence in the draft that hinted at Franklin's failure to inform him was deleted, and a doubly inked-out paragraph described his "despair" at Franklin's encouragement of duplicitous peace gestures and concluded once again that Congress should "release" him "from this Tye and appoint another Minister of that Commission" in his place.[56]

In not informing Adams, the senior member of the peace commission, of the August approach or of his numerous other exchanges with England, Franklin, who once had kept Arthur Lee similarly in the dark, lent more than a tinge of actuality to Adams's suspicions, though by now it had grown tit for tat with the two colleagues to keep information from one another. Adams believed that Franklin was trying to outshine *him*—to

56. See Adams to Franklin, May 29, 1782, Adams Papers, Reel 107. Franklin later apologized for not writing, explaining that he had been ill. The opposition between Franklin and Adams on handling England was complicated by rapid changes of English ministries. Adams believed that Lord Shelburne should be resisted in order to bring him around to Charles James Fox's more acquiescent position toward America; Franklin favored Shelburne, with whom he was in contact. Adams appears to have been wrong about Fox's real intentions but right about the advisability of holding out against Shelburne. Fitzherbert's commission, about which Franklin failed to inform Adams, mentioned treating with "the four powers [rather than nations] at war with Great Britain," an expression that left United States sovereignty an open question. See Adams to Jay, Aug. 13, 1782, *Works of John Adams*, VII, 609.

For the letter accompanying the copy of the commission that Adams sent to Congress, see Adams to Livingston, Aug. 18, 1782, Adams Papers, Reel 106. Readings of the inked-out portions of this letter were conjecturally supplied to me by the editors and staff of the Adams Papers. "Despair" is my own conjecture. "If I were now the Sole Minister for treating of Peace," Adams wrote in one of the crossed-out portions, "I should decidedly refuse to enter into any Conferences with any one whatever, without full and express Powers to treat with the United States of America. . . . If my opinion had been asked by Dr. Franklin. . . ." He obviously still hoped that Congress would realize that Franklin had not kept him informed. When Adams printed part of one of the inked-out passages of this letter in the *Boston Patriot*, May 11, 1810, he added that he had decided not to pursue his resignation after concluding that he might after all be able to influence Jay.

"make himself a Man of Consequence by piddling with Men who had no title" to treat with the United States of America—and he believed that Franklin had conspired with Vergennes to expand the peace commission. Adams could not expose Franklin's attempt to get all the glory of negotiating a peace because with "Men of great Reputations . . . to remark their Mistakes is to envy them."[57] Nor could he go to Paris and take the play away from Franklin, because this, too, might appear as motivated by envy—to himself no less than to imagined critics.

Knowing as much as he did about English peace overtures, Adams had sufficient official cause to leave for Paris. There joined with Franklin and Jay, who had left Spain on the same news, he would stand at the head of the peace commission and be able to demand full prior recognition as he had in the case of the abortive Austrian mediation. But he did not challenge Franklin's diplomacy with his own stubborn independence. He satisfied himself with urging Jay to stand fast, thereby losing the distinction of being the one to hold out for prior recognition from the English. As a result, the question of his and Jay's relative contributions to the peace haunted Adams for the rest of his life.

Adams offered good reasons for remaining in the Netherlands —too many of them, as at other times of reluctance to act. He had not completed his Dutch treaty. His presence in Paris would have the effect of a seeming capitulation, he explained to Jay, and would fill "at once another year's loan for the English." (The English, too, were borrowing, partly from the Dutch, to pay for the war.) To the last he predicted "no peace until 1784, if then," marking his return to a belief that first had emerged after the loss of his sole peace commission. "It is very possible they may be in earnest about terms of peace," he had then predicted,

<hr />

57. Adams to Jenings, July 20, 1782, Adams Papers, Reel 357. The letter goes on to accuse Franklin of "base Jealousy of me and . . . Sordid Envy of my Commission for making Peace and especially of my Commission for making a Treaty of Commerce" (see above) and charges Franklin with "an assassination upon my Character at Philadelphia, of which the world has not yet heard." A heavily inked-out line follows. In 1775 Adams called John Dickinson "piddling" for wanting to negotiate with England. See chap. 4.

"before I shall believe it."[58] Yet, neither Adams's good reasons nor his bad ones sufficiently explained his remaining in the Netherlands in the face of British overtures and his misgivings about Franklin. While he attended to the formalities of a substantially completed treaty with the Dutch, Jay and Franklin spent summer 1782 with various English emissaries sketching the basis of a peace. Adams's reluctance to be near Franklin had begun to have political consequences.

At about this time Adams paused significantly at a passage in the letters of Frederick the Great: "When your heart has received a wound, the Stoic tells you: you ought not to feel pain; but *I feel it in spite of myself*, it consumes me, it rends me." In the margin he wrote, "True."[59] Adams still felt the wound of losing the peace commission, and he still regarded Franklin as responsible for his suffering. Yet, Paris represented not an opportunity to get even but "millions of Perplexities, and millions of Humiliations and Mortifications." A self-denier rather than a fighter, Adams responded to aggression such as Franklin's with self-doubt instead of a thirst for revenge. As a result, for the first time in his life Adams's battle with himself left him unable to act at a critical moment. Heretofore, when events called for action his sense of himself as a moral agent and, beginning with the Revolution, his identification with his country, had helped him to shrug aside the personal. But now he felt abandoned by both his country and the moral order of things. By "disarming" him the "providence" that had helped him bring about Dutch recognition seemed to prevent his stopping

58. Adams to Jay, Aug. 10, 1782, and to Dana, Sept. 17, 1782, *Works of John Adams*, VII, 632, 606; Adams to William Lee, Apr. 2, 1780, Wharton, ed., *Diplomatic Correspondence*, III, 588. Charles Francis Adams's selection of letters from this period seems calculated to give the impression of good reasons for Adams's not going to Paris. Was Charles Francis's uneasiness expressed in the rare misdate of this letter as 1752 instead of 1782? In May, Adams had written to Franklin that he did not expect serious negotiations for a long time—even though he had just written to one of his agents that he might have to leave "at a short warning" for the "serious negotiation *going on*" in Paris. Adams to Alexandre Dumas, May 2, 1782, *Works of John Adams*, VII, 578 (italics added). Adams also had word from the marquis de Lafayette of the seriousness of the negotiations. *Ibid.*, 581.

59. Zoltán Haraszti, "John Adams and Frederick the Great," *More Books*, 6th Ser., IX (1934), 166 (italics in original). Adams's comment is dated Sept. 8, 1782.

the false negotiations.[60] His proud independence had degenerated into personal isolation.

Adams was still explaining to John Jay why he could not pay even a short visit to Paris to consult, and was counterproposing a meeting, without Franklin, either in the Netherlands or Brussels, when Jay announced that negotiations were about to begin. The English had not quite accorded prior recognition, but they were willing to treat with the representatives of the United States of America.[61] Thus Adams learned, September 29, 1782, that the peace negotiation was to begin in a matter of days without the senior American commissioner—himself. He prepared to join his colleagues, but even at this juncture delayed leaving for another three weeks.

60. Adams to Abigail Adams, Aug. 17, 1782, and to Matthew Ridley, Sept. 29, 1782, Adams Papers, Reels 357, 107. Jay conceded more than was necessary on fishing rights and the northeast boundary, both of which were issues that particularly interested Adams, who would have been certain to secure better terms on them for the United States at the outset had he been present. See Hutson, "John Adams and Diplomacy," 162–164.

61. Adams to Jenings, Aug. 30, 1782, Adams Papers, Reel 357. It is possible, as well, that Adams elected to remain in the Netherlands to secure some measure of recognition for himself. Being present for the formal signing of a Dutch-American treaty on Oct. 8, 1782, may have appeared to him a more significant act than it proved to be.

VII
Peace
1782–1783

At the peace conference in November 1782 John Adams contributed to a rare diplomatic victory by a weak nation over the great powers of Europe. But he obscured his record by erratic behavior before, during, and after the negotiations. Later he and his descendants privately admired but publicly underplayed his contribution to peace with England. They preferred to name recognition by the Dutch as his greatest diplomatic achievement—a lesser event than the peace, but his own.

When John Jay's summons to Paris reached Holland, Adams not only responded with several reasons for having to delay his departure but also warned that once on his way his health would make it "impossible for me to ride with as much rapidity as I could formerly, although never remarkable for a quick traveller." Instead of setting out immediately, he elected to sign his commercial treaty with the Dutch, put ministerial and personal affairs in order, finish signing for loans, write his reports to Congress, and to take correct, formal leave of the court. These activities consumed eleven days. In contrast, during the previous summer Adams had immediately broken off important business in Holland to discuss the mediation offer in Paris since, he wrote, "the world would consider my commission for peace as the most important of all my employments."[1]

This time, though he later said "every moment" had been directed to securing a quick departure, his diary suggests un-

1. Adams to John Jay, Oct. 7, 1782, *Works of John Adams*, VII, 646; *ibid.*, 431n (from the *Boston Patriot*, 1812).

conscious delay. Inspired by his friend the comte de Sarsfield, a French diarist with philosophical pretensions, Adams had resumed keeping his own diary October 1, less than a week before the summons from Paris. On October 6, the day it arrived, he mentioned reading Sarsfield but omitted the important news. (The omission recalled Adams's failure to record the news of a Franco-American treaty on his arrival in Bordeaux in 1778. Both times he turned away from developments that reduced his own role.) On October 10 he copied several pages in French from Sarsfield's diary into his own. On the morning of the next day he had "a hours Conversation" with Sarsfield about these, after which he took a stroll. Adams noted that he had "spent most of the day in signing [loan] Obligations, for the United States. It is hard work to sign ones Name 1600 times after dinner."[2] There can be no doubt that he kept himself busy. But his rare detailing of his leisure moments betrayed uneasiness over what kind of work it was. Diary writing, literary talk, prodigies of work—all these had sustained Adams in the past as they would in the future. But this time they served as devices of avoidance: he did not wish to see either the comte de Vergennes or Benjamin Franklin.

If he had held himself in readiness to leave on short notice, Adams could have been in Paris three days after receiving Jay's note on October 6. Instead he left the Hague on October 17, 1782, and then consumed a week more than the usual time for the trip, arriving on October 26. He later explained that "rains of unusual violence and duration had ruined the roads," which was true. On two successive days his party's carriage, which had to be dragged through the mud, suffered breaks in its axletree. Far from kindling anxiety, however, the delays seemed to fall in with his mood.

On the trip Adams assiduously viewed the churches, historical sites, and principal towns in his way, recording his impressions of them in detail. He also either composed or copied several poems: a Scottish ballad spoken by a lass mourning her

2. *Boston Patriot*, July 17, 1811; *Diary and Autobiography*, III, 24.

young "Jemmy" and four drinking and hunting songs. Adams professed a taste for instructional art, though in practice he was attracted to the sensual. In all his travels, in any case, only on this trip to Paris did he allow himself the dalliance of writing out pages of merely diversionary poetry. He might have defended as morally uplifting his ballad of the lonely lass for properly evoking feelings of loss like those he and his wife were suffering in each other's absence. But the drinking songs that he wrote out express primarily one theme: release from responsibility.

On his way to dispatching the great responsibility of a peace with England, rather than chafing at his delays Adams was writing in his diary: "Then Let Us, Let us now enjoy, all We can while We may" and

> How Sweet with a Bottle and Lass to refresh
> And loose the Fatigues of the Day.
>
> . . . .
> Since Life is no more than a Passage at best
> Let's strew the Way over with Flowers.[3]

The following day, while touring the grounds of the castle at Chantilly, he recorded a romantic episode: "While We were viewing the Statue of Montmorency Mademoiselle de Bourbon came out into the Round house at the Corner of the Castle dressed in beautifull White, her Hair uncombed hanging and flowing about her Showlders, with a Book in her Hand, and leaned over the Bar of Iron, but soon perceiving that she had caught my Eye, and that I viewed her more attentively than she fancied, she . . . turned her Hair off of both her Showlders . . . and decently stepped back into the Chamber."[4] This remark-

---

3. *Boston Patriot*, July 24, 1811; *Diary and Autobiography*, III, 33, 35. In the *Patriot*, Adams also wrote: "I have several times performed this journey of about three hundred and twenty-five miles in three days." See Adams to R. R. Livingston, Oct. 31, 1782, *Works of John Adams*, VII, 653, while on his way (a letter that omitted the date of Adams's departure) and Adams's account in the *Patriot*, continued June 26, 1811, in which he took pains to explain the delay.
4. *Diary and Autobiography*, III, 35–36.

able entry, in evocative prose rare for Adams, appeared at the one time when he could be expected to be too busy either to experience or record such an incident.

When he reached Paris, Adams uncharacteristically noted not his duty to inform himself about the peace negotiations but his recollection that "the first Thing to be done, in Paris is always to send for a Taylor, Peruke maker and Shoemaker." He had just learned, again failing to note it in his diary, that John Jay and Richard Oswald, the English representative, had negotiated a preliminary treaty during Franklin's illness. They had sent a draft to London on October 7, the day before Adams signed the Dutch treaty. In addition to being put off by this news, "Mr. Adams," Charles Francis Adams wrote, was "not much disposed to be subject, without strong necessity to a renewal of the rude and menacing tone which Count de Vergennes had not forborne again to use on his last visit [i.e., during the previous summer's discussions of the Austrian mediation offer]."[5]

Adams delayed calling on both Vergennes and Franklin. He went first to see his new confidant, Matthew Ridley (who had sent Adams a letter hinting at differences between Jay and Franklin) and then to John Jay. Ridley acquainted Adams with Jay's "Firmness"—presumably in holding out for a satisfactory degree of recognition—and his "Independence"—for taking "upon himself, to act without asking Advice or even communicating with the Comte de Vergennes—and this even in opposition to an Instruction [from Congress]." Franklin could be expected to favor complete openness with the French, both from personal inclination and in accordance with the congressional instruction, but Jay had taken up an independent line exactly like Adams's own. Naturally Adams threw in with Jay.

Instead of calling a meeting of the three commissioners, however, Adams brooded. He conceived of himself as being in a similar position between contending parties as on his first arrival in France, when he had visited Lee and Franklin in turn. This time, referring first to Franklin and then to Jay, he wrote:

5. *Ibid.*, 37; *Works of John Adams*, I, 354. Charles Francis Adams did not document this explanation, a rarity that suggests his having heard it directly from his grandfather.

"Between two as subtle Spirits, as any in this World, the one malicious, the other I think honest, I shall have a delicate, a nice, a critical Part to Act. F.s cunning will be to divide Us. To this End he will provoke, he will insinuate, he will intrigue, he will maneuvre."[6] Had Adams been a junior member of the peace commission, it is hardly conceivable that he would have been kept so long from Paris, or that once there he would have hesitated to bring his colleagues together to air their differences. As the senior member, though, he remained indecisive. From such a position of strength Adams proved constitutionally incapable of forcing an advantage over Franklin.

In the meantime, for three days Adams could not bring himself to visit or write to Franklin. At Jay's on Sunday (the day after his arrival) he "spoke freely what he thought of Dr Franklin." On Tuesday, when Ridley urged that he call on Franklin, Adams said that "after the usage he had received from him he could not bear to go near him." Finally, persuaded by the argument that even though he was "first" in the peace commission he ought to call in order to announce his arrival, Adams did so reluctantly, simply noting in his diary: "In the Evening, I went out to Passy to make my Visit to Franklin."[7]

A few weeks later Adams outlined the resultant conversation with Franklin. Adams did most of the talking—his recollections of this and other conversations with Franklin at this period are full of the phrase, "I told him." In closing, Adams "told" Franklin "without Reserve . . . that I was determined to support Mr. Jay to the Utmost of my Power." He also outlined his position on the disputed issues with the English. As in other of their confrontations, Franklin listened "patiently but said nothing." In a later account Adams described Franklin's con-

6. *Diary and Autobiography*, III, 38. See Matthew Ridley to Adams, Sept. 20, 1782, Adams Papers, Reel 359: "I find Mr. J firm—I wish however he was supported." Richard B. Morris, *The Peacemakers: The Great Powers and American Independence* (New York, 1965), 355, has Ridley say this to Adams in Paris, but Adams had been set thinking by the phrase in Ridley's letter while still in the Netherlands; apparently it added to his reluctance to see Franklin. Ridley, a merchant, was an agent in Europe for his state, Maryland.

7. Frank Monaghan, ed., *Diary of John Jay during the Peace Negotiations of 1782* . . . (New Haven, Conn., 1934), 12; *Diary and Autobiography*, III, 40, 39.

versation on this, and presumably other occasions, as consisting of "solemn, frigid silence on the subject of our public affairs, merry and pleasant enough about trifles and tittle-tattle."[8]

On the following day Franklin concurred in proceeding without French advice. But the manner in which he did so reflected his strained relationship with Adams, to whom as head of the commission he owed a private communication of his decision. At "the first Conference We had [with the English] . . . ," Adams wrote, "in considering one Point and another, Dr. Franklin turned to Mr. Jay [not Adams] and said, I am of your Opinion and will go on with these Gentlemen in the Business without consulting this Court [i.e., the French]."[9] As a result of this decision the Americans were able to present a united front. But Adams had no way of knowing that this would be the case when he failed to secure a commitment from Franklin in advance of the first session. As it developed, Adams could neither take full credit for Franklin's change of heart nor ever fully clarify his contribution to the peace.

When Franklin announced his decision to Jay he not only snubbed Adams but revenged himself on Vergennes, ostensibly for neglecting the American commissioners, but more likely in resentment at Vergennes's forcing him to take sides in the devaluation dispute with Adams. On any other theory than revenge Franklin's "joining in the Mutiny" against the French appears, as it later did to Adams, as "the most curious and inexplicable Part of the History." Charles Francis Adams called it "a singular fact," while a recent study of the peace negotiations calls it, as John Adams did, simply "inexplicable." Franklin's behavior makes sense, however, as an example of his pattern of conciliation. Publicly favoring complete openness with the French, Franklin had secretly deceived them even before going along with Adams and Jay. Later, completing his

8. *Diary and Autobiography*, III, 43, 82; Adams to Mercy Warren, Aug. 8, 1807, "Correspondence between Adams and Mercy Warren," Mass. Hist. Soc., *Colls.*, 5th Ser., IV, 427.
9. *Diary and Autobiography*, III, 82. Adams recalled the incident a few weeks after it took place. Franklin may have turned to the English negotiators rather than to Jay, in which case "these Gentlemen" referred to Adams and Jay.

pattern, he acted to mollify Vergennes after the Frenchman complained of not being informed when the Americans signed their treaty with the English on November 30.[10]

The congressional instruction, which the commissioners finally decided to ignore, directed them "to undertake nothing" without informing the French and "ultimately to govern yourselves by their advice and opinion." Historians have for the most part followed Adams and Jay in characterizing the last phrase as an effective surrender of sovereignty.[11] Yet, where Jay favored an outright refusal to obey Congress, the unusual indirectness and delayed timing of Adams's response suggest not outrage but a rare case of calculated deception on his part. Without quite admitting it to himself, he appears to have chosen to pretend that he never fully received Congress's unwelcome instruction.

Soon after he reached Paris, Adams protested to Livingston about the instruction, threatening to resign if Congress intended it literally to mean what it said. In his diary he wrote: "This Instruction . . . has never yet been communicated to me. It seems to have been concealed, designedly from me."[12] But he supposedly had received it in August 1781, in code, with the

10. John Adams to Arthur Lee, Apr. 12, 1783, Adams Papers, Reel 360; Morris, *Peacemakers*, 264. In a later recollection of Franklin's announcement, Adams, this time describing Franklin as having turned "to his colleagues," added that Franklin said he would "treat without consulting the court, the rather because they communicate nothing to us." For another Vergennes provocation see Stourzh, *Benjamin Franklin*, 172; Adams to Mercy Warren, Aug. 8, 1807, "Correspondence between Adams and Mercy Warren," Mass. Hist. Soc., *Colls.*, 5th Ser., IV, 427. Franklin had accepted Vergennes's advice that the Americans treat with Oswald under his first, unacceptable commission, reminding Jay, in a "heated argument," that they were bound by their instructions to accept French advice. But at the same time he "confidentially suggested to Oswald the cession of Canada" to the United States. Stourzh, *Benjamin Franklin*, 173, and see 168–175; Morris, *Peacemakers*, 309–310. Also see Bemis, *Diplomacy of the American Revolution*, 196. Franklin's mollifying letter has "often been called a diplomatic masterpiece." Stourzh, *Benjamin Franklin*, 178.

11. Instructions to the Commissioners for Peace, June 15, 1781, Wharton, ed., *Diplomatic Correspondence*, IV, 505. See Bemis, *Diplomacy of the American Revolution*, 190; Morris, *Peacemakers, passim*; William C. Stinchcombe, *The American Revolution and the French Alliance* (Syracuse, N.Y., 1969), 169; Adams to R. R. Livingston, Nov. 18, 1782, *Works of John Adams*, VIII, 13.

12. *Diary and Autobiography*, III, 38 (Oct. 27, 1782). See also Adams to Livingston, Oct. 31, 1782, *Works of John Adams*, VII, 653. Adams's account in the *Boston Patriot*, Aug. 10, 1811, agrees that he had not seen the instruction earlier.

letter announcing the expansion of his peace commission (immediately after which he suffered his breakdown).

From James Lovell's letter, which accompanied the instructions from Congress, Adams had been able to decipher the following: "Blush blush America consult & ultimately concur in," which hinted at some kind of subservience, followed by, "Gravier . . . strongly pressed for orders of that kind . . . under the Spur of at least Marbois," which revealed the French origin of the instruction (the French minister was *Gravier* de Vergennes; Luzerne's secretary was Barbé-*Marbois*). Rather than being unable to follow Lovell's code, as he complained, Adams had given up his correct deciphering of it at just this point.[13]

There were good reasons why Adams might have put off looking further into the matter as minister to Holland. At the time he received the new peace commission, he had been "instructed to confer in the most confidential manner" with La Vauguyon, whom he was about to defy by pressing for recognition. He hardly wanted at that point to learn about an instruction having to do with France and containing the words "consult & ultimately concur in." (Such an instruction, moreover, represented a clear rebuke to Adams by Congress.) Not until six months later had he written to Franklin to ask for "a copy, in letters [i.e., deciphered], of our peace instructions. I have not been able to decipher one quarter part of mine." Adams's suspicion that the instruction was being concealed from him evidently arose as a result of Franklin's failure to answer this letter.[14]

Adams had done his duty in requesting a decipherment, yet he could make an advantage out of not receiving it. If, on being

13. James Lovell to Adams, June 21, 1781, Burnett, ed., *Letters of Continental Congress*, VI, 125. "America" and "under the spur of " were not in cipher; see Adams's working copy, deciphered in Aug. 1781, Adams Papers, Reel 355.

14. Adams Papers, Reel 355, in Adams's instructions from Congress, Aug. 16, 1781, to form a triple alliance; Adams to Benjamin Franklin, Mar. 26, 1782, *Works of John Adams*, VII, 555. The instruction to obey the French was voted to control Adams as a sole peace commissioner. William T. Hutchinson and William M. E. Rachel, eds., *The Papers of James Madison*, III (Chicago, 1963), 154n. It was retained when other commissioners were added a few days later. Whether Adams immediately recognized this "personal rebuke" is not clear. Stinchcombe, *American Revolution and French Alliance*, 161.

sent a clear copy, he had been forced to request of Congress a clarification and had been informed that its words were to be taken literally, then his hands would be tied at a peace conference. As matters stood, he could (honestly) profess ignorance of the instruction at his initial meetings with his colleagues and proceed to interpret it in the "liberal" way he had handled the similar instruction to confer with La Vauguyon.

Such was the method by which Adams resisted incursions on his own independence and that of the United States. Rather than attempt to prevent Congress's moves, he maneuvered so as to be able to defy them on moral grounds. In disdaining to exert influence over Congress he was hewing to the suprapolitical stand that he had maintained in Massachusetts politics and, with nearly as much success, in the national Congress. Given the primitive state of parties, it is questionable whether he could have exerted influence in Congress even if he had tried. His support there continued to come from men of similar temperament like Samuel Adams and Elbridge Gerry. Without having to consult with him they fought, unsuccessfully, to save his prerogatives and his commissions in what amounted to "one of the most protracted, as it was probably the most hotly contested parliamentary battles ever waged in Congress."[15]

The point at which the American commissioners in Europe united in defiance of Congress marked the beginning of real negotiations with the English. Richard Oswald, who was friendly to the United States, had forwarded to London, substantially without change, Jay's proposals for a treaty. They were sent back with instructions to demand far more than Oswald had asked and were accompanied by Henry Strachey, an added negotiator sent to stiffen Oswald's posture. Strachey was to secure promises of reparations to injured loyalists, payment of debts to English creditors, and more constricted boundary lines where the United States touched Canada.[16]

15. Burnett, *Continental Congress*, 433. See also *Boston Patriot*, Aug. 10, 1811. Edmund S. Morgan has described congressional alignments in moral and regional terms—interestingly enough in connection with support and opposition to Silas Deane. "Puritan Ethic and the American Revolution," *WMQ*, 3d Ser., XXIV (1967), 25.

16. Morris, *Peacemakers*, 350–358. Adams had met Strachey (1736–1810), now a British

Adams, announcing that he had no intention of cheating anyone, surprised both his colleagues and the English by recommending a clause that permitted the loyalists to seek legal compensation. (On the other hand, no one knew better than he how complicated lawsuits could prove to be in American courts.) On the Massachusetts-Maine border with Canada, Adams brought from America maps and documents that confounded the English records clerk sent with Strachey to bolster English claims. Yet, Adams took a "mild" position here as well, agreeing to a boundary acceptable to the English.[17] Between October 24 and November 4 a new draft treaty was agreed on with relatively little difficulty and was sent with Strachey to London for approval.

Without a real crisis having developed or any distinct call on Adams for special sacrifice or effort, suddenly there remained nothing to do but wait—until November 23—for word of the draft's reception in London. It made yet another pause after great exertion, and another bad time for Adams. If his delay in the Netherlands had ruined his chance to take the leading role on the commission, he had nevertheless managed to make an important contribution so far. Now he proceeded to cloud his achievement.

When outdated letters from Livingston arrived containing criticisms of his work in Holland, Adams responded with superfluous self-vindication. This led him to familiar complaints that his services were not recognized, to anti-Franklin innuendo, and finally, in a letter home, to self-pity. "I am obliged, to differ in opinion So often from Dr Franklin and the C. de Vergennes," he wrote, "that I do not expect to hold any Place in Europe longer than next Spring." He now explained that because he had confounded French policy, the court had

---

undersecretary of state, on board Adm. Richard Lord Howe's ship when he and Franklin traveled to Staten Island to discuss conciliation in 1775. Richard Oswald (1705–1748) was a Scottish merchant sent by Shelburne to Paris in answer to Franklin's first overtures because he was their common friend. See Morris, *ibid.*, for sketches of the other English negotiators.

17. Morris, *Peacemakers*, 364, and see *Diary and Autobiography*, III, 50n.

organized a campaign against him in which "one man [Franklin], who is submission itself, is puffed up to the top of Jacob's ladder in the clouds, and every other man depressed to the bottom of it in the dust."[18]

In this state of mind Adams underwent a crucial incident with the comte de Vergennes, whom he had not forgotten in his complaints. Although he could not avoid speaking to Franklin, he indulged his reluctance to see Vergennes by omitting for a month to pay the call demanded by diplomatic etiquette. Only after both Lafayette and Franklin brought messages that Vergennes expected him did Adams go to Versailles. When he did he was astonished to receive royal treatment from the man who had broken off correspondence with him as he had left for Holland, then intrigued to strip him of his commissions, and finally dealt so peremptorily and unwillingly with him the previous summer in the affair of the proposed Austrian-Russian mediation. Privately, in a morning conference, Vergennes suggested objections to the American positions on loyalists and boundaries. Adams produced the documents that he had just shown to the British and overwhelmed Vergennes with arguments in his familiar fashion. Even though Vergennes officially knew of Adams's instruction to submit himself to French advice he made no mention of it.

Vergennes's motives in supporting the British even though his country was at war with them remain a subject of debate. Adams believed that he wished to clip America's wings, keeping her divided internally by maintaining the loyalists within her borders, and constricting those borders by maintaining a British power to the north and a Spanish one to the south and west. Others have argued, in support of Franklin, that Vergennes wished nothing but the best to the new nation. Whatever his political intentions, he did not like Adams; yet he invited him to stay to lunch, privately escorting him into the dining room where his wife sat Adams on her right "and was

18. Adams to Abigail Adams, Nov. 8, 1782, Adams Papers, Reel 359, and to Livingston, Nov. 8, 1782, *Works of John Adams*, VIII, 5.

remarkably attentive" to him "the whole Time." The comte, who sat opposite Adams, "was constantly calling out" to him, Adams noted, "to know what I would eat and to offer me petits Gateaux, Claret and Madeira &c. &c."[19]

Adams reported to Livingston the next day that he had been treated "with more attention and complaisance than ever" before at Versailles. Then, as if to emphasize that flattery did not touch him, he warned that Vergennes's arguments on the loyalists and boundaries amounted to support of the English position. Privately, though, Adams exulted at his triumph and wrote in his diary: "A few of these Compliments would kill Franklin if they should come to his Ears." Whatever Vergennes's reasons for treating Adams as he did, the luncheon amounted to a decided triumph over Franklin. As Adams's theory of diplomacy had it, Vergennes was motivated not by gallantry but by reasons of state.[20] Adams made clear that he understood the source of Vergennes's behavior, but he could not emulate it by suppressing his feelings about Franklin and the French. On the other hand, with his suspicions aroused by Vergennes's stated opposition to American aims, Adams correctly suspected that at the next round of negotiations the

19. *Diary and Autobiography*, III, 49. Congress had officially instructed Franklin to convey the peace instructions to the French king. See *Secret Journals of Congress*, II, 456. See Morris, *Peacemakers*, 357, for what was kept from Vergennes by the American commissioners. A recent defense of Vergennes is Orville T. Murphy, "The Comte de Vergennes, the Newfoundland Fisheries, and the Peace Negotiation of 1783: A Reconsideration," *Canadian Historical Review*, XLVI (1965), 32–46. Richard B. Morris argues against Murphy, pronouncing Vergennes's policy "ruinous" to the United States. *The American Revolution Reconsidered* (New York, 1967). See also Harlow, *Founding of the Second British Empire*, 241.

20. Adams to Livingston, Nov. 11, 1782, *Works of John Adams*, VIII, 8; *Diary and Autobiography*, III, 53. Bemis points out that Vergennes did not show great upset even in his remonstrance to the American commissioners for having proceeded without his advice. *Diplomacy of the American Revolution*, 240. O'Donnell argues that the Americans had "done him a good turn" by speeding Spanish acceptance of the separate English-French-Spanish treaty. *Chevalier de La Luzerne*, 233. Edward S. Corwin argues that the loan from France that followed the treaty was forthcoming not because of Franklin's mollifying note but because the money kept the United States dependent on France. *French Policy and the American Alliance of 1778* (Hamden, Conn., 1916), 343. Adams's sarcastic remark on Franklin's inability the following June to obtain further money when funds simply were no longer available in the French treasury makes the point: "One would have thought, that this letter, though by no means servile or unbecoming, was sufficiently courtly to have obtained the necessary loan; but not another louis d'or could be obtained." *Boston Patriot*, Feb. 5, 1813.

English would take a harder line on the issues raised by the Frenchman.

Adams responded by elevating these issues to a high ethical and global plane. His language reached for simile to express his conviction that only a refusal to be drawn into the orbit of either of the great powers could secure American independence. Lamenting that America "has been a football between contending nations from the beginning," he proceeded to impose his view on his colleagues and, surprisingly, on the French and English diplomats whom he met informally during the waiting period. Adopting a variation on his image of the United States as the fulcrum of the European "Ballances of Power," he told the Englishman, Oswald: "They will all wish to make of Us a Make Weight Candle. . . . for We shall very often if not always be able to turn the Scale. But I think it ought to be our Rule not to meddle, and that of all the Powers of Europe not to desire Us, or perhaps even to permit Us to interfere, if they can help it."[21] A football, a fulcrum, a scale, and a makeweight candle are all objects acted upon or used. With them Adams expressed an instinctive resistance to dependency that ran like a theme through his life.

Beginning with early defiance of his father Adams placed himself in situations testing his independence. His formula became: "To preserve my Independence, at the Expence of my Ambition." He avoided the intellectual constrictions of ecclesiastical councils. He refused the town of Worcester's offer to establish him as a lawyer. He argued against the absolute authority of Parliament on behalf of Braintree, Boston, the province of Massachusetts, and finally the United Colonies. The common description of the new American nation as an infant— a babe in swaddling clothes, an "infant Hercules"—spoke to Adams with special urgency.[22] Now, having fought to declare

---

21. Adams to Livingston, Nov. 11, 1782, *Works of John Adams*, VIII, 9; *Diary and Autobiography*, III, 61. Adams transcribed this passage with "pride" for the *Boston Patriot*, Sept. 11, 1811.

22. Adams to Abigail Adams, Dec. 3, 1778, *Adams Family Correspondence*, III, 129–130, and to Major Jackson, Dec. 1, 1781, Adams Papers, Reel 102. Among numerous examples of Adams's representative fascination with the infant republic, see his manuscript draft of a

independence, to make the Dutch and English recognize it, and then to prevent Congress from giving it up by making its commissioners subservient to the French, he prepared to resist English incursions on American sovereignty.

His means—the foreign policy of a balancing neutrality—reflected his character as surely as his emulation theory of human nature. He envisioned a United States that, like himself, with his aloof pride and independence of the help, influence, or flattery of others, would be impervious to either the threats or flattery of great powers. Adams's apprehensions of a helpless America held up only by Vergennes's "hand under our chin" once again recalled his description of himself in 1779 as left "dangling" by Congress. On this second mission Congress had weakened him by taking away first his exclusive peace commission and then that for commerce. In both instances removal of his powers spelled a loss of sovereignty for his country, as did the attempts to make him subject to the advice of La Vauguyon and Vergennes. It was not surprising that he imagined himself among European diplomats in similar terms to the United States among nations. "My fixed Principle never to be the Tool, of any Man, nor the Partisan of any Nation," he wrote, "would forever exclude me from the Smiles and favours of Courts."[23]

Once he had analyzed the situation and clarified his own role, Adams poured forth his views to Jay, Franklin, Oswald, Lafayette, and Vergennes. His troubles with the French he treated as matters of policy. Meeting with Franklin, "I told him," he recorded, "that I always considered their extraordinary Attack

reply to Hamilton, headed "Mr. Hamilton's Letter," [1800–1801], Adams Papers, Reel 399, and Adams to Abigail Adams, Feb. 28, 1779, *Adams Family Correspondence*, III, 181, and July 1, 1782, *ibid.*, IV, 337.

23. Adams to Livingston, Nov. 8, 1782, Wharton, ed., *Diplomatic Correspondence*, V, 865; *Diary and Autobiography*, III, 60. Elsewhere Adams called for a national state of mind equivalent to his own. "I humbly conceive," he wrote, "the congress ought, in all their proceedings, to consider the opinion that the United States or the people of America will entertain of themselves. We may call this national vanity or national pride, but it is the main principle of the national sense of its own dignity, and a passion in human nature, without which nations cannot preserve the character of man." Adams to the president of Congress, Sept. 5, 1783, *Works of John Adams*, VIII, 144.

upon me, not as arising from any Offence or any Thing personal, but as an Attack upon the Fishery." In fact, the French, by mistaking Adams as a man of one party and region, and therefore "liable to prove very stubborn on the questions of Canada and the fisheries," made him the champion of New England's fishing rights.[24] Holding "in the depths of his soul a conviction that his country's interests were safest under his guardianship," Adams prepared to take the most startling position of his career at the next bargaining session with the English: he personally would make American satisfaction with regard to the fishery a personal sine qua non for his signature to a peace treaty. Adams "had laid down a line," he told Matthew Ridley, "and beyond that he would not go let who would be ready."[25]

On November 25, having received instructions from London, the English representatives brought to the first of the six sessions that were to produce a definitive treaty newly worded clauses on both the loyalists and the fishery. Americans were to be prevented from fishing off Newfoundland within a limit of three leagues in some places and fifteen leagues at others. The Englishmen had not been given instructions to make these points ultimatums, but the Americans did not know how far they might be permitted to compromise. For six days, until

24. *Diary and Autobiography*, III, 64; La Luzerne to Vergennes, Aug. 4, 1779, in O'Donnell, *Chevalier de La Luzerne*, 43n. When Ralph Izard warned Adams against French designs to deny America the fishery in 1778, Adams tended to dismiss his fears and to suppose that even if they were realized the result would be to turn New England toward manufactures, a useful thing. See Adams to Izard, Sept. 25, 1778, *Works of John Adams*, VII, 47–48. On the other hand, preservation of fishing rights was regarded in the New England pulpit as part of the Revolutionary struggle. See Samuel Langdon's 1775 sermon in A. W. Plumstead, ed., *The Wall and the Garden: Selected Massachusetts Election Sermons, 1670–1775* (Minneapolis, Minn., 1968), 358. In September, Jay had been given an intercepted letter by Vergennes's secretary, François Barbé-Marbois, advocating surrender of United States fishery claims. Franklin never believed it genuine, which it was, but Jay and Adams were moved by it to their stand against obeying the congressional instruction to submit to French advice.

25. *Works of John Adams*, I, 381; Herbert E. Klingelhofer, ed., "Matthew Ridley's Diary during the Peace Negotiations of 1782," *WMQ*, 3d Ser., XX (1963), 132. Charles Francis Adams's phrase, a second rare departure from the historical record, has the appearance of reflecting John Adams's own words. Morris, *Peacemakers*, 376, points out that Adams announced his planned ultimatum to Ridley on the day that he had drafted some conciliatory clauses. See further in this chapter on later compromises during the negotiations.

November 30, Adams delivered a barrage of arguments showing why it was impossible for such restrictions to appear in the
treaty. His chief tactic remained that of all his dealings with the
English: appeal to self-interest. Their "Ideas respecting the
Fishery," he provocatively insinuated, appeared "to come pip-
ing hot from Versailles." For a myriad of reasons England
would "be compleatly the Dupe" of France if she imposed
fishing restrictions on the Americans.[26]

The English retreated step by step, as had others before them
in the face of Adams's detailed arguments. Finally, late on the
last night of negotiations, they held out for only one word: the
Americans should have the "liberty" to use the fishery, not the
"right," as the first sentence of each of Adams's drafts continued to read. "Mr. Fitsherbert [one of the English negotia-
tors] said the Word Right was an obnoxious Expression,"
Adams wrote. "Upon this I rose up and said, Gentlemen, is
there or can there be a clearer Right? . . . If Heaven in the
Creation gave a Right, it is ours at least as much as yours. If
Occupation, Use, and Possession give a Right, We have it as
clearly as you. If War and Blood and Treasure give a Right, ours
is as good as yours. . . . If then the Right cannot by denied,
Why should it not be acknowledged? . . . I said, I never could
put my hand to any Articles, without Satisfaction about the
Fishery." At this declaration Jay and Henry Laurens, who that
day had joined the negotiation, supported Adams, and he carried his point. It was his most dramatic moment.[27]

Adams soon designed a family seal containing a fish and, in
Latin, the proclamation, "We will fish and hunt as heretofore."
In 1815 he wrote to John Quincy Adams: "Of the importance of
the fisheries, my dear Son, I have a volume to write. But how
can I write it?" His family, if not history, understood his

26. *Diary and Autobiography*, III, 72–73. For the British instructions, see Morris, *Peacemakers*, 367–368.
27. *Diary and Autobiography*, III, 79, 81. Oswald's letter on the following day, Nov. 30,
confirms that Adams declared his refusal to sign. Wharton, ed., *Diplomatic Correspondence*,
VI, 94, also quoted by Chinard, *Honest John Adams*, 175. See also Adams's *Boston Patriot*
account, Dec. 11, 1811. An exchange about the possibility of sending once again to London
about the word "right" apparently intervened between Adams's speech and his ultimatum.

feelings. John Quincy Adams studied the negotiation several times in the course of his life, and Charles Francis Adams lent it prominence in his biography with the declaration that "such a victory is not often recorded in the annals of diplomacy."[28]

The stand assumed by Adams resolved a year's suffering over loss of his commissions. For, after being prevented by Vergennes for two years from assuming his full public character, by suddenly announcing his commerce commission he vindicated himself. "Congress," he revealed to all assembled at the negotiation, "had, 3 or 4 Years ago, when they did me the Honour to give me a Commission, to make a Treaty of Commerce with G. Britain, given me a positive Instruction, not to make any such Treaty, without an Article in the Treaty of Peace, acknowledging our Right to the Fishery." In the face of the Adams torrential righteousness no one in the room was prepared to raise what must seem like a niggling point, namely, that the commerce commission, along with its instructions, had been revoked.[29]

Adams came to Paris thanking God for the "Stubborness" and "Obstinacy" ("when I know I am right") that would explain his success in Holland if "an Historian . . . [should] compare my Negotiations . . . with those of Mr Franklin and of Mr Dana." But this was to adopt too readily the character ascribed to him by others. At the peace talks Adams took advantage of his reputation for stubbornness more than he exercised the quality itself. In fact, each of the American commissioners found his own way to cooperate in what proved to

28. Adams to John Quincy Adams, Feb. 7, 1815, Adams Papers, Reel 122; *Works of John Adams*, I, 381. The seal is stamped on the binding of Samuel Flagg Bemis's *John Quincy Adams and the Foundations of American Foreign Policy* (New York, 1949). John Quincy Adams studied his father's negotiation in 1814 and in 1823 (in a series of letters to Benjamin Vaughan, one of the English negotiators).

29. *Diary and Autobiography*, III, 81. Adams continued to keep the whole matter of commissions and instructions usefully vague. The present instructions read: "As to disputed boundaries and other particulars, we refer you to the instructions formerly given to Mr. Adams, dated 14 August, 1799, and 18 October, 1780." Ford *et al.*, eds., *Journals of Continental Congress*, XX, 651. Once the former instructions had been thus revived in part, then the commerce instructions to which they had been linked might also in some sense be revived. The fishery had been an ultimatum in the *draft* of Congress's peace instructions but had been deleted as such at the instance of the French minister; thus Adams did not carry with him such an ultimatum to Europe, except, in a sense, in his commerce commission.

be a successfully coordinated defense of America's prerogatives. Adams moved toward compromise, and Franklin away
from it; Jay, his major contributions of the summer behind
him, never relented in his francophobia but contented himself
with offering suggestions for the wording and rewording of
articles. Thus Adams, when he rose to defend his fishery article,
insisted on a "Right" to fish off Newfoundland, yet he already
had compromised by stipulating only a "Liberty" to fish closer
to the shores.[30]

After the preliminary articles were signed Adams committed
the indiscretion of exposing his exultation at Vergennes's flattery during their recent lunch. In order to defend the decision to
ignore Congress's instructions Adams directed that his personal
diary of the negotiations be copied. This contained an objective
account of the sessions, along with judicious praise for both Jay
and Franklin. But it included a fulsome description of his
reception by Vergennes as well. The praise accorded him there,
after all, concerned his achievement in the Netherlands. Here
was a chance to convey some information about French policy
while correcting American ignorance of the importance of
Dutch recognition. Accordingly, although Adams had intended the diary copy for Massachusetts congressional delegate
Jonathan Jackson, he changed his mind at the last minute:
"Considering that in the Conferences for the Peace, I had been
very free, which I had Reason to Expect would be misrepre-
sented by Franklin, I suddenly determined to throw into the
packet for Livingston [who might 'make the most and the
worst of it'] what was intended for another."[31]

30. Adams to Edmund Jenings, Sept. 27, 1782, Adams Papers, Reel 358; "The Definitive
Treaty of Peace," appendix to Morris, *Peacemakers*, 463. Adams cultivated his reputation
for stubbornness. He omitted from his peace journal, described immediately below, a draft
stipulating a "right" to dry fish on the shores, which was later amended, in the same
manner, to a "liberty." *Diary and Autobiography*, III, 45–46. Similarly, Adams hereafter
represented himself as adamant in holding out for unconditional recognition of the United
States in Oswald's credentials. Yet, he had suggested to Jay the compromise on which the
talks began.
31. Adams to Samuel Osgood, June 30, 1784, in *Diary and Autobiography*, III, 43n. In part
the gesture continued Adams's vindication of his diplomacy to Livingston, to whom he
exposed himself on this occasion despite knowing him for a political enemy.

When this "peace journal" was read in Congress, the negotiating sessions never came up for discussion. Instead laughter broke out over its description of Adams at Versailles. Although the Massachusetts delegates were able to stop the reading by claiming that the diary had been intended for one of their number and only sent to Livingston by mistake (something Adams let himself believe in later life), Adams never lived it down. In 1800 Alexander Hamilton contemptuously described the scene in Congress in a pamphlet that contributed to Adams's loss of the presidency.

Adams's mistake of sending his peace journal to Livingston was a prelude to other indiscretions as the period between the signing and ratification of the treaty stretched out into months of "perpetual uncertainty." First British, then American ratification of the peace treaty hung in question. In Parliament anger at the concessions granted to the Americans resulted in the resignation of the Shelburne ministry and delay of action until late in the spring. Word of Congress's approval was delayed until July. In the end, though the commissioners undertook commerical discussions with the English negotiators and planned revisions of the treaty, for ten months they did little more than wait, until September 3, 1783, to sign as the definitive treaty the draft that they had completed on November 30, 1782.[32]

Adams was left "with nothing to do but think of my Situation." During these months he went from feeling himself in a "dull Place" to feeling that he should "forever be a dull Man in Europe" to pronouncing himself "out of all Patience," in a "ridiculous State of Torture," "chained here on the only spot in the world where we can be of no use." "Weary, disgusted, affronted and disappointed" and no longer required to "stifle every feeling," he began to let out his resentments. In static, heraldic terms he described Vergennes's machinations as an attack upon his "honour" that had left a "Stain" on his "Livery." Congress, having so weakly acquiesced, could re-

---

32. Adams to Abigail Adams, May 30, 1783, Adams Papers, Reel 360. The treaty reached Congress on Mar. 12 and was ratified Apr. 15.

deem itself only by appointing him its first American ambassador to England.[33]

Adams did not take long to progress from privately making and writing such statements to sending Livingston a long letter showing why an ambassador was needed and, as when he had listed the requirements for a minister to France two years earlier, to giving a sketch of the ideal man—obviously himself. He said that his own vote would go to Jay (he could not himself be considered, presumably because he had sent Congress yet another resignation), but then added the phrase, "Provided that Injustice must finally be done to him, who was the first object of his Country's Choice." The letter only hurt his chances for the appointment.[34]

As the sense of identity between himself and his nation in crisis slipped away, Adams went from seeing America's danger as his own to projecting his own state of mind onto America. "Our Country will be envied," he told his wife; and, he warned Livingston, if it did not adhere to his plan of neutrality, "instead of being the happiest people under the sun . . . we may be the most miserable." America was "at Peace, but not out of Danger," not the least because those who saw through the schemes being laid against her were also endangered by being objects of envy.[35]

During this period Adams established his reputation for vanity and psychological instability. He aired his views and revealed his role in Anglo-American relations with seemingly everyone in Paris, the French and English included. He showed his revoked commerce commission to the English commis-

33. Adams to Abigail Adams, Apr. 16, 1783, to Jenings, Feb. 19, 1783, and to Abigail Adams, Mar. 28, 1783, Adams Papers, Reel 360; *Diary and Autobiography*, III, 103. On the necessity of appointing Adams to England see his letters to Abigail Adams, Feb. 9, 1783, Adams Papers, Reel 360; to Livingston, June 16, 1783, *Works of John Adams*, VIII, 72; to Francis Adrian Vanderkemp, Feb. 6, 1783, Vanderkemp Papers, Pa. Hist. Soc.; and to John Trumbull, Apr. 2, 1790, Adams Papers, Reel 115.

34. Adams to Livingston, Feb. 5, 1783, Adams Papers, Reel 108. See also Adams to Alexandre Dumas, Mar. 28, 1783, *ibid.*, and to Abigail Adams, Feb. 9, 1783, Adams Papers, Reel 360.

35. Adams to Abigail Adams, second letter of Apr. 16, 1783, Adams Papers, Reel 360; to Livingston, July 18, 1783, *Works of John Adams*, VIII, 108; and to James Warren, Apr. 16, 1783, *Warren-Adams Letters*, II, 213.

sioners and had it published in England. "No Wrestler," he told the Englishmen, "was ever so compleatly thrown upon his Back as the C. de Vergennes."[36]

It has been said that Adams's behavior during the months after the peace negotiations "does not make very pleasant reading" and that he "cast all reserve to the wind and started on an undignified and personal campaign against Vergennes, the French Court, and the house of Bourbon." They deserved the worst from Adams to be sure, but as a diplomat he had no right to give vent to his feelings, even in so difficult a time as this.

Yet, it should be recalled that he had been away from his wife and children for three years. This separation became insupportable with the restoration of safe travel across the ocean. On the signing of the preliminary treaty Adams had sent his resignation to Congress and informed his wife several times and by several routes that he planned to return "in the Spring Ships." But he wrote: "I dont love to go home in a Miff, Pet or Passion nor with an ill Grace."[37] He decided to wait awhile either for some mollifying gesture from Congress or for its acknowledgment of his resignation.

As late as September, Adams believed that he soon would be returning to America, and he sustained himself alternately with this belief and with the conviction that Congress was "bound" to send him to England. As the months went by he assured his wife that he would return in the spring, in the fall, during December at the latest, and he urged her in triplicate letters to await his almost certain arrival; if Congress failed to accept his resignation he would return "without Leave." He was not likely to receive an appointment, in any case, because of French influence. On the other hand, his enemies might prefer to isolate him in England rather than have him return to Congress

36. *Diary and Autobiography*, III, 105. Adams gave credit to Jay as well as himself. For publication of his former commission see Hutson, "John Adams and Diplomacy," 173.

37. Chinard, *Honest John Adams*, 180, 178–179; Adams to Abigail Adams, Jan. 22, 1783, Adams Papers, Reel 360. For his resignation see Adams to Livingston, Dec. 4, 1782, Wharton, ed., *Diplomatic Correspondence*, VI, 106, and for an explanation to Congress that his resignation amounted to a request for appointment to England, see Adams to Chief Justice Thomas McKean, Feb. 6, 1783, Vanderkemp Papers.

to expose them. If he should be appointed he could look forward to the worst kind of treatment in England (in this prediction he was, in fact, correct); furthermore, "it is the most difficult Mission in the Universe, and the most desperate, there is no Reputation to be got by it, but a great deal to be lost."[38]

Living in self-created uncertainty and "total Idleness . . . the most insipid and at the same Time disgusting and provoking . . . imaginable," Adams succumbed to his resentments. He insulted Congress by suggesting to Livingston that it had removed his commerce commission to assuage "the envy and green-eyed jealousy of copatriots." He complained with justification of Franklin's abandonment of him two years before during the paper money argument with Vergennes, but he went well beyond the facts when he charged: "Franklin's Motive was to get my Commission, and Vergennes's Motive was to get it for him." Congress's failure to support him against "the Treachery of a Colleague," he admitted to his friend Warren, had been "enough to poison the Life of a Man in its most secret Sources."[39]

Franklin's fame ("I expect Soon to See a proposition to name the 18th Century, the Franklinian Age, le Siecle Franklinnien," Adams wrote) and his patronizing treatment of Adams and Jay after the treaty understandably nettled his colleagues. Furthermore, letters from James Warren and Arthur Lee warned of congressional intrigues by Franklin's supporters. When Franklin began discussions with the Portuguese minister about a commercial treaty without informing either Adams or Jay, and later sent Congress a draft of a proposed treaty without consulting his colleagues, a frustrated Adams complained in letters to Livingston, then proceeded to a study of Portuguese and

38. Adams to Abigail Adams, May 18, 1783, July 13, 1783, Adams Papers, Reels 360, 361. See as well other letters to Abigail Adams on Reel 360, and letters to James Warren, Apr. 9, 1783, *Warren-Adams Letters*, II, 206; to Gerry, Aug. 15, 1783, Wharton, ed., *Diplomatic Correspondence*, VI, 650; and to the president of Congress, Sept. 1, 1783, *ibid.*, 688.

39. Adams to Abigail Adams, May 30, 1783, Adams Papers, Reel 360; to Livingston, Feb. 5, 1783, *Works of John Adams*, VIII, 34; and to James Warren, Mar. 21, 1783 (with another emendation concerning Franklin in the draft, Adams Papers, Reel 108), and Apr. 9, 1783, *Warren-Adams Letters*, II, 197, 206.

South American commerce, pointing out certain stipulations that Franklin should seek. As in other matters concerning Franklin, Adams took infinite pains to demonstrate the difference in energy and comprehensive knowledge between them. Waiting to hear from Congress about his future, he began to think of his vindication as involving at least an equality of standing with Franklin. Adams was indeed undergoing "Jobs Tryals," though they were largely self-inflicted.[40]

As his suffering grew acute his mention of "anxiety" pointed toward a breakdown. (Adams wrote to his wife, "Nothing in Life ever cost me So much Sleep, or made me So many grey Hairs, as the Anxiety, I have Suffered for these Three Years.") He had stopped talking about his health a few months after recovering from his Amsterdam "fever," but now he informed several correspondents that he never had recovered from it. His symptoms, including "my Fidgets"—the term he had used to describe his avowedly nervous complaints while at Congress during 1776—coincided once again with respite and resent-

40. Adams to Arthur Lee, Apr. 10, 1783, and to Abigail Adams, Apr. 16, 1783, Adams Papers, Reels 108, 360. Adams claimed that European and American newspapers were "continually under the influence of the French ministers" and that they manipulated the public opinion that had made Franklin famous. Adams to Livingston, Sept. 8, 1783, *Works of John Adams*, VIII, 149. For the warning letters to Adams see James Warren to Adams, Nov. 1, 1782, and Arthur Lee to Warren, Dec. 12, 1782, *Warren-Adams Letters*, II, 182, 185. About Franklin's negotiations with the Portuguese, Adams protested to Livingston that the only authority under which Franklin could be proceeding would be the joint commission of 1779, of which he too was a member. Adams to Livingston, July 12, 1783, Wharton, ed., *Diplomatic Correspondence*, VI, 538; see also Franklin's letters, *ibid.*, 480, 655, 583. For Adams's further complaints about not seeing the proposed treaty (or another with Denmark) and for his demonstrations of his own knowledge, see his Aug. 1783 letters to Livingston, in *Works of John Adams*, VIII, 128, 130, 131; also 138, 140. Although he wanted vindication and wished that Franklin "was out of public Service, and in Retirement, repenting of his past Life," Adams did not believe that Franklin should be recalled lest public opinion be shocked. To James Warren, Apr. 13, 1783, *Warren-Adams Letters*, II, 211.

Adams believed that Dana, in his embassy to Russia, had also been foiled by Franklin and that Franklin had encroached on Dana's authority by dealing secretly with Sweden, as he had done with Portugal. Adams to James Warren, Sept. 10, 1783, *ibid.*, 222, and to Livingston, Aug. 3, 1783, *Works of John Adams*, VIII, 131. Dana's letter to Adams, June 1, 1783, seems to hint at some such intrigue. *Works of John Adams*, VIII, 65. See also W. P. Cresson, "Francis Dana: An Early Envoy of Trade," *New England Quarterly*, III (1930), 732.

For other complaints about Franklin (and Vergennes) see Adams to Gerry, Sept. 10, 1783, Adams Papers, Reel 107, and Sept. 3, 1783, Wharton, ed., *Diplomatic Correspondence*, VI, 670: "No man will ever be pleasing at a court in general who is not depraved in his morals or warped from your interests."

ment. Adams connected his symptoms to his state of mind when he described to his wife the "Sharp fiery humours which break out in the back of my Neck & in other Parts of me and plague me as much as the uncertainty in which I am in of my future destination."[41]

A brief reunion in Holland with John Quincy Adams, in whose progress he took great pride, combined with the approaching responsibility of signing the definitive treaty of peace, revived Adams for the time being, and he renewed a lapsed correspondence with his wife and children. But he had already gone too far. Franklin now wrote to Congress that Adams "imagined" slights and plots against him. He concluded with the famous estimate that Adams never lived down: "I am persuaded . . . that he means well for his Country, is always an Honest Man, often a wise one, but sometimes, and in some things, absolutely out of his senses." This second clandestine attack on Adams, like his turning on Vergennes, was a typical stroke of Franklinian revenge for having been forced to take sides—this time during the peace negotiations. But Franklin's letter—not his first imputation that a colleague was mad—showed that he knew his man. If not the products of mental disturbance, Adams's suspicions promised to become its cause.[42]

Within a few days, at the beginning of September, the year's frustrations came to a head. On September 3 the definitive treaty of peace was formally signed. Four days later came word that Congress intended to appoint Adams, Franklin, and Jay

41. Adams to Abigail Adams, Mar. 28, 1783, and May 10, 1783, Adams Papers, Reels 360, 361. See also Adams to Livingston, July 9, 1783, *Works of John Adams*, VIII, 86.

42. Franklin to Livingston, July 22, 1783, Smyth, ed., *Writings of Benjamin Franklin*, VIII, 62. Franklin had imputed insanity to Arthur Lee (in an unsent letter), suggesting that he should control his "Sick Mind, which is forever tormenting itself, with its Jealousies, Suspicions, and Fancies." Henderson, "Congressional Factionalism," *WMQ*, 3d Ser., XXVII (1970), 249. Page Smith provides perspective when he writes that Adams's "dislike of Franklin was certainly an obsession, one that was shared by every American envoy with the exception of the unhappy Silas Deane." *John Adams*, I, 570. For the falling off of Adams's letters home from his arrival in the Netherlands to the peace signing see Peter Shaw, "Diplomacy and Domesticity: An Intimate Record," review of *Adams Family Correspondence*, III–IV, *American Scholar*, XLII (1973), 688–689.

joint commissioners of commerce to all European countries. Adams had not been made ambassador to England, nor had his commerce commission been restored exclusively to himself. His services in Europe either were at an end or would be reduced to more such negotiations as those that had dragged out over the summer.

Just as before his breakdown in Holland, Adams reacted to his change of status with apparent equanimity. He wrote to his wife that "this Resolution of Congress deserves my Gratitude, it is highly honourable to me, and restores me my Feelings, which a former Proceeding had taken away." He noted that the commission was being established in response to one of his letters to Congress and that it listed his name first. He declared: "I am now indifferent who goes to England." As for working with Franklin, "Jay and I, do admirably well with the old Man," he wrote to Elbridge Gerry. "We go on very Smoothly, and make him know what is right and do it for absolutely he does not know of himself." Only the number and excessiveness of Adams's professions that he was satisfied gave a hint of his real feelings.[43]

Adams was compensating for his disappointment by inflating the importance of the new commission. At the same time, contradictorily, he convinced himself that he would remain in Europe no more than another six months. For more than a year he had been announcing his imminent departure in letters home, each time mentioning that he would send for his family if it appeared that he would be forced to remain on duty in Europe. Now he urged his wife to set out immediately, even though he believed that she probably would have to return to America with him soon after arriving. Ominously, he gave as an important excuse for staying the need to combat Franklin's

43. Adams to Abigail Adams, Sept. 7, 1783, Adams Papers, Reel 361 (the word "restores" is conjectural); to James Warren, Sept. 10, 1783, *Warren-Adams Letters*, II, 221; and to Gerry, Sept. 8, 1783, Adams Papers, Reel 106. An incomplete version of the last letter, lacking the quoted sentence, appears in Wharton, ed., *Diplomatic Correspondence*, VI, 684, under an incorrect date, Sept. 9, 1783. For professions of gratitude to Congress see Adams to James Warren, Sept. 10, 1783, *Warren-Adams Letters*, II, 221, and to the president of Congress, Sept. 8, 1783, *Works of John Adams*, VIII, 147.

"low cunning and mean craft" from which "the publick" otherwise would suffer.[44]

The situation repeated the circumstances of Adams's break-downs in 1771 and 1781. Overwork, this time self-induced, a sudden respite followed by lack of adequate recognition, and a nominal success without clear defeat of his nemesis—once Hutchinson, now Franklin for the second time—confronted Adams in uncanny repetition, down to the detail of Franklin's being the first to receive news of the new commerce commission, just as he had first received news of the new peace commission two years before.

On September 10, 1783, after finishing a series of letters assuring his friends that he was satisfied, Adams had to sign a joint letter of the commissioners that amounted to an endorsement of Franklin. It informed Congress, "As we are satisfied with the conduct of Mr. [William Temple] Franklin . . . we propose to appoint him" as secretary. Adams had complained when Franklin, without consulting, appointed his grandson acting secretary of the peace commission, and he had grown convinced that "the Plan is laid between the C. de Vergennes and the Dr., to get Billy made Minister to this Court and not improbably the Dr. to London."[45]

On this same day Adams received a note from Franklin that quoted a letter "from a very respectable person in America." "It is confidently reported, propagated, and believed by some among us," it stated, "that the court of France was at the bottom against our obtaining the fishery and territory in that great extent in which both are secured to us by the treaty; that our minister at that court [Franklin] favored, or did not oppose this design against us, and that it was entirely owing to the firmness, sagacity, and disinterestedness of Mr. Adams, with whom Mr. Jay united, that we have obtained these important advantages." Appealing to Adams as "a brother commissioner,"

44. Adams to Gerry, Sept. 10, 1783, and to Abigail Adams, Sept. 10, 1783, Adams Papers, Reels 107, 361.

45. Adams, Franklin, and Jay to the president of Congress, Sept. 10, 1783, Wharton, ed., *Diplomatic Correspondence*, VI, 691; *Diary and Autobiography*, III, 103 (Jan. 11, 1783).

Franklin wrote that he had "no doubt" of Adams's "readiness" to supply him with "certificates, that will entirely destroy the effect of that accusation." Franklin averred, "I cannot allow that I was behind any . . . in zeal and faithfulness. I therefore think that I ought not to suffer an accusation, which falls little short of treason to my country."[46]

Franklin's construction of the matter, in which he made the question one of his "fidelity," "zeal," and "faithfulness" rather than whether or not he had agreed with Vergennes, put Adams in a difficult position. Jay, who received the same letter from Franklin, wrote back on the next day: "I do not recollect the least difference in sentiment between us respecting the boundaries or fisheries"—he did not mention the disagreement over how they should have been defended. Whether or not Adams, then intimate with Jay and his family, learned of this reply, he decided not to bring his opinion of Franklin out in the open. Three days after receiving Franklin's request he wrote to him: "It is unnecessary for me to say anything upon this subject more than to quote the words which I wrote in the evening of the 30th of November, 1782, and which have been received and read in Congress."[47] Adams enclosed the passage from his peace journal on their unproductive, one-sided conversation before the negotiations, transcribing as far as Franklin's turning to Jay to announce his agreement with his colleagues. The entry did include Adams's acknowledgment of Franklin's usefulness at the rest of the sessions.

In view of Adams's real feelings his response was the feeblest imaginable. Yet, sending his peace journal to Congress and then providing Franklin with this excerpt represented the

46. Franklin to Jay, Sept. 10, 1783, Wharton, ed., *Diplomatic Correspondence*, VI, 686. This is identical to the letter that Franklin sent to Adams on the same day. Franklin omitted to transcribe from the letter he had received a passage that Adams would have wished to comment on: the charge that "the court of France secretly traversed Mr. Adams' views in Holland for obtaining . . . an acknowledgement of our independence, and that the same part has been acted in Spain and Russia." Wharton, ed., *Diplomatic Correspondence*, VI, 686n. One wonders if Franklin had noticed Adams's special association of the word "zeal" with himself.

47. Jay to Franklin, Sept. 11, 1783, Wharton, ed., *Diplomatic Correspondence*, VI, 692–693; Adams to Franklin, Sept. 13, 1783, *ibid.*, 696.

closest he could bring himself to a public statement on the relative contributions of the peace commissioners. Faced with the opportunity to state his case, Adams proved incapable of self-serving denunciation. Indeed, the excerpt suggested his own failure to unite the commission more clearly than it did Franklin's dogged support of French policy. (Franklin forwarded it to Congress along with Jay's letter.) Hereafter he could not expect ever to be vindicated in his quarrel with Franklin. On the following day Adams collapsed.

This new fever, which proved to be his last, "cured" Adams, as he put it. Although it left him "emaciated and weak," he was "persuaded," he wrote his wife, that it would do him "much good." He meant spiritually, not physically, for he assumed a mental cause for his illness.[48] A different John Adams emerged from this breakdown. Still insistent upon due recognition, he appeared to have learned the personal cost of pursuing it. During his remaining five years in Europe he found an outlet in writing. For a while friendships instead of rivalries sustained him. Able in consequence to look at the world in a larger perspective, he dealt with his aspirations and disappointments in tracts on government.

48. *Diary and Autobiography*, III, 144n, and Adams to Abigail Adams from London, Oct. 14, 1783, Adams Papers, Reel 361. In this letter Adams attributed his illness to "too close an Application to writing" and "continued application of mind."

VIII
The Consolations of Philosophy
1783–1788

When Adams recovered in October from the illness fol-
lowing his answer to Franklin, he traveled to England for
his health. There Benjamin West and John Singleton Copley,
the leading painters of the day (and both Americans) took
portraits of him during his short vacation. Both showed a
portly, composed figure in middle age enjoying his recent
diplomatic achievement at Paris. In West's painting, which
includes the other Americans at the peace treaty, Adams is
more prominent than Franklin, whose position indicates but a
guiding spirit. Both portraits suggest that Adams expected to
be viewed not as a personality but as a man of accomplishment
and consequence. Copley's seven-foot, full-length figure in
formal diplomatic costume shows an aristocratic, self-possessed
professional rather than the harried, explosive, combination
scribe-and-bargainer that Adams was in actuality—Adams
quickly recognized the painting as a "Piece of Vanity" (see
figure 2).[1]

Yet, in the genuine serenity that underlies the attempted
aristocratic assurance in these paintings one sees that for once
his sense of vindication was not accompanied by resentment.
Copley's portrait conveys a new, philosophic calm. Its preten-
tious paraphernalia—the statesman's ceremonial sword; the

---

1. Andrew Oliver, *Portraits of John and Abigail Adams* (Cambridge, Mass., 1967), 25.

maps, parchments, and globe that Adams stands next to, and the allegorical statue of peace and innocence presiding over him—accurately symbolize the philosophical period of life begun with his trip to England. Adams sat for these portraits at a time when, out of frustration, he might have been busying himself. He had expected to begin commerce negotiations with the English but was delayed for want of credentials from an indecisive Congress. A commercial union with England, something offered by the colonies before they resorted to independence, would justify his own long-standing obsession with commerce. However, rather than expressing disappointment, he devoted himself to sightseeing. He viewed such sights as Buckingham Palace and the Houses of Parliament, was treated with deference by English officialdom, and took hope for Anglo-American relations.

In January 1784, two months along in his vacation for health, Adams reached Bath to take the waters. Almost immediately after arriving, he was summoned to rescue the unpaid American loan in Holland—a task he regarded as impossible as he set off. His crossing of the wintry North Sea has justly been called "heroic," and his later account of it is undoubtedly the most vivid passage of description he ever wrote. Adams wrote that on this voyage he had passed from one stage of life to the next: "The passengers were required to get out of the boat and walk upon the ice. . . . we were all day and till quite night in making the passage. . . . I was chilled to the heart, and looked I suppose, as I felt, like a withered old worn out carcase. Our polite skipper frequently eyed me and said he pitied the old man."[2] Soon after this trip he gave John Quincy Adams the maxim, "Let nothing frett you, or grieve you but your own faults."[3] He had felt old and above the battle before, but this time he held to a philosophical calm substantially until he left Europe in 1788.

During spring 1784 Adams learned more about the congressional struggle over his commissions and instructions. One of

2. *Diary and Autobiography*, III, 149n, and 153n, quoting Adams's *Boston Patriot* account.
3. Adams to John Quincy Adams, [May–June] 1784, Adams Papers, Reel 363.

his informants, Samuel Osgood, a Massachusetts representative and casual acquaintance, wrote him a gargantuan letter full of the jesuitical intrigues of the French "to clip your Wings, and make you more tame and docile," Franklin's maneuvers to make his grandson a minister, and the congressional "Party" (still a dreaded word) against Adams. Osgood revealed the laughter in Congress as Adams's peace journal was read, and the fact that "the infamous Instructions [were] made out for you." Adams was overwhelmed. The terms were his very own; the revelations confirmed his worst suspicions. He could not trust his "Temper" to write a response to Osgood. Yet, he could take satisfaction when Osgood wrote that "the Names of those Comm'rs who nobly dared to act contrary to the Intention of that inglorious restriction will be immortalized."[4] Although it took months for Adams to absorb these and other revelations reaching him from America during 1784, he eventually reacted with his usual mildness to direct attack. Once again he sought not revenge but justification—in the form of his receiving the ambassadorship to England.

Without his wife, however, Adams could not bring himself to live again near Franklin in Paris, and he delayed his return there with telltale multiple excuses: poor health, important money negotiations in Holland, and claims that his presence was not needed. In the meantime, though, Abigail Adams had responded to his contradictory instructions by finally setting sail. When Adams learned in July that she had reached England, he announced, after eight months of avoiding Franklin, that it was essential for him to join his "colleagues in Paris without Loss of Time" and even added that he felt "lucky" to be going.[5]

4. Osgood to Adams, Dec. 7, 1783, Burnett, ed., *Letters of Continental Congress*, II, 383, 380, 381. "Temper": Adams to Osgood, Dec. 13, 1784, Osgood Papers, N.-Y. Hist. Soc. See also two drafts of an apparently unsent letter to Osgood, Apr. 9, 1784, Adams Papers, Reel 362. Page Smith describes one of these letters about Franklin as containing "almost pathological bitterness." *John Adams*, I, 569.

5. Adams to Abigail Adams, Aug. 1, 1784, and July 26, 1784, Adams Papers, Reel 363. For Adams's excuses see his letters to the president of Congress: Feb. 10, 1784, Adams Papers, Reel 107, also in *Works of John Adams*, VIII, 178; Mar. 9, 1784, Wharton, ed., *Diplomatic Correspondence*, VI, 785; and July 5, 1784, Adams Papers, Reel 363; and also Lyman H. Butterfield, "John Adams and the Beginnings of Netherlands-American Friend-

In France, Adams settled in Auteuil, the suburb of Paris where he had convalesced after his breakdown during the previous fall. The latter half of 1784 and the first few months of 1785 made a domestic interval that seems to have been the happiest in his life. Making "a little America of my family" he had the "Indolence and Ease" to rest himself, study commercial treaties, read the books he had started buying in England, entertain his small circle of philosophical Frenchmen, and spend time with his family. He rented at a bargain a huge house of decayed, decadent elegance—"far Superiour to Dr Franklines at Passy!"—and mused on the salacious goings on its mirrored boudoir had entertained. Abigail Adams, their daughter, Abigail, then nineteen, John Quincy Adams, and their servants made up the household. Together the family strolled in the Tuileries, toured the city, and viewed the latest advance of the century, balloon ascensions.[6]

Adams helped John Quincy, who had decided to take a degree at Harvard, prepare himself in the classics and "geometry and science."[7] With Jefferson, who had arrived soon after Abigail Adams to replace John Jay, Adams could discuss any number of philosophical matters, including "the platonic philosophy of some of our articles" in a proposed treaty with Prussia's philosopher-king, Frederick II. Franklin's and Adams's intellectual circles differed but overlapped, so that the two men met together not only on business but at soirees. During this quiet period Franklin's ideas and conversation overcame Adams's grievances.

---

ship," in *Butterfield in Holland: A Record of L. H. Butterfield's Pursuit of the Adamses Abroad in 1959* (Cambridge, Mass., 1961), 57.

6. Adams to John Jay, Jan. 31, 1785, and to Francis Adrian Vanderkemp, Feb. 17, 1817, Adams Papers, Reels 107, 123. See also Gilbert Chinard, *Honest John Adams*, 189; [Caroline de Windt, ed.], *Journal and Correspondence of Miss Adams, Daughter of John Adams, Second President of the United States. Edited by Her Daughter* (New York, 1841), 40–41, hereafter cited as *Journal and Correspondence of Miss Adams*; Howard C. Rice, Jr., ed., *The Adams Family in Auteuil, 1784–1785, As Told in the Letters of Abigail Adams*, Massachusetts Historical Society pamphlet (Boston, 1956). In his autobiography Adams gave 1784, the year Abigail Adams joined him in Europe, instead of 1764 as his marriage date. The slip suggested that the later year amounted to a second honeymoon.

7. Memories dictated by Adams to Harriet Welsh, about 1813, Adams Papers, Reel 327.

Adams still looked for his appointment to England, but in the meantime he had the satisfaction of prevailing over Franklin in other ways. First, he learned that he had been put at the head of the long-delayed commerce commission and that William Temple Franklin was dismissed as its secretary. These decisions followed another congressional battle between Adams and Franklin supporters in which Franklin's shortcomings had been aired. Elbridge Gerry provided Adams with this information and added that when Franklin heard of the debate he would "have no reason to Suppose that his Conduct is much approved. Indeed We have not been reserved in Congress with respect to the Doctor, having declared in so many Words, that so far advanced in Years and so tractable is he . . . that it has become a matter of indifference to Us, whether we imploy him or the C——t d V——s to negotiate our Concerns at the C—— of V——s——."[8] Again the characterization was exactly Adams's own; with its unnecessarily veiled mention of Vergennes and the Court of Versailles it vindicated Adams in terms that could not have been more gratifying.

Within months of the Adams family's establishing in Auteuil in summer 1784, then, the contest with Franklin was over. Numerous letters from America about Franklin stirred Adams up, and a complete copy of Franklin's "out of his senses" letter moved him to another denunciation ("the most unprovoked, the most cruel, and the most malicious misrepresentations, which ever were put upon Paper"). But he also noted with softened feelings that Franklin's gout had confined him to his house for a year except for "four times to dine with me." Once he had the advantage Adams could not sustain his resentment.[9]

8. Adams to Baron de Thulemeier, Feb. 13, 1785, *Works of John Adams*, VIII, 225; Elbridge Gerry to Adams, June 16, 1784, Adams Papers, Reel 363. See also Stephen Higginson to [Jonathan Jackson], Apr. 1784, "Letters of Stephen Higginson, 1783–1804," American Historical Association, *Annual Report for the Year 1896* (Washington, D.C., 1897), I, 717–719, on the congressional contest.

9. Adams to Gerry, Dec. 12, 1784, Adams Papers, Reel 107. Abigail Adams, Jr., recorded at least eight visits from and to Franklin. See *Journal and Correspondence of Miss Adams*, 19–63 *passim*. For Adams's softened feelings about Franklin see his letter to Gerry, Jan. 31, 1785, Adams Papers, Reel 107; Smith, *John Adams*, II, 616; and his letters to

Both men, after all, had philosophical bents. With their rivalry abated they found much in common. Furthermore, each was sustained by the private contemplation of himself made possible by the quiet life in France. Franklin was writing the second, short portion of his autobiography, with its account of his youthful attempt to master a chart of virtues, humility among them. Franklin's autobiographical "strategy of humility," as it has been called, had a specially poignant application to Adams, who suffered all his life from being unable to adopt the conventional poses of humility.[10]

While Franklin thought over his career in Passy, Adams thought over his prospects in nearby Auteuil. With John Jay returned from France and appointed by Congress to manage foreign affairs, Adams could advance the idea of an ambassador to England with the likelihood of a better hearing than under Livingston in 1783. In April 1785, unaware that Congress had appointed him in February, Adams wrote that he would no longer "be intimidated from giving this advice [that a minister be sent] by any apprehension that I shall be suspected of a design or desire of going to England myself."[11] Two weeks later he learned both that he had been made ambassador and that his previous self-recommendation had led to a congressional discussion of his ambition and vanity. The details were again supplied by Elbridge Gerry in a letter justly called "tactless." That the debate in Congress "soiled" or "marred" the appointment for Adams is less clear. "I perceive, that I received a trouncing in Congress," he wrote, "& perhaps not wholly unmerited"; and he told Gerry that "of all the Letters I ever received in my Life . . . excepting one from Mr. Osgood, this is perhaps the most friendly & faithful."[12]

Jefferson in July and Oct. 1785, in Lester J. Cappon, ed., *The Adams-Jefferson Letters: The Complete Correspondence between Thomas Jefferson and Abigail and John Adams* (Chapel Hill, N.C., 1959), I, 40, 41, 42, 43, 85, 87.

10. On Franklin's guilt see Paul W. Conner, *Poor Richard's Politicks: Benjamin Franklin and His New American Order* (New York, 1965), 212–213, and, on Franklin's "strategy of humility," *ibid.*, 152–153.

11. Adams to Jay, Apr. 13, 1785, *Works of John Adams*, VIII, 234.

12. Smith, *John Adams*, II, 621; Howe, *Changing Political Thought of John Adams*, 124n;

The news of his appointment made Adams uneasy but did not presage another illness. This time his triumph had come gradually, in the presence of his family, and concerned the future rather than the past. As confident as at any time in his life, Adams produced his most searching self-analysis in two letters on vanity to Elbridge Gerry.

In his first letter Adams rebutted the charge of having a "weak Passion" by pointing out the simplicity of his manner of living. In his second he detailed several types of vanity and admitted to one. He was guilty neither of display nor of "empty boastings of Wealth, Birth, Power, Beauty, Parts learning, Virtues or Conduct." His vanity lay in being unable to suppress satisfaction over the "transcendant Success" of his long course of service to his country. Such vanity as his own, "although a Weakness," was "a real Proof of a valuable Character." Adams went on to demonstrate the inevitability, the universality, among public men of this weak passion for rejoicing in service to one's country and to show how much less dangerous it was than the strong, positive passions of "Avarice & Ambition" or "Craft, Cunning, Intrigue." Indeed, to deny having the weak passion showed more vanity than to admit it.

His own admission marked what Adams would have called an "epocha" in his life. Yet, it did not plumb the true nature of his passion. His present enjoyment of recognition and success made an exception in his life. Typically he felt resentment at the public—either for impeding his success or failing to recognize it. Although Adams might for a few days regard appointment to England as a proper recognition of his triumph, by the end of his letter to Gerry he revealed how tardy and insubstantial it seemed. He was not done with resentment, then, even in this letter. First the question of pretended humility led him inevitably to Franklin: "I never knew but one Man who pretended to be wholly free from it [vanity], . . . and him I know to be in his heart the vainest Man, and the falsest Character I

Adams to Richard Henry Lee (then the president of Congress), Apr. 29, 1785, and to Gerry, Apr. 28, 1785, Adams Papers, Reel 107.

have ever met with in life." Then, contemplating Franklin led once more to the assertion that the congressional charges of vanity "smell, as rank as the Ripeness of a Rabits tail, of french Politicks."

Thus, without realizing it, Adams admitted to his special kind of combative resentment. For if the French were responsible for the charge that he was vain, then he was referring not to the present time of success but to 1778 and 1779, when he had lived resentfully in Franklin's shadow. Confusing old and new charges of vanity, Adams showed that he felt guilty of them all. Just as with his theory of emulation, when it came to his own case Adams forgot his distinction between justified pride and illusory vanity. "Instead of mortifying me," he wrote, "I declare that I believe it [the French 'Insinuation of Vanity'] has increased my Vanity and made me more careless of avoiding the Appearance of it, than any Thing that ever happened to me in my whole life."

In this letter Adams expressed the hurt that he had nursed since his return to Europe in 1779—a period of five years. He mentioned the conspiracy of "English French and American Politicks watching the Moment to push me over," then reiterated his wish to return home in order to be away from constant exposure to attacks, and closed by repeating that he could have made himself loved and famous if, like Franklin (again not named), he had cooperated with French designs against America. "When a Man is hurt," he concluded, "he loves to talk of his wound, and I know of no other way to account for this long letter."[13] Although he had admitted to no more than a minor form of vanity, Adams refrained from sending his letter to Gerry. Yet, the act of writing seems to have enabled him thereafter to allude to his reputation for vanity. He joked about it for the rest of his life—rather awkwardly and unsatisfyingly, but with perhaps some relief from his weight of guilt.

Within weeks of receiving his appointment as ambassador, Adams reached London. He officially announced his arrival on

13. Adams to Gerry, May 2, 1785, Adams Papers, Reel 364.

the day he reached the city and was presented to George III less than a week later, on June 1, 1785. For all his optimistic dispatch, though, Adams had prepared himself for disappointment, and it was well that he did so.

The embassy represented a test of the theory that an American minister could eliminate the restrictive trade decrees imposed by the English after the preliminary treaty of November 1782. Adams did not plan to go as a supplicant from a minor to a major power, but rather with appeals to British self-interest similar to those he had employed at the peace talks. But not only trade was involved. According to its conduct toward America, England would go down to "Perdition" or "redeem" itself "from total destruction."[14] Adams proposed to convince the English that the war with America threatened by their unfriendly trade policies was in the interest of neither side. England should not wish to see American neutrality broken in any way—not even by the two countries' joining together in a war against a third power: "It is so much the interest of England that we should be neutral in a future war, that I am persuaded cool and candid reasoning with their ministers upon the subject would convince them of it. The force of truth is greater, even in the minds of politicans, than the world in general is aware of."[15] The closing remark told more about Adams's faith in the Enlightenment than it did about politicians' minds, as a few months in England sufficed to demonstrate.

George III showed "so marked an attention" when he received him at court that initially Adams hoped for "a residence less painful than I once expected." Wisely, he kept his confidence to himself, toning down in his first report to Jay his enthusiastic notes on the king's manners and his own elaborate deference during their interview.[16] He quickly realized, however, that he had no chance of success in the main objects of his

14. Adams to Richard Cranch, Apr. 27, 1785, Adams Papers, Reel 107, and to the president of Congress, Nov. 13, 1783, *Works of John Adams*, VIII, 160.
15. Adams to Jay, Apr. 13, 1785, *Works of John Adams*, VIII, 235.
16. Adams to Jay, June 2, 1785, *ibid.*, 258. On Adams's interview with the king see this

embassy. Despite the peace treaty the English would not evacuate or even discuss their northern forts in America until the debts being held up in American courts had been paid to English creditors. Nor would they discuss a commercial treaty or adjust their crippling trade restrictions while the American confederacy remained powerless to retaliate with effective counter restrictions. Surprised, but without bitterness, Adams concluded by the end of 1785: "No step that I can take, no language I can hold, will do any good, or, indeed, much harm."[17]

The equanimity of his response to failure typified Adams's handling of a series of both serious and trivial annoyances such as would have brought him near to despair at any other time in his life. To begin with, Congress cut ministerial salaries by one-fifth. Without an independent income Adams was hard put to dress himself, his wife, daughter, and servants to be received properly at court. Unable to entertain as elegantly or as often as he was entertained, he was ridiculed for his parsimony by the London press. Nevertheless, he reasoned, "I am the best man in the world to bear it, and so be it." In London he took pleasure in visits to William Herschel's astronomical observatory.[18] He found a circle of unpretentious, philosophical Englishmen whom he could informally have to either breakfast or dinner, and he filled out his table with resident or visiting Americans. When he had to dine with British ministers he left his wife at home.

Congress had let Adams down yet again, not only in cutting his salary but in ensuring his failure: first, by not carrying out its side of the peace treaty—an omission that gave the English

---

letter with changes in Adams Papers, Reel 107. On Adams's report to Jefferson, see Boyd *et al.*, eds., *Jefferson Papers*, VIII, 526; also L. H. Butterfield, "New Light on the North Atlantic Triangle in the 1780's," *WMQ*, 3d Ser., XXI (1964), 596–606.

17. Adams to Jay, Dec. 3, 1785, *Works of John Adams*, VIII, 355. Needless to say, Adams was tireless in pursuing his assignments. See his letter to Jay, Aug. 25, 1785, *ibid.*, 302, 308, for his masterly interviews with Pitt and Lord Carmarthen.

18. Adams to James Warren, Aug. 27, 1784, *ibid.*, IX, 526. On the relative poverty of the Adamses as dealt with by the press see Smith, *John Adams*, II, 646; *Journal and Correspondence of Miss Adams*, 83–84.

an excuse for not evacuating their forts—and second, by not retaliating against English commercial measures—which left Adams without any bargaining leverage in trade talks. Adams complained about his "lot." He talked "as usual," as his daughter put it, of taking an early leave from England, and he declared himself almost ready to forsake his neutralist principles and take up a defensive alliance with France. Yet, Charles Francis Adams rightly called the frustration arising from his country's actions and inaction but "a single drop of bitterness."[19]

More striking than Adams's disappointment were his balanced manner in urging the measures necessary to provide him with a bargaining position and his realization that he could not indulge in "high language" to the English. He typified his frame of mind when, urging that loyalist refugees be allowed to return to their homes, he wrote: "Angry Passions and especially personal resentments we Should Sacrifice like men." With the same philosophical practicality he favored what proved to be the only workable approach with the Algerine pirates: to pay tribute money along with the major European powers. When Jefferson, Franklin's replacement in Paris, advocated fighting the pirates, Adams showed how paying would be cheaper, though "humiliating," then added with genial realism that, because of congressional penury and indecisiveness, "your Plan of fighting will no more be adopted than mine of negotiating."[20]

In the meantime, while Adams's diplomatic notes were ignored at court, English society ostracized him along with all Americans unlucky enough to have chosen to spend this period in England. Charles Francis Adams in his biography described the treatment accorded his grandfather: "Of civility, cold and formal, such as only the English know how in perfection to

19. Adams to Gerry, May 24, 1786, and Abigail Adams, Jr., to John Quincy Adams, Oct. 18, 1785, Adams Papers, Reels 113, 366; *Works of John Adams*, I, 436. On forming a French alliance, see Adams to Jefferson, July 31, 1786, Cappon, ed., *Adams-Jefferson Letters*, I, 147.

20. Adams to Jay, Dec. 3, 1785, *Works of John Adams*, VIII, 355; to Rufus King, Jan. 22, 1786, Adams Papers, Reel 113; and to Jefferson, July 31, 1786, Cappon, ed., *Adams-Jefferson Letters*, I, 147.

make offensive, there was enough. No marked offence; but supercilious indifference." Adams gradually lost faith in his idea of a salvation for England dependent on America, the country "destined beyond a doubt to be the greatest power on earth, and that within the life of man." "The mistaken Policy of G Britain" not only gave rise to "all" of America's "difficulties" but would cripple the mother country as well. The real reasons for England's anti-American policy were fear and envy of the new country's coming greatness. The maritime laws attempted to slow the growth of an American navy, while newspaper propaganda was calculated to discourage emigration—"so humiliating to their pride—so mortifying to their vanity"—because it threatened to depopulate England while speeding American growth.[21]

Nevertheless, Adams relinquished without complaint the hope of introducing into an Anglo-American treaty the same ideals that Jefferson and he had projected for a treaty with Frederick the Great. Realizing that England would never interest itself in these ideals, he wrote to Jay, "We have hitherto been the bubbles of our own philosophical and equitable liberality," and, free tradesman though he was, he recommended restrictive American laws in retaliation. Similarly, his original commitment to American independence had conceived of a country made up of state governments with a Congress elected to act for the states chiefly in diplomatic affairs. The English believed Congress incapable of retaliatory trade measures; in effect, they told Adams: "You have no government." He therefore changed to urging "supremacy" for Congress in regulating all American trade.[22]

21. *Works of John Adams*, I, 425; Adams to Jay, May 8, 1785, *ibid.*, VIII, 246; to Matthew Robinson, Mar. 4, 1786, and to R. H. Lee, July 15, 1785, Adams Papers, Reels 113, 107.

22. Adams to Jay, Aug. 10, 1785, June 26, 1785, and July 29, 1785, all in *Works of John Adams*, VIII, 299, 274, 289. For the treaty ideas see *ibid.*, I, 416–417, VIII, 308; Chinard, *Honest John Adams*, 188. Adams's later claim that he was against the philosophical parts of the treaty may be dismissed as a residue of his anger at Jefferson. See his letter to Mercy Warren, July 11, 1807, "Correspondence between Adams and Mercy Warren," Mass. Hist. Soc., *Colls.*, 5th Ser., IV, 323. Adams may have recalled that it was to Jefferson that he recommended American restrictive trade decrees in opposition to the principles of their treaty. Nov. 4, 1785, Cappon, ed., *Adams-Jefferson Letters*, I, 89.

In America, too, England's challenge appeared as another threat to independence. Once again an English assault on American trade spurred calls for the self-denial of nonimportation and for the formation of a new government (with the latter resulting in a Constitutional Convention). With these calls came a revival of old fears about a decline into luxury and vice. In fall 1786 news reached England of Shays's Rebellion, a tax revolt in ever-recalcitrant western Massachusetts. Unlike his American correspondents Adams did not view the disturbances as signs of the imminent dissolution of government. But they reawakened his disapproval of mob violence and his dislike of innovation. The same people who now made up the Shaysites had opposed his Massachusetts Constitution in 1779; they continued to oppose his governor and senate, as well as property qualifications for voting and officeholding.[23]

The years of war had done much to muffle the tone of Enlightenment speculativeness notable during the Declaration of Independence period of the American Revolution. In Europe, where the American struggle was viewed as an "experiment" as much as a war, Adams continued to find the general principle in particular questions. With American independence recognized by Great Britain, both Europe and America wondered if the republican experiment could succeed. The inability of the states and Congress to pay their debts or concert a maritime policy in response to England's shipping decrees suggested not only difficulties of the moment but also an inherent weakness

23. See Patterson, *Political Parties*, 247. On the revival of fears about American decline see Morgan, "Puritan Ethic and the American Revolution," *WMQ*, 3d Ser., XXIV (1967), 36–38. For Adams on mobs see his letter to Benjamin Hichborne, Jan. 27, 1787, Adams Papers, Reel 113. On the Shaysites as dangerous innovators see Adams to Jay, Nov. 30, 1786, written on "the same day that he penned his 'don't worry' comment to Jefferson." Quoted by Adrienne Koch, ed., *Adams and Jefferson: "Posterity Must Judge,"* Berkeley Series in American History (Chicago, 1963), 21. Later comments on Shays's Rebellion by Adams emphasized the resolutions of Massachusetts county conventions as much as the violence as reasons for his deciding to write his *Defence of the Constitutions*. See Adams to Thomas Boylston Adams, Jan. 24, 1801, Adams Papers, Reel 400, and to Samuel Perley, June 19, 1809, *Works of John Adams*, IX, 623. Joyce Appleby, "The New Republican Synthesis and the Changing Political Ideas of John Adams," *American Quarterly*, XXV (1973), 583n, corrects the tendency of scholars to accept Adams's later claims that Shays's Rebellion caused him to write the *Defence*.

of republican government. Similarly, many believed that if America should manage to survive foreign threats, pressures from within would eventually bring it to monarchy. The country might succumb in the very process of correcting its weaknesses; thus, in an attempt to avoid anarchy Americans might turn to a dictator in the characteristic manner of democratic governments.

This last possibility was by no means dismissed when Washington showed himself uninterested in becoming the king of America; for, if not by a man on horseback, monarchy could come in quietly and slowly with the gradual introduction of aristocratic distinctions. With their classical educations the thinkers of the day agreed when they learned of the Cincinnati, a society of retired military officers, that such aristocratic distinctions had been introduced. Eventually these could become hereditary, as they were with the Cincinnati, and so lead to a European social order and then inevitably to monarchy.

At first Adams saw the Cincinnati in this light, only to decide that, as with Shays's Rebellion, his friends in America exaggerated the dangers. They suggested that the Cincinnati was part of a French plot calculated to exacerbate a process of generalized internal decay in the United States. They reported to Adams a frightening picture of bankruptcies, a falling off of trade, the ineffectiveness of a Congress that could not command a quorum, a rising spirit of aristocratic luxury, and, finally, disorder, anarchy, and the immediate threat of civil war.[24] Taking a broader view, in summer 1786 Adams went to Holland to sign his philosophical Prussian treaty. There, buoyed up by his one satisfactory accomplishment since the peace, he experienced a "profound effect" when he attended

24. See Samuel Osgood to Adams, Dec. 14, 1783, Adams Papers, Reel 362; James Warren to Adams, Sept. 4, 1785, Oct. 2, 1786, and May 18, 1787, *Warren-Adams Letters*, II, 264, 278–279, 291–292; undated manuscript "from Mr. Higginson" to Adams, [Feb. 9, 1784?], Adams Papers, Reel 362. See also Smith, *John Adams*, II, 617–685 *passim*; Abigail Adams to Adams, Feb. 13, 1779, and Abigail Adams to John Thaxter, June 17, 1782, *Adams Family Correspondence*, III, 168, IV, 331. For Adams's mild reaction see his letters to [Arthur Lee?], Apr. 6, 1784, and to Gerry, Apr. 25, 1785, Adams Papers, Reels 362, 107; and Cappon, ed., *Adams-Jefferson Letters*, I, 207.

206 / *The Character of John Adams*

ceremonies in Utrecht installing a new government of his patriot friends in that city. He saw the dawning of a millennium. "In no Instance of ancient or modern History," he wrote Jefferson, "have the People ever asserted more unequivocally their own inherent and unalienable Sovereignty."[25]

Yet, more than confidence in republicanism and America was called for in view of the reports from home. A French philosophical school represented by Turgot and Franklin advocated the abandonment of the tripartite governments that had been adopted by most of the states (on the model, Adams believed, of his Massachusetts Constitution). The new theorists favored the old, 1776 innovation of a single assembly that had been adopted in Pennsylvania (where Franklin had presided over the state constitutional convention). For Adams, balance in government, like the balance of power among nations, represented a logical extension of his lifelong attempt to harness self-interest. Attacks on the idea of balance (which informed his international no less than his domestic outlook) returned Adams to "Politicks," the subject he described as "the most interesting that can engage the understanding or the heart."[26]

Adams decided both to correct the error of the single-assembly idea (put forth a few years earlier in a letter from Turgot to Adams's friend Richard Price) and to express his faith in the American experiment. In 1776, against a similar background of anarchic violence, attempted constitutional innovation, and calls for a renewed morality, Adams had written *Thoughts on Government*, his defense of the ancient, New England constitutional system. In 1786 he responded to the combined challenge of English arrogance and American disorders by looking back to the same constitutional system that he had embodied in the Massachusetts Constitution. "The

25. *Diary and Autobiography*, III, 201. Thus Adams's optimism coincided with the inception of Shays's Rebellion, his pessimism, discussed below, with its resolution.

26. Preface to *Thoughts on Government*, in *Works of John Adams*, IV, 294. The *Defence* was partly a contribution to the attacks on the Pennsylvania Constitution that resulted in its reform in 1790. See J. Paul Selsam, *The Pennsylvania Constitution of 1776: A Study in Revolutionary Democracy* (Philadelphia, 1936), 147, 149, 186. See further on the *Defence* and Franklin in chap. 11 below.

following work," he wrote in the preface to *A Defence of the Constitutions*, "was really written to lay before the public a specimen of that kind of reading and reasoning which produced the American constitutions."[27] He began the first of three volumes in October 1786, a little over a year after reaching England, and he spent much of the rest of his time there finishing the next two.

He set out in his typical fashion of writing entire volumes on a single point (here Turgot's unicameralism) while expressing at the same time his broadest ideas about society, government, and the American commonwealth: the book was called *A Defence of the Constitutions of Government of the United States of America, Against the Attack of M. Turgot, in His Letter to Dr. Price, Dated the Twenty-Second Day of March, 1778*, by John Adams. As Adams wrote, mounting concern over Shays's Rebellion stimulated him to rush his first volume to press. Thus the perennial Adams ingredient of haste was added, and with it his habitual infirmities as a writer: absence of form, repetitiousness, inconsistencies, all of which he confessed to at the end of the third volume.

The *Defence of the Constitutions*—a work that has been called "the finest fruit of the American Enlightenment . . . [a] bulky, disordered, conglomeration of glosses on a single theme"— intended to conduct, as Abigail Adams summarized its intention, "an investigation into the different forms of government both ancient and modern—Monarchical Aristocratical Democratical and Republican, pointing out their different balances" —with the purpose of demonstrating the superiority of mixed forms over simple ones.[28] Adams began with modern democracies (represented by a few Swiss cantons hidden away in mountain fastnesses), aristocracies, and monarchics. After sur-

27. *Works of John Adams*, IV, 293–294. Among the numerous examples of Adams's absorption in earlier times at this period: in the *Defence*, *ibid.*, III, 34, IV, 393, 395, VI, 67. And, on the peace of 1763–1764, which seemed to him like the present one, see his letter to Richard Cranch, Dec. 12, 1785, Adams Papers, Reel 113.

28. Gordon S. Wood, *The Creation of the American Republic, 1776–1787* (Chapel Hill, N.C., 1969), 568; Abigail Adams to John Quincy Adams, Nov. 22, 1786, Adams Papers, Reel 369.

veying the "Opinions of Philosophers," the "Writers on Government," and the "Opinions of Historians," he completed his first volume by surveying ancient democracy, aristocracy, and monarchy. This was the work that influenced the Constitutional Convention.

Adams's theory of mixed government repeated the old, whig view that human nature required control by a government structured to meliorate its weaknesses. All societies were subject to dangerous internal competitions. If men could live by the precepts of the Bible or by their reason, then government would be unnecessary. But nothing like a group of unselfish politicians, let alone an entire population of unselfish citizens, had ever existed in history, including—and here Adams threatened the myth of unique American virtue that earlier in life he had come near to sharing—the United States of America. Ideally, as the English constitution provided and American practice had brought into effect, control of government should rest in the possession of all the people. But historically, "to our inexpressible mortification, we must have observed, that the people have preserved a share of power, or an existence in the government, in no country out of England, except upon the tops of a few inaccessible mountains, among rocks and precipices, in territories so narrow that you may span them with a hand's breadth." Here, although men "exhibit the most charming picture of life, and the most dignified character of human nature," they live "unenvied, in extreme poverty, chiefly upon pasturage, destitute of manufactures and commerce." The United States would never return to such a stage.[29] As every complex society since the beginning of time demonstrated— and Adams cited examples from Greece, Rome, the Italian middle ages, and modern Europe, as well as from ancient and biblical legends—one class of ambitious men always managed to secure all the power for themselves. This was the aristocracy.

29. *Works of John Adams*, IV, 380–381. For the connection between fallen human nature and the need for "checks and balances" in government see John B. Kirby, "Early American Politics—The Search for Ideology: An Historiographical Analysis and Critique of the Concept of 'Deference,' " *Journal of Politics*, XXXII (1970), 823.

It appeared in America under the guise of the better sort, the better educated, or the better placed; it had existed universally since the beginning of time and would until the end.

The purpose of upper and lower legislative houses was to isolate (or "ostracize") the aristocrats into the upper house. So able and ambitious were they that they would quickly come to dominate Turgot's single assembly and thus seize control of the state. But as senators in a bicameral system, their "subtlety" and "sagacity" became useful. Under any other arrangement the people's "characteristic simplicity and unbounded confidence in their rulers" would make them the dupes of the aristocrats, who would establish an oligarchy.[30] Adams's solution amounted to an institutional version of his earliest fears about inequality. His isolated aristocrats were a late version of the dangerous, simultaneously feared and elevated "exalted Geniuses" of his Worcester diary. In his early works on government Adams praised "the better sort," proudly claiming that as many of them joined the patriots as joined the tories. He called the Massachusetts Council a body as similar to the aristocratic House of Lords as it was possible to make it. Yet, in standard whig fashion he "ostracized" the better sort in all his plans of government.[31]

When the Constitutional Convention adopted Adams's two houses it was not with the purpose of again creating a kind of Lords and Commons to balance the opposed forces in society,

30. *Works of John Adams*, IV, 344. The essential balance was between the upper and lower houses, but Adams also referred to a balance among executive, legislative, and judicial powers. See *ibid.*, VI, 80, 106.

31. For Adams on "the better sort" see *Diary and Autobiography*, I, 226–227, and *ibid.*, II, 3, for an opposite opinion; also *Works of John Adams*, IV, 32. See also "Novanglus," no. 14, in Bernard Mason, ed., *The American Colonial Crisis: The Daniel Leonard–John Adams Letters to the Press, 1774–1775* (New York, 1972), 264. On the House of Lords and the Massachusetts Council see *Works of John Adams*, IV, 117. W. B. Gwyn, *The Meaning of the Separation of Powers: An Analysis of the Doctrine from Its Origin to the Adoption of the United States Constitution*, Tulane Studies in Political Science, IX (New Orleans, 1965), 111n, calls the comparison "a commonplace in English constitutional thought." In pointing to the influence of Jean Louis De Lolme on the *Defence*, Joyce Appleby, "New Republican Synthesis and John Adams," *Am. Qtly.*, XXV (1973), 588, suggests that he adopted the term and concept of ostracism from De Lolme. But once again the concept may be found in whig theory, and the term in Adams's writings as early as 1772. John B. Kirby, "Early American Politics," *Journal of Politics*, XXXII (1970), 826; *Diary and Autobiography*, II, 59.

but rather to balance the parts of *government* one from another. Adams, without advocating anything new, in adhering to the old idea of a social balance, set himself at odds with another "emerging American myth," that of equality. Apparently unaware of the new prestige of equality, he defended the people while emphasizing their inferiority. As a result he forged an enduring reputation as a champion of aristocracy by the manner in which he opposed himself to it: namely, by warning that aristocrats were dangerous because superior. He further offended democrats with his adherence to the old, whig belief that, properly, the people will choose their representatives from among those "most conspicuous for fortune, family, and wealth."[32]

It has been supposed that along with his view of aristocracy Adams changed his attitude toward the American people and their democracy. His experience of Europe, according to this view, led to an increasing skepticism that emerged in the *Defence*. In fact, Adams's fears about the people accompanied optimistic pronouncements about them in his writings before, during, and after he wrote the *Defence*. In England, it is true, he had reached a height of disappointment with Americans for their failure to pay the debts specified in the peace treaty. Yet, he expressed an ultimate faith when he wrote, "I long to see my countrymen acting as if they felt their own great souls." He expatiated to his dinner guests in England, moreover, on the sources of the New Englanders' "Temperance, Patience, Fortitude, Prudence, and Justice, as well as their Sagacity, Knowledge, Judgment, Taste, Skill, Ingenuity, Dexterity, and Industry."[33]

When in the *Defence* he both praised and attacked the American people, Adams continued an old habit. Beginning in doubt and elevation of Braintree, he went on to similar ambivalence toward his fellow Bostonians, Massachusettsians, New En-

32. Wood, *Creation of the American Republic*, 571; *Works of John Adams*, VI, 93.

33. Adams to Cotton Tufts, May 26, 1786, *Works of John Adams*, IX, 548; *Diary and Autobiography*, III, 195. On Americans' "Depravity of Heart" see Adams to Gerry, Dec. 13, 1785, Adams Papers, Reel 113.

glanders, Americans. He had lashed out at "the Multitude" when he failed in his campaign against Braintree taverns in 1760, when his campaign against Governor Hutchinson went unrewarded in the 1770s, and when his securing of Dutch recognition was neglected in the 1780s. In an early essay on government, moreover, he wrote that "the Popular Power" in a mixed government can become "as dangerous as any other."[34] Adams's pronouncements reflected not only the ups and downs of his career but also a philosophical conundrum over the special virtue of Americans.

Like the Puritan jeremiads, both Adams's early and late works on government expressed a mixture of disillusionment and faith in the people. The seventeenth-century leaders had perceived a falling away from selflessness and had called for a renewal of the people's compact with their God. In 1775 Samuel Danforth continued the tradition in a sermon on the contemporary decline in morality. He announced that it was "high time to restore the corrupted dying state to its original perfection" by erecting a new government.[35] In 1787 Adams countered the general decline reported from America as he had in 1776—by calling for renewal, like Danforth, through the contemporary equivalent of the Puritan covenant: the compact of government.

In this approach to spiritual decline Adams's *Defence* was prefigured by Cotton Mather's *Magnalia Christi Americana* of 1700. For, in his mixture of disillusionment with Americans combined with a defense of their constitutions, Adams repeated Mather's unremitting doubt about the individual combined with ever renewed faith in the special calling of the community. Mather, writing for "an evil Generation," as he put it in his diary, countered his private belief "that the colony had strayed beyond recall" by treating its corporate mission as the grand culmination of universal history.[36] Like the *Defence* the *Magnalia*

---

34. *Diary and Autobiography*, I, 132, II, 60 (1772).

35. Plumstead, ed., *Wall and the Garden*, 365.

36. Sacvan Bercovitch, "New England Epic: Cotton Mather's *Magnalia Christi Americana*," *ELH: Journal of English Literary History*, XXXIII (1966), 337, 342.

made America the perfection of biblical, ancient, and medieval history. Both authors regarded Americans as fallen, but extolled their errand: in the *Magnalia* to illuminate the world with the example of the New England church-state; in the *Defence* to demonstrate the efficacy of the English tripartite balance perfected in the constitutions of the American states.

Adams's underlying conception of man derived from the seventeenth century, as did his belief in a special American destiny. Like a Puritan divine assuring a New Jerusalem to the community that kept its covenant with the Lord, Adams in 1776 had told his readers that if the people remained faithful to the traditional system of his *Thoughts on Government*, then "you will fancy yourself in Arcadia or Elysium." The *Defence* maintained this view of a chosen community: "The people in America have now the best opportunity and the greatest trust in their hands, that Providence ever committed to so small a number, since the transgression of the first pair." But, conceiving of America as both fallen and risen—again in good Puritan fashion—Adams shockingly could declare, "There is no special providence for Americans, and their nature is the same with that of others," within a few pages of exclaiming that if we "compare every constitution we have seen with those of the United States of America," we shall "feel the strongest motives to fall upon our knees, in gratitude to heaven for having been graciously pleased to give us birth and education in that country, and for having destined us to live under her laws!"[37] Such was the paradoxical vision of the first volume of the *Defence*.

Adams, because of the anachronism of his assumptions, gained a reputation as the author of a work of recently imbibed European pessimism and antidemocratic prejudice. Absent from America since 1779, he appeared unaware, for example,

37. *Works of John Adams*, IV, 200, 290, 401, 382. On Adams's political thought and the Puritans see Frank Washburn Grinnell, "John Winthrop and the Constitutional Thinking of John Adams," Massachusetts Historical Society, *Proceedings*, LXIII (1929–1930). For public reaction to Adams's statement that America had "no special providence" see Adams to Benjamin Rush, Oct. 22, 1812, Schutz and Adair, eds., *Spur of Fame*, 158; also Adams to Rush, Oct. 22, 1812, Adams Papers, Reel 118.

that it was no longer politic to call the English constitution "the most stupendous fabric of human invention." And even though he continued to follow Montesquieu in classifying England as a republic, as he had in "Novanglus," his terms "monarchical republic" and "aristocratic republic" sounded like the expressions of a preference for monarchy and aristocracy. Even the relatively optimistic first volume of the *Defence* was received with misgivings by the delegates to the American Constitutional Convention, although they appropriated its demonstrations in favor of bicameralism.[38]

If Adams failed to realize the import of his discussion of the people and the aristocracy, he understood that his advocacy of a strong executive, which had raised opposition when he presented his draft of the Massachusetts Constitution, would suggest a predilection on his part for monarchism. Never a king hater, even during the Revolution (when his opposition had focused on Governor Hutchinson), Adams now insisted that his arguments for a powerful head of state concerned not monarchy but the executive branch of government. "Is the cause of liberty," he asked, "are the rights of mankind, to stand for ever on no better a foundation than a blind superstition, and a popular prejudice against a word, a mere name?" The people had the authority "to appoint the executive power, by appointing a prince, president, governor, podestà, doge, or king, and to call him by which of these names they please." But Adams grew increasingly disposed to call the executive power, the king. In a personal letter he recognized the implication of his use of the term, asserting that he was "not Solicitous about the Name of the first Magistrate," who might be called "even King Sir! I am not afraid of the Word." But he then crossed out

38. *Works of John Adams*, IV, 358. In 1819 Adams remarked the attacks on him for his use of the word "republic." To J. H. Tiffany, Apr. 30, 1819, *ibid.*, X, 378. For Adams's source in Montesquieu see Robert W. Schoemaker, " 'Democracy' and 'Republic' as Understood in Late 18th Century America," *American Speech*, XLI (1966), 93. For the reception of the *Defence*, especially at the Constitutional Convention, see Haraszti, *John Adams and the Prophets of Progress*, 31, 38. For Adams's classification of England as a republic in "Novanglus" see *Works of John Adams*, IV, 106.

all mentions of the word "King" before mailing the letter.[39]

Adams's Revolutionary defiance of King George III followed the pattern of all his struggles with authority. With success came the softened feelings apparent in his personal liking for the king when they finally met, followed by a leaning toward the principles of the figure whom he had defied. During the Revolution, Adams had appeared a radical by opposing first Parliament, then George III's monarchical power. But, depending on how he thought the ideal balance of government was being threatened, he could become the champion of any of its three parts. In the Massachusetts Constitution he switched to defending the executive by attempting to give it the negative, and he adhered to that position in the first volume of the *Defence*. By the last volume of the *Defence* he was trying to right the balance in favor of the upper house. This, together with opposing the king without hating him and championing the people without loving them, aroused suspicions about Adams's republicanism. Yet, though he anticipated his critics he refused to mollify them. To maintain his reputation he depended upon his technical adherence to the outline of balanced government set forth in his earliest writings.[40]

Nevertheless, the changed feelings that underlay Adams's surface consistency expressed themselves in an anomalous sec-

39. *Works of John Adams*, VI, 81, 172; Adams to Thomas Brand Hollis, Oct. 18, 1787, Adams Papers, Reel 370. Adams may have written "Ay King Sir!" rather than "even King Sir!" See further on Adams, Hutchinson, and honorary titles in chap. 9.

40. In fact, Adams changed technically as well as in emphasis. He went from advocating annual elections to suggesting long or even permanent tenure for officeholders, and from election of the executive by the legislature to election by some other, unspecified method. See Gwyn, *Meaning of the Separation of Powers*, 122. Jesse Lemisch points out the contradiction between early and late Adams on the frequency of elections in "The American Revolution Seen from the Bottom Up," in Bernstein, ed., *Towards a New Past*, 38n. Those who speak of Adams's changing thought have in mind not these changes but rather a growth toward conservatism. John R. Howe, Jr., is followed by Gordon Wood in arguing the cause as a progressive disillusionment in Adams, though both quote post-*Defence* writings to support this view. They assume a contrasting "early optimism about American society" in Adams's earlier political writings. Howe, *Changing Political Thought of John Adams*, 147; Wood, *Creation of the American Republic*, 571. Adams is judged consistent, on the whole, by Richard M. Gummere, "Classical Politics of John Adams," *Boston Pub. Lib. Qtly.*, IX (1957), 168; Haraszti, *John Adams and the Prophets of Progress*, 27 (agreeing with Charles Francis Adams in his biography); and Richard B. Morris, *Seven Who Shaped Our Destiny: The Founding Fathers as Revolutionaries* (New York, 1973), 110.

tion of the *Defence* on Benjamin Franklin. Turgot, along with other of the philosophes, had praised his friend Franklin for Pennsylvania's unicameral assembly. Adams's defense of the other, bicameral state constitutions "against the attack of Turgot" aimed to correct European impressions about the philosophy of American governments and to halt Franklin from again usurping his reputation. Accordingly, for the digressive section of the *Defence* called "Opinions of Philosophers," Adams eccentrically chose three men to discuss: his friend "Dr. Price," to whom Turgot's letter had been addressed; "Dr. Swift," "one who [is] seldom quoted as a legislator" (but who agreed with Adams); and "Dr. Franklin," with whose "reputed opinion" on single assemblies Adams was "obliged" to deal. (Adams was implying that Franklin had neither written on government nor, as Adams once had told the Chevalier de La Luzerne, even made "the Constitution of Pennsylvania, bad as it is.") "The intention" of Turgot's letter, Adams later wrote, "was to celebrate Franklin's Constitution and condemn mine. I understood it, and undertook to defend my Constitution, and it cost me three volumes."[41]

Franklin's only statement on the science of government was "the common anecdote which is known to everybody" (and was destined to be better remembered than the three volumes of the *Defence*). Having two legislative houses, Franklin suggested, resembled the practice of moving heavily laden wagons down steep hills by hitching teams of oxen at opposite ends to achieve a slow, safe descent. Adams argued that "the real force of the simile . . . is clearly in favor of two assemblies." Recalling the Franklin invention most fascinating to him, Adams suggested that he "might have alluded" to the lightning rod, which acts upon disorders in "those angry assemblies in the

41. *Works of John Adams*, IV, 389; *Diary and Autobiography*, II, 391; Adams to Samuel Perley, June 19, 1809, *Works of John Adams*, IX, 623. Adams first saw Turgot's letter to Price while living in Auteuil. He showed Franklin his written comments on it, which Franklin had "copied and bound into his own volume." Haraszti, *John Adams and the Prophets of Progress*, 142.

heavens" by "restoring between them the *balance of* the *power*ful fluid."[42]

If Adams gave Franklin's "anecdote" more importance than it deserved, he showed an understanding of how well his and Franklin's governmental theories expressed their opposed temperaments. He seemed to recognize in Franklin's unicameral system an expression of the man's exasperating serenity of character. Expressing his own characteristic of intellectual perpetual motion, he cited against Franklin, Newton's "there can never be any *rest*." The opposing systems reflected their authors' views of mankind, as well. For if it is true that Adams viewed balance of powers more archaically than some of his American contemporaries (following James Otis in this as in other details of his governmental theory), Franklin and the philosophes shared his assumption that a single assembly expressed confidence in the people. It gave the people the most immediate representation possible, while a divided system, by complicating and balancing representation, expressed reservations about all orders in society.[43]

The great change in Adams's political thought, then, lay not in a growing conservatism but in his increasing mistrust of the behavior of mankind. His views of the aristocracy, for example, cannot be explained in liberal-conservative terms. He did not grow more conservative when he went from a conception in *Thoughts on Government* in which the aristocracy constituted "the ablest and wisest men of the state, different from the people but by no means opposed to the people's welfare," to a view of "the aristocratic interest set in opposition to the people's or the democratic interest."[44] As part of a rising skepticism of all classes of men, however, Adams's changed view of aristocracy fits a pattern. Yet, not even this skepticism was entirely new in Adams's political thought. It was discernible in

42. *Works of John Adams*, IV, 389, 391, 390 (italics added).

43. *Ibid.*, 390 (italics in original). For Otis's and Adams's common source in Puritan theory of balance of powers, see B. Katherine Brown, "A Note on the Puritan Concept of Aristocracy," *Mississippi Valley Historical Review*, XLI (1954), 110.

44. Wood, *Creation of the American Republic*, 579.

a slight shift of purpose between his "Dissertation on Canon and Feudal Law" and "Clarendon" of 1765, and the later "Novanglus" (1775), *Thoughts on Government* (1776), and the Massachusetts Constitution (1779). Originally viewing government as an expression of the virtue of New Englanders, by 1775 Adams looked to it rather than to men to foster and renew virtue, as his clause in the Massachusetts Constitution on the encouragement of literature and the arts made explicit. Without significantly changing the method of representation or the form of government, Adams gradually elevated government over the people, a trend that later culminated in his "Discourses on Davila" (1791).

In his long drift toward his "Davila" essays the most striking shift in Adams's views occurred within the *Defence of the Constitutions*. Neither the growth of pessimism between his works of the late 1760s and 1770s, nor the further growth between the latter and the first volume of the *Defence* in 1787, matched the change in his views that Adams underwent from 1787 to 1788. The change was apparent in the third, largely unread volume of this work. Objections by contemporaries to Adams's pessimism about the people seem largely to have been based on the first volume. Yet, between this volume and the third Adams went far beyond the hints sensed by his first readers. The defense of American constitutions led him from the American people, whom he addressed in the first volume, to mankind, and from the American system to universal principles of politics. By the second volume he was writing that America had a "destiny . . . common to all mankind," while in a letter to James Warren he wrote, "Our Countrymen have never merited the Character of very exalted Virtue." By the last volume Adams began to write of "the populace, the rabble, the *canaille*," and of man in general, whose "heart is deceitful above all things, and desperately wicked."[45]

Historical developments in Europe and America evidently

45. *Works of John Adams*, V, 45; Adams to James Warren, Jan. 9, 1787, *Warren-Adams Letters*, II, 280; *Works of John Adams*, VI, 10, 61.

had something to do with Adams's deepening gloom in the
Defence. In part he was disillusioned by Prussia's defeat of the
Netherlands while he was writing in 1787. The resultant
"downfall of liberty in Holland" reversed his initial elation at
the seeming triumph of the patriot party there. In a letter
Adams wrote, "Such is the melancholly Lot of Humanity, that
I cannot pretend to promise Immortality to Liberty or to Virtue
in any nation or Country of great numbers and large Extent
from any Constitution of Government within human Contri-
vance." Dutch events suggested a "severe trial" for the United
States "in a few years."[46] Other news to some extent balanced
the reports from Holland. Shays's Rebellion in Massachusetts,
which also had coincided with the inception of the *Defence*, was
put down, prompting Adams to write that "government appears now in its Majesty."

More important than events in Holland and America, however, was Adams's extensive culling of history while writing
the *Defence*. To sustain his effort he lived "in a State of Phylo-
sophic Solitude." In his isolation he was affected most by the
unhappy spectacle of Italian history. Volumes two and three
consisted of long passages copied from Italian history in a city-
by-city survey of "Italian Republics of the Middle Age." Adams
kept breaking off his accounts as he realized that "this essay is
already too long" and that "the history of one [city] is . . . the
history of all."[47] Adams believed that he was amassing proofs
that systems other than his own did not work: the history of

46. Adams to Brand Hollis, Oct. 18, 1787, Adams Papers, Reel 370; to Jay, Nov. 30,
1787, *Works of John Adams*, VIII, 464; and to Abigail Adams, Dec. 27, 1786, Adams Papers,
Reel 369. The letter to Brand Hollis contains the passage quoted above at n. 40 on not
fearing to call the executive a king. The connection supports R. R. Palmer's suggestion that
Adams was influenced by his experience of the weak executive power in the Dutch system.
The Age of the Democratic Revolution: A Political History of Europe and America, 1760–1800
(Princeton, N.J., 1959), 73. For Adams's response to the downfall of the Dutch patriots see
Abigail Adams to John Quincy Adams, Oct. 12, 1787, Adams Papers, Reel 369. For the
influence on Adams of the patriot movement see also Edward Handler, *America and Europe
in the Political Thought of John Adams* (Cambridge, Mass., 1964), 110 *ff*. Adams had been
interrupted from his second volume by a trip to the Netherlands, May–June 1787, to save
American loans through renegotiation.
47. Abigail Adams to John Quincy Adams, Nov. 22, 1786, Adams Papers, Reel 369;
Works of John Adams, V, 403, 332.

Florence, for example, appeared to him as "a satire, written with the express and only purpose of exposing to contempt, ridicule, and indignation, the idea of 'a government in one centre.'" But as he proceeded he found himself copying a volume and a half of examples amounting to an indictment of mankind. He jumped from city to city and historian to historian, each time arbitrarily breaking off as he realized that in his fascination with one or another poisoning or stabbing plot he had wandered from politics into intrigue. His own comments grew sparse—down to probably less than 10 percent of the text—and they showed him beginning to view horrors like mob violence as inevitable even in America.[48]

In the middle of the third volume, evidently realizing that he had room neither to finish his survey of Italy nor to include the study of modern confederations with which that volume was to have begun, he undertook a discussion of a book sent to him soon after he finished his first volume. Marchamont Nedham's *Right Constitution of a Commonwealth* was a Cromwellian, anti-monarchical apology written in the previous century. In his "Dissertation on Canon and Feudal Law," Adams had listed Nedham as a worthy predecessor in the fight against tyranny, and his fellow patriot Josiah Quincy had used "Nedham" as his pseudonym. But because Nedham advocated the single assembly Adams now grouped him with Turgot and Franklin. Subsequently, as his commentary on Nedham's book took him over the ground of his own first volume, Adams expressed himself differently on each of his major themes: democracy, monarchy, aristocracy, human nature, America. Where in the first volume he continued to fear aristocratic takeover in a republic because of the "simplicity and unbounded confidence" of the people, he now pronounced the people "as unjust, tyrannical, brutal, barbarous, and cruel, as any king or senate." (He had come a long way since writing in his diary in 1756, "The greatest men have been the most envious, malicious, and re-

48. *Works of John Adams*, V, 179. On mob violence see *ibid.*, 456–457, 39, 57; on America's destiny see *ibid.*, 40, 488.

vengeful.") He began to fear aristocracy less than democracy. "Intemperance and excess," he wrote, "are more indulged in the lowest ranks than in the highest." Accordingly, while the degenerate form of democracy "lets in vice, profligacy, and corruption," the parallel degenerate form, "the despotism of aristocracy," preserves "the morals of the people."[49]

The aristocrats remained a danger, "but it must be remembered, that the rich are *people* as well as the poor; . . . they have as clear and as *sacred* a right to their large property as others have to theirs which is smaller." Properly managed, "they are, in general, the best men, citizens, magistrates; . . . they are the guardians, ornaments, and glory of the community."[50] As with the subject of monarchy, Adams had said as much years earlier. Indeed, in 1756 he had read the bloody pages of Tacitus with a horror similar to that stimulated by the Italian histories, and he had remarked in his diary the excellence of aristocracy. He had disapproved of Tiberius's pretended contempt of fame on the ground that one should not deny the aristocratic virtues in response to the leveling impulse of the common people. But now his reading suggested to him that the bloodbath of civilization is delayed by a few choice souls from among the well-born and then inevitably begun by the people.

In his fear of the people and reliance on the virtues of "the better sort," Adams underwent a fundamental change in the Nedham section of the *Defence*. So corruptible in elections were the people, Adams had come to believe, that "first magistrates and senators had better be made hereditary at once, than that the people should be universally debauched." In "Novanglus" he had written that the American people had a "hereditary aversion to lordships." He had associated frequent elections with republican freedom itself (indeed, had been among those in favor of impractical annual elections) and, in 1776, had expressed his "dread" of the idea of life appointments. Now he

49. *Ibid.*, IV, 344, VI, 10, 94, 62. For Adams's reference to Marchamont Nedham in the "Dissertation on Canon and Feudal Law" see *Works of John Adams*, III, 463. On Adams's incomprehension of Nedham see Gwyn, *Meaning of the Separation of Powers*, 119.

50. *Ibid.*, VI, 65, 73. With his italics Adams pointedly referred to Jefferson's Declaration of Independence.

would not permit "the delicacy or the dread of unpopularity" to conceal the "important truth" that hereditary offices might have to be instituted. Whig theory, it was true, held that each form of government had its degenerate side, but never before had Adams seized on the idea of the people as a potential force of evil. On the contrary, earlier in the *Defence* he had gone further than Franklin's dictum that any form of government will suffice for a virtuous people when he wrote, "The people can live and increase . . . without any government at all." Still earlier, in "Novanglus," Adams wrote, "A democratical despotism is a contradiction in terms." By the third volume of the *Defence*, however, such a despotism had grown into his greatest fear.[51]

In his early volumes Adams frequently warned that America was not unique; in this third he began systematically to demonstrate this proposition. Ancient Greece provided the first example of decline in a republican government. There "a never-failing passion for tyranny, possessing republicans born in the air of liberty," had "astonished" historians. With ancient history and especially the histories of the Italian city-states in mind, Adams indulged his habit of prediction in detailing not the glories of a well-ordered republic for America but the almost unpreventable horrors to which it was liable.[52]

The Italian histories had moved Adams from fearing unbalanced government to fearing the beast in man set loose. He now required not only a bicameral system but one containing "an equal mixture"—a formula that suggested an ostracism of the popular rather than the aristocratic branch. For once the "democratical" element became too strong, which seemed to occur when it "*approached* to, an equality of power with the senate," it let loose luxury and rendered property "insecure." By the end of the *Defence*, Adams had come to Hobbes's view of savage human nature, with the addition of the idea that the war of nature amounted to a contest for dictatorial powers

51. *Ibid.*, 57, IV, 54 ("Novanglus"); Adams to Hugh Hughes, June 4, 1776, *ibid.*, IX, 388; *ibid.*, VI, 67, IV, 587, and 79 ("Novanglus").
52. *Ibid.*, VI, 102.

unabated even by the institution of civilization. "In the state of nature," Adams wrote, "when savage, brutal man ranged the forests with all his fellow-creatures, this mighty contest was decided with nails and teeth, fists, stones, and clubs, in single combats, between all that dared to pretend. Amidst all the refinements of humanity, and all the improvements of civil life, the same nature remains, and war, with more serious and dreadful preparations, and rencounters of greater numbers, must prevail, until the decision takes place."[53]

Adams's inward journey to philosophical despair took place during a period that continued the outward calm of his Auteuil interlude. He maintained health better than Abigail Adams had known him to have for several years.[54] In addition, during the summer before the *Defence* was begun, his daughter married his secretary, Colonel William Stephens Smith, to whom Adams nominally addressed the series of letters that made up the *Defence*. In the two years that he spent on the *Defence*, Adams had gained a son-in-law and grandson, received frequent news of John Quincy Adams's success at Harvard, taken another pleasant excursion in England, and with his resignation in 1787 (to take effect at the end of his official term the next year) anticipated moving into the fine Vassal-Borland house in Braintree, which he had arranged to buy.

Neither these circumstances nor completing the *Defence* fully satisfied Adams. From the time he distributed private copies of his first volume, two of which went to Franklin, he expressed the fear that his ideas would be taken as heresy and would make him "unpopular," that is, would cut short his political career. But if he anticipated misunderstandings, why did he not explain himself? He might not have had time in the first volume, which needed to reach America as soon as possible, but he had

53. *Ibid.*, 124, 108, 87 (italics added), 134, 166.
54. See Abigail Adams to John Quincy Adams, Nov. 22, 1786, Adams Papers, Reel 369. Years later, in dedicating a copy of the *Defence*, Adams connected it with Auteuil and the mirror-lined boudoir in his rented house by suggesting that it should be titled "The American Boudoir, or a Looking Glass for Monarchists, Aristocrats and Democrats. 1804." Worthington Chauncey Ford, ed., *A Catalogue of the Books of John Quincy Adams Deposited in the Boston Athenaeum . . .* (Boston, 1938), 79.

room enough and time in the next two. Instead he failed even to correct his text for the printer. Partly, of course, Adams would not deign to profess good intentions. Then, being misunderstood, unappreciated, and too prescient for the public mind had become a habit with him. He could hardly conceive of an undertaking that did not involve brave unpopularity followed by eventual vindication. Thus he expected the *Defence* to remain unpopular "for a long time" until its principles were proved right.[55] Brilliant but discontinuous, disordered, and sporadic, the *Defence* reflected his personality. He did not stand before the world represented by a finished work because, even at the age of fifty-three, he remained uncomposed. Events had formed him, and on events he continued to depend. He could make the *Defence of the Constitutions* a political act, a defense, but not the rounded statement of political philosophy that its length made it appear. It was not surprising that, as with all his works, Adams expressed dissatisfaction when he finished.[56]

Next to this disappointment, the annoyances of his last months in Europe in 1787 and early 1788 hardly mattered. He had twice to rush to the Netherlands in symbolic recapitulation of the frustrations of his entire European experience. In 1787 he arranged a final, again desperately needed loan, and in 1788 he returned to take formal leave when Congress failed to send him long-requested papers of recall (these belatedly arrived just before he set sail for America).

John Adams did not know that he was returning to a career in the national government. His ambition, in so far as he would express it, pointed to state politics—he seems not to have realized that the new national system would be more important than the government of Massachusetts. He entertained the possibility of returning to law practice seriously enough to ask John Quincy Adams if he would like to apprentice with him.

55. Adams to Benjamin Franklin, Jan. 27, 1787, Adams Papers, Reel 113, and to Jefferson, Mar. 1, 1787, Cappon, ed., *Adams-Jefferson Letters*, I, 176. See also Adams to Benjamin Hichborne, Jan. 27, 1787, Adams Papers, Reel 113, and to James Warren, *Warren-Adams Letters*, II, 281.

56. See Adams to Mercy Warren, *Warren-Adams Letters*, II, 275, and *Diary and Autobiography*, III, 209 (July–Aug. 1787).

The years in England left Adams a confirmed pessimist and at least theoretically a stoic accepter of inevitable neglect and unpopularity. Although he continued to agonize in practice over his fate, at least he had arrived at a stance in which to receive the blows of providence. Mather Brown's portrait of him the month before he left England shows a dispirited, melancholic scholar at his table seeming to ponder the vicissitudes of history (see figure 3). The fire of personality, formerly apparent in a vigorous fleshiness and slightly protruding eyes, seems to have gone out of this sallow, expressionless man. No doubt Adams felt the results of his failure to obtain a serious hearing for American interests in England. Yet, as in the *Defence* itself, his melancholy was of a philosophical order; not just a town, a province, or a state, but mankind itself had disappointed him.

IX
Great Sacrifices
to Union
1789–1796

John Adams returned to the United States in 1788 to find himself a personage of far greater popularity than he had anticipated. Every high office in government was urged on him but that of president: governor of Massachusetts, senator, and vice-president (in addition he was made a member of but did not attend the expiring Continental Congress). Once he decided that the new federal government was more important than the states, it appeared to him that the only position in which he would not be "descending as a public man beneath himself" was the vice-presidency, to which he was elected in November 1788.[1] He took office under Washington in March 1789 and served two terms, at the end of which, in 1797, he succeeded as president.

When the government assembled in New York no one knew what the duties of the vice-president were to comprise beyond the constitutional specification that he preside over the Senate. During his eight years in office Adams remained limited to this largely ceremonial function. Theoretically he could have taken a part in the executive direction of government—many expected that he would act as a kind of prime minister. But partly out of Washington's coolness toward him and partly out of an

1. Abigail Adams to Abigail Adams, Jr., July 16, 1788, *Journal and Correspondence of Miss Adams*, II, 89.

instinct to avoid rather than appropriate power, Adams remained in the Senate chamber; he met with the cabinet "only two or three times in eight years."[2]

The post of vice-president could not have been better devised to torture Adams. Officially in power but lacking any useful function, he was deprived of his protesting, essentially oppositionist eloquence and left either to sit idly by or to create make-work for himself. Unhappy, he did a little of each. In the meantime, while he wrestled with the ethical question of his own ambition, others took power, and while he pondered the historical significance of the new government, others gave it its initial direction.

Taking a long view of the fate of republics, Adams feared that the American experiment might not last for so much as four years, an opinion that he unfortunately voiced in public. The executive lacked a strong negative, the states had too much power and prestige compared to the central government, and elections were likely to prove corrupt. He had outlined the almost inevitable pattern in his *Defence of the Constitutions:* good men preserved a new republic for a while, then were succeeded by others unable to compensate for its inherent weaknesses. And now, significantly, the younger members of the new administration, soon to replace his own generation, ignored him. They "know not Joseph," he complained.[3]

Adams's fears about the success of the new nation were shared by others. It was well known that the chief cause of failure for republican governments lay in the likelihood of election irregularities. Thus, when Alexander Hamilton engineered an intrigue in the first election that humiliatingly reduced Adams's electoral votes, those observers with classical

2. Stephen G. Kurtz, *The Presidency of John Adams: The Collapse of Federalism, 1795–1800* (New York, 1957), 222.

3. Adams to John Trumbull, Mar. 9, 1790, Adams Papers, Reel 115. For Adams's forebodings see his letters to Abigail Adams, May 30, 1789, Adams Papers, Reel 372; to William Tudor, June 4–14, 1789, and to Roger Sherman, July 20, 1789, *ibid.*, Reel 115; to Richard Price, Apr. 19, 1790, and to John Trumbull, Jan. 23, 1791, *Works of John Adams*, IX, 564, 573. Also see William Maclay, *Sketches of Debate in the First Senate of the United States, in 1789–90–91*, ed. George W. Harris (Harrisburg, Pa., 1880), 63.

educations found ample cause for worry. Feeling himself thwarted by his office from acting directly to preserve the Union, Adams busied himself with issues of protocol. In questions that held but a pale resemblance to earlier preparations for new responsibilities, he asked for votes on how he should comport himself as presiding officer of the Senate. How should he address the president of the United States? What should his own title be? Should he give up his chair when the president made his first visit to the Senate? (He did.) Another man, less uneasy about being prominent, could have handled such problems without drawing attention to himself. But Adams could not assume any title or prerogative unless it was first made impersonal by official sanction. Far from advocating a regal title for Washington in order to secure one for himself, as it was charged, he was attempting to raise the embarrassing matter of deference to an impersonal plane.

By implying a liking for panoply Adams's questions prompted objections on republican grounds. He pointed out that all governments in the history of the world had supported themselves to some extent by show. The new American government could employ impressive titles as a device for attracting to it men of talent from the more prestigious state governments. Internationally, the new government would secure respect only if it designated a title for the president equal to those of other heads of state. As the debate continued, and Adams, his enthusiasm quickened, began to think the subject through, he went so far as to predict that without the title "Majesty," George Washington would be so scorned in Europe that America would be forced into war to support his dignity. "This is all nonsense to the philosopher," Adams admitted, "but so is all government, whatever."[4]

Adams's titles campaign, as it has come to be known, was both a product of his European experience and, as another attempt to utilize emulation for the state, a logical culmination

---

4. Adams to Jabez Bowen, June 26, 1789, Adams Papers, Reel 115; Maclay, *Sketches of Debate*, ed. Harris, 41.

of his thought. He clearly had been impressed by the awe for government generated by princely display and pageantry in Europe. But if he was willing to institute a vice-presidential throne, he did not think of himself as an aristocrat or change his private manners. Indeed, he persisted in his contempt for "laced waistcoats" and ritual until the end of his stay in Europe. In the "Dissertation on Canon and Feudal Law" he objected to the "glare of mystery" surrounding priests. Since "no mortal could deserve" the sanctity in which priests were held, their elevation was "dangerous in society." "Formalities and Ceremonies are an abomination in my sight," he wrote in 1770; "I hate them, in Religion, Government, Science, Life." In 1776 he expressed his contempt for the "burlesque Extream" of ritual that the Dutch republic found necessary in order to instill deference for its leaders. As recently as 1782 he asserted Americans' dislike of titles.[5] At the same time, he upheld the seventeenth-century whig concept of deference to leaders, arguing during the Revolution that the patriot party showed no disrespect to constituted authority. But never before had he advocated the ostentatious display of authority.

On the contrary, when Thomas Hutchinson came to the head of the Massachusetts judiciary in 1761 Adams was disgusted when he introduced in the courts "that scenery," "so theatrical and so ecclesiastical," consisting of "scarlet and sable robes" and "enormous tie wigs." In advocating virtually the same costumery for the new federal government Adams offered a final retribution for his violent rejection of patriarchal authority in the person of Hutchinson. Formerly Adams had attempted to reinstate that authority by advocating the executive negative in the Massachusetts Constitution and the *Defence of the Constitutions*. Now he called again for a strong negative to give stability to the new government, while wishing the new Senate to open with a regal panoply reminiscent of Hutchinson's conduct of the General Court's annual opening session. In more general terms, after becoming vice-president, Adams

5. *Works of John Adams*, III, 453; *Diary and Autobiography*, I, 355; Adams to James Warren, Apr. 22, 1776, *Warren-Adams Letters*, I, 234.

moved from his early emphasis on man's potentialities to an emphasis on his limitations—that is to say, back to the old-fashioned Christian view taken by Hutchinson in his *History of Massachusetts-Bay*. In reparation for his most thoroughgoing revolt from authority, the Revolution, Adams made his most thoroughgoing amends when he succeeded to power. (He had succeeded to Hutchinson's chief justiceship of Massachusetts during the Revolution; as vice-president he was the equivalent of Hutchinson as lieutenant-governor with a similar likelihood of advancing to become chief executive.) James Otis had ridiculed Hutchinson by calling him "Summa Potestatis" or "Summa." Now Adams was recommending chief executive titles that sounded quite as absurd to his opponents.[6]

Adams increasingly tortured himself with the irony of appearing as the aristocrat among men with more money and of better family than he. Committed to support the dignity of his office, he kept his wife busy entertaining diplomats and members of the government. But Massachusetts successfully had moved a bill to keep the vice-president's salary low, and in order to save money Adams had taken a house some distance from New York City, where the first Congress convened. At first he felt that he could not afford to have his wife join him but, missing her, he urged her to borrow or "sell Horses oxen Sheeps Cowes, any Thing at any Rate [price] rather than not come on." Thus he waged and lost his campaign for governmental shows of extravagance to the accompaniment of personal frugality. Then, without admitting error he gradually abandoned his position, though not before enlarging his repu-

6. Adams to Tudor, Dec. 18, 1816, and to Hezekiah Niles, Feb. 13, 1818, *Works of John Adams*, X, 233, 286. For Adams's renewed Revolutionary spirit typified by these 1816 and 1818 recollections see chap. 12. Merle Curti, *Human Nature in American Historical Thought*, 18–19, makes Thomas Hutchinson the representative of the older, Christian view. Adams's attempt to associate the American presidency with kingly authority prompts the speculation that he was restoring authority not only to the governor but to the king himself. Although he had the right to deny ever having been a king hater (see the previous chapter), he had flirted with parricide during the Revolution and perhaps was making ill-timed amends for it now. See *Works of John Adams*, III, 17–18, 461. For the influence on Adams of Jonathan Mayhew, who celebrated the murder of Charles I and was praised by Adams in "Novanglus," see *Diary and Autobiography*, I, 6n.

tation for absurd vanity. After being ridiculed by the newspapers in doggerel verse and given the titles "the Duke of
Braintree" and "His Rotundity," he stopped wearing his sword
and then his wig to the Senate. Soon he was complaining that
he continued to wear his European diplomatic costume only
because he could not afford to replace it. He regretted the
"Monarchical Trumpery" of his expensive coach and four and
vowed never to be taken in again by such vanities.[7]

Before Adams changed his position, however, the titles
question grew in importance. The new American government
of 1788 was born into the arms of the French Revolution of
1789. The titles debate, when put in the context of the recent
French practice of calling everyone "citizen," became part of the
battle for the rights of man. Adams began by attacking the
French pretense at the abolition of inequality by the universal
use of this word. Within a family, he argued, modifying his
Revolutionary position, father and mother, children and servants all retained their titles and places, which not even the
most rabid francophiles proposed to do away with.[8] Then, in
1790, regarding the issue on a higher philosophical plane than
his opponents, Adams transformed it into a study of the nature
of man and the special condition of Americans.

In a series of newspaper essays in the form of a commentary
on the Italian historian Davila's account of the French civil wars
of the sixteenth century, Adams viewed the recent uprising in
France in the light of the lessons of French history. His "Discourses on Davila" set out to show that the French, requiring
their aristocratic institutions in order to maintain stability,
could not sustain a thorough social revolution. The lesson
applied to America, which was not merely subject to the same
laws of history as Europe, as he had proclaimed to the shock of
some in his *Defence of the Constitutions*, but was susceptible to

7. Adams to Trumbull, Apr. 2, 1790, and to Abigail Adams, May 19, 1789, Adams
Papers, Reels 115, 372. On his clothing see Adams to Abigail Adams, Mar. 2, 1793, *ibid.*,
Reel 376. On his sword and wig see Smith, *John Adams*, II, 758–759, 825.

8. See Adams to Tudor, May 4, 1789, Adams Papers, Reel 372; also in "Davila," *Works of
John Adams*, VI, 270. For Adams's previous position on the family see *ibid.*, III, 15.

even more virulent forms of corruption. In Adams's early writings innocent America faced particular dangers from corruption but had a brighter outlook than Europe if it maintained its republican institutions. Now America required for its survival its own, natural, nonhereditary aristocracy. If, like France, it failed to encourage its superior men by offering them recognition in the form of titles, its very existence would be threatened. At that point hereditary aristocracy would have to be instituted (with a hereditary monarch to balance it). Adams did not go quite so far in "Davila" as he had privately in averring that without titles "one half" of the Senate would "resign before two years."[9] Nevertheless, he conveyed his doubts about the new American system clearly enough to shake the confidence of friends and to provide damaging evidence for enemies that he was an aristocrat and monarchist.

Needless to say, Adams anticipated and looked forward to this response in his proud, combative way. "The Cry of monarchy" always greeted advocates of the strong executive. "I have run the gauntlet too long among libels, halters, axes, daggers, cannonballs and pistol bullit, in the Service of this people, to be at this age afraid of their injustice." But the inevitable attacks on Adams, crude as they were, stumbled on a truth that he did not admit to himself. He was leaning toward monarchy and aristocracy (as distinct from kings and aristocrats) at the time he wrote "Davila," though he did not directly reveal this in its essays. Decidedly, some time after he became vice-president, Adams concluded that the United States would have to adopt a hereditary legislature and a monarch. In the course of writing "Davila" he retreated from and denied ever having held such an opinion. He insisted that he had imagined such an arrangement only as a contingency, and a distant one at that. In fact, however, stung by Hamilton's electoral manipulations he had written that "elections of President and Senators

9. Adams to Tudor, June 4–14, 1789, Adams Papers, Reel 115. For Adams's early view of American corruption see *Diary and Autobiography*, II, 58–59. On the likely need for hereditary aristocracy see Adams to Benjamin Rush, July 24, 1789, Adams Papers, Reel 115.

cannot be long conducted in a populous, oppulent, and commercial Nation without corruption Sedition and civil war," and he outlined a plan by which state conventions would appoint hereditary senators while a national one appointed a president for life.[10]

In the meantime "Davila" itself grew from a tract implying these necessities into a study of human psychology. Beginning in the manner of the *Defence*, Adams copied and commented on passages from Davila's *History* in order to illustrate the need for titles. After only one number, however, he decided that his opponents misunderstood man's nature. He could proceed no further without turning his readers' "thoughts for a few moments to the constitution of the human mind." There followed twelve essays on this subject, the most sustained effort of his writing career.

Adams returned to the theory of emulation he had first expressed while teaching in Worcester: man was activated less by fear, hunger, or any other primitive impulse than he was by "the *passion for distinction*." Approaching this truth from a political perspective, he now went so far as to claim that the desire to do better and thereby shine in others' eyes was more effective in controlling a population than "human reason" or "standing armies."[11] This was why he had advocated titles, he implied. Unless men were given objects to aspire toward they would not devote their energies to or properly respect the new central government.

In Worcester, Adams had attempted to come to terms with ambition by denying it to himself but allowing it to others. Now he built a theory making it the basis of all human behavior.

In the course of years his own ambition, and with it his emulation theory, had progressed from concern with the psy-

10. Adams to Gen. Benjamin Lincoln, June 19, 1789, to Judge James Sullivan, Sept. 21, 1789, and to Francis Adrian Vanderkemp, Feb. 27, 1790, all in Adams Papers, Reel 115. For Adams's denials of having had monarchical leanings, see *Works of John Adams*, VIII, 512–513. For his plan of conventions to appoint senators for life see his letter to Vanderkemp, Mar. 27, 1790, Vanderkemp Papers, Pa. Hist. Soc.

11. *Works of John Adams*, VI, 232 (italics in original), 234.

chology of striving to the question of recognition. Man's need for recognition, the subject of the titles debate, dominated "Davila," where Adams called it "the passion for distinction." Adams made a universal principle of the passion for distinction, offering an exclusive emphasis on it as his contribution to the great eighteenth-century discussion on the nature of man. The "desire of the attention, consideration, and congratulations of our fellow men . . . is the great spring of social activity," he wrote, and "the history of mankind is little more than a simple narration of its [this desire's] operation and effects."[12] As in the *Defence*'s single principle of balance, Adams was at his best when able to "seize on a permanent political truth" and "defend it wittily and with almost infinite resourcefulness." He grew particularly eloquent in describing "the awful feeling of a mortified emulation," for he had suffered the feeling of neglect and knew it as potentially destructive to personality itself.[13]

In Adam Smith's *Theory of Moral Sentiments*, Adams found a passage describing the horror of poverty as lying not in hunger but in "obscurity." The poor man, he expanded on the insight, "is not disapproved, censured, or reproached; *he is only not seen*." Like him, Adams had felt "insignificant" while waiting for a new appointment from Congress in 1779. Now he imagined the lives of those beneath the attention of society:

If you follow these persons . . . into their scenes of life, you will find that there is a kind of figure which the meanest of them all endeavors to make; a kind of little grandeur and respect, which the most insignificant study and labor to procure in the small circle of their acquaintances. Not only the poorest mechanic, but the man who lives upon common charity, nay, the common beggars in the streets; and not only those who may be all innocent, but even those who have abandoned themselves to common infamy, as pirates, highwaymen, and common thieves, court a set of admirers, and plume themselves upon that superiority which they have, or fancy they have, over some others. There must be one, indeed, who is the last and lowest of the human species. But there is no risk in asserting, that there is no one

12. *Ibid.*, 245, 234.
13. Lyman H. Butterfield, review of Zoltán Haraszti's *John Adams and the Prophets of Progress*, in *American Historical Review*, LVII (1951–1952), 984; *Works of John Adams*, VI, 247.

who believes and will acknowledge himself to be the man. To be wholly overlooked, and to know it, are intolerable. Instances of this are not uncommon. When a wretch could no longer attract the notice of a man, woman, or child, he must be respectable in the eyes of his dog. "Who will love me then?" was the pathetic reply of one, who starved himself to feed his mastiff, to a charitable passenger, who advised him to kill or sell the animal. In this *"who will love me then?"* there is a key to the human heart; to the history of human life and manners; and to the rise and fall of empires.[14]

Passages such as this would make the "Discourses on Davila" an American classic were it not for the characteristic Adams shortcomings of the work as a whole. After his essays on "the human mind" Adams returned to quotations and commentary from Davila as unfocused as the weakest parts of the *Defence*. He shifted as usual from one object to another. "Why all this of emulation and rivalry?" he asked at one point, then answered that it was because the whole of Davila's *History of the Civil Wars* "is no more than a relation of rivalries" that "will assist us . . . to form a right judgment of the state of affairs in France at the present moment." Later, as he became immersed in history, he wrote that his purpose, "at present, is only to relate the fortunes and catastrophe of the great actors in those scenes of emulation, which have been before described." And still later: "With a view of vindicating republics, commonwealths, and free states from unmerited reproaches, we have detailed these anecdotes from the history of France." The chief obstacle to recognition of sporadic eloquence in "Davila" lies in Adams's use of Adam Smith. So taken was he with finding his own ideas and many of the ideas of the age treated skillfully in Smith's *Theory of Moral Sentiments* that he not only transcribed long passages from the work but often gave a running paraphrase of it. Thus, though Adams sometimes improved on his original— the passage on the poor quoted above is his own though the sentences preceding and succeeding it are paraphrases—his

14. *Works of John Adams*, VI, 239 (Adams's italics). The charitable passenger, with his offer of alternative means of disposing of the dog, sounds as if he was Adams himself.

method of composition again precluded his leaving a work that he might be remembered by.[15]

From his theory of human motivation Adams turned to an attack on the optimism of the philosophes, especially Condorcet. "The world grows more enlightened," he admitted. But, he asked, "are riches, honors, and beauty going out of fashion? . . . the more knowledge is diffused, the more the passions are extended, and the more furious they grow." Partly Adams was pitting against the optimists his old belief that bounties such as those they wished to spread—education, success, fame—only stimulate ambition. But partly, too, he was using the Christian-conservative view of imperfect human nature against the idea of progress. "Cold will still freeze," he wrote in a classic statement of this position, "and fire will never cease to burn; disease and vice will continue to disorder, and death to terrify mankind."[16]

Despite his darkest fears, or rather because of them, Adams adhered to his ancient millennarian hope for America. He conceived the defense of aristocratic titles as a defense of the American republics. If human passions—seen in pride of attainments and competition for places in government—were stronger in America than in the Old World, so was America's republican solution. By maintaining a proper balance of powers the new United States could contain the dangers of ambition more successfully than aristocratic or monarchical systems. In 1777 Adams wrote, "Ambition in a Republic . . . is but another Name for . . . Virtue." Now virtue flowed from the balance itself, which functioned to restrain rather than free republicans. Nevertheless, Adams continued to follow the Puritans in thinking of America as "our Israel," a land meant to illuminate the Old World with the principles of the Massachusetts town meet-

15. *Ibid.*, 269, 377–378, 394. For the comparable passages on poverty see *ibid.*, 239, and Adam Smith, *The Theory of Moral Sentiments . . .* (1759), H. G. Bohn edition (London, 1911; orig. publ. London, 1853), 71–72. As Zoltán Haraszti, who discovered Adams's borrowing from Smith, put it, Adams's "own phrasing is often more powerful than Smith's; his passion for stringing together epithets and metaphors makes his presentation particularly vivid." *John Adams and the Prophets of Progress*, 169.

16. *Works of John Adams*, VI, 274–275, 279.

ing. "AMERICANS!" he announced, if you "advert to the principles on which you commenced" your "glorious self-defence," then you "may ultimately loosen the chains of all mankind."[17]

The eternal principles that Adams had in mind, however, remained the ancient practices of the English constitution. This hardly made a program to fire the imagination during the first years of the French Revolution. The closest Adams approached to the new spirit of the age was to call for an end to class hatred. "The way of wisdom to happiness is to make mankind more friendly to each other." Aristocrats should not be hated. "We, the plebeians," he wrote, significantly identifying himself with the lower classes, "find them the workmanship of God and nature, like ourselves." Understanding between the classes evoked Christian charity, not revolutionism. And Adams spiced his call for accommodation with a view of man certain to alienate both of the classes to which he addressed himself: "Let the rich and poor unite in the bands of mutual affection, be mutually sensible of each other's ignorance, weakness, and error, and unite in concerting measures for their mutual defence against each other's vices and follies."[18]

It would be difficult to imagine a more impolitic appeal than this, or a more impolitic act than writing "Davila." Once again Adams consulted with no one. Far from feeling responsible to his political party he continued to feel uneasy as long as he failed to show his independence by outraging at least half of the electorate. This he proceeded to do in "Davila" by working himself into an intellectual fix similar to that in the last volume of the *Defence*. As he there placed himself on the side of monarchy by attacking the antimonarchical Marchamont Nedham, in the thirty-second "Davila" essay he turned to the "vehement Phillipic against monarchy and aristocracy" of Étienne de La Boétie. Typically, Adams drove straight at the logical question

17. Adams to [James Warren?], Apr. 27, 1777, and to Gen. Lincoln, June 19, 1789, Adams Papers, Reels 91, 115; *Works of John Adams*, VI, 276–277. Adams increasingly emphasized the special dangers of the passions in a republican system; see his letter to Tudor, June 4–14, 1789, Adams Papers, Reel 115, and *Works of John Adams*, VI, 243–244.
18. *Works of John Adams*, VI, 395, 396.

of why men had so often chosen to live under kings. It was because "they had almost unanimously been convinced that hereditary succession was attended with fewer evils than frequent elections. This is the true answer, and the only one, as I believe."[19] True or not, Adams had gone too far; the "Davila" essays were suspended. When they were collected in a volume he allowed this last number to be omitted.

Heretofore Adams's instinct for unpopularity had served his country, if not himself. Once elected vice-president, however, he could be of use only if he established connections with men of like convictions and learned to wield power in a political way. The politician needs to establish a web of influence in anticipation of the moment when, wishing to do good, he will need allies. In the Netherlands, Adams organized merchants and intellectuals to petition the newspapers in favor of recognizing the United States. But he also expressed a creed of "Independence" that later would spell disaster for him as a politician: "I never in my Life observed any one endeavouring to lay me under particular Obligations to him, but I suspected he had a design to make me his dependant, and to have claims upon my Gratitude. This I should have no objection to— Because Gratitude is always in ones Power. But the Danger is that Men will expect and require more of Us, than Honour and Innocence and Rectitude will permit Us to perform."[20] It is true that the techniques of political parties were not yet understood early in the 1790s—Washington warned against their very existence in his Farewell Address. Furthermore, Adams had succeeded while remaining above party in Massachusetts politics through the 1779 constitutional convention, his latest experience in American politics. Yet, while others adapted to the new realities Adams continued to follow ancient models like Demosthenes and Cicero, both of whom achieved their glory in lonely unpopularity and defeat.

19. *Gazette of the United States* (Philadelphia), Apr. 27, 1791, 829.
20. Adams to Abigail Adams, Dec. 18, 1780, *Adams Family Correspondence*, IV, 35. On the continuing fear of party in the United States during the 1790s see Howe, *Changing Political Thought of John Adams*, 194.

When he took office as vice-president, Adams refused to use his influence on behalf of office seekers. Among the flood of requests sent him—all of which he referred to Washington on the theory that the chief executive should have the appointing power entirely in his hands—came several from deserving old friends. His refusal to intercede for James Warren at the request of his wife, Mercy Otis Warren, gave birth to a political enemy. In the meantime Adams also alienated two old associates in France and fellow sufferers at the hands of Franklin, Ralph Izard and Arthur Lee, both senators in the first Congress during the titles debate. Far from meeting and concerting with these men, Adams contrived to insult each of them in the course of debate by handing down embarrassing rulings on procedural questions. (It was Izard who subsequently coined the term "his Rotundity" for Adams.)[21]

This unpolitical and impolitic behavior derived partly from the frustrations of the vice-presidency and partly from the abuses of an ideologically heightened period of history. Popular responses to the French Revolution dominated the political climate of the 1790s. After news of France's military successes during the "extraordinary year" 1793, the "French frenzy" took the form of gigantic civic feasts. In Boston, after a celebratory procession replete with symbolic representations of liberty and tyranny, the prison doors were "thrown open" and "those who had long been immured therein were invited to join their festive brethren and again breathe the air of Liberty." The execution of the French king was widely acclaimed. The hysteria of the radicals was matched by the conservatives, who politicized even the 1793 yellow fever epidemic. Adams for the most part held himself aloof both as vice-president and president, but failed to take the lead in moderating the political climate. He adopted an isolated, philosophical purity instead of rallying the men above party.[22]

21. Haraszti, *John Adams and the Prophets of Progress*, 38. On Adams's rulings see Maclay, *Sketches of Debate*, ed. Harris, 21, 109. Adams's rebuff of the Warrens: Adams to Mercy Warren, Feb. 14, 1791, Adams Papers, Reel 115. See also below, chap. 11.
22. Charles Downer Hazen, *Contemporary American Opinion of the French Revolution*,

The reigning issue of one's attitude toward the French Revolution affected Adams all the more in his isolation. Within a few years it culminated in the main business of his presidential administration: the very palpable matter of threatened war with France. When the French minister, Genet, whose father Adams had known, arrived in 1793, he seemed to sweep the country before him. He lost much of his support by fitting out American privateers to sail against the English, however, and his triumphal tour of the states ended in his recall. In the meantime the new pro-French democratic societies seemed to threaten government until Washington finally denounced them. Proclaiming themselves upholders of the rights of man, these secret clubs developed into vigilante groups. They polarized domestic issues into questions of allegiance to France or England, twisting into an attack on France and its principles even John Jay's mission to secure a treaty with England. Again Adams held himself aloof from both issues.

The manner in which the French issue affected lives and political fortunes is well illustrated by the break it caused in the friendship between Adams and Jefferson. When a printer put out an American edition of Paine's *Rights of Man* in 1791 he prefaced it with a letter from Jefferson containing an obvious slur on Adams's current ideas. John Quincy Adams opposed Paine and the Jefferson preface in a series of anonymous pieces by "Publicola," whom many believed to be the senior Adams. Jefferson apologized to Adams for the unauthorized preface, and Adams accepted, explaining that John Quincy Adams had written entirely without consultation with his father. In replying to Adams, Jefferson speciously suggested that Publicola, not he, had been responsible for the public excitement over the

---

Johns Hopkins University Studies in History and Political Science, XVI (Baltimore, 1897), 169. On the climate of the times see Marshall Smelser, "The Federalist Period as an Age of Passion," *American Quarterly*, X (1950), 407, which shows that John Quincy Adams contributed to conservative fears; Claude G. Bowers, "An American Spasm of Passion," in Allan Nevins, ed., *Times of Trial* (New York, 1958); and Martin S. Pernick, "Politics, Parties, and Pestilence: Epidemic Yellow Fever in Philadelphia and the Rise of the First Party System," *WMQ*, 3d Ser., XXIX (1972), 559–586. For Adams's one moment of terror see his letter to Thomas Jefferson, June 30, 1813, Cappon, ed., *Adams-Jefferson Letters*, II, 346–347.

issue. Then, though he had admitted to Madison that his letter referred to Adams, he damaged his credibility by claiming that he had not written it with Adams in mind.[23]

Such disputes consumed Adams's attention because of his increasing disappointment with his office. As with his periods of idleness in Europe he found the vice-presidency "not quite adapted to my Character.—I mean it is too inactive, and mechanical." He complained, sometimes in bitterness, more often in self-deprecation, of his powerlessness and, like the outcasts in "Davila," his "insignificance." Years later he revealed that while vice-president and president political intelligence was withheld from him by both deceiving enemies and too delicate friends. From this vice-presidential isolation Adams issued such politically ill-advised writings as "Davila." Federalists like Alexander Hamilton and Fisher Ames agreed or held still more conservative views than his but found Adams an embarrassment. (Hamilton's remarkable intrigues against Adams had at least part of their inception in his realization that Adams absolutely could not be talked to as a party man.)[24] Adams's political influence diminished until he was left with little more than the prestige of his name. This sufficed to reelect him vice-president and then to make him president but left him unequipped to manage the federal administration of the United States of America.

Although not yet sixty Adams felt his age. He complained increasingly of his old, minor physical troubles. By 1795 he

23. Dumas Malone, *Jefferson and the Rights of Man* (Boston, 1951), 370, discusses Jefferson's disingenuousness on this occasion. See also Cappon, ed., *Adams-Jefferson Letters*, I, 245–252, and Smith, *John Adams*, II, 772.

24. Adams to John Quincy Adams, July 9, 1789, and to Abigail Adams, Dec. 12, 1793, Adams Papers, Reels 372, 376. For Adams's later revelations about his lack of political intelligence while president see his letter to Theodore Foster, Oct. 6, 1811, *ibid.*, Reel 118. For Adams's naïveté compared with Hamilton see Manning J. Dauer, *The Adams Federalists* (Baltimore, 1953), 56. For Fisher Ames's wish that Adams might be less blunt in expressing his opinions see Claude G. Bowers, *Jefferson and Hamilton: The Struggle for Democracy in America* (Boston, 1925), 6. Adams spoke more often while chairing the Senate than he admitted, especially to give information and opinions about the foreign service; he cast numerous, often important, tie-breaking votes as well. That he could have influenced procedure far more than he did was evident from two resolutions from France on the death of Franklin. Both the House and Senate answered them, but under Adams's influence the Senate responded more coldly. Hazen, *American Opinion of the French Revolution*, 149–150.

could hold his pen only long enough to explain to John Quincy Adams that he wrote "in great Pain and under Embarrassments." With his "weak Eyes and . . . a trembling hand" he had grown unused to writing; as a result his brains were "rusty."[25] He lived increasingly in his son's career and in memories of his own when it had been more active. John Quincy's loss of his first case as a lawyer reminded him of his own, and the young man's instinct for the unpopular side of public issues delighted him. Adams grew convinced that his son was the most accomplished man in the country. Far from criticizing him as of old, Adams began to write in awe and praise, though still with much good advice. He addressed John Quincy Adams respectfully as "Dear Sir," excused him for not writing often enough, and could add to his praises only the hope that he would continue always to think and act as he did now. Adams wrote to his wife, "I have often thought he has more Prudence at 27, than his Father at 58." Adams's reluctance for political battle seems partly attributable to his premature wish to pass the mantle on to his eldest son. "All my hopes are in him," Adams wrote in 1794, "both for my Family and Country."[26]

Adams grew silent. He viewed the world with, if anything, increasing despair and bitterness, frequently commenting on mankind's fulfillment of his most dire prophecies. Without admitting it he began to moderate his views. By 1794, for example, he regarded the presence of the public at Senate debates as a benign practice, though accompanied by some difficulties. Yet, in 1789 he had reversed his Revolutionary position to write that public galleries, presumably because of the spectators' dangerous influence over the legislators, "will establish the national Government, or break the Confederation. I can conceive of no medium between these Extremes."[27] For all his

25. Adams to John Quincy Adams, Apr. 21, 1795, and Apr. 26, 1795, Adams Papers, Reel 379, and to Abigail Adams, Jan. 31, 1796, *ibid*., Reel 381.

26. Adams to Abigail Adams, May 19, 1794, and Apr. 5, 1794, *ibid.*, Reel 377. For Adams on his age see *ibid.*, Reels 115, 377 *passim*. On John Quincy Adams see Reels 376, 377, 380, 372, 375, *passim*, and Adams to Thomas Welsh, Sept. 13, 1790, *Works of John Adams*, IX, 571–572.

27. Adams to Abigail Adams, Apr. 19, 1789, Adams Papers, Reel 372. Adams praised the

diary keeping, preservation of letterbooks, and extensive marginalia and note taking, Adams rarely checked his past writings, even while composing his books. Now, in self-serving reminiscences about his career he made forgetfulness an aging man's convenience.

An isolated life with prolonged, sedentary periods in the Senate took its toll on Adams. In addition he lived in increasing anxiety while away from his wife, whose health was also failing. Rather than turning to his fellow men in his loneliness Adams took to books. When he felt "Ennui, of an Evening" he read until he exclaimed, "I Shall Stiffle myself with reading." Otherwise, he wrote in 1794, "I go to Senate every day . . . see a few Friends once a Week, go to Church on Sundays." Living in boardinghouses during legislative sessions, he refused invitations to dine in order "not to be wholly ignorant of what is passing in the litterary World." His description of an evening out suggests the tenor of his life in the arcadian years of the new government. At Robert Morris's for dinner: "Sat Smoaking Segars, drinking burgundy & Madeira & talking Politicks till almost Eleven o Clock. This will do once in a great While: not often for me."[28]

The pace of Adams's reading from the peace of 1783 until his retirement seventeen years later, partly reflected in the epigraphs and poetic tags abounding in "Davila," hardly abated whether he was at home or in the capital. Although he continued to ransom his life to his political fortunes Adams cared above all for books and ideas. He had emerged in 1765 from ten years of study to lend his erudition to the fight against the Stamp Act. Then from 1765 to 1776 he contributed his studious writings to the Revolutionary struggle—in the newspapers and

---

open galleries of the Massachusetts General Court in "Novanglus," *Works of John Adams*, IV, 53. On the other hand, James Otis once had moved to open the General Court gallery with the result of mob-like intimidation of the legislators. Shipton, *Sibley's Harvard Graduates*, XI, 269–270.

28. Adams to Abigail Adams, letters of Dec. 14, 1794, and Dec. 17, 1794, Adams Papers, Reel 378; Jan. 21, 1794, *ibid.*, Reel 377; Dec. 26, 1793, *ibid.*, Reel 376; and Jan. 29, 1795, *ibid.*, Reel 379. Smith, *John Adams*, II, 883, suggests a regeneration in Adams of the sort described below in this chapter as taking place some months later.

in the form of committee reports. From 1778 to 1788 he wrote newspaper propaganda for Europeans and diplomatic reports for Congress (as well as preparing the Massachusetts Constitution in 1779 and his *Defence of the Constitutions* in 1786–1787). For his twelve years as vice-president and president, however, Adams had little outlet for his erudite approach to politics—the reception of his "Davila" essays demonstrated that.

During the 1790s, as a result, Adams's studiousness ran underground, turning him into a recluse and an eccentric. He continued to view events in the same philosophical and bookish manner as before but could find no way to express himself publicly. The follies of the times struck him increasingly as products of the philosophy of the French Enlightenment. And so while Congress debated measures that might have drawn the country into war, Adams occupied himself with an unpublished attack on Rousseau's *Discourse on Inequality*.[29]

With Adams's decline into age, forgetfulness, and isolation came flareups of his resentment toward and pessimism about America. When he had to make the uncomfortable trip by public coaches to and from Philadelphia, he thought about his lack of rewards. Once, he fancied himself treated by the people worse than Benedict Arnold. Comparing his country with Great Britain, he called America "in points of Insolence her very image and Superscription. As true a Game Cock as She and I warrant you Shall become as great a Scourge to Mankind." The Senate, still trying to force British evacuation of the forts left over from the Revolutionary War, was threatening to suspend debt payments arranged by the peace that Adams had signed in 1783. Unable to join in the debate, he anguished in his letters: "Oh Liberty! O my Country! Oh Debt and Oh Sin." As for humanity, he saw "no tendency to any Thing but Anarchy, Licentiousness and Despotism. Mankind will not learn Wisdom from Experience."[30]

29. See the series of letters from Adams to Thomas Boylston Adams, Mar. 16, 1796, and following, Adams Papers, Reel 377. Also see Smith, *John Adams*, II, 855–857.

30. Adams to Abigail Adams, Apr. 15, 1794, May 10, 1794, and Feb. 9, 1794, all in Adams Papers, Reel 377. For Adams's complaints see his letters to Abigail Adams, Jan. 23, 1795, and Apr. 2, 1790, Adams Papers, Reels 379, 115.

Without his feeling of neglect by the people, of course, Adams would not have been Adams. But during the 1790s he began to express himself with the resigned sarcasm of disillusionment. In the past, despite an official pessimism about mankind of the sort that easily lends itself to irony, Adams's broad humor had signaled his essential optimism. While vice-president, however, he developed a self-deprecatory, ironic wit. "I have held the office of libellee-general long enough," he quipped in 1794; "the burden of it ought to be participated and equalized, according to modern republican principles."[31] In such moments Adams became the conservative who subsists on exposing the excesses of the party of hope rather than on a vision of his own.

By summer 1796, after which he would be elected president, Adams seemed to occupy himself far less with politics than with the careers of his three sons (Charles as a lawyer, John Quincy as minister to the Netherlands, and Thomas Boylston as his secretary) and with his wife, his books, and his farm. His letters from the capital began and ended with inquiries and directives pertaining to agriculture. Warm, fall weather in Philadelphia alerted him to the possibility of late plowing at home; an east wind suggested "Treasures" of seaweed washed up on his shores to be carted onto next year's fields; frozen winter roads signaled the time to haul manure out of the barns. Adams began to write letters to his wife during Senate hours and confessed that he could hardly get through his week without a letter from her. He said that he could survive without one on Thursday, but "Should be inconsolable on a disappointment a Monday."[32]

Adams returned home in May 1796 with only one more session of the Senate before him. Not until September would it be known for certain that Washington intended to retire, but Adams had to prepare himself for the likelihood of becoming president. Accordingly he took up his diary, not kept regularly

---

31. Adams to Abigail Adams, Jan. 2, 1794, *Works of John Adams*, I, 461.
32. Adams to Abigail Adams, Jan. 29, 1795, Adams Papers, Reel 379. For Adams's homesickness see Reels 377 and 378 *passim*.

for ten years, to prepare himself a last time for a new challenge. His task no longer involved introspection, study, or exercises in humility; he needed to reconstitute his debilitated energies. "This Journal is commenced," he wrote, "to allure me into the habit of Writing again, long lost. This habit is easily lost but not easily regained. I have, in the Course of Life, lost it several times and regained it as often. So I will now."

Adams set his farm hands to work building a new barn, clearing fields, setting up walls, and carting manure. With the growth of his crops and the improvements on his lands he revived, and an old delight and gentleness returned to his language. "It rains at 11. O Clock. The Barley is growing white for the Harvest. My Men are hilling the Corn over the Road. A soft fine rain, in a clock calm is falling as sweetly as I ever saw in April, May or June. It distills as gently as We can wish. Will beat down the grain as little as possible, refresh the Gardens and Pastures, revive the Corn, make the fruit grow rapidly, and lay the foundation of fine Rowen and After feed." The day before, he "arose by four O Clock and enjoyed the Charm of earliest Birds. Their Songs were never more various, universal, animating or delightful." One could almost mistake Adams's diary entries, weather notations included, for those written thirty years earlier. Parson Wibird, still alive, "dined with Us." Adams borrowed his brother's oxen to plough. On August 4: "Went over to Weymouth with Mrs. A., visited Mr. Norton and dined with Dr. Tufts whose salted Beef and shell beans with a Whortleberry Pudden and his Cyder is a Luxurious Treat." Adams's complaints concerned his land taxes; his worries, the laziness of some of the hired men. His strongest expressions were reserved for the "Tyranny" of the man who mishandled horses with women and children nearby and for the thoughtless people who "murdered" a fine walnut tree. No wonder that he dated his entry for August 19 as 1769 instead of 1796.[33]

33. *Diary and Autobiography*, III, 226, 228, 227, 238, 242. Wherever he traveled Adams sought out "recipes" for making compost, the local materials for which were seaweed; "slimy Mud from the Brook"; horse, cow, and pig manure; and purchased lime. During this summer he corresponded about a recent English agricultural *Report . . . On the Subject of Manures. Diary and Autobiography*, III, 238n.

Through the summer he continued to read widely and randomly. One of his observations hinted at a returning optimism about America. "Tyranny," Adams wrote, "can scarcely be practiced upon a virtuous and wise People." A week later he expressed familiar hopes about the American errand: "A Nation that should never do wrong must necessarily govern the World." Late in August, Adams grew unwell for a few days with symptoms that reminded him of his two collapses in Europe. But his home remedies of "Rhubarb and Salt of Wormwood" and "balm Tea" seemed to work; he felt reborn: "The shower last night has refreshed Us. The Corn, the Gardens, the Pastures, The After feed, the Fruit trees all feel it."[34] Thoughts, discussion, and correspondence about politics now resumed. John Adams was ready for Philadelphia and the election.

34. *Ibid.*, 236, 238, 243, 244. In the course of the summer Adams read a Christian critique of Thomas Paine, a life of Petrarch, Cicero, and a book on mythology returned by a borrower. See *ibid.*, 231–245 and notes.

X
President John Adams
1796–1801

In Adams's mind preparing to be president had nothing to do with preparing to win an election. He neither solicited for the office nor campaigned to win it after the Federalist caucus put up his name. He regarded the presidency as his due by seniority, natural "Succession," and a due recognition of his services. Jefferson, his Republican opponent, agreed. He, too, did not campaign, and when it seemed as if the electoral votes might be even, he decided privately to cede the election to Adams, his senior. Jefferson had been chosen as his party's standard bearer as early as 1794 and emerged during Adams's presidency as a formidable political tactician.[1] But in 1796 the aloofness of the candidates represented a still lively idealism about presidential politics. Adams proved himself the least sophisticated one of all, carrying over into the partisan era after his election the vague, idealistic conception of the executive office expressed in the Constitutional Convention and his own *Defence of the Constitutions*. This anachronism accounted for many of his eccentricities as president.

For all his talk about the importance of the executive veto Adams conceived of the presidency not so much as a strong office as an independent one. A man of integrity stood above contending factions in the Senate and House of Representatives, and above parties as well. He represented the dignity of government and the interests of all the people. In Quincy during

---

1. Adams to Abigail Adams, Feb. 15, 1796, Adams Papers, Reel 381, phrase crossed out then replaced by Adams. On Jefferson see Kurtz, *Presidency of John Adams*, 95, 90.

the summer of 1796 Adams readied himself psychologically to take up this position. He failed to contact party leaders, arrange appointments, or, most surprising of all, to develop a program for his administration. His preparation was no more practical than those for the case of farmer Field in 1758, for his second voyage to Europe (when despite his previous experience he left without consulting about his instructions), or most recently for his vice-presidency in 1788.

At the end of the summer Adams traveled to Philadelphia in his usual simplicity of public conveyances and then watched philosophically as the election returns slowly came in during November and December. He did not learn the common knowledge among influential men in both parties—that Hamilton had once again plotted to reduce his vote, this time in the hope that Adams's running mate, Charles Cotesworth Pinckney, would receive more votes than he and slip in as president. While others counted the key votes of electors in New York, Pennsylvania, and South Carolina, Adams treated the election process as a generalized expression of approval or disapproval of his character. In his mind the contest pitted his principles against Jefferson's dangerous, jacobinical tendencies; it had nothing to do with party organizations, local issues (which were of great importance in this election), or the pressures that might be brought to bear on certain members of the Electoral College.

As ever, Adams prepared himself for the equally difficult pains of winning and losing, probing his consciousness in the process. "It really Seems to me as if I wished to be left out," he wrote. "Let me See! do I know my own heart? I am not Sure." His detachment testified that his character would not give way to concupiscence even when the highest honor came within grasp. But his philosophical nature cost him more than ever before. His preparation for defeat was admirable—"then for Frugality and Independence.—Poverty and Patriotism. Love and a Carrot bed."—but he should have been developing a legislative program.[2]

2. Adams to Abigail Adams, Dec. 7, 1796, Adams Papers, Reel 382. For Adams's

In four years as president, Adams split the Federalist party, suffered a rising crescendo of criticism and abuse, and left public life feeling himself an outcast. He looked forward to recognition for having left the country flourishing and at peace when he went out of office—in every important way better off than when he came in. Yet, his behavior as president was, as Adrienne Koch has described it, "almost as enigmatic as his complex personality." By the end of his term Adams had gained a reputation for vanity and suspiciousness. His grandson and later writers have pointed out, though, that rather than suspicion his behavior displayed excessive trust—"a childlike optimism," in fact. However, these comments in turn raise the question of how Adams could have been so trusting. Given his devastating insights into the foibles of men and his fierce sense of personal prerogative, what can have turned him to the self-destructive trustfulness and mistimed compromises of his presidency?[3]

Adams was elected in 1796 because the Federalist party was still dominant, but he received a minority of the votes cast. This placed him in an awkward but familiar situation, for in his whole career he gained office by a majority of popular votes only once: in 1776 he was elected Braintree selectman by "but one Vote more than half," with about a hundred votes.[4] He

---

preparations see Kurtz, *Presidency of John Adams*, 78–79, and Chinard, *Honest John Adams*, 259.

3. Adrienne Koch, *Power, Morals, and the Founding Fathers: Essays in Interpretation of the American Enlightenment* (Ithaca, N.Y., 1961), 94. After being set down as a weak, vacillating president by historians, Adams has had some recent defenders. His failures have been laid to insurmountable obstacles and dishonest subordinates, while his mysterious delays and changes of policy have been called "wise," only "apparent" hesitations. He has been described as "an astute politician" and molder of public opinion who left office more popular and with more electoral votes than when he came in. See Joseph Charles, "Adams and Jefferson: The Origins of the American Party System," *WMQ*, 3d Ser., XII (1955), 412, and Kurtz, *Presidency of John Adams*, 389, 383, 372. Similarly, Hutson, "John Adams's Titles Campaign," *NEQ*, XLI (1968), argues the politically explicable bases of Adams's troubles in 1789.

4. *Diary and Autobiography*, I, 302. Adams was elected to the General Court from Boston at a special town meeting to find a replacement for James Bowdoin. He won by 418 to 118 votes. In 1774 he was elected by Braintree to the Provincial Congress as an additional delegate. He was appointed, not elected, to the Continental Congresses. In 1775 he was elected to the Massachusetts Council by the lower house. Adams was a minority vice-

approached the presidency in his old spirit of lonely independence when the new party politics demanded an opposite approach.

Nearly the whole of Adams's administration was taken up with French affairs. No sooner had he entered office in 1797 than news came that the French Directory had dismissed the American ambassador and begun to violate American neutrality on the seas. Adams recommended a simultaneous military buildup and gesture of conciliation—the sending of a bipartisan commission of three to France. Early in 1798 it became known that the commissioners not only had been denied an official reception but had been asked for bribe money. This insult by the French agents, designated X, Y, and Z (from which letters the affair takes its name), roused American public opinion, giving rise to the famous toast, "Millions for defense, but not a cent for tribute." From 1798 until the end of Adams's administration clashes between French cruisers and American merchant ships and frigates amounted to a "quasi-war." The difficulties facing Adams were exceptional. He entered office to the accompaniment of simultaneous economic depression and inflation. Three cabinet members conducted an intrigue against him unmatched in American history. Virtually every Adams paper, statement, and gesture was retailed to Alexander Hamilton, who dictated the secretaries' actions from outside the government.

Yet, taken together with both French and English maritime violations, Adams's difficulties fail to account for his ineffectual responses. Despite warnings he failed for two years to detect anything amiss within his cabinet, then continued to tolerate the insubordination, and finally dismissed only two of the offenders, never realizing that, as Charles Francis Adams put it, he "retained in his bosom the most subtle and venomous serpent of them all." Still more remarkable was the way Adams suffered and trusted Hamilton despite knowledge of his plot in

---

president both times and was elected president with a plurality of only three electoral votes.

the 1788 election. At the time Adams called the reduced vice-presidential vote engineered by Hamilton both a "curse" and a "Stain," and he complained of it in public. Yet he allowed his son Charles to study law under Hamilton and wrote politely to him in connection with the arrangement. Insofar as he could support Hamilton's financial program, which included payment of Dutch loans signed for by Adams, he did so from the vice-presidential chair. (Coincidental agreement occasionally gave a misleading appearance of political collusion between the two throughout the 1790s, while it tended to mask from Adams the influence of Hamilton over the cabinet.) After Hamilton apparently supported him for reelection as vice-president in 1792 Adams called him "faithful." Then, when Hamilton repeated his scheming in the presidential canvass of 1796, Adams at first could not be persuaded that he had done so, though he agreed that Hamilton "must be attended to." Finally convinced, Adams insisted for months that Hamilton's "Motives were . . . for the publick Good" and declared, "I believe there were no very dishonest Intrigues in this Business."[5]

To some extent Adams restrained himself publicly in order to achieve political harmony, for he was more acerbic in writing to his wife: "Hamilton I know to be a proud Spirited, conceited, aspiring Mortal always pretending to Morality, with as debauched Morals as old Franklin who is more his Model

5. *Works of John Adams*, I, 570; Adams to Benjamin Rush, May 17, 1789, Adams Papers, Reel 115; to Abigail Adams, Jan. 24, 1793, Dec. 12, 1796, and Dec. 18, 1796, *ibid.*, Reels 376, 382; and to Rush, Feb. 13, 1797, *ibid.*, Reel 117. For Adams's letters to Hamilton about Charles's law study see July 19, 1789, *ibid.*, Reel 115, and Abigail Adams to Mary Cranch, Aug. 9, 1789, in Stewart Mitchell, ed., *New Letters of Abigail Adams, 1788–1801* (Boston, 1947), 21. The arrangement ended when Hamilton had to leave New York. Charles, "Adams and Jefferson," *WMQ*, 3d Ser., XII (1955), 428–429, attributes some of Adams's delay in moving against the cabinet to a change of political view during the 1790s that brought him close to Hamilton's aristocratic position. But see chap. 9 for the content and chronology of Adams's views of aristocracy. Howe, *Changing Political Thought of John Adams*, 159–214, describes a similar continuing drift away from democratic institutions during the 1790s. Yet, Adams continued the ambivalence described in chap. 9, affirming his confidence in America as often as his despair and continuing to express millennarian hopes based on its system and practice. "Our independence," he wrote, "will be one essential instrument for reclaiming the fermented world, and bringing good out of the mass of evil." "To the Young Men of the City of New York," June 1798, *Works of John Adams*, IX, 198–199. Compare his asserting his "unshaken confidence in . . . the American people" in his inaugural address. *Ibid.*, 110, and see 188.

than any one I know." But much more to the point—as "model" for Adams's behavior now—was his own ineffectual handling of Franklin. He had allowed himself to remain ignorant of Franklin's connections with speculators and British spies and had let pass Franklin's denunciation of him to Congress with no more than complaints in letters to friends. Now, despite warnings, he suffered Hamilton in the same way, balancing criticism with praise for his accomplishments as he always did with Franklin and planning only to "keep him at a distance." In 1798 Adams honored Hamilton's request that he give an appointment to his nephew. And in the same year, during the XYZ crisis, he apparently was ready to appoint Hamilton as secretary of war.

This last report has been called "astounding if true"; yet it fits a pattern of excessive trust and forgiveness.[6] From John Dickinson's snub, through Robert R. Livingston's French-inspired rebukes of his diplomacy, to the accusations on the floor of Congress that he was vain, Adams responded to direct aggression with surprising calm. Indeed, he tended to take to his bosom those who delivered it. Elbridge Gerry, whose report that certain congressmen found him vain produced Adams's significant avowal of his weakness along with thanks to Gerry for having been candid with him, remained his confidant while Adams was in Europe. Then John Trumbull and William Tudor, two other purveyors of criticism, succeeded as confidants in 1789 and 1790. Later, after Gerry criticized his politics Adams again drew close to him.

In 1797 Adams appointed Gerry one of the commissioners to France over protests that he was not a Federalist. When Gerry drew criticism for his apparently inconsistent behavior as an envoy, Adams, who despite similar reports about himself from France in 1779 had been supported by Gerry, stood by his old friend. The two were among the few left from the old party of

---

6. Adams to Abigail Adams, Jan. 9, 1797, Adams Papers, Reel 383; Kurtz, *Presidency of John Adams*, 302. On the appointment of Hamilton's nephew see Adams to James McHenry, Sept. 3, 1798, *Works of John Adams*, VIII, 591. For warnings about Hamilton see Charles, "Adams and Jefferson," *WMQ*, 3d Ser., XII (1955), 414.

Revolutionaries who prided themselves on standing above party. Another was Samuel Adams, whom Adams supported for governor of Massachusetts despite his opposition to Adams's reelection to the vice-presidency in 1792. (Samuel Adams replied with a warm note congratulating him on becoming president.) As he put it in 1805, "There is something in my composition, which restrains me from rancour against any man, with whom I have once lived in friendship."[7]

Adams went furthest in ignoring personal resentment in the case of Franklin's grandnephew, Jonathan Williams, the manager of Silas Deane's and Benjamin Franklin's speculations and a British spy. Despite the warning that Williams opposed his administration, Adams nominated him for a government position. Not surprisingly, rather than inspiring a bipartisan spirit, Adams's disposition to trust and forgive gave rise to a remarkable series of betrayals. So long is the list that one is forced to look for the cause in Adams's own conduct, especially his failures to respond to opponents' attacks. His restraint was the product of a long-standing fear of giving vent to his true feelings. Feeling incipient rage at minor fallings off of affection he began to exercise self-control at the point where anyone else would begin to lose patience. The result was that his behavior appeared alternately warlike and compromising. It was characteristic that Adams's first published essay, on "private revenge," contained the advice, "Sit down and bear it."[8]

7. Adams to Rush, July 7, 1805, Adams Papers, Reel 118. Adams supported Gerry despite personal annoyance. See Mitchell, ed., *New Letters of Abigail Adams*, 186. On Gerry's return from France, Adams listened sympathetically to him despite Federalist pressure not to meet with him at all. For Gerry's similar support of Adams in the 1780s see *Adams Family Correspondence*, III, 232n, and IV, 190n. After a frank exchange of letters on government Samuel Adams attacked Adams in 1790. See Cappon, ed., *Adams-Jefferson Letters*, I, 248n. For Adams's loyalty to Samuel Adams see his letters to Abigail Adams, Feb. 10, 1794, Apr. 19, 1794, and May 12, 1794, Adams Papers, Reel 377. In 1800 Gerry was against Adams for reelection to the presidency.

8. "On Private Revenge," *Works of John Adams*, III, 427 (from the *Boston Gazette*, Sept. 5, 1763). On Jonathan Williams see Adams to Timothy Pickering, Sept. 13, 1797, Adams Papers, Reel 114. A partial list of those who turned against Adams includes John Trumbull, Gen. Henry Knox, Theodore Sedgwick, Tench Coxe, the Muhlenbergs, and George Washington. Trumbull: Adams to Trumbull, Aug. 12, 1800, *Works of John Adams*, IX, 74, 74n; Dauer, *Adams Federalists*, 249. Knox: Dauer, *Adams Federalists*, 78–79; Bernhard Knollenberg, "John Adams, Knox, and Washington," American Antiquarian Society,

As president, Adams showed the strain by growing, in the words of his friend Benjamin Rush, "more irritable in temper, and less cautious in speaking of men and things, than he had been in the early and middle stages of his life." In 1797 Adams himself wrote: "I believe honesty is always anxious and consequently peevish and fretful. It is always afraid of doing wrong, or making mistakes." He rendered himself an ineffectual president by a combination of ill-timed restraint, his old uneasiness with any condition but unpopularity, and a self-destructive fatalism. Because he "always expected" to be attacked, he had "always submitted to it; perhaps often with too much tameness."[9]

Of all the betrayals to which Adams left himself open, the cabinet plot was the most remarkable, not only because its disloyalties to a president were unique in American history but because Adams ignored explicit warnings against it for so long. From the beginning Gerry warned that Pickering, the secretary of state and most able of the three plotters, intended to keep him in the background. Gerry pointed out that Pickering had published an account of the peace diplomacy of 1782–1783 that minimized Adams's contribution while enlarging Jay's. No doubt just because the issue was that most tender one with Adams, his own reputation, and especially because it touched on his temporary failure to leave Holland for Paris in 1782, he excused Pickering. "There are none whom I distrust," he wrote Gerry.[10] Neither Pickering's unchallenged insolence during a

Proceedings, LVI (1946), 207–238. Sedgwick: Kurtz, *Presidency of John Adams*, 378. Coxe: *ibid.*, 292; Smith, *John Adams*, II, 900. Muhlenbergs: Paul A. W. Wallace, *The Muhlenbergs of Pennsylvania* (Philadelphia, 1950), 292–293. Washington: James Thomas Flexner, *George Washington: Anguish and Farewell (1793–1799)* (Boston, 1972), 401, 409–410. For Adams's later comments on these and other deceptions see Biddle, ed., *Old Family Letters*, I, 76, and Adams to Rush, June 23, 1807, Adams Papers, Reel 118.

9. Corner, ed., *Autobiography of Rush*, 143; Adams to Abigail Adams, Apr. 3, 1797, Adams Papers, Reel 384, and to Jefferson, June 30, 1813, Cappon, ed., *Adams-Jefferson Letters*, II, 348.

10. Adams to Elbridge Gerry, Feb. 20, 1897, Adams Papers, Reel 117. See also Adams to Gerry, Feb. 13, 1797, *Works of John Adams*, VIII, 523. On Pickering's insubordinations, which included maliciously blocking an army appointment for Adams's ne'er-do-well son-in-law, see Kurtz, *Presidency of John Adams*, 280–282. For a final Pickering gesture of insolence see *Works of John Adams*, I, 539.

cabinet meeting nor his flat refusal to execute an order turned Adams against him.

Adams's first presidential act had been to retain Washington's cabinet, thereby setting a self-destructive pattern of abrogating power. Toward opposition from the cabinet Adams suppressed not only natural resentment but his normal suspicions—just as in Paris he had ignored the spying so apparent to Arthur Lee and as head of the peace commission had suppressed another form of suspicion—jealousy of prerogative—and refrained from forcing Franklin's hand. Now he responded to Gerry's warning against Pickering by writing, "Pickering and all his Colleagues are as much Attached to me as I desire: I have no *Jealousies* from that quarter." Suspected while vice-president of casting his tie-breaking Senate votes for executive privilege in anticipation of succeeding Washington, Adams yielded one prerogative after another once he became president. Suspected of malice toward opponents, he took revenge on none. Suspected of ambition, he consistently avoided acting with an eye to reelection. It was in this spirit that he retained Washington's cabinet, resolving to remove from office "not one from personal motives."[11]

Adams correctly predicted that his administration, "like Popes Woman will have no Character at all." It gained the reputation of inconsistency from Adams's behavior during the three years of the French crisis. During this period his pattern was one of self-righteous response to events (he still had not become an initiator) followed by ill-timed compromise that failed to achieve conciliation. The first act of his administration, the sending of a commission to France despite the rebuff of America's envoy in 1797, initiated this pattern of behavior. At first Adams reacted with high resentment at the French insult. When his temper cooled he favored another attempt to negotiate. At his first cabinet meeting, in an intended gesture of

11. Adams to Gerry, Feb. 13, 1797, Adams Papers, Reel 117 (italics added), and to Benjamin Lincoln, Mar. 10, 1800, *Works of John Adams*, IX, 47. The sentence continued, "[and] not one from party considerations." For a defense of retaining Washington's cabinet see Kurtz, *Presidency of John Adams*, 237–240.

bipartisanship, he proposed a Republican as the new envoy. But he gave way when the three Hamiltonian intimates threatened to resign in protest. After settling on a commission of three (on which Gerry served), Adams called a special session of Congress to recommend the commission along with preparations for defense: the arming of merchant vessels, the establishment of a navy, and bringing the militia into a state of readiness. One of the first bills subsequently to come before him was a "Stamp Tax" to raise money not only for a navy but for an army as well. Americans tended to oppose taxes whether levied by the English or their own government; they were certain to dislike one so unfortunately named. Adams, who had been born into politics as an opponent of the Stamp Act in 1765 and who opposed raising an army, realized the dangers but refrained from vetoing the measure.

In 1798 Adams again urged a naval but not an army establishment, only to see Hamilton's program go through Congress to saddle the country with the unnecessary expense of both. A year later came the news that the United States had been insulted by the XYZ request for bribe money. Again Adams grew angry on behalf of his country, drafting a message to Congress little short of a declaration of war. Then he replaced it with more restrained language drawn at Hamilton's instance by a cabinet member.[12] Adams was unaware that Hamilton often influenced his speeches, most of which from 1797 to 1799 were extensively revised by the cabinet. It was thus that the constant pressure of Hamilton's secret influence reacted on Adams's periodic compliance to help give the administration its reputation for inconsistency. Typical of his failure to assert authority at this time was his permitting Congress to make "the most serious attempt in American history to declare war without a recommendation by the President." The effort failed without his taking a hand against it, Congress adjourned,

12. Adams to Jefferson, July 3, 1813, Cappon, ed., *Adams-Jefferson Letters*, II, 349. The extent of Hamilton's influence over Adams's state papers is a matter of dispute. See Smith, *John Adams*, II, 954–957, and Jacob E. Cooke, "Country above Party: John Adams and the 1799 Mission to France," in Edmund P. Willis, ed., *Fame and the Founding Fathers* (Bethlehem, Pa., 1967), 58n.

and Adams left the capital to spend the summer in Quincy. Most damaging of all to Adams were the Alien and Sedition Acts passed by Congress and quickly associated with his supposedly reactionary ideas. He responded to the XYZ hysteria with far less enthusiasm than most Federalists but was sufficiently alarmed to permit his subordinates to prosecute the opposition press. Continuing his vice-presidential passivity, Adams attracted responsibility not by any complicity in framing the acts but by his failure to take up against them the moderate position that his administration stood for. He soon grew disenchanted, issued pardons, and went on to appoint John Marshall to the Supreme Court despite his politically embarrassing denunciation of the acts. Nevertheless, Adams remained guilty of passive acceptance.[13]

Government administration—what there was of it—effectively ceased over the long summers between congressional sessions, and though Adams was no different from Washington or Jefferson in remaining at his farm until October or November each year, he stayed away during crises of a sort never faced by either of them. On the other hand, it should be remembered that to a great extent Adams was justified in managing affairs as he did. He was basically correct in his confidence that the people continued to regard him as a Revolutionary figure whose long services merited trust. Certain contemporaries and later students might make much of newspaper misrepresentations of his views on monarchy or imagine a universal uproar over the twenty-five Sedition Act cases (which resulted in ten convictions) because of Madison and Jefferson's Virginia and Kentucky Resolutions. But Adams stood at a high point of popularity in 1798 for his measured, patriotic stand against

13. Dauer, *Adams Federalists*, 169–170. For Adams's messages see James D. Richardson, ed., *A Compilation of the Messages and Papers of the Presidents, 1789–1897*, I ([Washington, D.C.], 1897), 223–229, 261–265. For an indictment of Adams for the Alien and Sedition Acts see John C. Miller, *Crisis in Freedom: The Alien and Sedition Acts* (Boston, 1951); for a defense see Smith, *John Adams*, II, 976–977. Also see James Morton Smith, "John Adams Pardons William Durell: A Note on Sedition Proceedings, 1798–1800," *New-York Historical Society Quarterly*, XL (1956), 176–181. On Adams's immunity to the anti-Jesuit hysteria of 1799 see Haraszti, "John Adams and Frederick the Great," *More Books*, 6th Ser., IX (1934), 166.

French insults. His presence in the capital was required not so much to manage the government as to head off his enemies.[14]

In Quincy, with the country at a height of excitement (including clashes in the streets of Philadelphia between pro- and anti-French groups), Adams became distracted by a series of family crises. His son Charles suffered financial ruin and began a decline that ended two years later in his death. His wife became so sick that by August, Adams believed her "at the point of death." He called it "the most gloomy Summer of my Life" and "the severest trial I ever endured." Adams's letters to his wife from Philadelphia near the end of his second term as vice-president had expressed a reawakening of feeling for her, and even sexual innuendo. Now, with her suffering from fever, diarrhea, and "diabetes," Adams, who was himself suffering from pyorrhea and beginning painfully to lose his teeth, fell into despair. During this summer he became convinced of Hamilton's scheme to become head of the army, but he responded to appeals to deal with the matter by pleading his "state of depression, agitation, and *anxiety*." In writing to George Washington he repeatedly expressed the wish that he could resign the presidency to him.[15]

By the time Adams returned to the capital in fall 1798 he had received several indications that the French would be amenable to diplomatic talks. He drafted his annual speech for the opening of Congress on a conciliatory note but then acquiesced in a more aggressive one by the same secretary—Oliver Wolcott—who had changed his speech the previous year. Charles Francis Adams pointed out that Adams insisted on a "small" but "significant" modification of a sentence in Wolcott's draft with

14. "President Jefferson absented himself from Washington one day in four during his eight years as President." Marshall Smelser, *The Democratic Republic, 1801–1815* (New York, 1968), 45n. Adams remarked the impossibility of gathering quorums until "gentlemen" had returned from their estates each fall—Nov. 15 at the earliest. Adams to Abigail Adams, Nov. 15, 1794, Adams Papers, Reel 378, and see Nov. 18, 1794, *ibid*.

15. Adams to James McHenry, Aug. 29, 1798, *Works of John Adams*, VIII, 589, and Oct. 22, 1798, Adams Papers, Reel 391; to Abigail Adams, Feb. 22, 1799, *Works of John Adams*, I, 545; and to John Quincy Adams, Oct. 16, 1798, Adams Papers, Reel 391; Smith, *John Adams*, II, 982 (italics added). On his wish to resign his office to Washington see Adams to McHenry, Aug. 29, 1798, *Works of John Adams*, VIII, 588.

the effect of keeping open the door to accommodation. "But this explanation," as Gilbert Chinard has written, "is no excuse for the President's unwillingness to assume full responsibility for foreign affairs. On the whole, he had compromised, if he had not surrendered, to the demands of his cabinet, and against his better judgment had yielded." Of two minds about war with France, Adams wavered in his position throughout his administration. When he thought of France's insults to American sovereignty he renewed his patriotic insistence on the recognition of American independence. When he recalled himself to his diplomatic principle of neutrality he grew conciliatory. Thus, he remained bellicose during most of the summer, then returned to the capital with a conciliatory speech—which he proceeded to abandon. He soon changed back to conciliation, yet as late as 1800 he returned to the conviction that war was imminent.[16]

The two months following Adams's return after his trying summer saw the advancement of Hamilton's program even as additional evidences of French willingness to treat were arriving. The culmination of Federalist preparations for war was congressional approval of a thirty-thousand-man army. Adams withdrew himself in characteristic fashion, then acted with stunning suddenness. His behavior continued a habit as old as his decision to study law. What appeared as a sudden act actually was the product of long consideration, though with little or no consideration of the impression it was likely to give. In his public life an emotional outburst, such as his initial, warlike speech in response to the XYZ affair, characteristically preceded retreat, study, consideration of the personal consequences of taking an unpopular stand (as in the Boston Massacre trials), and finally the abrupt, surprising deed itself. During the two months following his December 1798 speech Adams

16. *Works of John Adams*, I, 536–537; Chinard, *Honest John Adams*, 281. See also Adams's letter to John Marshall, Sept. 4, 1800, *Works of John Adams*, IX, 80–81. Adams's fluctuations have occasioned remarks like Gilbert Chinard's observation of a "curious change of heart" during summer 1798 or Stephen Kurtz's "just what kind of a game Adams was playing it is almost impossible to ascertain," on his capitulation to the cabinet when he returned to the capital. *Honest John Adams*, 279; *Presidency of John Adams*, 346.

read over his own diplomatic correspondence. He called himself the "Solitudinarian," and he echoed the 1768 phrase that had preceded his return to provincial politics from his retreat in Quincy (then still called Braintree): "It is time for me to bid farewell to Politics." Then, acting for the first time without a hint to his "thunderstruck" cabinet, on February 18, 1799, Adams sent to the Senate his nomination of another envoy to France: William Vans Murray, John Quincy Adams's friend and fellow diplomat in Europe.[17]

In after years Adams and his descendants pointed to this decision, which eventuated in the convention of 1800 with France, as his great contribution as president. Fraught with political danger for himself—"perhaps no President ever made an announcement which had such violent political repercussions"—it amounted to a classic Adams gesture of selflessness. And the obscure peace that followed it was another achievement destined to be remembered only by the family.[18] As the Adamses saw it, he had placed his country before party and personal considerations, won the peace, and consequently lost the presidency. Once again, though, as Adams perhaps never realized, he had made a gesture only. Had he pursued his initiative, he might not have lost his office. Capable of the statesmanlike gesture in a crisis, he lacked the instinct for the required follow-up.

When a Senate committee came to dissuade him from the nomination of a new French envoy—a procedure that Adams suffered though he considered it presumptuous—he behaved testily, threatening to resign. Then, with "reluctance" he compromised by adding two commissioners to serve with the youthful Murray, thus expanding this peace commission just as his own had been expanded to his distress in 1781. Having done so, he left hurriedly for eight fatal months in Quincy, not to

17. Adams to Thomas Boylston Adams, Jan. 16, 1799, and to Abigail Adams, Feb. 9, 1799, Adams Papers, Reel 393; Howe, *Changing Political Thought of John Adams*, 201, quoting Pickering to King, Feb. 19, 1799. For Adams's reading see Reel 106 where Adams's note dated Jan. 18, 1799, on a letter of Sept. 4, 1782, indicates his reading of his diplomatic correspondence. See also Haraszti, *John Adams and the Prophets of Progress*, 270.

18. Charles, "Adams and Jefferson," *WMQ*, 3d Ser., XII (1955), 418.

"dramatize" his break from the Hamiltonians, but in the exhaustion that overcomes one who gathers his life into a few intense moments.[19] It was the turning point of his presidency.

With Adams gone, Pickering "deliberately delayed" the sailing of the commissioners for approximately two months.[20] Had they completed their mission only one month sooner than they did, word of their eventual success would have reached America in time to affect the presidential election lost by Adams. But Adams was not in complete command. In Quincy he insulated himself from the world, this time for escape, not preparation. When a letter arrived hinting at chicanery in the capital during his absence, Abigail Adams "did not think proper to communicate" it to him, evidently because of his anger at any suggestion that he return to oversee the government. He could, as he pointed out, conduct the business of government by mail. For his tendency to make of his presidency a few grand gestures and his lack of an administrative program did not mean that he shirked the daily labors of his office. Adams waded through masses of paper work both in Philadelphia and in Quincy (appointments and military commissions, largely). In addition, from the onset of the French crisis he received patriotic messages of support from towns, private associations, and college students, and he continued during the summer to write elaborate replies to these. When he might have been pursuing measures, Adams sententiously and with much rewording (which was rare for him) lectured his countrymen on political philosophy and the nature of man. In Quincy he read the correspondence of Frederick the Great with Voltaire and

19. Smith, *John Adams*, II, 1003, quoting Theodore Sedgwick, who headed the delegation. Kurtz, *Presidency of John Adams*, 372.

20. Chinard, *Honest John Adams*, 286. Pickering, in addition, apparently without Adams's realizing it, failed to announce publicly that Patrick Henry, one of the two men originally added to the commission with Murray, had been replaced after refusing the appointment. This omission fostered an impression of administration lack of interest in the matter. See Smith, *John Adams*, II, 1011. Jacob Cooke and Stephen G. Kurtz have argued that Pickering was not responsible for later delays often charged to him by historians. But they do not discuss this earlier delay. Cooke, "Country above Party," in Willis, ed., *Fame and the Founding Fathers*; Kurtz, "The French Mission of 1799–1800: Concluding Chapter in the Statecraft of John Adams," *Political Science Quarterly*, LXXX (1965), 543–557.

attended ceremonial events like the Harvard commencement and fourth of July observances.[21]

When word came of Talleyrand's assurance that the envoys would be treated properly, Adams responded in a letter to Pickering in which he called for dispatch in readying their departure. Yet, he added that he had "little confidence in the issue of this business." Pickering had called his attention to an "insult" by Talleyrand in claiming that Adams had unnecessarily delayed negotiations by insisting on an official assurance. In response to the Frenchman's "impertinent regrets, and insinuations of superfluities," Adams, referring to himself as "the President of the United States," proceeded alternately to speed and suspend the mission, as if to show Pickering that he was determined to proceed and Talleyrand that he could not be rushed.[22] He ignored warnings from Benjamin Stoddert, the loyal secretary of the newly formed navy, that he should come to oversee the government. Adams knew that on the way he would have to face his son Charles's abandoned wife. (When he did reach New York he wrote, "I renounce him.") Then, once in front of the recalcitrant cabinet he would be obliged to maintain his self-imposed restraint. (His volcanic fury when he later dismissed James McHenry as secretary of war suggests the cost of this effort.) He therefore put off Stoddert with the lamest excuse of all—that he could not come to Trenton because of its unsuitable accommodations![23]

21. Abigail Adams to her son, apparently Thomas Boylston Adams, June 23, 1799, Adams Papers, Reel 395. For Adams's work routine see Mitchell, ed., *New Letters of Abigail Adams*, 195. On the infinite detail of Adams's letters on shipbuilding to Benjamin Stoddert see Kurtz, "French Mission of 1799–1800," *Pol. Sci. Qtly.*, LXXX (1965), 556. On Adams's reading at this juncture see Haraszti, "John Adams and Frederick the Great," *More Books*, 6th Ser., IX (1934), 123–124.

22. Adams to Timothy Pickering, Aug. 6, 1799, *Works of John Adams*, IX, 10–11. For Pickering to Adams see *ibid.*, 10n. Adams inadvertently revealed that Talleyrand had stung him when, a year later in notes justifying his conduct he copied incorrectly and had to write over the offending sentence from Talleyrand's letter: "It was certainly Superfluous to Suffer So ~~much time~~ [crossed out] many months to elapse for the Simple confirmation of what I had already delivered to Mr. Gerry . . . and . . . you." Adams's unpublished draft of a reply to Hamilton, headed "Mr. Hamilton's Letter," [1800–1801], [p. 152], Adams Papers, Reel 399.

23. Adams to Abigail Adams, Oct. 12, 1799, Adams Papers, Reel 396. See also Adams to Stoddert, Sept. 4, 1799, *Works of John Adams*, IX, 19–20. When Adams left for Trenton he

On two previous occasions Adams had refused to leave Quincy when Congress was assembling. Now, in offering unconvincing excuses for his immobility, including his wife's health, though he admitted that it was much improved, Adams rehearsed his unwillingness in 1782 to go from the Netherlands to Paris. Abigail Adams had undergone an early summer fright that her previous year's condition might be returning. Husband and wife believed, with good justification, in the periodicity of their illnesses: Adams caught a severe cold every fall when he left Quincy, as he would this year when he finally reached Trenton (the temporary capital during an outbreak of yellow fever in Philadelphia). This time, though, neither of them fell ill during the summer.[24] Instead Adams was undergoing the conditions of his previous breakdowns without quite succumbing to them. It was significant that he conceived of himself as repeating the family crisis of the previous summer, when he had undergone the "anxiety" that usually preceded his collapses. Other ingredients were present as well: the respite after a crisis, an unsatisfying, temporary victory over Congress, the continued presence in affairs of his tormentor—once Hutchinson, then Franklin, now Hamilton.

In September, Pickering suggested that recent news of revolution within the French Directory dictated further delay of the envoys. Adams agreed, then suddenly decided to leave for Trenton. His departure gave the appearance of a belated but hurried response to signs and warnings of skulduggery. But he did not "rush" to Trenton. In fact, his suspicions about the

---

wrote to Stoddert: "I can and will put up, with my private secretary and two domestics only, at the first tavern or first private house I can find." Sept. 21, 1799, *ibid.*, 34. For Stoddert's warnings see his letters to Adams, Aug. 29, 1799, and Sept. 13, 1799, *ibid.*, 18, 25–29; but see n. 25 below. Benjamin Stoddert (1751–1813) was appointed secretary of the navy and hence a member of the cabinet, 1798–1801.

24. Hamilton had urged Adams to come to the capital in order to influence his reelection as vice-president. Hamilton to Adams, Sept. 9, 1792, *Works of John Adams*, VIII, 514. In 1793 Adams had delayed his return to Philadelphia because of the yellow fever there, and then in summer 1798 he had been urged to come to Trenton to oversee the organization of the army. Adams to McHenry, Oct. 22, 1798, *ibid.*, 612. On his wife's improved health see Adams to Uriah Forrest, May 13, 1799, *ibid.*, 645–646; Abigail Adams to [Thomas Boylston Adams?], June 12, 1799, Adams Papers, Reel 395. Both John and Abigail Adams took sick just before their marriage.

cabinet were no more pointed than before. The delays in sending off the envoys continued to be his own, though abetted by
Pickering, and his leisurely trip to Trenton suggests his ignorance of the machinations awaiting him there. All signs made
the cabinet members confident that Adams would be amenable
when he met with them.[25]

When Adams arrived Hamilton was on the scene. Although
he held no government position his influence had been felt from
the day Adams took office. But he never before had appeared in
person. He visited Adams to argue for further delay of the
envoys, addressing him "in a Style the most peremptory and

25. Kurtz, *Presidency of John Adams*, 388. My interpretation rests on Jacob Cooke's
demonstration that Stoddert's reference on Sept. 13 to "artful, designing men" was not a
warning against the cabinet and did not spur Adams to leave for Trenton. Cooke,
"Country above Party," in Willis, ed., *Fame and the Founding Fathers*, 68n. It is only
hindsight that makes Adams appear to have recognized the cabinet plot to delay the
envoys. For example, Howe describes his "rush" to get to Trenton in *Changing Political
Thought of John Adams*, 202. But Adams did not arrive until three weeks after the letter from
Stoddert that supposedly decided him to leave. Adams himself later implied but never
claimed a speedy departure, just as with his delayed trip from the Netherlands to Paris.
Furthermore, in recalling his "instantaneous determination to go to Trenton," Adams
ascribed his decision to letters from *Pickering* (of Sept. 11 and 17) that arrived a week after
Stoddert's. See *Works of John Adams*, X, 252, reprinted from the *Boston Patriot*. For a similar
later version see Adams's draft of a reply to Hamilton, [pp. 150–151], Adams Papers, Reel
399. Although these letters from Pickering counseled delaying the envoys, Adams by now
had no argument with their advice, as I have pointed out above. Indeed, by this time delay
made sense, since the news from France showed rapid, contradictory developments. (In the
sequel, the envoys sailed before the French news was sorted. As they did, Napoleon seized
power, with a result that turned out to be favorable to the mission.) Again, not hints of a
plot to delay the envoys but Pickering's request that he be allowed to make minor changes
in the instructions, in order to *save* time, appears to have decided Adams to leave—
apparently for the purpose of asserting his executive prerogative (Stoddert's reason, too,
according to Cooke, for wanting Adams in Trenton).

Charles Francis Adams, to whom Adams might well have communicated his having had
suspicions at this time, wrote that Adams seems to have had "no suspicion of the truth."
Works of John Adams, I, 554. Charles Francis believed that Adams sensed cabinet opposition
when letters recommending delay because of events in France arrived from both Pickering
and Ellsworth, one of the new envoys. (Pickering had arranged Ellsworth's letter, Charles
Francis noted.) But if Adams was alerted by this advice, which now made sense, he
responded not to disloyalty but to opposition.

Stephen Kurtz, while conceding a number of Cooke's points, defends Adams's statecraft
by calling the delay of the envoys "deliberate" on Adams's part while he waited for the
outfitting of a new squadron of American fighting ships. Kurtz, "French Mission of
1799–1800," *Pol. Sci. Qtly.*, LXXX (1965), 543, 556. But Kurtz accepts Adams's retrospec-
tive explanations, ignores the hollowness of Adams's excuses for remaining in Quincy, and
takes Adams's theory of executive strength for the practice of it. *Ibid.*, 551, 545–546.
Cooke and Kurtz agree, contrary to my analysis, that Adams acted out of political
expediency.

even Swaggering." Adams recalled, "I received him with great civility. . . . I was fortunately in a very happy temper and a very good humor." Adams used the words "a very happy temper" to describe his similar confrontation with John Dickinson outside the Continental Congress in 1775. His repetition of the phrase indicates that it was not coincidence that found him this way on these two occasions, but rather his habitually mild reaction to provocation.

In addition to allowing Hamilton's insolence Adams persisted in suppressing his own darkest suspicions. Indeed, with regard to his treatment of Hamilton in Trenton he later protested at being "accused of suspicion." He was, he insisted, "the most open, unsuspicious man alive."[26] When Adams suddenly ordered that the envoys set sail immediately he reacted defiantly to coercion rather than cannily at the discovery of a plot, as some have assumed. The decision was admirable—in its sacrifice of party support no less than in its successful outcome. But it hardly deserved Adams's later description of it as part of the "Steady pursuit of a Uniform regular Plan," any more than his sporadic campaign for Dutch recognition deserved his later descriptions of steadily applied pressure. Soon after issuing the order he again dropped the initiative. He consulted as usual with his cabinet on his speech to Congress and accepted their suggestions for toning down its intemperate first draft Adamsisms.[27]

Adams had an eventful year and a half to serve, but his important personal test was done. Despite the continued threat of war, the virulence of election rhetoric in 1800, and the stir

26. Draft of a reply to Hamilton, [1800–1801], [p. 153a], Adams Papers, Reel 399; *Correspondence of the Late President Adams. Originally Published in the Boston Patriot. In a Series of Letters* (Boston, 1809[–1810]), 29, 78.

27. Draft of a reply to Hamilton, [1800–1801], Adams Papers, Reel 399. Jacob Cooke shows that Adams's own view has generally been accepted by historians. Cooke, "Country above Party," in Willis, ed., *Fame and the Founding Fathers*, 53–54. See, for example, Richard B. Morris, *Great Presidential Decisions: State Papers That Changed the Course of History* (Philadelphia and New York, 1960), 51. Despite Page Smith's critique of the notion that Adams acted out of "political expediency," Stephen Kurtz and Jacob Cooke treat the decision and Adams's subsequent wavering with the cabinet as politically calculated: see Smith, *John Adams*, II, 1029–1031; Cooke, "Country above Party," in Willis, ed., *Fame and the Founding Fathers*, 61n; and Kurtz, *Presidency of John Adams*, 389.

caused by the attack on him in Hamilton's famous election pamphlet, the next seventeen months had an autumnal quality. Adams often considered retiring without serving out his term. In the meantime, calmly, thoughtfully, and correctly, and against the unanimous advice of his cabinet, he pardoned John Fries, the tax rebel who had been sentenced to death under the Sedition Act. Still suppressing personal resentment, and still ignorant of the extent of their betrayals, Adams procrastinated over dismissing the disloyal cabinet members. After he finally did, he nearly gave sinecures to each, even though McHenry was a proven incompetent.[28] Then, though he hoped until the last to win a second term, Adams faced the truth philosophically as he had in 1796: that the national prospects in the event of Jefferson's victory would not be as catastrophic as Federalist rhetoric suggested.

The usual, drawn-out process of counting electoral votes provided a series of ironies that seemed like comments on Adams's attitudes toward himself and the American public. Electors were chosen in some states by popular vote, in some by the state legislature, and in some by both methods. In all cases it was difficult to predict the outcome. In the key state of New York, where the legislature method operated, Aaron Burr, opposed by Hamilton, managed by the manipulation of a few hundred votes to ensure a Jeffersonian slate of electors. Not the people, then, but unscrupulous aristocrats right out of the *Defence of the Constitutions* and the "Davila" essays brought Adams down. And they were able to do so by using one of the checks on direct representation—legislative election of the chief execu-

28. On McHenry's sinecure see Adams to Stoddert, Nov. 16, 1811, Adams Papers, Reel 118, and to Samuel Dexter, Aug. 13, 1800, *Works of John Adams*, IX, 76. On Pickering's, a judgeship, see Benjamin Waterhouse to Adams, July 8, 1811, Worthington Chauncey Ford, ed., *Statesman and Friend: Correspondence of John Adams with Benjamin Waterhouse, 1784–1822* (Boston, 1927), 59. When two Federalist electors defected after the election, Adams, as he pointed out, "consented to the appointment" of one and "permitted the appointment of the other." Draft of a reply to Hamilton, [1800–1801], Adams Papers, Reel 399. Adams wrote of his dismissals of the cabinet members: "The opposition had been astonished for more than a year that it had not been done." *Ibid.*, [p. 155]. On Adams's wish to retire see Mitchell, ed., *New Letters of Abigail Adams*, 263, and Adams to Benjamin Stoddert, Nov. 16, 1811, Adams Papers, Reel 118.

tive—that he had advocated in those writings. Most unscrupulous of all was the extraordinary pamphlet of personal
denigration, *Letter from Alexander Hamilton, concerning the Public
Conduct and Character of John Adams, Esq., President of the United
States*. Uniformly treated by historians as an unbalanced act, it
gained Hamilton nothing, but it probably contributed to
Adams's defeat. Adams spent much of his first decade in retirement fuming over and preparing answers to this pamphlet.
But initially he responded to it with three months of silence
ended by a personal letter of "singular equanimity." Adams
contented himself with stating, "I am not his enemy, and never
was," and, "He has talents. . . . There is more burnish, however, on the outside, than sterling silver in the substance."[29]

As early as the June before election Adams began to speak of
Jefferson's certain victory, and by August he was addressing the
public in a valedictory strain. Later he wrote that he had been
"obliged to stand Candidate knowing that it would end in
disgrace." When defeat did come he and his family were ready
with quotations on the fate of virtuous public servants. John
Quincy Adams, writing from Europe in anticipation of the
outcome, reminded his father that "you have always made up
your account to meet sooner or later such treatment in return
for every sacrifice, and every toil." Adams himself revealed to
more than one correspondent, "All my life I expected it." An
ironical fate seemed to rain its blows on him at the end of 1800
and the beginning of 1801. The news of his son Charles's death
coincided with defeat in the Electoral College. Immediately
afterward it was learned that just before the election, on October 30, peace with France had been secured. Yet, though he had
expressed a bitter fatalism in anticipation, Adams found relative
equanimity in defeat itself. His health was good, and when he

29. Adams to Dr. Ogden, Dec. 3, 1800, *Works of John Adams*, IX, 576, quoted in Gilbert
Chinard, *Honest John Adams*, 306. On Hamilton's "luckless attack," see Broadus Mitchell,
Alexander Hamilton: The National Adventure, 1788–1804 (New York, 1962), 478. The
Hamilton pamphlet came after the popular vote, with the intention of influencing the
Electoral College. See Dauer, *Adams Federalists*, 256–258, for the suggestion that Adams's
popularity fell off in the Pennsylvania vote. But it is not clear whether Adams was more or
less popular at the end of his term than at the beginning.

examined himself, he declared, "Depressions of spirits . . . I have not perceived."[30]

Far from attempting to exploit whatever power remained to him, Adams focused on relinquishing the little that he had wielded. Even his notorious, last-minute appointments of judges showed not a clinging to power but the freedom that came from its being lifted. Having put aside his excessive fear of appearing to use his position for personal benefit, he appointed friends, relatives, and loyal supporters whom before he held reservations about favoring.

At the end of December the electoral vote showed a tie between Jefferson and Burr, which resulted in a week of congressional runoff balloting in February. Rather than taking a hand Adams frequently expressed his old wish to resign, this time in favor of Jefferson. Although a vigorous sixty-five—younger and stronger than Franklin had been in France—his thoughts were directed back over his administration and forward to his retirement rather than to the present. Like the spurned ancients whose examples had accompanied him through life, he must retire to his farm. He now faced the condition of the "displaced" ministers of state whom he prophetically described in "Davila" just ten years before. "Are they seen happy in a calm resignation to their fate? Do they turn their thoughts from their former employments, to private studies or business? Are they men of pleasant humor, and engaging conversation? Are their hearts at ease? Or is their conversation a constant effusion of complaints and murmurs, and their breast the residence of resentment and indignation, of grief and sorrow, of malice and revenge? Is it common to see a man get the better of his ambition, and despise the honors he once possessed; or is he commonly employed in projects upon projects, intrigues after intrigues, and manoeuvres on manoeuvres, to recover them?"[31] In fact, Adams again proved an exception

30. Adams to Stoddert, Nov. 16, 1811, Adams Papers, Reel 118; John Quincy Adams to John Adams, Nov. 25, 1800, *ibid.*, Reel 399; Adams to William Tudor, Jan. 20, 1801, *ibid.*, Reel 400, and to Joseph Ward, Feb. 4, 1801, *Works of John Adams*, IX, 97.

31. *Works of John Adams*, VI, 247.

to his own rule. Out of office he was no more susceptible to ambition than while in.

His last gesture was to slip away from Washington early on the morning of Jefferson's inaugural, giving the appearance of a man of disappointed ambition. One last time, though, his private agony came from a lack of recognition rather than a lack of power. He could not bear to sit at a fourth inauguration—two as vice-president, one as president, and now this as outgoing president—and for a third time see a less deserving man be the cynosure. As he took his last journey of more than a few miles, a quarter of a century lay ahead in which to contemplate the inequities of fortune.

XI
The Monarch
of Stoney Field
1801–1812

Adams approached his retirement as he had the earlier turning points of his life: with much psychic preparation and little practical planning. He imagined that he could reach the philosophical calm in a setting of agrarian simplicity recommended by Cicero's "De Senectute," the "very beautiful apology" for his life that he said he read every year. Yet he often wished himself a lawyer again, back at "the bauling bar."[1] And his emotions remained inflammable as ever. A question from a correspondent, an attack on him in a newspaper, or the warning of a national emergency set him going as of old. In response he would pour forth observations on the times, personal reminiscences, and philosophical speculations. These continued unabated until he was almost ninety and close to death.

During the next twenty-five years Adams sometimes admitted the fiery waywardness of his personality (though he never recognized how impulsive some of his acts had been). But he did not grow more calm. In taking Cicero for his model, for example, he enforced a disturbing rather than a settling

1. Adams to Thomas Boylston Adams, Aug. 20, 1810, Adams Papers, Reel 118; and to Benjamin Waterhouse, Jan. 3, 1806, Ford, ed., *Statesman and Friend*, 32. On Cicero see also Josiah Quincy, *Figures of the Past, from the Leaves of Old Journals*, ed. M .A. De Wolfe Howe (Boston, 1926), 64; Adams to Elihu Marshall, Mar. 7, 1820, *Works of John Adams*, X, 388, and to John Adams Smith, Mar. 15, 1820, Adams Papers, Reel 124. Naturally, Adams read Horace on farming, and, presumably, Virgil as well. For the age's ideal of retreat modeled on Horace's Sabine farm see Howard Mumford Jones, *O Strange New World. American Culture: The Formative Years* (New York, 1964), 245.

view of his own life. Both Cicero and Adams were men of the middle class who initially distinguished themselves as lawyers. As a law student and young lawyer Adams had modeled himself on Cicero's practice, down to studying the details of his legal oratory. Plutarch's observation about Cicero—"his readiness and address in sarcasm . . . offended many, and gave him the repute of ill nature"—applies equally to the "saucy," denunciatory courtroom style adopted by Adams.[2]

In looking back on his life Adams found parallels with Cicero everywhere. He went so far as to connect his supposed loss of public notice because of his ten years' service in Europe with Cicero's loss of popularity after his year in Sicily. Adams believed that as Mark Antony got rid of Cicero, "Jefferson got rid of . . ." He did not write his own name, but, continuing his old practice of complaining on behalf of others to express his disappointments, he substituted the name of John Jay, another righteous figure who deserved better from his country. (Adams did not mention his failure similar to Cicero's of not taking consistent, vigorous action once in office.) In Conyers Middleton's "melancholy" life of Cicero, Adams found himself reading the "history of our own country for forty years past. Change the names and every anecdote will be applicable to us."[3]

In 1759, when Adams lived not far up the road from his present house, Cicero's character was a common topic of discussion. Oxenbridge Thacher argued, "Tully was not a vain Man." Confessing his desire for fame in 1760, Adams compared his situation with Cicero's and tried to show that modern philosophy would prevent his ambition from similarly leading him on to vanity. In 1774, impatient with the policy of nonimportation, he was certain that Cicero would have put forward proposals in the Continental Congress "a little more

2. Plutarch, *The Lives of the Noble Grecians and Romans*, trans. John Dryden and rev. by Arthur Hugh Clough, Modern Library ed. (New York, 1932), 1043. For Adams's early study of Cicero see Butterfield *et al.*, eds., *Earliest Diary*, 39, 65, 75.

3. Adams to Benjamin Rush, Jan. 18, 1808, Adams Papers, Reel 405, and Dec. 4, 1805, Schutz and Adair, eds., *Spur of Fame*, 44. On Adams's Cicero-like loss of popularity see his letter to Judge Trumbull, [Nov.?] 1805, Adams Papers, Reel 118.

Sublime and Mettlesome." When in 1796 he retired like a Roman to his farm to prepare himself for the presidency, he naturally turned to Cicero's essays. In 1809 he came back to the familiar charges of Cicero's ambition and vanity: "In his Anguish at times and in the conscientiousness of his own Merit and Integrity, he was driven to those Assertions of his own actions which have been denominated Vanity. . . . I think them the most infallible demonstration of his Innocence and Purity. He declares that all honors are indifferent to him because he knows that it is not in the Power of his Country to reward him in any proportion to his Services." The defense amounted to Adams's own apologia, which he concluded, "I blush not to imitate that Roman."

Adams wrote but refrained from mailing to his friend Benjamin Rush another defense of Cicero, perhaps because its private definition of the word "naïveté" as well as its use of the word "independence" was too flattering to himself. He sent it to John Quincy Adams with instructions that it be read and burned. "What other People call Vanity in Cicero, I denominate Naivete," Adams wrote. Cicero was faced with "Jealousy and Envy" of his talents and surrounded by libelers. "In this distressing Situation he poured out the feelings of his tortured heart with the utmost Naivete. . . . He blazoned forth his own Virtues Talents and great Services in the Face of the Senate and the whole Roman People. . . . It was Self Defense, Independence, Intrepidity, or in one Word Naivete." Unlike Cicero, Adams had *not* given way to anguish by blazoning forth his own services, though his occasional outbursts of self-righteousness had been sufficient to fix him, too, with a reputation for vanity. When Adams wanted to defend his own record and settle with his detractors he remembered Cicero, whose philippics kept him from among "the highest grade of Statesmen."[4]

4. *Diary and Autobiography*, I, 110; Adams to James Warren, July 25, 1774, *Warren-Adams Letters*, I, 32; to Rush, Jan. 18, 1808, Adams Papers, Reel 405; and to William Cunningham, Feb. 22, 1809, *Correspondence between Adams and Cunningham*, 90. Adams's 1760 discussion came in a letter to Jonathan Sewall, *Works of John Adams*, I, 52. Sewall replied by wondering

Returned home to become a farmer, Adams slipped back into the Quincy orbit. He well expressed the physical limits of his new life when, with sardonic reference to the charges of his detractors, he called himself the "monarch of Stoney field, Count of Gull Island[,] Earl of Mount Arrarat, Marquis of Candlewood Hill, and Baron of Rocky Run." His intimates once again were Parson Wibird and his brother-in-law Richard Cranch. All three once had flirtations with Hannah Quincy, after which Adams and Cranch went courting the Smith sisters together in the early 1760s. Now Adams visited his brother-in-law Cranch virtually every day. He became interested in local and family history and began to trace the genealogy with which he would begin his autobiography. Childhood memories returned as he contemplated himself as an old man, and these often concerned his humble family origins.[5] Far from despising the local way of life of his ancestors, he wrote, "The greatest fault I ever found with any of them was that they did not educate me to their farms and trades." The family practice had been to farm in the summer and pursue one's trade after the harvest. In accordance with this tradition Adams waited until October 1802 to write "John Adams" at the top of an oversized sheet of paper and begin an account of his life.

On his return to Braintree, Adams instantly was cut off from all political ties, so tenuous had they been. He dropped from public view as well, having maintained no function or relationship to the public worthy of extended mention in the press. An autobiography would not break through this isolation, but by accounting for his lack of fame in the present—a mark of his proud refusal to curry favor with any party or public—it would secure his reputation with posterity. Specifically, autobiography meant one thing to Adams: vindication. He might observe the formality of providing his genealogy and a sketch of his youth,

if Adams was to become New England's Cicero. Sewall to Adams, Feb. 13, 1760, Adams Papers, Reel 343. In calling Cicero "conscientious" Adams again used the term with which he had described the father in "Clarendon."

5. Adams to Thomas Boylston Adams, Sept. 15, 1801, Adams Papers, Reel 118. On Richard Cranch see Adams to Waterhouse, Dec. 3, 1811, Ford, ed., *Statesman and Friend*, 71.

but his business was to answer charges, especially the aspersions on his character in Hamilton's election attack of 1800. As always there would be surrogates of his neglect: James Otis, Francis Dana, and John Jay. In contrast, Franklin and Washington held inflated reputations, while Thomas Paine and Alexander Hamilton deserved outright denunciation. In the event, no one received his due in Adams's autobiography, a work dominated throughout by all the ambiguities of his private quarrel with the public. (Through posterity he was addressing the public, after all, even though he did not intend publication.) He had done the state much service, and they had to know it. Yet, he could not bring himself to say so directly.

Thus Adams opened by mingling apology, excuse, and self-deprecation in his familiar, self-defeating fashion: "As the Lives of Phylosophers, Statesmen or Historians written by them selves have generally been suspected of Vanity, and therefore few People have been able to read them without disgust; there is no reason to expect that any Sketches I may leave of my own Times would be received by the Public with any favour, or read by individuals with much interest." The "disgust" cited by Adams did not apply to autobiography, a popular form, but it did reflect his distaste for the task before him. "My Excuse," he went on, "is, that having been the Object of much Misrepresentation, some of my Posterity may probably wish to see in my own hand Writing a proof of the falsehood of that Mass of odious Abuse of my Character, with which News Papers, private Letters and public Pamphlets and Histories have been disgraced for thirty Years."[6]

In the three fragments of his uncompleted autobiography Adams touched briefly on the record that he set out to correct. He denied the "Calumnies and Insinuations" that he had taken the Boston Massacre case in order to earn a large fee and had accepted the chief justiceship of Massachusetts in 1776 out of

---

6. Adams to John Trumbull, Mar. 9, 1790, Adams Papers, Reel 115; *Diary and Autobiography*, III, 253. "My principal business is in my garden, at this season," Adams wrote to John Taylor in June 1814. "Next Winter I may write more Essays on Man." June 3, 1814, Adams Papers, Reel 122.

ambition. He also refuted the false charge that he had participated in a cabal against Washington during the Revolution. But
he drifted from one aim to another, accomplishing none. He
could not write for long without abandoning his design, especially when it concerned himself. As a result his autobiography
soon became what its first sentence inadvertently predicted,
"Sketches . . . of my own Times."[7] Like so many of his acts the
writing evolved into a sacrifice to duty, as personal justification
gave way to public duty—in this case the responsibility to copy
documents from his private collection of papers and make them
available to posterity.

Adopting a common autobiographical convention, Adams
thought of "these Memoirs" as "not for the Public but for my
Children," whom they would instruct in morality. After lecturing them on "Licentiousness" and "Innocence," however, he
stopped writing for two years. In 1804 John Quincy Adams,
apparently unaware of the partial manuscript, urged his father
to write his autobiography. Adams informed him that he could
not trust his passions to such an undertaking—"in many Passages it would set me on fire and I should have Occasion for a
Bucket of Water constantly by my side to put it out." With this
observation he resumed writing. He must have been reminded
of the patriotic fire attributed to him during the Revolution
(when Colonel Otis had said, "The zeal pot boils over"), for
he skipped over the rest of his youth to dilate on that period. At
this point, for the first time since he had begun his narrative, he
consulted a source—his set of the original *Journals* of the Continental Congress—and quickly fell into his old habit of composition by extract and commentary. He began to copy his
own letters into the text, consulting them in most cases for the
first time since writing them. Many of them had no relation to
what little design the autobiography retained, but once involved in providing documents he vowed, "I will conceal

7. *Diary and Autobiography*, III, 293, 253. On Adams and the supposed "Conway Cabal"
against Washington see Bernhard Knollenberg, *Washington and the Revolution: A Reappraisal*
(New York, 1940), chap. 7, and appendix. On the literary form of the autobiography see
Earl N. Harbert, "John Adams' Private Voice: The *Diary* and *Autobiography*," *Tulane Studies
in English*, XV (1967), 102–103.

nothing from Posterity."[8] In this manner he drew no closer to the diplomatic or presidential periods that he had set out to defend. Not surprisingly, he soon broke off again. When he next resumed, after a year and a half, he skipped over what remained of his congressional service to begin writing, in 1806, his "Travels and Negotiations."

He succeeded no better here, but he did write the most affecting parts of his work, for it occurred to him to transcribe and expand on his diary. This led to vivid recollections of his perilous ocean crossing to France in 1778 and of his reception in Bordeaux. He barely outlined the diplomatic situation, however, when he broke off again, this time to skip directly to his second, crucial mission in Europe.

Adams began this section, titled "Peace," intending to deal principally with Benjamin Franklin and the comte de Vergennes. Instead he wasted too many pages dilating (vividly again) on his diary account of crossing the mountains of Spain in 1779. He started a careful presentation of his initial exchanges of letters with Vergennes, in which the minister's deviousness first appeared, but broke off, never to return to his manuscript. As a result he left yet another compendium useful to biographers and students of his life and period but lacking the cohesion to stand as an independent work. Yet, an incidental pattern emerged as Adams went from one to another of the charges against him. Repeatedly he found it necessary to explain as well as answer these, and in the process he articulated a theory of why he had so often been betrayed.

Dating from an incident in 1773 involving Samuel Adams and John Hancock, "Jealousy and Envy" had stalked him. He believed that he had offended Samuel Adams by outdoing him in Revolutionary zeal, Hancock by favoring one of his rivals. In both of these cases, and in the many that followed them, his independent behavior implanted resentments. These eventually grew to such proportions as to destroy his presidency. This

8. *Diary and Autobiography*, III, 253, 261; Adams to John Quincy Adams, Nov. and Dec. 1804, quoted *ibid.*, I, lxix; *ibid.*, III, 437. For the rest of Butterfield's account of the autobiography's composition see *ibid.*, III, xlv, and I, 338n–339n.

Ciceronian formula of virtue resented had merit if pursued far enough. The enmities of Robert Treat Paine, Thomas Paine, John Dickinson, John Hancock, and Alexander Hamilton did grow out of political differences with Adams dating to the Revolution. Later, the comte de Vergennes, Benjamin Franklin, John Paul Jones, and others found themselves similarly thwarted by his stubborn independence and also turned against him. But rather than look into himself for the cause of his unpopularity with so many antagonists, Adams took his case as part of the world's way with its devoted servants. The popular heroes were ever the conquering Caesars and the Tiberius-like cultivators of the public, never the men of integrity like Cicero. Invariably, his own "Zeal" and independence "might recommend me to the Esteem of a very few, yet, it will be easily believed that it contributed nothing to my Popularity, among the many." Here lay the explanation for his failure to join the other leaders of the Revolution in the shrine of public adulation. "The Examples of Washington, Franklin and Jefferson," he added, "are enough to shew that Silence and reserve in public are more Efficacious than Argumentation or Oratory."[9]

His own public fate could be traced to the debate for American independence: "A public Speaker who inserts himself, or is urged by others into the Conduct of Affairs, by daily Exertions to justify his measures, and answer the Objections of Opponents, makes himself too familiar with the public, and unavoidably makes himself Ennemies. Few Persons can bare to be outdonc in Reasoning or declamation or Wit, or Sarcasm or Repartee, or Satyr, and all these things are very apt to grow out of public debate. In this Way in a Course of Years, a Nation becomes full of a Mans Ennemies," who "take a secret pleasure in assisting to humble and mortify him." "Wit," "Sarcasm," "Satyr"—the terms conveyed Adams's cutting style in debate and suggested his own responsibility for losing so many allies. The truth was that his "Repartee" all too well expressed the contempt for others that grew out of his own self-flagellation.

9. *Ibid.*, III, 305, 433, 336. Adams dealt with Thomas Paine, John Dickinson, and John Hancock, *ibid.*, 334, 316, 323.

As for his lack of fame, the manner in which he expressed his devotion explained the public's failure to elevate him: "I never would deceive the People, conceal from them any essential truth, nor especially make myself subservient to any of their Crimes, Follies or Excentricities."[10] It was no wonder that the nation became full of his enemies.

It is no wonder, either, that Adams satisfied himself with respect to them all no better in his autobiography than in life. He indulged in some premonitory hurling of epithets at Hamilton, whose "Petulance, Impertinence and Impudence, will make too great a figure in these memoires hereafter," but he never dealt with him except in fragments. Determined to expose every villain, he left behind little more than the impress of his own hurt: "If my Life should be spared to continue these memorials, more of this Marshall De Maillebois will be recorded." . . . "I am sorry that I shall be obliged to say something more of this Man [Dr. James Smith] hereafter." Similarly, his determination to expose the French Revolution ended with, "But more, much more of this hereafter." Eventually, Adams was reduced to expressions of frustration: "It cannot be known from the Journal [of the Continental Congress] how much debate" a minor proposal "occasioned. . . . It will never be known how much labour it cost Us, to accomplish it." Or else, his transcribing sputtered into inarticulateness:

April 3. 1776 great Things were done. The Naval System made great Progress.
April 4. 1776. We did great Things again.[11]

So much for setting straight the historical record.

Despite a growing sense of inefficacy accompanied by complaints of having "to rummage trunks, letter books, bits of journals, and great heaps and bundles of old papers," Adams declared to Rush, "I do not intend to let every lie impose upon posterity." He labored on in the conviction that there was "a Secret and deliberate design" against the "Principal Actors" in

10. *Ibid.*, 336, 290.
11. *Ibid.*, 447, IV, 80, 50, 147, III, 381, 377.

the Revolution, "not only to deprive" them "of all their Merit, of their Labours, of their Hazards, Sufferings and Sacrifices, but to leave their Characters with Posterity under Uncertainty, Suspicion and even odium."[12] Nevertheless, in 1807 he permanently gave up his autobiography, trailing off *in medias res*.

While he wrote Adams brooded on the contrast between "the illustrious and immortal Franklin and the obscure and mortal John Adams." He watched "the eternal puffing and trumpeting of Washington and Franklin and the incessant abuse of the real Fathers of their Country," yet he tried in his letters to write about Washington and Franklin so as to display their accomplishments as admirable but mortal. It was true that he had dropped into obscurity while they grew into mythical heroes celebrated in paintings and lithographs, literature, and epigram. As the power of the Jeffersonians grew after 1801 Adams was mentioned less and less, his name dropping even from Fourth of July toasts.[13] He seemed to deserve mention only when debates on public policy during Jefferson's two terms recalled one or another of the presumed errors of his own administration. In his autobiography Adams proved unable to become either a demythologizer of others or a mythologist of himself. The point is painfully clear when one compares his autobiography with Franklin's.

Adams's attempt to account for his failures has not even earned mention next to Benjamin Franklin's story of success. Franklin created the image of the American of humble origin who rises through hard work to success and international prominence. The story was Adams's as much as Franklin's, but it became associated with Franklin in life, autobiography, and the historical memory of Americans. Franklin's story reads like

12. Adams to Rush, July 23, 1806, Schutz and Adair, eds., *Spur of Fame*, 60; Adams to Rev. Abiel Holmes, May 6, 1807, Adams Papers, Reel 118.

13. Adams to John Quincy Adams, Jan. 29, 1806, Adams Papers, Reel 404, and to Francis Adrian Vanderkemp, Aug. 23, 1806, Vanderkemp Papers, Pa. Hist. Soc. On Adams's decline in prominence see Donald H. Stewart and George P. Clarke, "Misanthrope or Humanitarian? John Adams in Retirement," *NEQ*, XXVIII (1955), 216; L. H. Butterfield, "The Jubilee of Independence, July 4, 1826," *Virginia Magazine of History and Biography*, LXI (1953), 137; Schutz and Adair, eds., *Spur of Fame*, illustrations, and on Fourth of July toasts, 135n.

a lesson in what Adams should have done, Adams's as a cautionary tale of what might have become of Franklin. For vanity, ambition, and the problem of making enemies because of an abrasive wit were as prominent in Franklin's character as in Adams's or Cicero's. But, though originally a contentious Massachusetts Bay character in Adams's own mold, Franklin wrote that he "dropt" his "abrupt Contradiction, and positive Argumentation, and put on the humble Enquirer and Doubter." Thanks to his strategy of humility Franklin glided over difficulties with which Adams was still struggling when he wrote his autobiography. In contrast to Adams, for example, Franklin gracefully admitted that in writing his autobiography, "I may as well confess . . . since my Denial . . . will be believ'd by no body" that "perhaps I shall a good deal gratify my own *Vanity*."[14]

On reading Franklin's autobiography in 1818 Adams wrote, "My own appears, upon retrospection, a dull dreary unfruitful Waste." Though both told stories of self-improvement, the one by prudent self-interest, the other by self-denial, Franklin's alone conveyed an impression of profit. Both writers recalled, for example, taking up Cheyne's vegetarian diet as young men. But where Adams uselessly imposed eighteen months of near starvation on himself, Franklin made his diet the famous occasion for saving money and time for his studies. In a similar contrast, when the governor of Pennsylvania favored him, Franklin recalled, he fell in easily with the plan of setting up as his employer's rival. When Adams, too, was about twenty, in order to complete his planned self-improving tour of Rhode Island he refused the governor's "many polite Invitations to return with him to his home."[15] Where Franklin never lost

14. Adams to J. Watson, July 23, 1818, Vanderkemp Papers; Leonard W. Labaree *et al.*, eds., *The Autobiography of Benjamin Franklin* (New Haven, Conn., 1964), 64, 44. The phrase "strategy of humility" is from Conner, *Poor Richard's Politicks*, 152–153. Conner suggests that Franklin, too, wrote out of a sense of failure. Adams evidently did not read Franklin's autobiography until 1818, after William Temple Franklin sent John Quincy Adams a copy of his edition of Franklin's works. See Ford, ed., *Catalogue of the Books of John Quincy Adams*, 96.

15. Adams to J. Watson, July 23, 1818, Vanderkemp Papers; *Diary and Autobiography*, III, 267.

sight of the purpose of his self-improvement, unhesitatingly compromising to preserve his self-interest, Adams raised his programs to absolutes and adhered to them even when they no longer benefited him.

The certitude of Franklin's program has often been compared to the uplifting advice of Cotton Mather's *Essays to Do Good*, a book cited early in his autobiography for its profound effect on him. Adams's uncertainties derived from another side of Puritanism, best represented by its autobiographies. When writing autobiography Puritans avoided the anguishings of their diaries in order to set forth an exemplary pattern for their children, just as Adams and Franklin professed to do. Yet, whatever the spiritual certainties a father might present to his sons, these could not be demonstrated by Adams or the Puritans in terms of measurable earthly success of Franklin's sort. Adams resembled Puritan autobiographers in his conviction of having proceeded in the right way accompanied by a severe doubt about whether his course had procured its desired end (for them, salvation; for him, recognition by posterity).

Increase Mather left his son, Cotton, such an autobiography of doubt. It has been described as an attempt to achieve "the consolation of the Psalmist," for, like Adams, Increase Mather suffered what he regarded as popular neglect. Sensible of the wrongs done him, he wrote "less for the instruction of the son than for the reassurance of the father." In the end, if he could not say that he had been a success, Increase Mather could hope that "when I am gone, the Lord will make some of my people sensible of their neglects of me." For Adams's generation the Lord's ultimate dispensation of justice was replaced by the far less dependable workings of posterity. Thus Increase Mather adhered "undeviatingly to the notion that for the afflicted servant . . . withdrawal of mercy is only temporary and apparent. Were it otherwise, autobiography would lose its reason for being and become an instrument of despair." With Adams the conviction grew that the world's lack of appreciation would be permanent. Where his diary had been an instrument of ambition, his autobiography grew into one of despair.[16]

Unknown to Adams, though, during the decade in which he wrote about his life his contemporaries in their private writings were preparing a just image of his place in history. Jefferson and others separately agreed in calling him, if not the Cicero, then the "colossus" and the "Atlas" of the American Revolution. The heroic figure of Atlas staunchly holding up the heavens appealed to Adams himself, though he was drawn to the suffering more than the glory. He adjured John Quincy Adams to stand firm as Mount Atlas in his political life. As for himself, "They wore me out with hard service," he wrote just before abandoning his autobiography, "and then turned me adrift like an old Dray horse." Among his frequent references to himself as a helpless, dumb beast he tended to recur to one that he had attempted to turn against Franklin while defending balance of powers—the example of oxen straining to draw a load uphill as horses pulling in the other direction slowly prevailed to bring it safely down. "Sic vos non vobis fortis aratra boves," he quoted —"thus you become the oxen fit for the plows, but not to your benefit." He also likened himself to Aeneas, standing as firm in his resistance to expostulation as a well-rooted tree in a storm, and to a circus animal he once had seen pullied up into the air, holding on by its teeth while being abused.[17]

He might have compared himself to Ajax, the staunch warrior at Troy who engaged in what Adams once referred to as the "well-known" competition with Odysseus—the wily rival resented by Ajax as much as Franklin was by Adams.[18] Ajax and Ulysses conduct a public debate on the question of who

16. Daniel B. Shea, Jr., *Spiritual Autobiography in Early America* (Princeton, N.J., 1968), 158–160.

17. Adams to Rush, Feb. 2, 1807, and to Waterhouse, Aug. 22, 1805, Adams Papers, Reel 118; *Correspondence in the Boston Patriot*, 88–89. See also *Adams Family Correspondence*, III, 229n, and Adams to Abigail Adams, Feb. 28, 1779, *ibid.*, 181.

18. *Works of John Adams*, III, 442. Adams used Ovid's version of the Ajax-Odysseus dispute, *Metamorphoses*, Book XIII. But Sophocles' version offers the greater insight into Adams's psychology. One can guess Adams's approving response to Pindar's version, in which "the greatest prize hath been held forth to cunning falsehood. For the Danai, by their secret votes, unfairly favored Odysseus." Nemean Ode VIII, Sir John Sandys, ed. and trans., *Odes of Pindar* (Cambridge, Mass., 1915). Homer's Ajax has no application here.

shall have the honor of inheriting Agamemnon's armor. When it is awarded to Odysseus, Ajax is consumed with jealousy. Unbearably hurt because his own great contributions have been ignored, he broods until he goes mad but then harms only himself in his rage. In his *Ajax*, Sophocles set forth the psychology of the staunch, dependable patriot who labors self-lessly, then turns out to be desperately sensitive about the honors due him.

Adams made no such heroic parallels for himself. He continued to regard it a kind of cheating at life to take advantage of personal charm or reputation, however much importance he lent to both in his political writings. To impose a literary design on his autobiography would have amounted to similar chicanery. Instead Adams attempted to be factual, eventually preferring the documents themselves to any other mode of presentation.

Adams was attempting to convey the monumental quality of his often disastrously formal portraits, his stilted replies to petitions while president, and the opening passages of every work that he wrote with posterity in mind. He began each section of his autobiography by trying to tame his prose, changing words like "Clerk" to "Amanuensis" and "pay" to "imoluments," and he paused to apologize for "the abrupt uncouth freedom" of his personal letters—the very qualities for which they are praised today. He did not succeed in sounding like Cicero in translation, but neither did his recurrent informalities of diction help him to triumph over the sheer bulk of the documents that crowded his pages. Nor did he achieve self-knowledge. Once he admitted to being "like my Friend Chase of a temper naturally quick and warm," but he went no further in this promising direction.[19] Elsewhere, he recorded examples of his most characteristic behavior—withdrawing into self-denying regimens of self-improvement—without ever noticing a pattern.

If he never discovered the key of self-denial in his life, how-

19. *Diary and Autobiography*, IV, 1, III, 419, 311. Other attempts at formal diction occur *ibid.*, III, 334, IV, 65, 66, 107.

ever, Adams did eventually recognize his weaknesses. Just as he admitted his passion for fame when writing to college friends while denying it in his diary, in his late letters he admitted his incapacity to organize either his papers or his thoughts sufficiently to write a satisfactory autobiography. He began to suggest that he was writing only "hints" for his biographer. His *political* writings "would be a tolerable account of my own life." Alternately: "My Life is already written in my Letterbooks, as particularly as I wish it. There I shall appear as I wish with all my imperfections on my head." In any case he realized that the disorder of his autobiography was a reflection of character. "The few traces that remain of me," he wrote, "must, I believe, go down to posterity in much confusion and distraction, as my life has been passed." And, after breaking off for the last time, he wrote, "If I had not been a weak man, I should have explained myself so as to be better understood."[20]

In another letter he recalled his friends' telling him when he was in his twenties that he "had a little capillary vein of satire, meandering about in my soul, and it broke out so strangely, suddenly, and irregularly that it was impossible to foresee when it would come or how it would appear." He termed this quality "facetiousness," by which he meant verbal wit and liveliness, and said that it "was always awkward and seldom understood." He was beginning to accept his impulsiveness, though he did not regard such a seeming vagary of character as proper to mention in an autobiography. "What am I to say of my own vanity and levity?" he asked his friend Rush as he prepared to make a final attempt to complete his manuscript. "Crimes, I thank God, I have none to record. Follies, indiscretions, and trifles, enough and too many." He hesitated to record these because he could not connect his impulsive behavior, the real key to his actions, with the solemn matters that he planned to discuss. In the end, writing his autobiography brought

20. Adams to Rush, July 23, 1806, Schutz and Adair, eds., *Spur of Fame*, 60; to Vanderkemp, Apr. 30, 1806, Adams Papers, Reel 118; and to Rush, July 23, 1806, and Aug. 31, 1808, Schutz and Adair, eds., *Spur of Fame*, 61, 117. Adams republished some of his political writings in 1805 and 1819.

Adams to conclude: "I am not, never was, & never shall be a great man."[21] His somewhat disingenuous opening reference to "Men of extraordinary Fame, to which I have no pretensions," had betrayed a self-doubt that grew into a conviction during the five years over which he wrote.

The struggle that led to this state of mind anticipated one of the dominant modes of American literature: the tale of the outcast obsessed with injustice. Alone on his farm and largely forgotten by the public Adams resembled a small town philosopher with a secret manuscript. Although he wrote at length his output reduced itself to short, brilliant passages anticipating the epigrams of Puddin'head Wilson's calendar in Mark Twain's novel. Adams's aphoristic tendency appeared to best advantage in marginalia, a form suited to his genius because it avoided the requirements for literature. In one-word exclamations and arguments extending across the tops of pages then crawling onto the end papers of his books (until they equaled the number of words written by the author), Adams scrawled some of his most striking passages. Hardly an opinion, example, or narration existed that failed to exemplify for him one of his themes: the nature of aristocracy, democracy, and monarchy (with their attendant dangers of oligarchy, anarchy, and despotism); balance of powers and the dangers of a single assembly; ambition, envy, jealousy.

As if in illustration of his lifelong, self-defeating independence of everyone but his family and a few local friends, Adams lived in self-imposed isolation, broken occasionally by visitors interested in meeting the ex-president and patriot. In Boston, it is true, on the Fourth of July "in successive annual processions" Robert Treat Paine joined Adams and Elbridge Gerry "in the place of honor as signers." Adams's influence, though, hardly reached beyond the Quincy town meeting to affairs of the nation, state, or the city of Boston. From these he systematically cut himself off. When he traveled to nearby towns or into Boston a half-dozen times a year, it was invariably for

21. Adams to Rush, Feb. 27, 1805, Schutz and Adair, eds., *Spur of Fame*, 23–24, and to Vanderkemp, Jan. 29, 1807, Adams Papers, Reel 118.

private reasons: to hear a sermon, attend a picnic, or take books from the Boston Athenaeum. He occasionally provided young men with letters of recommendation to Jefferson, Madison, and Monroe, but in writing to his successors he elaborately avoided any suggestion of offering advice. "Mum!!!" he warned himself. When a diplomatic crisis with England in 1808 caught him up he refrained from offering his opinion in favor of war even in a private letter. For some years he attended the dinners of the American Academy of Arts and Sciences and the Massachusetts Society for Promoting Agriculture, organizations in which he held honorary presidencies, but he resigned from both because he felt that his presence put "a restraint upon conversation." Ironically, he now felt out of place for being the only one in those Federalist-dominated organizations who was not rabidly anti-Jefferson. So extreme was his conviction of unpopularity that he feared recriminations for opinions about agriculture expressed in letters to friends, which he accompanied with admonitions of secrecy.[22]

In general Adams lived in modest circumstances "like a Hermit." He spent most of his time alone in his garden and with his books and correspondence. Until 1816 John Quincy Adams was in the United States only between 1804 and 1808, and then spent most of his time in Washington. His children stayed with their grandparents when not in school, and the widow and children of John Quincy's brother Charles lived with them permanently. Otherwise, with old friends dying off Adams increasingly depended for companionship on his correspondents—his sons, son-in-law, and grandchildren, as well as men of letters and old political acquaintances and *their* children. In his physical isolation he continued his lifelong dependence on the stimulus of events, leaving his literary work incomplete

22. Shipton, *Sibley's Harvard Graduates*, XII, 482; Adams to Vanderkemp, Jan. 26, 1802, Adams Papers, Reel 118. On agriculture see Adams to Elkanah Watson, Sept. 11, 1812, Adams Papers, Reel 123. For other examples of diffidence see Adams to Pres. James Monroe, Mar. 8, 1820, Adams Papers, Reel 123; to Elbridge Gerry, Apr. 26, 1813, *Warren-Adams Letters*, II, 381; and to Rush, June 20, 1808, Adams Papers, Reel 118. Adams refrained, in general, from corresponding with his successors to the presidency until they were out of office.

whenever he felt himself called to some new project or crisis. He continued in retirement to break off his projects out of excess rather than deficiency of energy. In this manner he ended his autobiography when he stopped to reply to a history of the Revolution by his former neighbor Mercy Otis Warren.[23]

Wherever his name came up in her book it appeared to inspire one or another of the old political charges against him. Adams responded in ten agitated letters that may stand as the epitome of his fruitless battle for fame. Turning away from his one chance to alter the consciousness of his countrymen, his autobiography, he directed the full energy of his recollection and analysis at a target only as far away as Milton, Massachusetts, and wrote "another version of his autobiographical memoirs addressed solely to a person who did not want to read them." Adams dilated on himself and his views at length sufficient to provide his antagonist with proof of both her political charges and her characterization of him as vain and unstable. Furthermore, Mrs. Warren rightly stigmatized "the rambling manner in which your angry and indigested letters are written." "I shall observe no order," Adams wrote in the first letter, "in selecting the passages, but take them up as they occur by accident." True to his word, he began: "In the 392d page of the third volume, you say . . . "[24] Incomplete yet overlong, each of his attempts to clarify had the self-defeating effect of clouding his character and his services alike. The letters to Mrs. Warren, though, were written under circumstances making them more revealing than Adams's other autobiographical writings. At the

23. Adams to Rush, Sept. 12, 1811, Adams Papers, Reel 118. Adams broke off his draft of a reply to Hamilton just before the runoff election between Jefferson and Burr in 1801. In 1802 he broke off his autobiography when he became interested in Mount Wollaston, a nearby property that he bought in 1803. See "Scraps of the History of Mount Wollaston with Notes," Oct. 19, 1802, Adams Papers, Reel 401. After resuming his autobiography in 1804 Adams broke off sometime in 1806 after a growing excitement over public affairs beginning in 1805. "I feel more interested in public affairs now, than I have, for Some years past," he wrote to Rush, Jan. 25, 1806, Adams Papers, Reel 118. See also his letter to Rush, June 22, 1806, Schutz and Adair, eds., *Spur of Fame*, 55, and *ibid.*, 21n, on the trial of Justice Samuel Chase, which began in Feb. 1805.

24. *Diary and Autobiography*, I, lxxi; Adams to Mercy Warren, July 28, 1807, and July 11, 1807, "Correspondence between Adams and Mercy Warren," Mass. Hist. Soc., *Colls.*, 5th Ser., IV, 359, 320.

time of high Revolutionary sentiment the Adamses had felt especially close to the Warrens, who shared their classical sense of the times. With polished diction Adams had flattered Mercy Warren on her historian's abilities, as she now reminded him. (Had he consulted his letter file he could have reminded her that she had reciprocated his praise.) Mrs. Warren shared Adams's view of man and America, like him employing ambition as her key concept. Accordingly, when she described Adams in her book as ambitious she delivered a stunning blow. Adams's complaint of her "malignity of heart and a disposition to lessen me as much as you could in the opinion of your readers" has the appearance of excessive sensitivity, but he brought to her work the insight of the aggrieved. She had omitted from the printed version material in her original manuscript that would have supported his charge.

He knew that Mrs. Warren had not forgotten his refusal while vice-president to provide an appointment for her husband, James Warren. He now pleaded his rigid policy of not interfering with the executive but omitted to mention his "rough, ungentlemanly reply" at the time—one inspired by the spirit of party that both of them denounced. After this rebuff James Warren had joined with Samuel Adams to oppose Adams's second vice-presidential candidacy, the most intimate example of abandonment among many that Adams experienced in a lifetime of political estrangement from friends.[25] In the heady days of 1775–1776 Adams had confided to Warren, "I write every Thing to you, who know how to take me." Throughout their relationship Warren held the special moral

25. Adams to Mercy Warren, July 20, 1807, and Mercy Warren to Adams, Aug. 27, 1807, "Correspondence between Adams and Mercy Warren," Mass. Hist. Soc., *Colls.*, 5th Ser., IV, 354, 483. For Mercy Warren's early praise of Adams see *Warren-Adams Letters*, II, 215–216. Adams recalled a request while he was vice-president by Mrs. Warren for an appointment "for some of her family." To Mercy Warren, Aug. 19, 1807, "Correspondence between Adams and Mercy Warren," Mass. Hist. Soc., *Colls.*, 5th Ser., IV, 475. She took this as a reference to her husband and angrily insisted that it had been for her son (apparently she had both in mind at the time). On this unsuccessful son and the Adamses see Winslow Warren to Abigail Adams, May 26, 1780, *Adams Family Correspondence*, III, 358, 359n–360n. On "ambition" in Mercy Warren's *History* see Curti, *Human Nature in American Historical Thought*, 52–54. For changes in the manuscript concerning Adams see Alice Brown, *Mercy Warren* (New York, 1896), 224–225.

advantage, reflected in Adams's letters to him, of having repeatedly retired from public life instead of only promising to do so. Warren was one in a series of exaggerated alter egos who helped Adams temper his clashes of personality with such men as Franklin, Hamilton, and Jefferson. A provincial eccentric, both vain and jealous though strictly honest, Warren acted out Adams's guilt at attaining prominence. As a young man he had deserted his partner in the middle of a dance to walk mysteriously out into the night. Later in life he was known to rise similarly to leave his hosts in the middle of dinner, and he once walked out of a session of the provincial legislature.[26] Adams's own pains at enjoying himself in company and his periodic urges to retire take a different perspective when compared with the behavior of his eighteenth-century contemporaries—especially those of home growth.

Among these was "my pious and virtuous, Sensible and Learned, orthodox and rigid, odd, droll and excentric, Reverend spiritual Guide, Parson Anthony Wibirt." Joseph Dyer, a sort of frenetic, prototypical Thoreau, stood out among the freethinkers of Worcester for "being very sarcastic, and very bitter against almost every body, but especially the Clergy." Colonel Gooch of the Braintree militia had reminded Adams of Homer's Thersites in his insistence on quarreling with his neighbors. It was the "extremely ambitious" Gooch who tried to bribe Deacon Adams with a militia captaincy in his campaign to replace "Coll. Quincy," himself one of the eccentrics in Adams's diary. Robert Treat Paine, in an exaggerated version of Adams's desire to succeed as a young lawyer, repeatedly made a fool of himself in company. In 1775 Paine grew "peevish, passionate and violent" as he was consumed by suspicion and resentment of James Warren and, because Warren had written sarcastically about him to Adams, of Adams as well.[27] These characters set in a fairer light some of Adams's own excesses.

26. Adams to James Warren, Oct. 25, 1775, *Warren-Adams Letters*, I, 166. The story about Warren is told in Katherine Anthony, *First Lady of the Revolution: The Life of Mercy Otis Warren* (Garden City, N.Y., 1958), 39. See Shipton, *Sibley's Harvard Graduates*, XI, 247, for a similar story about Mercy Warren's brother.
27. Adams to Waterhouse, Mar. 29, 1811, Ford, ed., *Statesman and Friend*, 53; *Diary and*

Later characters offered Adams cautionary versions of his tendency toward paranoid suspiciousness. The demonizing of Hutchinson by Mercy Warren's brother, James Otis, for example, had warned Adams as he contemplated a similar political career for himself, "that way madness lies." Later the morbid suspicions of Ralph Izard and John Jay about the French and of Izard and Arthur Lee about Franklin tempered Adams's suspicions (as did Captain Landais's "jealousy" over his crew's respect for him). Franklin, it will be recalled, suggested that Izard, Lee, and Adams each had a touch of madness.

In Mercy Warren's *History*, James Warren seemed to look on in disapproval of Adams's rise to high places. Reading it, Adams, after rankling, like the Warrens toward him, for eighteen years, finally reacted to an old report "from Samuel Adams, who told me that General Warren had said that 'John Adams had been corrupted by his residence in England.'" In his belated reply Adams addressed himself to James Warren through Mrs. Warren: "Corrupted! On what Ground? On what color did he venture this assertion and expression? . . . Corrupted! Madam, what provocation, what evidence, what misrepresentation could he have received that could prompt him to utter this execrable calumny? Corruption is a charge that I cannot and will not bear. I challenge the whole human race, and angels and devils too, to produce an instance of it from my cradle to this hour." By habitually elevating critiques of his character to moral categories Adams kept himself from facing them. Nevertheless, his apologia, if inopportune and destined to obscurity, in this instance had merit. Republican opponents like the Warrens had excoriated and ridiculed him for years while he considered himself powerless to reply. Now, nearly all of his libelers had been discredited, suffering downfalls of which the death of Hamilton was only the most spectacular. Yet the old charges had not faded away with their perpetrators, as Mercy Warren's *History* showed. Adams might well be moved to

---

Autobiography, III, 265; *Works of John Adams*, II, 94n; *Adams Family Correspondence*, I, 351n. See further on Paine, *Diary and Autobiography*, I, 59–60.

declare his virtues in response to her charge that he had "much ambition." "If by 'ambition,' " he wrote, "you mean a love of power or a desire of public offices, I answer, I never solicited a vote in my life for any public office. I never swerved from any principle, I never professed any opinion. I never concealed even any speculative opinion, to obtain a vote. I never sacrificed a friend or betrayed a trust, I never hired scribblers to defame my rivals. I never wrote a line of slander against my bitterest enemy, nor encouraged it in any other."[28]

Mercy Warren's account of the Revolution suggested how little chance Adams stood of changing the public mind. To begin with, in treating his even-handed distrust of all classes as proof of his monarchism she showed that his adherence to balance-of-powers theory always would be open to misconstruction. (Thomas Paine continued to revile him as a monarchist during these years.) In the new nineteenth century one either had to elevate the people or be taken as a traitor to the American idea. Furthermore, her remarks on his personal style suggested that he who lived in spartan retirement more simply than Washington, Franklin, or Jefferson was to be pursued to his grave by the charge of aristocratic habits coupled with ridicule of his blunt Yankee provincialism.

When, in one of his letters to Mrs. Warren, Adams used the word "mortified," he expressed a lifetime's self-castigating shame, along with resentment at being misunderstood. "In page 140 of the 2d volume," he wrote, "you say that 'Mr. Adams returned [to the United States] rather disgusted at the early revocation of his Commission [in 1779], and the unexpected order thus speedily to leave the Court of France.' . . . When you proceed to say, Madam, that 'Mr. Adams continued in this retired and *mortified* situation for some months,' I am astonished at the spirit that guided your pen. With how much apparent delight do you insert that word 'mortified'!" Mrs.

28. For "that way madness lies" see above, chap. 3, n. 60. Adams to Mercy Warren, July 20, 1807, and Aug. 19, 1807, "Correspondence between Adams and Mercy Warren," Mass. Hist. Soc., *Colls.*, 5th Ser., IV, 335, 474. For Adams on the fates of his detractors see his letter to Rush, June 23, 1807, Adams Papers, Reel 118.

Warren shrewdly read the significance of Adams's outburst: "Your strange suggestion that I had dwelt with pleasure on the word *mortified*, a word only once used—I can impute only to the mortified and vexatious state of mind you were then in." Adams might explain that he had *not* been recalled by Congress, but rather ignored by that body; he might copy for Mercy Warren his letter to Samuel Adams recommending his own recall in favor of Franklin's appointment as sole American representative in France; and he might assert that it was *Franklin*'s vanity that had been "mortified" by Adams's appointment as sole commissioner to treat for peace. No matter. He had complained to the Warrens about Franklin when he wrote from Europe. With them as with history the intricacies of his diplomatic service and relationship to Franklin were to come down to the single memory of his disappointment.[29]

Adams frequently used the word "mortification," notably in his description of "mortified emulation" in "Davila," to express the feeling of being outcast, neglected, misunderstood, or unfairly ignored. Now he inadvertently used it again, revealing the view of himself to which he had been brought by reconsidering his life. He denied ever having "pride of talents": "I never in my life believed that I had any talents beyond mediocrity. I have always been sensible, to my mortification, that all I have done has been accomplished by the severest and most incessant labor. . . . I will open my whole soul to you on this subject. I have great satisfaction in believing that I have done more labor, run through more and greater dangers, and made greater sacrifices than any man among my contemporaries, living or dead, in the service of my country; and I should not hesitate to hazard all reputation, if I did not convince the public of it too, if I should ever undertake it."[30] Mrs. Warren had

29. Adams to Mercy Warren, July 28, 1807, and Mercy Warren to Adams, Aug. 1, 1807, "Correspondence between Adams and Mercy Warren," Mass. Hist. Soc., *Colls.*, 5th Ser., IV, 372, 376–377, 396. Mercy Warren recalled Adams's letters about Franklin written when James Warren was still Adams's confidant. See her letter, Aug. 1, 1807, *ibid.*, 394–395. For Thomas Paine's attacks see Philip S. Foner, ed., *The Complete Writings of Thomas Paine* (New York, 1945), 914–916, 949 *ff*, and esp. 956. For Adams's response see his letter to Rush, June 25, 1807, Adams Papers, Reel 118, and n. 9 above.

30. Adams to Mercy Warren, Aug. 19, 1807, "Correspondence between Adams and

singled out a word that illuminated Adams's experience. For the Puritans, mortification meant the feeling that accompanied the process of humbling oneself in order to receive grace. Adams experienced a similar emotion without an equivalent return. Mortification came to express for him the dilemma of unrequited, righteous ambition. As an old definition put it, "The loss of a prize, or the circumstance of coming into disgrace where we expected honour, is a *mortification* to an ambitious person." Adams recurred to the word in this sense at critical points in his life, tracing with it the recurring conviction of lonely, suffering right that so frequently governed his actions.

He used the word when, right after starting out as a lawyer in 1759, he had no clients. In 1765 it expressed his resentment over the public's neglect of his services against the Stamp Act (the unique, heavily inked-out passage in his diary included the word). In 1771, he later recalled, he never had been so mortified in his life as when Hutchinson prevented him from delivering an eloquent speech in court. Looking forward in 1773 to possible election to the General Court, Adams asked himself, as he would before every election in which he was involved, what self-denials and mortifications he should have to bear if chosen. Neglected by Congress on his first mission to France in 1779, he "confessed" his mortification. At his breakdown in the Netherlands in 1782 he wrote Francis Dana that the "dastardly meannesses of Jealousy and Envey" shown to him had been mortifying to him "to the last degree." Later in the same year he explained to his wife that he was loath to leave the Netherlands for the peace conference because in Paris he would find "millions of Humiliations and Mortifications," presumably at the hands of Franklin and Vergennes. In 1785 in the letter to Elbridge Gerry in which he admitted his vanity he compared his lot to Bolingbroke's "ill success and never ending Mortifications." Not surprisingly, the word came frequently to mind when Adams dealt with Franklin. In 1811 he wrote, "I must acknowledge, after all, that nothing in life has mortified or grieved me more than the necessity which compelled me to oppose him so often as I have." Finally, in 1804 he intended to abandon his autobiography because, "I wish not to be reminded of my Mortifications Disappointments or Resentments."[31] In 1807, when Adams did permanently abandon the autobiography after receiving Mercy Warren's unmoved replies to his letters, political events provided sufficient distractions to divert a man concerned with the welfare of his country.

In June the British ship *Leopard* fired on the Chesapeake, setting in motion events that led to the War of 1812. At the end of the year came the Embargo Act (Jefferson's attempt to preserve peace) and John Quincy Adams's surprising break with the Federalist party to endorse it. Events began to repeat in outline the provocations and threats of war during Adams's administration, while the terms of controversy harked back to cases and precedents that he had argued in Admiralty Court in the 1760s. He began to lecture his correspondents on impressments, maritime law, and embargoes, and to prepare an exhaustive essay on the subjects. "I know not," he wrote to Benjamin Rush in March 1808, "that I ever was more attentive to public affairs or more concerned about them." His essays revealed an intimate familiarity with national affairs since his administration. As he advanced into his seventies, the more he complained of his age the stronger he seemed to grow, and the more he lamented his inability to help his country the closer he came to publishing his opinions for the first time since his first term as vice-president. The pattern was familiar. Adams's youthful choice between the public career of a lawyer and the private career of a minister had given way to the choice between entering or bidding farewell to politics, and then to that between going on in public life or retiring. In retirement the

---

31. Crabb, *English Synonyms Explained*, new ed., s.v. "vexation." Adams's uses of the word "mortification" not mentioned in previous chapters are: Adams to Francis Dana, Apr. 28, 1782, Dana Papers, Mass. Hist. Soc., Boston; to Abigail Adams, Aug. 17, 1782, Adams Papers, Reel 357; to Elbridge Gerry, May 2, 1785, *ibid.*, Reel 364; *Boston Patriot*, 1811, in *Works of John Adams*, I, 664; and in 1804, *Diary and Autobiography*, I, lxix. For two letters to Franklin in which the word appears see *Works of John Adams*, VII, 316, 387.

question became one of publishing or withholding first his autobiography and then his opinions about current affairs. After eight years "Fundamental Errors in Doctrine and Practice, drew me once more out of my obscurity"—to challenge British naval impressments.[32]

He wrote a newspaper essay reminiscent of Revolutionary days in its argument from English legal sources. Then, in what amounted to a repetition of Hamilton's charges, he was attacked for his handling of the similar crisis with France. With Jefferson's two administrations at an end and John Quincy Adams out of office he could not be accused of either interfering with his former rival or attempting to influence his son's career if he now answered Hamilton. Only a few months earlier he had refused to write his vindication. But there had been "a systematical policy of both parties . . . to conceal from the people all the services of my life." At once vowing to "throw off that intolerable load of obloquy and insolence they have thrown upon me, or . . . perish in the struggle," and predicting "I shall not be believed," he finally addressed the public on his own behalf.[33]

In April 1809 there began to appear a series of letters from "the late President Adams" to the recently founded *Boston Patriot* newspaper. Appearing usually twice a week, they grew in length until abruptly breaking off in 1812. Adams began with "Diplomatic History," as Abigail Adams put it, about the crisis with France (1798–1800) and his earlier European diplomacy (especially in the peace of 1782–1783)—neither of which he more than touched on in his autobiography. But in his eighth letter he addressed the printers: "At first I intended to encumber your paper with no documents but such as were absolutely necessary for my own vindication. But . . . I hope you will allow me room for such other papers as may serve to throw

32. Adams to Rush, Apr. 18, 1808, Adams Papers, Reel 118, and Aug. 7, 1809, Vanderkemp Papers. For Adams's 1808 draft of a reply to "Mr. Pickering's Letter," see Adams Papers, Reel 405.

33. Adams to William Cunningham, Nov. 25, 1808, Mar. 20, 1809, and Apr. 24, 1809, *Correspondence between Adams and Cunningham*, 55, 101, 114.

light."[34] Hereafter commentary shrank, as it had in the *Defence* and in "Davila." Eventually Adams conceived the idea of using publication as a form of safekeeping for his papers, and any thought of formal development was gone. At this point he had repeated the pattern of his active life. Both spurred on and made guiltily diffident by his lust for fame, he found a public crisis to justify his appearing in print. Very soon fame was replaced by the desire of recognition for his services, and this desire in turn by an antiquarian impulse to set straight the historical record.

Just as Adams took his public acts without consultation, so did he unexpectedly issue the *Patriot* correspondence to the world. Subsequently, though the letters continued for three years Adams used no resources other than his memory and such of his papers as it occurred to him to consult. Thus, from the time he began his notes for a reply to Hamilton in 1801 to the end of the *Patriot* correspondence in 1812, he increasingly voiced suspicions about Franklin, Vergennes, and the members of his cabinet, but he never undertook the research to learn the details of what they had done.

One of the few sustained passages in the *Patriot* was occasioned by Adams's coming across a 1782 letter about Franklin. In the Netherlands before the Paris peace negotiations Adams had complained to Secretary Livingston about Franklin's behavior, tendered his resignation, and then crossed out what he had written. His renewal of old emotions as he copied his heavily inked-out lines for the printer moved Adams finally to set down the pith of what he thought about Franklin. A fellow commissioner should not have implied disapproval by secretly forwarding Adams's correspondence with Vergennes to Congress. Franklin's adding later that Adams was "sometimes out of his senses," allowed of only one interpretation: a "low intrigue" to "get possession of his commission for peace." Adams wrote that he was dealing with "the most disagreeable part . . . in my whole life" and pronounced it "a severe mortification to

34. Abigail Adams to John Quincy Adams, Dec. 31, 1809, Adams Papers, Reel 408; *Correspondence in the Boston Patriot*, 7.

me to find myself obliged to enter into so much egotistical history." But he went on, for he had the right of "explaining this dark transaction to posterity."[35]

By the time he finished he had pronounced his complete triumph over Franklin. In signing a joint letter with Jay and Adams justifying the conduct of the peace negotiations in Paris, for example, Franklin had acquiesced in a "perfect vindication of me, and condemnation of himself." Later, when Adams's *Defence of the Constitutions* was received by the Constitutional Convention, it "soon dissipated the vapours of Franklin's foggy system, demolished Hamilton's airy castles, and united the convention in the plan they finally adopted." Adams believed that as a result "the venerable Franklin could not subscribe his name [to the Constitution] without shedding tears." (Adams's two periods of diplomacy as envoy and president were only ostensibly his subject in the *Patriot* letters: for the earlier period one could read "exposure of Franklin" and, for the later, "Hamilton.") Once again, of course, Adams failed to carry out his plan. Among the few deletions from his personal letters copied for the *Patriot*, for example, were his more extreme passages about Franklin. Nevertheless, scattered among these letters in the long, narrow columns of the *Patriot*—all but indistinguishable from the news because of the typography— was Adams's only public defense of his career. With it he finally "replaced on the Shoulders of Franklin, burthens he shifted on mine." Thereafter he could not be enticed into criticizing Franklin.[36]

Adams also stated his own importance in American history. In his 1800 reply to Hamilton, the basis for the first *Patriot* letters, he had written for the most part with resentment so controlled that it lost its point. His subjects were "Mr. A.," "Mr. H.," and numerous questions raised by "Mr. Hamilton's

35. *Boston Patriot*, May 15, 1811, May 8, 1811, May 18, 1811.
36. *Ibid.*, Feb. 19, 1812, May 5, 1812, Apr. 15, 1812; Adams to Jefferson, July 12, 1813, Cappon, ed., *Adams-Jefferson Letters*, II, 353. For Adams's silence on Franklin see *The Adamses at Home: Accounts by Visitors in the Old House in Quincy, 1788–1886*, Colonial Society of Massachusetts pamphlet (Boston, 1970), 21–22.

Letter"—the title of the reply. In reviewing Hamilton's charge of "a vanity without bounds" supposedly evidenced in sending his peace journal to Congress, Adams succeeded in 1800 only in exposing his suffering over that indiscretion. "To be Sure," he admitted, "there are anecdotes in it one or two at least, which appear ~~exquisitely ridiculous~~ [crossed out] extraordinary, and have cost Mr. Adams a repentance more Sincere and more bitter than Mr. Hamilton has ever Shown for any of his faults." To this he had added the sort of passage that kept him from printing the reply. Now he repeated that passage verbatim in the *Patriot*. The French courtiers' praise for gaining Dutch recognition recorded in his peace journal was in fact deserved, for it was a response to "the greatest Event of the Whole War," which "had more decisive Influence in producing peace than the Capture of Burgoin and Cornwallis both together."[37]

Even as Adams decided to publish such assertions his need to do so was diminishing. The contemporaries whom he wished to enlighten were dying away while later generations faded to an abstraction before the cares of a growing family of grand-children and great grandchildren. "Witnesses to whom I intended to have appealed," he wrote the publishers of the *Patriot* on terminating, "have even while I have been writing, a [Francis] Dana, a [Benjamin] Lincoln, a [General] Knox, been summoned to a higher Tribunal." He could have added to this list the classmate who had advised that he become a minister, Judge William Cushing (d. 1810), his brother-in-law Richard Cranch (d. 1811)—"my Guide Philosopher and friend for Sixty years"—and, amid family deaths and illnesses that made 1811 "the most afflictive [year] of my life," an operation for cancer on his daughter, Abigail, from which she died in 1813.[38]

---

37. Henry Cabot Lodge, ed., *The Works of Alexander Hamilton*, VII (New York, 1904), 314; draft of a reply to Hamilton, [1800–1801], Adams Papers, Reel 399, and *Boston Patriot*, Sept. 7, 1811. As early as 1783 Adams wrote to Gerry: "Now I say and I can demonstrate, that the Negotiations in holland [word crossed out] advanced the American Cause, more than the Capture of either of those Armies did." Sept. 8, 1783, Adams Papers, Reel 106.

38. Adams to Monroe and French (editors of the *Boston Patriot*), May 12, 1812, and to Rush, Nov. 2, 1811, Adams Papers, Reel 118.

As his animating resentment drained away in the course of writing, Adams complained of boring himself and the public, which received his letters with "profound silence." He grew increasingly skeptical, if possible, about history until he concluded: "That man is in a poor case who is reduced to the necessity of looking to posterity for justice or charity." Then he stopped. "My Reputation," he soon wrote, "has been so much the Sport of the public for fifty Years, and will be with Posterity, that I hold it, a bubble, a Gossameur, that idles in the wanton Summers Air." By 1819 he no longer owned a complete copy of the *Patriot* correspondence. "I now think I was very idly employed in vindicating my Conduct," he wrote.[39] Though an unsatisfactory testament Adams's "second autobiography" proved to be a final one. After over a decade of obsession with the idea of vindication, the battle with himself and for himself was ended. Only at this point did Adams prove free enough to accomplish some of the aims of his retirement.

39. Adams to Cunningham, June 7, 1809, *Correspondence between Adams and Cunningham*, 124; to Rush, May 14, 1812 (the month Adams stopped writing), Schutz and Adair, eds., *Spur of Fame*, 216; to Jefferson, June 25, 1813, Cappon, ed., *Adams-Jefferson Letters*, II, 333; and to Nicholas Boylston, Nov. 3, 1819, Adams Papers, Reel 124. On contemporary reactions to the *Patriot* letters see Schutz and Adair, eds., *Spur of Fame*, 196–197.

XII
The Garrulity of
Narrative Old Age
1813–1826

Adams halted his correspondence in the Boston Patriot with complaints of his own and the public's weariness with his writings. But he was not tired. He wrote to Benjamin Rush: "The astonishment of your Family at my vivacity is very just. Rochefoucault says when a mans vivacity increases with years it becomes frenzy at last. Nothing is indeed more ridiculous than an old man more than three quarters of a hundred rattling like a boy of fifteen at school or at College. I am ashamed of it yet ten to one I shall fall into it again before I finish this letter." His passion to defend himself now gave way to a concern for history. "It is in my opinion our duty," he wrote to Elbridge Gerry, "to brave the Imputation of Vanity and Egotism by recording Facts that no other human Beings know"—especially those concerning the Revolutionary period.[1]

His reminiscences gradually had been leading him backward in time, and now some inquiries focused him on the most successful part of his life, the Revolutionary struggle from 1761 to 1776. He wrote a number of private letters about his fellow patriots that proved to be more influential than all the volumes, published or private, that he had devoted to himself. At the same time, events again began to buffet him. In June 1812 war

---

1. Adams to Benjamin Rush, Feb. 26, 1812, Adams Papers, Reel 118, and to Elbridge Gerry, Apr. 26, 1813, *Warren-Adams Letters*, II, 381.

with England was declared. Adams regarded it as another "furnace of Affliction" like the Revolutionary War and hoped that it would further refine the country's greatness. He dreamed of great fleets of American frigates (built in accordance with his naval policy from the Revolution to his presidency). The American naval victories over the English he found "sublime things . . . immortal, eternal," and in his old, zealous fashion he asked his grandson, "Is not your Soul on Fire?" For a time he immersed himself in naval history; then, as a peace settlement with England offered and the fisheries seemed to be threatened, "lost in an Ocean of Ideas" he turned to his negotiations of 1782 in Paris. He nearly broke his vow of silence when he wrote a letter to President Madison confessing his urge to visit Washington to discuss with him the state of the nation.[2]

Then, unexpectedly, there appeared in 1813 a work on political theory by John Taylor of Virginia based on a twenty-year study of Adams's *Defence of the Constitutions*. In *An Inquiry into the Principles and Policy of the Government of the United States*, Taylor argued that Adams's classical terminology of the one, the few, and the many did not apply to the American system. It has been said that Adams never quite understood Taylor, his tired reply showing that "age had mellowed his passion." In fact, no longer concerned with the infinitude of detail over which he had labored through his administrative life and in which he usually drowned his writings, Adams achieved a simplification without loss of passion. Once under way, just as with Mercy Warren he more than justified his critic's accusation of antidemocratic leanings, this time by dilating on "democratical dupery, credulity, adulation, corruption, adoration, superstition, and enthusiasm." Nevertheless, his thirty-three letters of reply to Taylor during 1814 are his most eloquent statement of his political philosophy.

His old faults remained. Rather than an analysis he gave a commentary on the passages that caught his eye as he went

2. Adams to Richard Rush, Dec. 12, 1813, Vanderkemp Papers, Pa. Hist. Soc.; to John Adams Smith, Dec. 14, 1812, and to John Quincy Adams, June 8, 1813, Adams Papers, Reels 118, 95. Adams's letter to Madison: May 19, 1813, *ibid.*, Reel 95.

through Taylor's book. In his thirtieth letter he observed that he was only on page twelve and that at that rate it would take him thirty or forty years to finish. After two more letters he left off, having just proven, again, that inequality, which now constituted his definition of aristocracy, would never be abolished. But Adams's digressions and verbal prolixity appear less as stylistic defects than they do as evidences of intellectual vigor in a man of seventy-nine. As a young man he regarded conciseness as the essence of a good style. Verbosity, though, came to dominate his disputatious works. "My great misfortune, through a pretty long life," he confessed to Taylor, "has been, that I have never had time to make my poor productions shorter." Yet, it was not brevity but organization that Adams lacked. Without his technically unnecessary elaboration his distinctiveness as a writer would be gone. One has to accept the "democratical hurricane, inundation, earthquake, pestilence, call it which you will," as well as "the ranks of society, or, if you are shocked at the word *rank*, say all the classes, degrees, the ladder, the theatrical benches of society, from the first planter."[3]

To a degree Adams's style of elaboration had assumed a useful function, for each time he included the planter, or the southerner, or the slaveholder in one of his lists of aristocrats, he was twitting John Taylor. Instead of agonizing under the familiar irony of arguing inequality as a small landholder against southern plantation owners like Jefferson and Taylor, Adams turned the paradox to his advantage. "Should you detect a conspiracy among your domestics," Adams wrote the theoretically democratic Taylor, "which I hope you will, if it should exist, while I devoutly pray it may never exist, you would find . . . a *one*, a *few*, and a *many*." Elsewhere he indirectly inserted himself into his lists, as when he wrote, "Birth and wealth are commonly so entangled together, from an emperor

3. Wood, *Creation of the American Republic*, 592; *Works of John Adams*, VI, 454, 514; Butterfield *et al.*, eds., *Earliest Diary*, 59; *Works of John Adams*, VI, 515, 485, 509 (Adams's italics). Roy F. Nichols, in his introduction to Taylor's *An Inquiry into the Principles and Policy of the Government of the United States* (New Haven, Conn., 1950), gives Adams better of the argument than does Gordon Wood.

down to a constable or tithing-man" (the last being two of his father's professions), or when he illustrated the respect for wealth implied in what he represented as a common saying, " 'His great grandfather, who was only a shoemaker . . . ' " (another of his father's callings).

If his ideas about governmental form had changed over the years, Adams was not aware of it. He supported the tripartite governments of the American colonial period, as they had been maintained during the Revolution and under the Articles of Confederation and the present Federal government. In his early works he emphasized the *moral* superiority of Americans. In the Massachusetts Constitution his concerns became *structural*. In the *Defence of the Constitutions* he exposed *social* inequality, and in "Davila," man's *psychological* predilection in favor of inequality. In his letters to Taylor, Adams defended his social and psychological insights in the form of a single *philosophical* point. Nature and society conspired to form two classes of men, superior and inferior. Adams recalled touring the foundling hospital in Paris: "Fifty babes in one room;—all under four days old; all in cradles alike; . . . all equally neat. I went from one end to the other of the whole row. . . . And I never saw a greater variety, or more striking inequalities. . . . These were all born to equal rights, but to very different fortunes." This natural inequality, Adams argued persuasively, is reenforced by the institutions of the most democratic society. Education, for example, serves to widen rather than narrow the gap.

But Adams had no such love of privilege as Taylor tried to suggest. His overriding political emotion was hatred of tyranny. For years an anger had been building in him at the world's loss of historical records. He had scolded Rush for destroying some of his papers and had recently been horrified by accounts of the Spanish Inquisition. Now he asked Taylor:

Where shall I begin, and where end? Shall I begin with the library at Alexandria, and finish with that at Washington [burned during the War of 1812], the latter Saracens more ferocious than the former, in proportion as they lived in a more civilized age? Where are the languages of antiquity? all the dialects of the Chaldean tongue? Where is Aristotle's history of eighteen hundred republics, that had existed before his time? Where are Cicero's writings upon government? What havoc has been made of books through every century of the Christian era? Where are fifty gospels, condemned as spurious by the bull of Pope Gelasius? Where are the forty wagon-loads of Hebrew manuscripts burned in France. . . . Remember the *index expurgatorius*, the inquisition, the stake, the axe, the halter, and the guillotine; and, oh! horrible, the rack![4]

It was a familiar note of high-minded outrage at the evils of mankind, and it was evoked by old adversaries: the church and the English nation. He had begun his career in politics by attacking both of them in "A Dissertation on Canon and Feudal Law." Now, reexperiencing former emotions and renewing his Revolutionary spirit, Adams returned to his youthful willingness to criticize both church and state.

Before and after the letters to Taylor the ever recurrent subject of his presidency inevitably interrupted this process, though Adams wished less and less to discuss the past. He shifted from one simple explanation to another for losing his office, though after a while he began to admit his error in allowing Hamilton's ascendancy. He revealed the extent to which he had been manipulated when he ironically referred to his cabinet members as his "masters," all of them "viceroys" "chained" by "the Sovereign Pontiff of Federalism," "Commander in Chief" Hamilton. As for himself, he had been the "Slave of a Senate, twenty to ten, Slaves of Hamilton," and had ended as "a mere sipher."[5] He could come no closer to an explanation for the disaster than to posit Hamilton's madness and to regard his presidency as a "tale told by an Ideot." He had mounted his Rocinante in what he now counted "a tragic-comic farce."[6]

4. *Works of John Adams*, VI, 464 (Adams's italics), 505, 502, 452, 478–479.
5. Adams to Benjamin Rush, Aug. 23, 1805, Sept. 30, 1805, and Nov. 11, 1807, Schutz and Adair, eds., *Spur of Fame*, 36, 42, 99; to James Lloyd, Apr. 24, 1815, *Works of John Adams*, X, 162; to Richard Rush, Aug. 7, 1809, and Oct. 18, 1813, Vanderkemp Papers; and to Harrison Gray Otis, Apr. 9, 1823, Adams Papers, Reel 124.
6. Adams to Benjamin Rush, Jan. 4, 1813, and to Harrison Gray Otis, Apr. 9, 1823, Adams Papers, Reels 121, 124. On the Rocinante of the presidency and Adams's explanations of how he lost the office see Schutz and Adair, eds., *Spur of Fame*, 241, 42, 224.

Adams could be spurred into writing at length on his presidency as late as 1823. But from 1813 his greatest writing effort went into letters on the Revolution. A question about Governor Thomas Pownall "excited" an "explosion of reminiscences . . . in me!" "You . . . have 'brought the old man out,'" he warned one correspondent, "and, I fear, he will never be driven in again till he falls into the grave." "You shall not escape me," he told another. After looking into the state of his papers he answered a request for copies (in an unmistakable prelude to a new correspondence): "In plain English, and in few words Mr. Niles, I consider the true history of the American revolution & of the establishment of our present Constitutions as lost forever." He set whichever relatives he could find about the house to copying documents, especially ancient English statutes, complaining of having to read so much at his age. But he later admitted, "I never read them without being set on fire."[7]

As long as he remained absorbed in his own life, he viewed the period from 1760 to 1776 as a "dark Valley of Grief Gloom and disappointment." As his reading drew him into the history of the period, however, he returned to his former patriot view of events. This posited a moral decline among the people, which stimulated the New England Revolutionaries, as it had their Puritan forebears, to equally righteous denunciations of their opponents and their own people. Adams now wrote, "From 1760 to 1766, was the purest period of patriotism; from 1766 to 1776 was the period of corruption; from 1775 to 1783 was the period of war." Again he made Thomas Hutchinson responsible for the corruption, though since Hutchinson's death Adams had labored to erase his animosity.[8] The purity of patriotism was exemplified by James Otis, Adams's first political model and last representative of his principles. "I seem to live over again, ten or fifteen years of my early life," Adams

7. Adams to William Tudor, Feb. 4, 1817, and Feb. 25, 1818, *Works of John Adams*, X, 241, 292; to Tudor, Jan. 11, 1817, and to Hezekiah Niles, Jan. 3, 1817, Adams Papers, Reel 123; and to Tudor, July 27, 1818, *Works of John Adams*, X, 336.

8. Adams to John Quincy Adams, Jan. 8, 1805, Adams Papers, Reel 404, and to Jedidiah Morse, Jan. 1, 1816, *Works of John Adams*, X, 197. For Adams's late feelings about Thomas Hutchinson see *ibid.*, 262, and Adams to Tudor, Nov. 16, 1816, Adams Papers, Reel 123.

wrote as late as 1823 on reading a life of Otis to which he had contributed his reminiscences. He had followed Otis in the content and style of his anti-Hutchinson politics during the 1760s. Now it appeared that he had followed his subsequent neglect by history as well. In the account that he proceeded to give of Otis's life and services, Adams projected an idealized version of his own idealistic life. He made the Writs of Assistance case the birth of American independence and Otis a figure resembling himself: "Otis was a flame of fire!—with a promptitude of classical allusions, a depth of research, a rapid summary of historical events and dates, a profusion of legal authorities, a prophetic glance of his eyes into futurity, and a torrent of impetuous eloquence, he hurried away every thing before him."[9]

Like Adams, Otis employed Ciceronian wit, humor, irony, and satire. In a series of letters Adams tried exhaustively to reproduce from memory Otis's speech on Writs of Assistance. Otis, after identifying himself with the patriot cause, had withdrawn amid rumors, credited at the time by Adams, of having made a deal with Hutchinson. Adams, whose behavior in the late 1760s appeared as a similar abandonment of the cause, defended Otis from his "false accusers and vile calumniators in abundance." Adams compared Otis to Demosthenes, Cicero, Luther, Isaiah, Ezekiel, and St. Paul, against whom a similar charge of self-seeking "has lasted more than seventeen hundred years." After William Wirt presumed to make Patrick Henry the father of American independence instead of Otis, Adams wished on Otis the sort of fate that he ordinarily reserved for himself: "I hope, the defamation of Otis will last as long, because it will be an immortal proof of the malice and revenge of the scurrilous, persecuting tyrants, against whom he had to contend."[10]

9. Adams to Tudor, Feb. 23, 1819, Adams Papers, Reel 124, and Mar. 29, 1817, *Works of John Adams*, X, 247. Adams wrote Tudor a series of letters on Otis between 1816 and 1819. For parallels between Adams and Otis see especially Adams to Tudor, June 24, 1817, Adams Papers, Reel 123.

10. Adams to Tudor, June 24, 1818, Apr. 5, 1818, *Works of John Adams*, X, 324, 310, and to Waterhouse, Feb. 6, 1818, *ibid.*, 281. "The wit, the humor, the irony, the satire played off

Through 1813 Adams continued to express his personal dissatisfactions by complaining on behalf of other Revolutionary leaders neglected by the public. Otis represented not only the fate of Adams in history but the principles of the early Revolutionary struggle as well. In writing about him Adams completed his return to the outlook of early days. For years he had complained about Samuel Adams and John Hancock, both of whom he had broken with. By 1817, dismissing justified resentments, he wrote that if Hancock's "vanity and caprice made me sometimes sputter," conversely his own identical failings undoubtedly "had often a similar effect upon him." In 1807 he began to lament the unavailability of Samuel Adams's and Hancock's papers. But he recalled the draft of a reply to Hutchinson by Samuel Adams as being "filled with . . . silly democratical nonsense" which he had managed to have expunged. Now he no longer recalled having so revised it, for "to strike out Principles which I loved as well as any of the People, would be odious and unpopular."[11]

Toward the English, the church, and all tyrannies, Adams felt the outrage of old. His sympathies went out to the Spanish and Greek patriots, and his patriotism and love of the American Union prevailed again over his eternal complaints about the people. His anticlerical fervor marked a return to the religious iconoclasm of his youth. He had rebelled not only against his family's expectation that he would become a minister but, in his disapproval of imposed religious views, against the church establishment of which his father was a member. Since then Adams had made some recompense to his father's memory. His

by Mr. Otis in his observations on these acts of navigation . . ." Adams to Tudor, June 24, 1818, *ibid.*, 324.

11. Adams to Tudor, June 1, 1817, *Works of John Adams*, X, 259; to Mercy Warren, July 20, 1807, "Correspondence between Adams and Mercy Warren," Mass. Hist. Soc., *Colls.*, 5th Ser., IV, 347; and to Tudor, Mar. 8, 1817, Adams Papers, Reel 123. In his autobiography Adams gave the same version as that he gave to Mercy Warren. *Diary and Autobiography*, III, 305. Charles Francis Adams reprinted the letter to Tudor but deleted from the autobiography the less liberal version: see *Works of John Adams*, II, 310–312. Adams had good cause to resent John Hancock, who abandoned him in the late 1760s in his own pursuit of higher office. For Adams's lament over the missing papers of Samuel Adams and Hancock see his letter to Rev. Abiel Holmes, May 6, 1807, Adams Papers, Reel 118.

"Dissertation on Canon and Feudal Law" had the structure and tone of a sermon. In his draft of the Massachusetts Constitution he favored taxation to support religion; while president he continued the ancient practice of declaring fast days in time of national emergency. When in Quincy he attended church twice on Sundays, and in his retirement he returned to the Bible and sermon literature. He also returned to the sort of disputatious theological works that had stimulated him from his teens through his years in Worcester, then a "hotbed of deistic belief."[12]

The most daring of these was Charles François Dupuis's *Origine de tous les cultes*, a twelve-volume rationalistic survey of religion and superstition that was the *Golden Bough* of its age. Adams read it in its entirety and emerged a confirmed skeptic— not about Christianity but about the ability of any ecclesiastical body to fathom the mysteries of the universe. In 1813 Jedidiah Morse and William Ellery Channing began a dispute over Unitarianism reminiscent of the Puritan age in its intensity. The old opposition between conservative and liberal theology flared up, exposing Adams's Unitarian leanings and reminding him of the intolerance his ideas had faced when he was a young man. He now revealed his sympathy with Lemuel Briant, the Braintree minister who had been called before an ecclesiastical council for preaching rational religion. When in 1815 Jedidiah Morse tried to draw Adams into the controversy on the conservative side, Adams pointed to Briant, declaring him to have been a Unitarian. He made it clear that he opposed Morse's attempt to impose orthodoxy.

As a reader and debater of theology Adams inherited "the speculative passion of the New England divines," but did not adopt their intolerance. He had tried unsuccessfully to declare

12. Howard Ioan Fielding, "John Adams: Puritan, Deist, Humanist," *Journal of Religion*, XX (1940), 34. For Adams's sympathy with contemporary revolutionary movements see his letter to one of his grandsons, Oct. 10, 1808, Adams Papers, Reel 118. See also Adams to Jefferson, Dec. 29, 1823, Cappon, ed., *Adams-Jefferson Letters*, II, 602. On Adams's churchgoing see Stewart and Clarke, "Misanthrope or Humanitarian?" *NEQ*, XXVIII (1955), 218; Muzzey, *Prime Movers of the Revolution*, 54. After rejecting religious trinitarianism, it may be noted, Adams went on to a religious-like support of political tripartism.

universal religious freedom in the Massachusetts Constitution's bill of rights. In 1813 he welcomed the British Parliament's religious toleration act. Then, in 1820, when invited to a convention to amend the Massachusetts Constitution he created a stir by proposing to change the clause on religion that had been substituted for his original one of 1779. In 1820 the Constitution continued to restrict religious liberty to "men of every denomination of Christians." Adams called for it to proclaim that "all men, of all religions, demeaning themselves as good subjects, shall enjoy the equal protection of the laws." The defeat of this liberalization spoke for the daring of Adams's belief in "Universal toleration."[13]

In general his mood was one of forgiveness. He recalled Bolingbroke's saying of the duke of Marlborough that he had forgotten his faults, and he tried to forget those of his own enemies. He succeeded with many, going so far as to "forgive" Great Britain. He would include "Alec Hamilton and Tim Pick," he declared, "if I could perceive a Symptom of sincere Penitence in either." But, "I say of Dr. Franklin he was so great a Man that I wish I could forget his faults and follies."[14]

In 1812 Adams resumed contact with Thomas Jefferson. For years he had described Jefferson as "ambitious" and "cunning," terms he reserved for Thomas Hutchinson, Benjamin Franklin, and the devil. Jefferson was a mere "party man," "an intriguer"; his presidential administration made Adams "shudder," in capital letters, "at the calamities, which I fear his conduct is preparing for his country: from a mean thirst of popularity, an

13. Haraszti, *John Adams and the Prophets of Progress*, 46; *Works of John Adams*, IV, 223n; Adams to Richard Rush, Nov. 13, 1816, Adams Papers, Reel 123. For Adams's response to Dupuis see Adams to Waterhouse, Feb. 22, 1817, Adams Papers, Reel 123. For his marginalia on Dupuis see Frank E. Manuel, *The Eighteenth Century Confronts the Gods* (Cambridge, Mass., 1959), 271–280. For Adams on Lemuel Briant see Stewart and Clarke, "Misanthrope or Humanitarian?" *NEQ*, XXVIII (1955), 227; Adams to Waterhouse, Dec. 19, 1815, Ford, ed., *Statesman and Friend*, 121. On the British religious toleration act see Cappon, ed., *Adams-Jefferson Letters*, II, 373.
14. Adams to Susan Adams, Oct. 10, 1820, Adams Papers, Reel 124; to Waterhouse, Jan. 10, 1810, Ford, ed., *Statesman and Friend*, 47; to Jefferson, May 29, 1818, Cappon, ed., *Adams-Jefferson Letters*, II, 526; and to Francis Adrian Vanderkemp, Feb. 21, 1823, Adams Papers, Reel 124.

inordinate ambition, and a want of sincerity."[15] As he found himself supporting policies like the Louisiana Purchase, though, Adams went from claiming credit for having laid the ground-work for Jefferson's policies; to complaining that Jefferson had stolen, via Washington, the Adams policy of neutrality; to calling Jefferson "Honourable" as his second term drew to an end. By 1808 Adams had arrived at a notably balanced view of Jefferson's achievements and failures as president. He could not help viewing his own administration as having been in practice more republican, and there was much that he disagreed with, especially the neglect of the navy that he had bequeathed to the nation, but he could "give him up to censure" only for his repeal of the judiciary act.[16]

Jefferson had originally held high regard for Adams, though he found his irascibility amusing. Under Madison's influence he revised his view, first to maintaining that, despite Adams's unbalancing hatred of Franklin, "he has a sound head on sub-stantial points, and I think he has integrity." Later he called Adams vain but "disinterested as the being which made him." After being persuaded by Madison not to send a congratulatory letter on Adams's election to the presidency, Jefferson grew

15. Adams to Thomas Boylston Adams, July 12, 1801, and to Richard Cranch, May 23, 1801, Adams Papers, Reels 401, 118; to Benjamin Rush, Sept. 1807, Schutz and Adair, eds., *Spur of Fame*, 93; and to William Cunningham, Jan. 16, 1814, *Correspondence between Adams and Cunningham*, 10–11 (words all in capitals). Adams also credited the story that Jefferson had fled British troops during the Revolution while governor of Virginia and the rumor that Jefferson refused to cross the ocean until after the peace of 1783 even though nominated for diplomatic posts and voted a member of Adams's peace commission. Adams to Mercy Warren, July 20, 1807, and Aug. 15, 1807, "Correspondence between Adams and Mercy Warren," Mass. Hist. Soc., *Colls.*, 5th Ser., IV, 337, 461; and to James Lloyd, Mar. 12, 1815, *Works of John Adams*, X, 138. Adams credited the story of Jefferson's Negro children. Adams to Col. Ward, Jan. 8, 1810, Adams Papers, Reel 118. He once called Jefferson "a dastardly poltroon." On the other hand, Adams did not descend to petty resentment. He forwarded a manuscript by Vanderkemp to the "Accademy" in Boston with the observation that its introductory compliments to Jefferson were likely to prevent its publication though they did not offend him personally. Adams to Vanderkemp, Aug. 1, 1803, Vanderkemp Papers. After his reconciliation with Jefferson, Adams did not revise his view of Jefferson's presidency, writing to John Quincy Adams in 1813 of Jefferson's and Madison's "total Incapacity for practical Government or War." July 15, 1813, Adams Papers, Reel 95.

16. Adams to Vanderkemp, Mar. 9, 1806, and to Col. Ward, Jan. 8, 1810, Adams Papers, Reel 118. See also to Benjamin Rush, July 7, 1805, *ibid.*, Reel 403, Sept. 4, 1812, Schutz and Adair, eds., *Spur of Fame*, 244.

convinced of Adams's monarchism, called his presidential policy toward France "almost insane," and collected stories of his eccentricity.[17]

Adams tried to deny his past intimacy with Jefferson, but Abigail Adams did not forget the elegant compliments she once had received from him; and she tried unsuccessfully to extract a suitable apology several times between 1801 and 1812. After Benjamin Rush effected a reconciliation in the latter year, she participated in the correspondence. Both presidents recalled not only their association in the Continental Congress but rare good times like their tour of English country houses in 1786. Jefferson had enjoyed the nude Venuses in the formal gardens, while Adams, equally moved, called them "quite unnecessary as Mankind have no need of artificial Incitements, to such Amuzements." Adams finally wrote to Jefferson because, "You and I ought not to die, before we have explained ourselves to each other."[18] His first letter contained a typically self-denigrating irony, which expressed his complicated emotions. In sending a copy of John Quincy Adams's *Lectures* by separate post he wrote misleadingly that he was sending a gift of "Homespun." Jefferson had been one of those aristocrats who turned the tables on Adams by adopting manners putatively more democratic than his. When he called his estate Monticello, Adams wrote, "Jefferson has had the affectation to go to Italy for an outlandish name for his Hill. . . . I have retained the homespun name of Wollaston." Later, presumably to point up

17. Jefferson to Madison, Feb. 2, 1783, and Jan. 30, 1787, Boyd *et al.*, eds., *Jefferson Papers*, VI, 241 (original in code), XI, 94. Adrienne Koch, ed., *Adams and Jefferson*, 41. See also Jefferson's "Anas," in Paul Leicester Ford, ed., *The Works of Thomas Jefferson*, Federal Edition (New York, 1904), introduction, 341, 375. In his 1797 letter on Adams (summarized though never shown to Adams), Jefferson, writes Dumas Malone, "had made unprovable assertions and voiced unwarrantable suspicions so far as Adams was concerned. Unquestionably he engaged in exaggeration when communicating his fears to the faithful, and as a partisan he was often injudicious." *Jefferson and the Ordeal of Liberty* (Boston, 1962), 332.

18. *Diary and Autobiography*, III, 185–186; Adams to Jefferson, July 15, 1813, Cappon, ed., *Adams-Jefferson Letters*, 358. For Jefferson's responses see Boyd *et al.*, eds., *Jefferson Papers*, IX, 369–373. For Adams's recollections of the tour see Adams to John Adams, Jr., Sept. 11, 1815, Adams Papers, Reel 122.

the irony of Jefferson's reputation for humbleness and to contrast his obscurity to Jefferson's fame, Adams adopted the name "Montezillo" for his estate. "Mr. Jefferson lives at Monticello the lofty Mountain," he explained. "I live at *Montezillo* a little Hill."[19] He did not realize that both words mean the same thing.

For years after the renewal of their correspondence Adams salted his letters to Jefferson with telling jibes on the Virginian's errors and inconsistencies: his authorship of the possibly seditious Kentucky Resolutions, his being "fast asleep in philosophical Tranquility" when the United States teetered on the brink of revolutionary disturbances during Adams's administration, his championing of the bloody French Revolution. But Adams's old affection was reawakened, and he grew dependent on Jefferson, whom he called the only man in the country with whom he could exchange certain ideas. Adams was thinking of their daring religious speculations, but this was not the only area in which he and Jefferson proved philosophically similar. Both retained a Puritan-Enlightenment skepticism about human nature, sought to control it through a governmental system of checks and balances, and looked to Americans as the people chosen to institute such a system. The extended argument on aristocracy in their correspondence has been justly praised, though on Adams's side the wonder is that he should have been able to summon up eloquence on what he admitted (in an underestimate) to have been his subject for thirty years, and on which he was writing to John Taylor at the same time. But for the most part Adams and Jefferson avoided argument, preferring to report their own interests—Jefferson in history and science, Adams in religious books "whose Titles you have never seen." Soon, with what he termed "the garrulity of narrative old age," Adams began to write twice, then three times as often as his correspondent—in lengthening letters—

19. Adams to Jefferson, Jan. 1, 1812, Cappon, ed., *Adams-Jefferson Letters*, II, 290; to John Trumbull, July 8, 1805, Adams Papers, Reel 118; and to Richard Rush, Nov. 24, 1814, Vanderkemp Papers.

and then, unable to write "a hundreth part of what I wish to say to you," to apologize for it.[20]

Adams's reading between 1801 and 1826 is a subject unto itself. Zoltán Haraszti's *John Adams and the Prophets of Progress* conveys its extent by reproducing some of Adams's marginalia. Adams also accumulated what amounted to marginalia on marginalia when he reread his own "Discourses on Davila." He felt himself justified in all that he had said about aristocracy even though his new comments reflected his rebirth of hatred for privilege. In 1805 he read Shakespeare twice through (with the single comment that the balance of powers had been lacking in his time). His classical reading was constant, and increased after 1815 when he began to follow his grandsons' studies. Newspapers, pamphlets, and congressional speeches never lost their interest. Adams loved travel books and Scott's romances, all of which he read as they appeared. Always a reader of history, in 1822 he plunged with new enthusiasm into histories of New England. After an exhaustive list of religious works he had studied, he asked Jefferson, "And all to what purpose? I verily believe I was as wise and good, seventy Years ago, as I am now." Adams's intellectual enthusiasm—"School Boy criticisms" in his phrase—remained unaffected by the ravages of time. He responded with the agitation of old to his honorary appointment to the new constitutional convention for Massachusetts. "I fear," he wrote, "the Town of Quincy will acquire little Credit by this Election." He never stopped urging his grandchildren to educate themselves for the next age, and in 1825 was recommending to Charles Francis Adams that he strengthen himself with horseback riding since "the times will require activity & agility as well as mind."

Adams remained a prophetic observer of events, always able to list both the local and national issues of the day. He vigor-

20. Adams to Jefferson, June 30, 1813, and July 18, 1813, Cappon, ed., *Adams-Jefferson Letters*, II, 346, 361; to Benjamin Rush, Feb. 27, 1805, Schutz and Adair, eds., *Spur of Fame*, 24; and to Jefferson, June 20, 1815, Cappon, ed., *Adams-Jefferson Letters*, II, 446. On Jefferson's philosophical ideas see Curti, *Human Nature in American Historical Thought*, 42–44. For similarities between Adams's and Jefferson's economic beliefs see Joseph Dorfman, *The Economic Mind in American Civilization, 1606–1865*, I (New York, 1946), 417–433.

ously opposed the potentially secessionist Hartford Convention, then trembled at the possible outcome of the Missouri issue. Viewing the world in 1821, he found "an Effervescence among Mankind at present, which is portentous of Changes in Religion and Government—I hope for the better in both."[21]

The observation expressed his own hopeful vigor. He pronounced himself satisfied with the life he had led, confident of a future state, and unable to be a misanthrope. His longevity, colossal memory, and "astonishing" health, appeared as confirmations of the way he had lived. It was not serenity that Adams achieved but an accommodation with his own, craggy personality. The New Englanders among whom he retired accepted him, too. The eighteen-year-old George Bancroft, later a historian sympathetic to him, visited Quincy in 1818. He was "presented," he later recalled, "as one who before many days was to embark for purposes of study at a German University." "The venerable man," Bancroft wrote, "with a frankness which did not at all clash with the welcome of my reception, . . . broke out in somewhat abrupt and very decisive words against educating young Americans in European schools, insisting, and from a certain point of view very correctly, that a home education is the best for an American."[22] Adams's mode remained that of denunciation. Even when he was pleased, he was one of those who could praise only by exposing the faults of some opposite example from that which he approved.

The family circle in Quincy began to contract when Adams's grandsons, who usually spent much of the year there, went to college. The return of John Quincy Adams and his wife to the United States in 1817 was followed by his appointment as secretary of state, which took him to Washington. Abigail Adams was ill in 1816, recovered, then died in 1818. Adams afforded few glimpses of his wife in his letters. He credited her

21. Adams to Jefferson, Apr. 19, 1817, Cappon, ed., *Adams-Jefferson Letters*, II, 509; to Louisa Catherine Adams (Mrs. John Quincy Adams), Oct. 21, 1820, Adams Papers, Reel 124; to Charles Francis Adams, Aug. 17, 1825, *ibid.*, Reel 471; and to John Jay, May 13, 1821, *ibid.*, Reel 124.
22. *The Adamses at Home*, 21.

with the upbringing of John Quincy Adams, and regarded her letters as comparable to Madame de Staël's. Their relationship, along with their manners, grew formal, it would appear, though the recollections of visitors suggest that she remained his bulwark.[23]

Not his books, philosophy, or the personal tributes that finally came his way when he reached his eighties sustained Adams in his growing solitude. Rather, he breathed life in living his life over again in a different kind of autobiography: the contemplation of John Quincy Adams's career as the epitome of his own. His deepest affections were engaged by "My Great and good son"—"Virtuous and Studious beyond any other" man. His own unguarded spontaneity contrasted with John Quincy Adams's controlled indirectness, yet he mistook his vicarious emotions for his son's. "Shall I recommend to you the eternal Taciturnity of Franklin and Washington?" he asked him; "I believe your nature is as incapable of it as mine." He admitted to being "as Solicitous about your responsibility as I was formerly for my own" and found parallels with his own and Cicero's career at every turn. The son could expect his independence to lead only to one result: "Happy will you be if you can be *turned out* as your Father has been, and as you have already had the honour to be, and retire to Obscurity till you become a candidate for Octoginarianism."[24]

The two men's careers showed similarities more striking than the instances of ingratitude that Adams kept pointing out. John Quincy Adams emerged from the obscurity of a law practice by writing newspaper tracts, served as a diplomat, negotiated a peace treaty with the English in which the Newfoundland fishery became a major issue, and then served as minister to England. No wonder that his father's anxiety mounted as he progressed toward the presidency. In 1802

23. On Abigail Adams see Adams to Richard Rush, Jan. 15, 1811, and to Vanderkemp, Oct. 4, 1813, Vanderkemp Papers. Also Adams to John Quincy Adams, Nov. 18, 1818, Adams Papers, Reel 123.

24. Adams to John Quincy Adams, Jan. 8, 1808, Adams Papers, Reel 118; Nov. 9, 1804, *ibid.*, Reel 403; May 19, 1815, *ibid.*, Reel 122; Jan. 17, 1808, *ibid.*, Reel 405; and Aug. 27, 1815, *ibid.*, Reel 122 (Adams's italics).

Adams wrote, "In the failure of my Sons Election to Congress I rejoice." In 1813 Adams wrote John Quincy that he had "little faith" in the success of his peace negotiations to end the War of 1812. In 1815 he wrote him that as minister he would "lose in England, as I did, all the popularity you have acquired." Looking forward from 1822 to the next election in 1824 (at which John Quincy became president), Adams tried to conjure away his anticipations by predicting in a letter to his daughter-in-law the time "two years hence when Mr. A. will be disgraced and turned out of office."[25]

But Adams went further than this. In the last, great denial of his life, he refrained from writing to his son as often as he wished. He gave familiar, telltale multiple reasons: fear of spies during the War of 1812; fear, later, "least I should hurt your Feelings, embarrass your Employments, give you unnecessary Solicitude for your Country or excite a useless gloom on the prospect before Mankind"; and, finally, the certainty "that you would answer every scratch of a pen from me, but I know the importance of your occupations." He did not mention the Newfoundland fishery until after the peace negotiations of 1814 and never mentioned the presidential election until it was over. "The multitude of my thoughts," he then wrote, "and the intensity of my feelings are too much for a mind like mine, in its ninetieth year." Adams suffered as in youth from what he regarded as his vanity when his friends praised John Quincy. "Every word I write or Say in Praise of my Son I consider an Egotism," he wrote to one correspondent. But he could not control himself from writing to another, "A more dutiful and affectionate Son there can not be," or from sending Benjamin Rush a disquisition on John Quincy's literary accomplishments.[26]

25. Adams to Vanderkemp, Dec. 14, 1802, Adams Papers, Reel 118; to John Quincy Adams, June 18, 1813, *ibid.*, Reel 95, to Vanderkemp, Feb. 7, 1815, *ibid.*, Reel 122; and to Louisa Catherine Adams, Dec. 25, 1822, *ibid.*, Reel 124.

26. Adams to John Quincy Adams, Aug. 30, 1815, and June 12, 1821, *ibid.*, Reels 122, 124, and Feb. 18, 1825, *Works of John Adams*, X, 416; to Vanderkemp, Nov. 13, 1810, and to Benjamin Rush, Aug. 7, 1809, Vanderkemp Papers. See also Adams to James Monroe, Feb. 23, 1813, *Works of John Adams*, X, 33.

Intensity of feelings remained with Adams to the end as surely as it marked his personality from the beginning. He watched his physical frame decay, annoyed by the tremors, weak vision, and weaker limbs of age as if they were excrescences on a basically sound constitution. In 1812 he was complaining about the unsteadiness of his handwriting in script remarkably steady for a man of seventy-seven. He relied increasingly on dictation, especially after 1818, but wrote his own letters as late as 1821, when he was eighty-six. In 1819 he still rode horseback and worked in his garden. In 1822 he could walk three miles, though no longer ride. In 1823 he wrote, "Last year I could walk a mile—now I can not walk an 100 rod without falling down." In the same year Gilbert Stuart came to Quincy to paint him (see figure 4). He "caught," as Josiah Quincy put it when the work was done, "a glimpse of the living spirit shining through the feeble and decrepit body. He saw the old man at one of those happy moments when the intelligence lights up its wasted envelope."[27] Adams felt his end coming, but erupted in enthusiasms like an old volcano. His daughter-in-law's diary set him "on fire," and at eighty-eight he wrote, "my old brain boils up, so many reminiscences of ancient facts, and conversations which I think ought to be committed to writing, but which I am utterly incapable of doing that they sometimes over balance my reason." His letters to his grandchildren were filled with warnings to make the choice of Hercules and control their passions. "Be very careful to avoid all exultation," he warned Thomas Boylston Adams, Jr., when he won a school prize, and when his father won the presidency he warned Thomas's cousin John: "Command down every petty passion, John. This is not an event to excite vanity, John." ("Sobrius esto John"—be sober, John—was his warning to himself when he grew too excited over his books.)[28]

27. Adams to [?], June 23, 1823, Adams Papers, Reel 124; Oliver, *Portraits of John and Abigail Adams*, 189.
28. Adams to Vanderkemp, Feb. 21, 1823, to Thomas Boylston Adams, Jr., Mar. 29, 1823, and to his grandson John, Feb. 19, 1825, all in Adams Papers, Reel 124; and to

The end came as an outpouring of feeling for the one enthu-siasm more sustaining to John Adams than self-love or pride in his son: love of country. He had grown to resent the Fourth of July, not the least because it celebrated the document that he believed Jefferson to have copied largely from himself and James Otis.[29] But in his reconciliation with both history and his old rival, in his ninety-first year he sent the local committee a toast for the Fourth that applied to both the country and himself: "Independence forever."

The words may stand as his motto. "I must think myself independent, as long as I live," he wrote in 1815. "The feeling is essential to my existence."[30] Jefferson held body together until July 4, 1826, the fiftieth anniversary of his Declaration. Adams, eight years his senior at ninety-one, kept death off, too, until he could be carried a last time to his chair on that Independence Day. It was his final exertion of patriotic fervor.

Jefferson, Nov. 4, 1816, Cappon, ed., *Adams-Jefferson Letters*, II, 493. For Adams's hand-writing see his letters to Vanderkemp, July 15, 1812, Aug. 19, 1818, and May 30, 1821, Vanderkemp Papers.

29. See Zoltán Haraszti's transcripts of Adams's marginalia on "Davila," p. 7. Transcripts lent by the staff of the Adams Papers.

30. Adams to John Quincy Adams, May 16, 1815, Adams Papers, Reel 122.

Index